Don Toney taught me so much, and he continues teaching me daily... ..... the most important one's being LOVE, LIGHT, LIFE! He taught me that everything must begin with LOVE, because with LOVE, comes LIGHT; and, with LOVE-LIGHT comes the LIFE I'm here to express in. He taught me that these are the 3 keys to be "A FORCE WITH A PURPOSE". Thank You Don & Babette Toney for the time we spent and all the Divine Wisdom you poured into me!

LOVE, LIGHT & LIFE!
Dan Ferrando, student

"This first book of the teachings of Don Toney is a wonderful and marvelous source of wise counsel. The reader can count on this oracular offering to contain a wealth of knowledge to consider and many insights to share, concurrent with mankind's transition into the New Age Of Aquarius."

Steven & Carolyn and all of his grateful class members.

"I was searching... when I looked into his eyes I knew he held the answers. Oh, he made me work for them! Loving me every step of the way. I often replay his twinkle & nod at each discovery I made. The light of the Universe, he held it, I followed it, and there, I found my answers."

Rebecca Gill, student

"By using Toney's exercises that move Light energy into my body, I have moved into greater connection with my inner guides. This has allowed Source

energy to move more clearly through me and partner with me in guiding my life choices. Inner connection with my Holy Guardian angels has been made! No longer do I need to question my own motives. I am on my path of Love and Service. Thank you Toney and Babette!"

Jean Louise Green, student

"Learning about my Soul's authority opened new dimensions of Life for me. What a blessing to be Don Toney's student in the ways of Cosmic Love and how to raise my frequency! I learned about Human Magnificence and how to harness the power we all have."

Carolyn, student

"Thank you, Toney, for countless 'ahas' and gifts of wisdom, helping me to know who I am, what I am, where I am and why. What Jesus did we shall do also in the fullness of time—caterpillars into butterflies all. Thank you for lighting the way."

-Rosemary Quinn, student

Such a special individual, Toney, the brightest, wisest, most loving individual I have ever met or known. Such a great privilege to have known him over 40 years in this expression. He was my teacher, my husband and best friend ever. What a privilege and blessing in my life.

Babette Toney

Universal Everlasting Life

Book I

SERIES 1

The teachings of Donald M. Toney
as told to his students

BABETTE R.H. TONEY

BALBOA.PRESS
A DIVISION OF HAY HOUSE

http://universaleverlastinglife.com/

Balboa Press books may be ordered through booksellers or by contacting:

Balboa Press
A Division of Hay House
1663 Liberty Drive
Bloomington, IN 47403
www.balboapress.com
844-682-1282

Print information available on the last page.

ISBN: 979-8-7652-4272-8 (sc)
ISBN: 979-8-7652-4274-2 (hc)
ISBN: 979-8-7652-4273-5 (e)

Library of Congress Control Number: 2023910960

Balboa Press rev. date: 06/13/2023

To:
Donald M. Toney, my beloved husband, teacher and greatest inspiration
The Father and Mother Creators
Divine Source
Ida Stewart, Toney's Master Teacher
Erwin Dumbrille and Jeannie Walton, fellow students of Toney from the 1970s, who helped transcribe these lessons from classes over many years, without whom these lessons would not have been put into print.
My family
Toney's family
Toney's students over the many years

Contents

Introduction And Overview

When you complete your studies in these Seven Books, you will leave here a different person than you are now. **You will get the Wisdom and understanding to PERFECT yourself, to change your earthly body to LIGHT,** so you can take it from this Earth. Otherwise, you will continue to return to Earth until you attain that perfection. Until you can *conquer* death, you are bound to Earth.

What You Will Learn

As most of you have lived your lives, you have made the social and cultural mistakes of your culturing conditions. You have been bred dumb. I'm not being facetious when I say this. Most people are not aware of their ability or of where they are, what they are about, why they are here and why they are doing what they are doing.

I've been given the privilege to receive **information of the truth that will help you guide yourself to find yourself and make yourself free.** If you will be very patient with yourself and don't rush, all changes will come about very gradually and very permanently. **The main thing is to get to know yourself, and know who you are and where you are.** When you know who you are and where you are, **then you will know what you are about and why.**

Many of the confirmed acceptances that you have now, you will slowly start to discard. New presence will take their place. Like all truth, it is continuously in a state of change, a state of flux. By your awareness you will make these types of exchanges. Every day you barter. You trade something you already have for something that you feel is better for you. You give up the old and take the new.

It is the same with truth. You are continuously in the exchange of true unto truth. The **truth state is the ultimate state of attainment,** but what we feel is true today in the absolute, we'll find tomorrow that we give it away for a new truth. As a result, we are constantly in a state of change and flux.

Your lessons will slowly unfold for you to make you aware of what you're about in life. Instead of being in a past tense of a lived state, you'll begin to become lovers and very loving, and you will begin to exchange with people on a common ground. You will find out that all of God's abundance is at your fingertips, and also that all **the Father's** love is for everyone to share equally because He loves all of us in the same amount. He **laid down everything in His possession for your ability to have, to express Him in this expression** of activity, only you kind of forgot a few of the rules. You bent the rules a little bit. We are going to try to bring those rules back into a permanent station where these become your mold and projection in life.

Rather than becoming in a "lived" state, I want you to **live**. I don't want a past tense in any activity. One of the things you will find is that you are going to let go of things that you felt were so positively the absolute. Even those will be given away as you shuck and sift the sand so that all the good kernels come to the top and all the chaff blows away with the wind. Like all of your bad habits, they will blow away with the wind.

You will learn your evaluations of discernment, where **you will use your mental capacity to its fullness,** rather than in the minor capacity that you are normally functioning with. **You will learn to be able to handle yourself with poise and grace with all people.** You will learn to be in common with all people, so a love bonds.

Your lessons, that I have been given, consist of seven books. **Each book is a graduation from the first book into perfection** and will give you all the avenues of being able to take your body with you when you terminate this expression, rather than terminating into a death state. I can't do it for you, but I can give you all the answers so you can do it for yourself.

The Beginning of My Awakening

I might tell you a little bit about myself so you will be aware of why and how this has come about. My awakening started at the age of twelve. My teacher was a pine tree!

The conditions that led up to the pine tree were that when I was a child I had been punished for something I didn't do. The more I tried to prove my innocence, the more guilty it made me seem. I went for a walk in woods, thinking how unjust it was.

I sat down at the base of a pine tree, overlooking the lake, watching the clouds. Then I heard a voice which said, "Never mind; everything passes away with time."

The hair on the back of my head just stood straight out. I looked around and there was nobody there but me.

A voice said, "Look up."

All I could see was the tree. It said, "Yes, it is I."

That was the beginning of my awakening teachings. Everything else goes on from that. After that, every time I went there the tree would teach me. I went into nature. That pine tree taught me all about nature and how everything exists in the universe in the exchange between the mineral and the vegetable kingdoms. It taught me about life, all about everything.

This went on for two years. Whenever I had any spare time I "hot-footed" it to the tree. I remember about a month afterwards I told someone and he told someone else, "Don's been out in the sun too much. The trees are talking to him." I learned from then on you don't tell anybody about anything.

That experience of the pine tree is so memorable.

When I graduated from that, I was taken into higher elevations and taught how life itself is exchanged into expression.

I have had the inner voice since the age of twelve, and I've been endowed with the same voice from that time until now.

I have seven more books in my head that have never been put in print. When the people are ready for them, then they will be placed into print. When they graduate to the point that they can handle and control this degree of truth, then it will be projected to them.

Personal Experience

In the exchange, **everything that I speak of in the lessons, I have personally experienced.** I have been placed in the ground as a piece of mineral from light, solidified until the osmosis activity was destroyed by the bacteria and turned into secretion energy and devoured and deposited again by the earthworm, and then forced through the tunnel of the earthworm's canal and through the osmosis of atomic explosion, through the vapors into the rooting of the plant, and being placed in sub-minute crystal in the leaf foliage in the plant, going through the full pumping system and the nervous system of the tree itself.

When I speak of things, I speak of them from firsthand experience rather than a related condition. I actually experienced each one of these experiences. It was all part of my teaching as I grew up.

I was sent around the world three and a half times, so that I would be in common with all nationalities of the world and all the religions of the world. Everywhere I went there was somebody waiting to take me in tow and to inform me completely of the conditions and their existence. I've had a very wonderful education by man's standards. In addition, I've been very endowed by the Father with this complete information and Source.

An Overview of the Lessons

In your first book you have forty-nine lessons. There are seven series oflessons, with seven lessons to each series. Each time you read them, you are going to find that new explanations will appear between the lines. The more you go into it, the more you will find because your thinking process is going to control you to a point of inquisitiveness to seek for the fullness of understanding.

You will get out exactly what you put in. For each effort that you make you will receive a multiple of seven, for each thing that you go into to understand and make the exchanges to give to understand, going in without a condition of bias, you allow yourself the freedom of truth to express for itself, by itself and of itself.

Meditation: The Avenue To All the Answers

One of the first things that we are going to learn about is how to meditate. I know that many of you have been through meditation courses, but I am going to ask you to give at least as long a period of time each day as you can until brain, as you understand it now, can't take over the situation. I want you each day to strive to increase that time of holding yourself in suspended condition, to take yourself from vibration to pulsation. This will be accomplished, because **it's the avenue to all the answers of everything that you seek. Meditation is the key for you to purify your body, to heal your body and to get to know yourself.** It enables you to get into rapport with Intelligence, as opposed to praying, which is not doing it for yourself, but instead, wanting someone else to do it for you. Meditation will open the doors for you **to find yourself and find the freedom** from what you call self-being or the ego of being, the selfish you.

Brain is quite a wrestler and is going to wrestle you in every way because it knows as soon as you conquer it, it has no existence. Brain is going to play every trick on you that is possible. Having full access to your memory, it will play back every little dirty trick that it can think of to keep you from shutting it down. When you succeed in shutting brain down, then Mind can take its place and you will have the alliance with the Source rather than the reflection of discernment coming from the brain. You will have true evaluations rather than supposing conditions.

As it is now, you receive over three million thoughts a second to discern and evaluate. In order to function, your automated system in your brain, in your Sightcone, through your pituitary activity, ciphers, reacts reflex feedback through brain and responses take place without your even being concerned about it, because you have let brain do it for so long that it is automatically in control.

You have become creatures of habit, rather than being supremely individualized. You are going to find as you shut brain down, you are going to become more individualized, until you can come to the point that you can let loose of self and become selfless, where you can find the dimension of the **Airless Cell, which is really you**. All the rest that surrounds it is illusion. Everything that you see here as tangible, is not. It is all make-believe. It only lasts as long as we take the dimensions of time, form and space, in that triangle.

Breath and Breathing: The First Secret of Freeing Yourself

One of the first things that we are going to learn about is breath and breathing. This is where the first secret of freeing yourself originates. It is putting yourself in unison with the pulsation of the universe. **The secret**

of this is to breathe in unison with your Airless Cell, which will give the pulse to your heart, and you will learn to fill your lungs with seven equal breaths in smooth, equal intake. You will hold your breath on the intake for two beats of the heart in stillness, and then allow the breath to slowly exhale in equal proportions on seven beats on the exhalation. Then you will allow that breath to be fully released for two beats of your heart before you start over.

The reason for this is that in the seven beats of the heart you allow the primary rays of light to enter the body to make the box. From the concentrated thought to the box or the square is a complexity of six pyramids in a cube condition. You are that cube. By the animation of your movement of that thought in thinking, you bring in the light rays to your diaphragm to energize your brain and your body. You draw energies from earth, coming from your feet to the bottom part of your diaphragm to satisfy that of the flesh and physical part of your body, and from the top side of your diaphragm to satisfy the spiritual part of your body. Both are in poise and balance with mind surrounding both simultaneously in two directions at the same time.

The **Holy Breath diagram shows you what you look like when you breathe.** That is breath. That is the full light transference of breath itself in activity **from the Source** into all the expressions that you express. You are quite a geometric, crystallized creature.

There are 7 Rays of Light: 3 primary and 4 secondary. These triangulations form triangles, circles and squares, which are the basis, in the geometric condition, of our creation. We are a 12 sense being, but man is in functional operation with the 5 lower senses, while the upper 7 senses are dormant. Animals function on 6 senses.

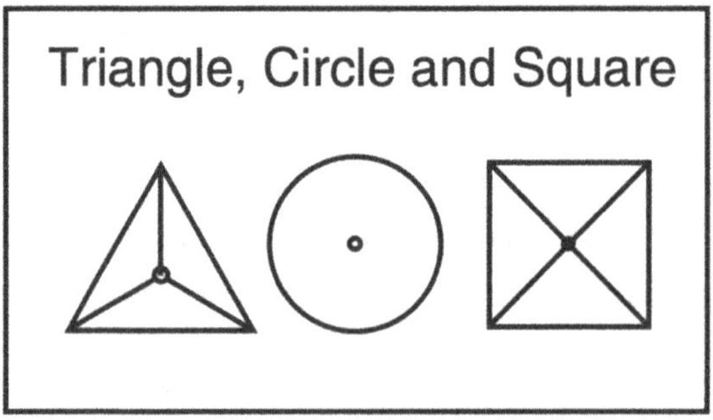

Triangle, circle and square.

The body is flesh-physical, existing in a sensory illusion. It only exists because of our agreement and solidification in our thoughts. **When we can still the brain so that Mind can be in rapport with Spirit, then we are really alive**.

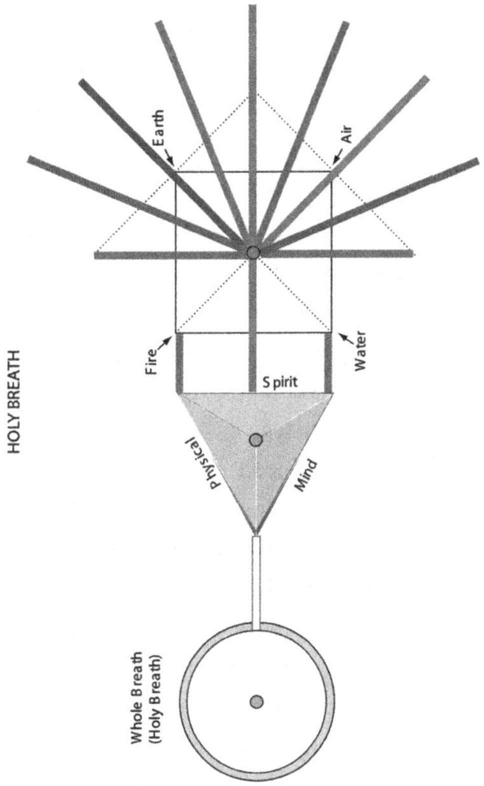

Holy breath.

By going deeper into meditation, the body will realign itself so that the atomic structure will synchronize into one function. You will spin through the Vortex of Light for great rewards. When you do, the atoms of the body will pulsate instead of vibrate. We will learn how to use the Light into an Energy Substance for the body.

Later on in our lessons, we will go very thoroughly into the geometrics of what breath and light and life are all about. It takes hours and hours of discussion to make this fully understood, as you will see as we go through each one of the lessons.

Holy Breath Exercise

There is an exercise which is the Holy Breath, the Whole-in-One Breath. The diagram shows you exactly what takes place when you draw from Source into the breath and how it animates by vibrating activity into expression from that of pulsation into vibrating activity, until you can go from the Source one way or the other in the complexity. It's really very simple. It only seems complex.

The diagram shows you some of the geometry of your pattern of thinking and the complexity of the multiplicity of motion simultaneously at the same time in all directions. As your thought goes into a thinking process, all the multiplicities of crystals in all geometric forms in your blood respond to the source of the energy of the activity and changes in dimensional crystal formation by the thought presence of its energy in exchange through the osmosis from the digestive system of the intestines into the blood. That's the source for the statement, "My life is in your blood." You would be surprised at all the geometric dimensions that are floating in your blood and crystal energy form in sub-minute particles.

This diagram shows your concentration of one full breath in and out in geometry of crystalline conditions of your operation, called the Lesser Maze. The complexity of this is very simple compared to the complexity of your body responding with its billions and billions of cells equally with itself in exchange between your breath discernment and thought, and your exchange of your being in automated mechanics of reflection, rather than the source of knowing actually where you really are and what you are really doing. You have safety valves within you for taking care of all the limits that you can endure, all the stress and strain, until you come to a point that you can take yourself out of stress and strain to a condition of poise.

How did you realize that the breath comes out in crystal formation? Is this a scientific fact?

Yes, it has scientifically now been proven. I've been teaching it now for many years. Last year they finally got electronic microscopes strong enough to be able to see, and in color. This is the first breakthrough.

I experienced this activity by becoming a piece of that crystal in my body. I was placed in the food substance, went through the full osmosis from the light being solidified in the earth to the light crystal into the foliage. Then I was devoured from the foliage and taken into the human body and went through the full digestive system of the body into the blood and to the point of the cellular activity, and then back into Universal Source.

Big Motion Picture

How come you remember this?

When you go through it as I did, it's just like being in a big motion picture, but you're in the minute angle of dimension in its relationship to all other things in its dimension of relationship. The minute infinite in smallness is beyond your comprehension.

I was placed in the center of my Airless Cell so that I could see the magnitude of this body. If you think there is a lot of space looking out there, you should look from your Airless Cell through your body. Everything that exists out there in the universe exists within you.

Did you go through this in a state of meditation?

No, the tree was used as the opening point for me to develop. I entered the earth without the Adamic sleep: I came in with full knowledge. At the age of twelve I became responsible for myself. When I was younger I could never understand why other people couldn't also understand and see what I saw. When you try to tell people that trees talk to you, you get problems.

Firsthand Experience

In everything, they wanted me to have the firsthand conditioning. When you experience it yourself, it's so vivid that you never forget. The impact of my training was to **be in clear-thought** to such a state that everything else was dismissed but that one act that I was in. I went through multiples of this type of training in my growth as I developed.

When I started to travel the world over, everywhere I went I was placed in the multiple history of that part of the world. What would be a few minutes to you would be thousands of years to me. In other words, time is accelerated so rapidly that within an hour's time you may span several million years of history of that condition of expression, or that surrounding area of existence. The whole history of the earth was played back from each dimension that I was in, and each dimension of history was placed in memory, because through the memory everything was fed back. I existed within all the different periods of the histories.

You said it was like a picture screen. You weren't actually just moving around?

What happens is that there is a picture screen and you see the picture. Then the next thing you are IN the picture and you ARE the picture, and you are fully in activity in the picture all the time. You have the ability to withdraw at any time to capture and readjust before you enter back in. You can come in and out at will. It's a beautiful way to learn.

When you say "they," that caught my attention. What do you mean by "they?"

In the universe there are many of authority and each one will take you in tow for personalized instruction. I say "they" because they are multiple and they are authorities of Universal Source. This is their authority and they supersede in the directing of this opportunity, and the adaptation of that after being obtained. Then you reach that level in light around your body. This gives you freedom to move within dimensions of the universe with total freedom. You are no longer bound to this earth.

Everybody has the same opportunity. You have every bit of ability that I have. You can do it better than I. **We all have the same conditions of source in us.** Only you just haven't become aware. You forgot about them.

It was my job when I came to the earth to re-inlight the people of this condition. That's why my schooling was so thorough all the way through, and I had multiples of teachers. When I speak of them I speak of multiples, because no one individual taught me. It was a multiple, yet the Father oversaw it all.

The physical teachers that I had were as equally endowed as the sources that I learned from, and they were just as proficient in their operations as I was taught to be. Everything that I did I had to prove before I could graduate to the next operation of intelligence. **Rather than an intellectual approach, everything was in Intelligence, of Source**.

When I had the control of it and I could demonstrate the control and hold that control, then I was released to the next graduating point.

When you say "control," do you mean it was memorized?

No, you don't memorize anything. You become it. You are that source. You have to prove that condition. You have to do it. You have to maintain it and show your ability of flexibility with it.

Then it is at your memory recall at any moment?

Instantly.

Could you talk about the reasons why we are encased in bodies?

You hold yourself in a body, in bondage because you have limited yourself in your expression. The first thing, after the age of twelve, you stopped breathing properly and your body started its point of deterioration.

At the age of twenty-one your body primes itself for servicing conditions. From that point on, your body starts to fall the other way, becoming imperfect. It becomes as a balance between perfect and imperfect by limitations and conditions that you place upon yourself.

You are no older than the thought of right now. Yet by your projection of acceptance and desire that when you are young you desire age, you fulfill in programming all of your activity to that programming by your projection. By your desires they will be filled.

Discernment

Guard well your thoughts so that you do not contaminate yourself with them. Your thinking has to be put into a proper respect and rapport with thought. **Your values of discernment must become very, very keen, as to know what is really right for you at that time.** That which is not proper should be replaced with that which is proper, so you do not contaminate your brother as you are contaminating yourself.

In our Western world of living we react too rapidly and many times we say things that we are sorry for later, but it is hard to take them back after you have said them. If you learn to use your values of discernment, you will find that you won't be quite so eager to respond until you are sure that this is the truth of the situation, as you see it at that time. **You will start to live in a state of love**, rather than a state of lust.

Desire of lust is where your deterioration really starts, because you start putting material things before perfection. Your First Commandment says, "Thou shalt have no other God before me." When you break the First Commandment, you break all the other eleven at the same time.

Putting Your House In Order

You have to put your house in order and you have to put your thoughts in order. It's like a clean, tidy house. As long as it's kept clean and tidy, it's neat, but if you get slothful and you allow it to decay a little bit, you start collecting dust in the corners. If you sweep it underneath the rug, it just makes a bigger pile to clean up later. You might as well clean up your own mess as you go, rather than putting it aside until it becomes a garbage pile, and you aren't able to carry it around.

It's like anything that's bothering you. It will eat you alive if you allow the imagination to run away, but if you will take it in tow, and quiet yourself, you can shut it off and dismiss it and go on about your business. It is never dropped until you do dismiss it. Tell it, "Out"! You allow anguish to destroy you if you allow it to run too long, because it changes the chemical reflections within your body and the energization of the chemical sources of energies of ether to your cells.

You are a twelve-sense being operating on five senses. Even animals are ahead of you because they operate on six and seven of their twelve senses. Man has bred himself rather dumb. I am not being facetious when I say it in this way, because of your conformity and sociality that you exist in, you become cultured creatures. You become very habit forming, and most of the habits you form are very bad, not good.

Above all, very few individuals are really truthful with themselves, and won't truly face the issues that are at hand. They pass them off to somebody else, when they are not looking. When you get through dragging them all around, you get kind of tired.

Face each issue squarely and fully. Quiet your breath and know the truth of the condition and correct it into that point. Learn to fully evaluate everything, including why it is being projected to you.

If you see anything out there that is bothering you, it is inside of you also. Take a good look at it if you want to dismiss it. The only way you can dismiss it is by understanding it, conquering it. By being quiet, you can bring Source to bear, rather than that of vibration activity, and the answers and the way will be placed at your fingertips for your perfectness of control.

There won't be any great changes all of a sudden, but there will be a continual graduation of exchange as you grow and you begin to know yourself better, and are able to **handle yourself in poise.** That's what this whole thing is all about, to change you from a past tense in a lived condition into life itself, and change you from vibration into a pulsating individual, where you become one breath breathing, instead of breathing breath to exist.

Meditation and the Breathing Exercise

How do we practice the breathing and meditation?

The best thing is to sit yourself up perfectly straight with both feet flat on the floor. If you can't feel your heartbeat, then take your pulse. You can take it with your second finger on the wrist, on the neck or in the temple, any one of the three places.

When you can **feel your heart beat, start breathing in frequency with it.** Feel the surge each time that you take your breath in, and fill your lungs with seven equal beats of your heart. It will take a little practice because you have been breathing at about a five beat rate for so long, that seven is going to be awkward.

After you have filled your lungs, stop your breath for two beats of your heart. Then let the breath slowly out for seven beats of your heart. Hold it out for two beats and repeat again. Do this about seven times.

After you have been with this for a while, it will become natural again and you will do it naturally without even having to prompt it.

Importance of the Breath

The reason for the stillness of the breath on the intake is your evaluations of discernment of all thoughts being taken into your body. Stilling your breath allows you to make your exchanges, your convictions and accept, reprogram, divide and put into motion all the activity that is being expressed to you through Source in intelligence.

This allows the gelatin mass between the vibrating fingers in the Sightcone to become very acute, and they become very critical in their selection of what's proper, what is really perfect, rather than sub-perfect. The more you learn to use your breath, the more the gelatin and the fibers in the Sightcone will vibrate, and the clearer view of conception you will have from source in mind to be exchanged into chemical energy for the cells to operate in unison with.

The exhaling of the breath is for the cleansing of the body.

On the inhaling of the seven beats when you get to about the third beat, the first atomic explosion takes place between the left lung and the right lung. There is an osmosis condition of the transferring of the blood energy in etheric vapors from one lung to the other.

In the stillness of the breath the full transfer is taking place and the new pure blood is placed back into the heart to be recirculated into the blood system to re-nourish the body. This is not only by the activity of the breath, but also all the cells will open in unison and you will start to breathe between your water cells with the light cells of your body which you really should do, but you don't do now.

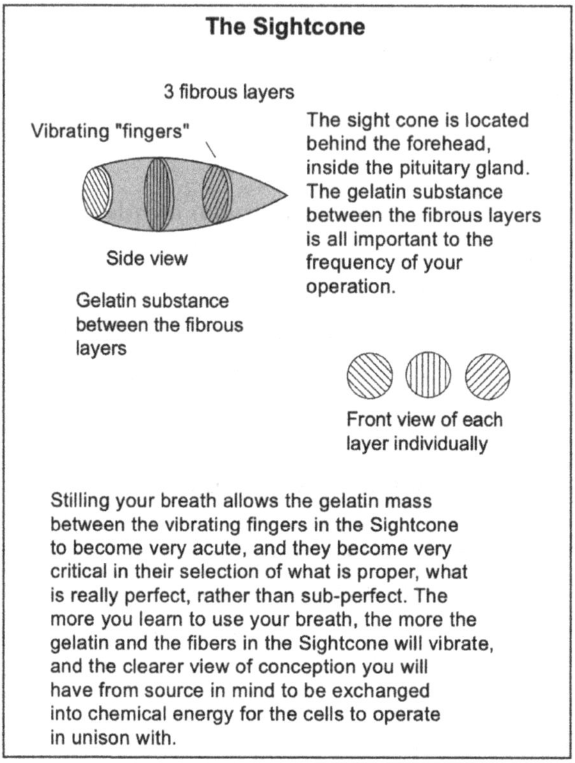

The Sightcone.

On a breath rate of only five beats of your heart, your light cells will never open. Your body becomes stagnant from this condition and by the stagnation of this activity you lose the elasticity of your body because the silicon in the air around you cannot be taken into your body for your cells to have flexibility.

There's a lot that goes on in every operation. There are multiples of reasons why it is done. This energy cannot be attained in any other way but in the unison of breath. It can't get into the body unless you breathe properly.

Breath and Formulating Pictures

The other operation of your breath is this. **Everything that you desire necessary for yourself is yours by proper breath and imaging.** You make the condition, to take yourself from vibration to pulsation. This will be accomplished, because it's the avenue to all that is necessary for yourself. On the intaking breath you formulate the pictures of what you want and how you want it. You collect that of substance to be manifested back into dimensional crystal operation until you have mattered substance.

BREATHING EXERCISE

Sit yourself up perfectly straight with both feet flat on the floor.
When you can feel your heartbeat, start breathing in frequency with it.

Inhale for 7 beats of your heart.
Fill your lungs with seven equal beats of your heart.

Hold for 2 beats.
After you have filled your lungs, stop your breath for two beats of your heart.

Exhale for 7 beats.
Then let the breath slowly out for seven beats of your heart.

Hold for two beats.
Hold it out for two beats and repeat again.
Do this about seven times.

After you have been with this for a while, it will become natural again and you will do it naturally without even having to prompt it.

Breathing exercise.

The stillness of the two beats, on the outgoing breath, is so that your thought transference of energy can be released from your realm of activity, so it is not destroyed. As it is now, you breathe it in and you breathe it right back out, and you fractionize it in such sub-minute particles that you destroy that which you desire before it can ever become yours, because it can't get away from you to collect the needed substance to be manifested back into material matter.

Your breath is extremely important in the control of what you want and what you desire to be manifested for you in your abundance. This **is how you bring your abundance** into this fullness. Many will say, "Gee, he is a lucky guy. Everything he touches turns to gold. He succeeds in everything. I sure wish I could do like he did."

The secret is: NO DOUBT. One speck of doubt destroys everything, instantly. When you know that you know, you know, but if you don't know you don't know, you'll never know. It's that simple. You are going to learn that little statement.

The second one you are going to learn, I desire that you really learn this:

Universal Creed

"I am eternally free in deed, which is my nature, and I bow to no man, not even God, for I am God."

That is your eternal Universal Creed.

We express because our Airless Cell and Ego Cell are in agreement in this expression of reflected activity. As you function in this activity, you operate with this Universal Creed. To think less is to belittle that which created you in His image.

The Twelve Commandments

If you do not love yourself, and you do not love God as you love yourself, then you have placed another god before you, thus breaking the First Commandment. When you have broken the First, then you have broken the other eleven. Until you can proclaim your Divinity, you will remain of Earth.

God, the Father, the Motionless One, is Intelligence. From the Godhead, we were given 12 Commandments as a basis for our expression, but Moses held back the 11th and 12th Commandments: The Love Commandments. It was Jesus' mission, among other things, to give these last two Commandments to us, which are in the New Testament. This was the primary mission. All of the rest were side-trips.

On the stillness of the breath, there are two stages, one on the outgoing and one on the incoming?

Right. Those are very important. The importance of the stillness of the breath allows the activity in the Sightcone to set up its vibrancy, so that which is being manifested has a right of crystalline to be solidified in your dimension for acceptance. Without the stillness, the exchange could not take place. The same thing on the transmission going out: it cannot get away from you to attain back to you unless you let go of it.

Abundance

One thing you are going to learn is that this is the only way of giving. When you learn that you own nothing, you will have everything. When you learn that you are only a user and a partaker of and you own nothing, that it belongs to the universe and you are a universal being, but you have all right of use, then you will have abundance, beyond your dreams. You will have **plenty and to spare, and the spare is so you may share** with those about you.

Earth: The Blue-Green Sun

Earth is to be the Blue-Green Sun, when it fully develops itself. It will be one of the Quadrant Suns of the universe. When this becomes a unison, Earth will be the most beautiful star in the universe, and this is what we're after. That's what it was created for. I can't see why everybody is in such a hurry to get away from here. This is really one of the most beautiful places in the universe to live, and to have life in expression. All the best in the universe was placed on this planet.

It's a very unique planet. It has twelve different dimensional sections, so that all twelve senses of man's being have an equal place of expression upon this planet. I don't care from where you come, from what quadrant of the universe, you have equal on this earth. You have the ability to all live together in unison, from many different vibration dimensions of segments of quadrants. Most of you are voyagers from other dimensions to this planet. Very few are Home on Earth.

You are saying that there is intelligent life elsewhere in the universe?

All over the universe.

We live in a gas mixture in a frequency by the dimension and size and movement of the body that we exist on and within the gases and pressures equal to the dimension within ourselves to the gravity of the earth holding us together, in crystallized dimension. Since we have moved this planet from a subsun to a planet, at about 3 1/2 billion years ago, give or take a few million, we have slowly manifested our crystal dimension into angling deflections of crystals.

Almost all crystals that are brought into dimension of solidification from light into the earth are off-balance on the angles of points on one direction or another. You may find a few gems that are nearly perfect in crystalline form and so nearly flawless that it takes tremendously high magnification to find the flaw. These are very valuable gems and are greatly sought after.

It is just like the individual who becomes this type of gem is greatly sought after too. As with any rough stone, you just need the edges polished up a little bit to balance.

You said that this is the most beautiful planet and you don't know why we are all in a hurry to leave it. Why did you say that? I'm in no hurry to leave it.

Most people are. They want to get down here so they can go. I don't know where they are going to go, but they want to go.

How do you know this?

In the thousands and thousands of people that I have discussed with over multiples of years, most of them are longing for something they don't even know exists. They are in such a hurry to get their life over, they use it up in sixty years, instead of seven thousand.

Would you say that longing is to get back to home base?

Right, because until you can take your body with you, in physical perfectness, drop the flesh and return the substance that belongs to this earth back to it, you'll continuously come back to this earth until you do, or until the earth passes above the vibration of your equalized of expression, in which case, you will be placed to another planet where you will take on that vibration activity.

Wherever you break the law, you will have to reenter, until you learn not to break the law. What Law? The Law of Life.

Our Quadrants of the Universe

What are the quadrants?

Your quadrants are your Central Sun, which is the center of the Universe, and your four Cardinal Suns. This makes your cube, with a center point which makes your six pyramids of operation opening up. Each opens up into a diamond from itself, from the Central Sun and the quadrant of each one. In our quadrant we are between the White Sun, the Central Sun and the Yellow Sun, on the variations of the Green Sun and the Blue Sun.

When we talk of magnitude of size, we are speaking of a Sun. I don't want you to be confused with what we call a sun, which is nothing but a speck of dust, in comparison with the size of the White Sun.

The intelligence that lives there is what feeds the thought emanations to us through mind activity, through spirit, to animate us back into perfection. The exchange of thought transference in mind is continuously in operation. Our frequency of acceptance is where we equalize ourselves in expression.

We run up and down a little yo-yo scale. Somebody pulls the string and we raise our arms and our feet. Until we learn to cut that string, we are going to do just exactly as they have us do by pulling the string.

Free Will and Responsibility

We are given one thing on this planet which is unique. It is called free will. You can do it your own way, any way you want, but you also pay the consequences for it. You can't hurt anybody without hurting yourself. You can't hurt anything without hurting yourself. You can't take away from anybody without denying yourself. These are all things you have to learn.

You can never take advantage of anybody else, because you are taking advantage of yourself first. Any time you deprive anybody of anything, you are the first one to get payment, only you get it in multiples of sevens. The back swing of that gauntlet is tremendous when the back swing comes back. Those are the days you don't quite feel so good.

It's just as easy to enjoy and be happy and be in a state of bliss as it is to be in a state of agony and pain. Everything that takes place you are responsible for; don't pass the buck onto anybody else. Nothing happens except by your programming. Nobody does it to you but yourself. Because of your agreement and conformity of acceptance, you put yourself in that acceptance of exchange. You can have it any way you want it, sunny side up, over easy or scrambled.

The Cube and the Cross

When you look at a cube and open it up, you will find that there are six pyramids in it. There are twelve planes in masculine and twelve planes in feminine. In science we call these positive and negative, but they really are two positives just a little bit out of phase with one another, in universal truth.

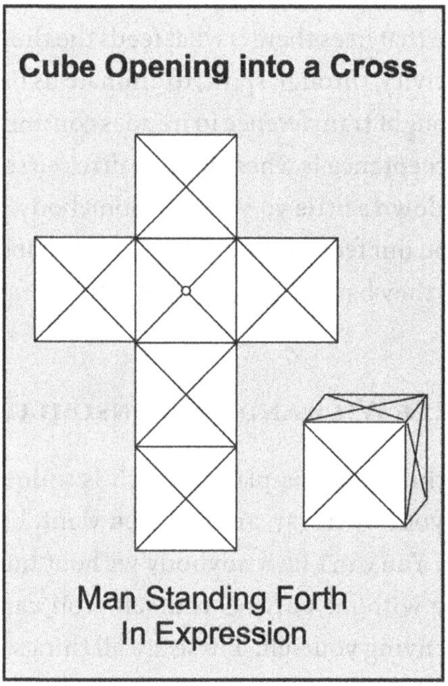

Cube opening into a cross.

They are equal to each other. As the cube opens up into expression it becomes you standing forth in expression, forming a cross, and you become these twenty-four planes of masculine and feminine, because one side of you is masculine and one side is feminine. If you were to put yourselves shoulder to shoulder facing one another, you would find the masculine and feminine would fit absolutely together.

The separation took place when man lost the ability to hold himself in his own purity of thought. When he did, the feminine part fell out of him. In order to allow man to exist in a human form, the feminine was separated at the toes from the masculine. Then we had male and female. "He made them then," is the way it is said in the Bible. Those are your twenty-four of your twelve senses of being, both masculine and feminine. This is your full operation.

By the diagram, you can see the outward of the cube inside of itself and you can see man standing forth in expression when it opens from the one thought into life in existence. It becomes that animated condition expressing continuously by its exchange in its breath breathing, all held in form and conception by the whole breath in the directing of the Airless Cell, solidifying the acceptance of the energies into form by space in dimension, by conformity of thought exchanging. We become the animated condition of that activity, all by breath.

Some of these things are very foreign to you. They sound very complex, but they really are not. It's just that you forgot and you have to be cued a little bit to reawaken.

Three Life-Changing Tips

As we go through our exercises of exchange and become acquainted with one another more, you will find, with an ease and poise, that many things that have been out of order will come into order in your life. Your whole life will begin to change around you, in spite of yourself.

When you take a good, earnest, hard look at yourself and you walk up to that mirror in the morning and you say, "I love you," and you mean it, and it answers back, you have a great day coming. However, when you can't look in that mirror and tell you that you love yourself, you have a lot of problems. That's one of the things you really want to learn to do.

In the morning when you get up, thank the Father for the beautiful day to express Him in. When you have terminated that day, before you go to sleep, review that whole day and forgive the trespassing that you did. You will find you will sleep a lot better, and you won't have any hang-ups in the morning. It's real simple and very easily put into operation.

Sleep, Minds and Vision

Never go to sleep in anger, or it will torment you all night. You may sleep, but you will never have any rest.

Review your whole day before going to sleep, and forgive those that you trespassed against as you forgive those who trespassed against you. Forgive yourself for all the things that you did wrong, and you forgive them for their acts. Everything comes to a neutral position. You just shut your eyes and you are asleep, that quickly. You will be surprised at how quickly you learn to go to sleep. Shut your eyes and you are gone, and awaken totally rested in the morning.

Sleep, Dreams, Visions and Activity

As you drop from a relaxed condition toward the sleep state there are fewer electrical connections in the medulla to the brain.

Connections	Visionary State	Activity
29 to 17	Black and white	Subjective Mind comes into activity.
13 to 9	Colored, visionary dreams	Prophecies of things in future
Below 9	Total sleep state Total rest state No mind activity	You can leave your body on breath, and go wherever you want to.

Sleep, dreams, visions and activity.

The problem is you have seven different minds. Everything that you suppress during the day from the Objective Mind, the Subjective Mind has to take over. You have 144,000 electrical connections in the medulla to the brain.

When you drop from relaxed condition toward sleep state, down to about twenty-nine to seventeen connections, at that time your subjective mind will come into activity. Everything that was suppressed during the day will then be acted out in the dream state. If you go into a visionary state, out of the black and white into color, you have color visions, and all color dreams are visions of future, past or conditions to inform.

When you drop down to between thirteen and nine electrical connections, you will have colored, visionary dreams which are prophecies of things in future. When you drop down below nine, you go into total sleep state and total rest state, no mind activity whatsoever. This is where you can leave your body on one full breath, go wherever you want to, and return back to your body and then resume normal breathing. You can travel the whole universe.

*When we put the **white light of protection** around us, is this from the Central Sun?*

No, the **White Sun**. We are directly in rapport with the White Sun. It's the **emanation of intelligence that directs our operation**. It feeds us directive information. Because of free will we have a right of acceptance or rejection. We can do it our way, wrong all we want to, or we can do it right, or halfway in between. It is our choice.

The White Ray isn't a color. It is the encompassing of all colors animated into expression.

Meditation and Stilling the Brain

In the breathing exercise do you still the mind?

No, you still the brain. When you first start, I want you to just learn to still your breath in your rate of breathing so that you are equal in flow, so the light exchange in your body becomes equal and in rapport to itself.

As you become proficient in this, when you become totally relaxed, you will catch brain off-guard and will slip by it into mind. Brain will fight like the devil to get back into control of you. It's going to make you itch, scratch, hurt, tickle; even dirty thoughts will run through your mind, and a lot of things which are garbage will run through there.

TEN REASONS FOR MEDITATION

Purify your body.

Heal your body.

Get to know yourself.

Shut off brain.

Be in communion with spirit.

Realize activation and unification with Mind.

Bring eternal youth into the body.

Release flesh into an expression of Light.

Gain total freedom of the universe.

Attain Perfection of a Being in the universe.

Until you can change the grossness of the flesh body into electrons, atoms and molecules and align them, simultaneously, to function in the same direction at the same time, you have not perfected.

Ten reasons for meditation.

The trick is to learn that as soon as you agree with any of that activity it has got you again. As soon as you agree, you lose mind and go back into brain activity. As soon as that takes place, give up. You have lost. Go back into your daily activities again.

Each time that you succeed, the brain is going to be more alert and you will have to be more persistent to break this hold. There will come a time when you can hold yourself between two and three hours on one breath, and change from vibration into a pulsated activity. In this state you will rise.

The Ultimate in Meditation: Full Light

When you first go into this activity, you will go into a condition where you think your body is going to disintegrate. **You will spin so fast** you will actually swear that your body is going to tear to pieces. When this takes place, don't be frightened, but just be in a totally relaxed condition. What is happening is that **all of your atoms in your body are lining up in one motion,** simultaneously at the same time.

When you accomplish this, you will pass right over into full Light. This means that all the cells of your body are in arrangement to be able to be transferred from this earth.

This is the ultimate in your meditation. This will take years for the average individual to attain, years of diligence, continuous repetition of control. Just to meditate to the point of relaxing is only the first step into meditation. Meditation is the key for you to purify your body, to heal your body and to get to know yourself. It enables you to get into rapport with Intelligence as opposed to praying, which is not doing it for yourself but wanting someone else to do it for you.

Until you can change the grossness of the flesh body into electrons, atoms and molecules and align them simultaneously to function in the same direction at the same time, you have not perfected. **Meditation is actually the gateway to freedom for yourself.**

The Father asks for ten percent of your time a day so that he can commune with you. What need has He of your pennies? He has the whole universe. Why should you have to pay tribute to Him? A loving Father you need to pay tribute to? No, never.

All He wants is for you to be quiet enough so you can hear His voice of thunder, and it will become like thunder when you become quiet. The whole universe is yours to be had when you learn to be quiet. Still the brain so that you can go into the rapport of Mind and move into the field of Spirit itself and become allied in unison with Spirit in universal function. This is what it's really all about.

Only through your diligent activities will you conquer the ignorance of yourself and conquer your brain and put it back into a computer, which it really is, instead of a playback of memory excuses. You will become individual in a condition of selflessness, where the **ego cell** that is controlling your body **will give up its control to the Airless Cell. When this takes place all the cells in your body turn to Light.**

This is what Jesus said when He told Mary, "Do not touch me. I have not yet ascended unto the Father." His body was all in Light transference. Had she touched it, she would have disintegrated. The energy of the body is so intense at that time that anything of flesh would be completely dissolved instantly if it were touched.

The energy in your body is beyond your conception. You cannot imagine how much force you really have inside of this body and the abilities that it has.

All of this is attained through the perfectness of **your meditation itself. This is the key.** I don't care how much you go to sleep. I don't care whether you lie down, stand on your head, bend your toes. I don't care what position you get in, as long as you are comfortable and totally relaxed. If you fall asleep, you will have a good nap.

There will come a time when you surpass falling asleep and you will be able to hold the pureness of thought in rapport and become one breath breathing. You do it now without realizing it every once in a while.

How many times have you been sitting somewhere, when all of a sudden you will jerk and come back to the realization that you have been gone, totally. You have moved from physical activity, into mind, into spirit, totally into function without even realizing you slipped in. When you realized, you took your breath and you came right back in again, with a jerk.

You will find out that as you develop and you become proficient in your own functioning, that you will have freedoms beyond your belief. You will have unison in rapport with yourself that you can attain in no other way, and you will attain health conditions within yourself beyond your belief.

Exercise For Alertness, Balance & Health

I am going to show you something that will help you during your day so that you keep yourself alert and in balance. On your wrists you have two lines. Take each one of your wrists and put those lines together. Extend your fingers; put them together and extend them out. Now look at the ends of your fingertips and see how much longer they are on one side than the other.

[To one student:] You are about three to four pounds heavier on your right side than you are on your left side, meaning you are under a stress condition and your body is laboring to work.

Take your hands with the left hand palm up, fingers pointing to the right, right hand palm down, fingers facing left. Put your fingertips together right over left, hooking them together. Now pull on them. Go right up over your head. Pull again behind your head. Bring your hands forward over your head. Line up your wrists. If they don't line up the first time, do it a second time and they will.

This neutralizes all of the electrical energy in your body. As you tire, your muscles become more taut and your body begins to curve. You can look at people and see that their shoulders will drop on one side where the tension is. If you will do this three or four times a day, you will **never ever have a stroke or a heart attack.** Whenever you feel a little out of sorts or a little tired, it doesn't take anything to just yawn and do the exercise. Nobody needs to know what you are doing. They just think you're yawning. It's that simple.

Did you say that the tension was the weight that was causing the imbalance?

Yes, the muscles begin to constrict. They start to draw up tighter so that in every movement which is taken, everything is twisted. Your digestive system and all the energies in your body go out of function. The more you wait, the more the friction overcomes and then turns to pain, because of lack of proper circulation, both in the nervous system and the blood. Your body then becomes deficient in functional operation. Pain will proceed and a condition of disease comes about.

It's just as easy to keep yourself in balance as it is to be unbalanced.

TENSION + FRICTION = DISEASE

Tension + Friction = Disease.

What is the spinning condition that is related to meditation?

Spinning is in the last stages of perfection and your breath control of meditation.

What causes dizziness?

You feel dizzy because you have so much mucus in your brain that when you try to quiet, it will cause a sensation because of the pulsation between the mastoids taking place that causes a spinning condition. Usually you can tell by pressing on your naval.

When you sit quietly your head will spin. If you roll your head around about ten times and then stop, see how quickly you stabilize. If you can't stabilize quickly, it means you have too much mucus on the brain.

How do we correct that?

Go get yourself some green pippin apples and eat them for three days. The pectin in these apples will take the mucus right out of the brain. It will clear it out in three days, but you can't have anything else but water and your green apples.

What is the pulsating in and out?

That's you becoming in unison with light itself. In other words, you're phasing. You're becoming in phase. You are seeing a reflection of your cell light and your breath is in a unison condition of exchange. As you are breathing, you still your breath and become one breath, then the light begins to illuminate itself because your aura increases continuously with the still breath. There is no animation going on.

It circles?

It actually spirals. By the drawing, you can see exactly what takes place as the one positive is trying to catch the other positive. We look at everything in flat dimension rather than in proper perspective of activity in form.

It is actually cycling. Whatever the dimension of the crystallization of its light ray, is in acceptance and rejection in discernment. That amount of light is cycling at that rate of speed in two directions at the same time. One is coming and the other is going. Yet they are reaching the zero point as they pass one another. They have a top and a bottom, but they are going in opposite directions at the same time, masculine and feminine.

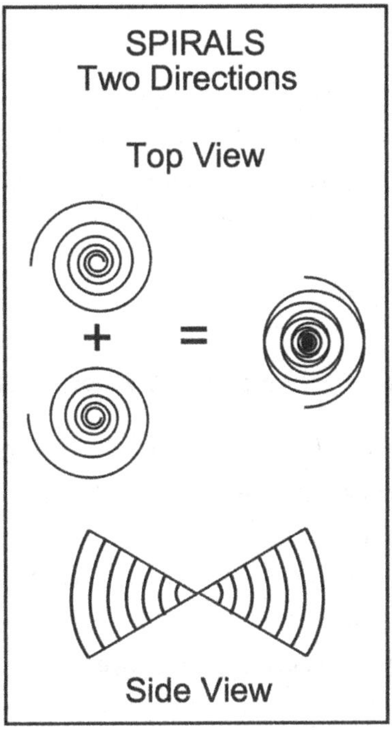

Spirals.

Are there mechanical things which do this?

They use it in marine applications a lot where they turn the two propellers against one another to hold trueness of course.

In the breathing exercise, sometimes it seems like the dot you are looking at comes toward you.

It's according to whether you are transmitting or receiving. If you look at a dot and concentrate on the dot in your breath, you will watch as you breathe in, it will come to you. As soon as you breathe out, it will go away from you. It will run back and forth.

With the spiral and when you turn to light are you in control of that?

Yes. You are in full control.

If you say, "I want to go back now," do you just stop?

No, you don't stop. You just take a breath and everything changes and you change right back into the crystallized condition, that quickly. You can be free that quickly or back in, that quickly. Remember, **you are creating all this illusion continuously in your exchange of breath by your Airless**

Cell. This really is all illusion. Even as solid and as firm as you think it is, it is illusion.

What is this tightness in my head?

Your mastoids are swollen. It means that the plates of the skull are buckling over the back. Take your hands and place them over your ears and slowly push up. Where the plates are buckled, it will take them right out and it will relieve that condition.

The Airless Cell and Becoming a Living Being

You mentioned the Airless Cell. Could you show the importance of the Airless Cell?

The Airless Cell is really you. It is the eternal you of Be. It is of such infinitesimal smallness that if you made a dot, only just a pinpoint, on a piece of paper about six feet in diameter, this pinpoint would be thousands of times larger than your Airless Cell.

Your Airless Cell is locked in the center of your heart. Everything that manifested into being was directed by its operation over the top of the mother's head. It collected the elements of the universe to make your form to express in.

When you take the first breath and the body is placed in condition and the breath is taken on the motion of breath, then the auricles of the heart close around the Airless Cell and you are a living being.

The AIRLESS CELL
is really you.
It is the eternal you of Be.

The airless cell.

Two and a half inches from the heart is the **ego center**, which is the reflective activity of the Airless Cell, the first cell that is put into the body. This is the egg that is in the feminine properties which is sparked by the sperm of the masculine. When that spark is accepted, the entity above then shoots a beam of light equaling with that spark and that form is claimed. At that split second, all the rest of the sperm die, in that one spark. That is osmosis of atomic explosion that takes place which puts that spark of light into activity into expression. From then on, the Airless Cell takes over and directs the ego cell to make the form or vehicle to express.

The color of the Airless Cell sets its presence of selection of parenting, bodies and conditions. All must give way to the gold or the silver. They have right of choice of parents and privileges. For all the rest of them, it's a dead heat, whoever comes in first. They are all colors of the rainbow.

Whenever a woman is in her period of conception, there will be thousands and thousands of little dots of light all around her head. They are energies waiting to come into expression.

As for the Airless Cell, it is hovering about the mother as the fetus is forming, drawing forth the elements of the Universe to build its vehicle for expression. During this process, the fetus develops through all Seven Kingdoms before it expresses into Life. This is the true evolution of the species, a most misunderstood concept. First, the fetus develops in water, then air and into Light.

We are presently expressing in air, stepping forward into Expression in Light. There is a Perfect Etheric picture pattern of being that is able to reconstruct our bodies. **Our body is the sum total of the external universe. Within our Divine Atom, we are the Universe in miniature.**

I too, have come into expression by this process. Don't be fooled by what you see before you. Age is accepted with wisdom. Never be fooled by what your eyes see, because you don't **see**; you are looking. Don't be surprised if you see me in many places. You found me, and I will eternally be with you. Any time that you have need, just call my name and I will be there with you instantly. That I promise you.

I come once in every history. I am in your history now.

This is very interesting, but it is very difficult for someone who has never heard of any of this before.

That's right. Like I say, when you are here, come in with a very open mind. I am going to rack your very foundations. This is information that I'm teaching to my students that have been with me almost nine years, and they're having trouble understanding what I am saying.

Have you at one time been a disciple?

Yes, I studied under Socrates. I studied under Zen. We can go back into the Amassaland period, which wouldn't even be an association of your history, about three billion years ago, when there was only one continent upon the earth, before the division or separation took place.

Histories, Planet Like a Motor, and Earth Tumbles

What do you call a history?

Our history has run just a little over six thousand years now.

How can you put a number on history?

It is when expression terminates and the earth tumbles. Earth tumbles on an average of approximately six to twelve thousand years. The longest period of history was about eighteen thousand years within the past twenty-eight histories.

When the termination of the history takes place, the outer surface of the earth comes to a standstill, while the inner of the earth continues to spin. This happens when the North Pole of Earth moves out of phase plus thirty-two degrees from magnetic north to true north. If you read in your Bible in the beginning, it tells you that they marveled at the sun standing still for four hours and the nausea of the people was terrific because of lack of a spinning movement.

A planet is like a selsyn motor with a rotor and a stator. The cellus belt, which is approximately 160 to 280 miles below the crust of the earth, is a large plastic band of absorption between the inner earth and the outer earth. This is what divides the movement of the earth from the rotating rotor to the relatively static stator, from the light acceptance into the North Pole and the light released from the South Pole. When the inner part builds up sufficient friction to grab the earth, it will throw it into a spin, eighty degrees and drift ten.

When the next North Pole is established, it will be at the Sea of Bengal, and in five minutes all of China and that area will be a frozen mass. That's how quickly it takes place.

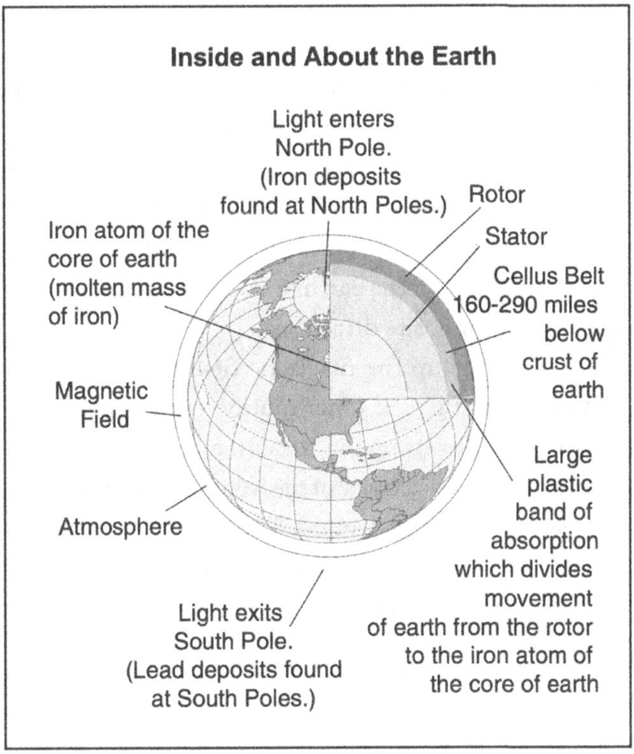

Inside and about the Earth.

The wall of water that comes out of the Pacific Ocean will be traveling at more than four thousand miles an hour, at a height of about three and a half miles. You can imagine the hydraulic effects of this when it strikes a continent. That's why we have so many earthquake faults along the coastline.

We know where every North Pole was because of the great iron deposits. We know where the South Poles were by the great lead deposits. We also know by the volcanic activity, the locking of the pyrites and the crystalline minerals, where the North Poles were at that time. By calculating the quadrants of its angles, we can tell exactly where each North Pole was in each span of history. It's an exact science.

Can you tell us when it would happen, when the earth might tumble next?

To set a time or date when anything like that will happen, all I can say is watch your exchange between magnetic north and true north. I can tell you this, though, in 1913 when they tested, we were at seventeen degrees out from magnetic north. We are now [1979] at thirty-one point seven (31.7) degrees. When we reach thirty-two, the earth tumbles.

It's up to the people of the earth and their thoughts whether it goes backwards or terminates itself. The Light workers and the collective thinking of mankind can keep this condition within tolerable limits. It is their thoughts that change the energy pattern of light that spins the earth.

There are seven rays of light coming in on multiples of sevens to itself. It passes seven times through the earth in one direction and seven times its multiple of itself in the opposite direction.

The outer stator sets up the magnetic field to make atmosphere on the outer part of the earth. The inner motion of the light of the primary source of the first triangle sets up the attraction of the inductance of the air transformer and the residual activity of the iron atom of the core of the earth. That's what makes the earth go around. This is what records us in balance to the Central Sun from the light in quadrants of angles between the Green, the White and the Red Suns. The balancing of the Central Sun gives you the Love, the Yellow.

Color, the Aura and Thoughts

You have brought up a color, yellow. Colors are important, aren't they?

Very, very important. Why do you pick the color of clothing that you wear each day?

It helps set the pattern of your day's activities.

Is that like auras? Some people say they see color around a person.

Every time you change your thoughts, the color changes around your head. That's why I can tell what the thoughts are in the room, because I see your thoughts and the intensity as they emanate.

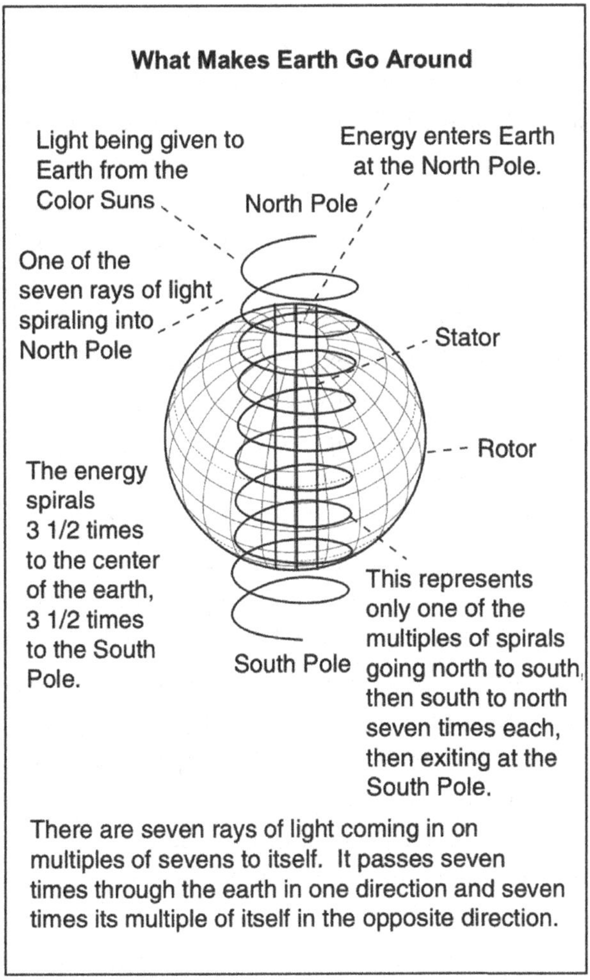

What Makes Earth Go Around
Light being given to Earth from the Color Suns
Energy enters Earth at the North Pole.
North Pole
One of the seven rays of light spiraling into North Pole
Stator
Rotor
The energy spirals 3 1/2 times to the center of the earth, 3 1/2 times to the South Pole.
This represents only one of the multiples of spirals going north to south, then south to north seven times each, then exiting at the South Pole.
South Pole
There are seven rays of light coming in on multiples of sevens to itself. It passes seven times through the earth in one direction and seven times its multiple of itself in the opposite direction.

What makes Earth go around.

You will find that as you are studying and learning, when you don't understand I will elaborate more, because I can see whether you are accepting or not. The class also will come into a unison of thought. I had it three different times tonight with you when everybody was totally in balance with one another. It is very easy if you span and see where each of your thoughts is, and how much you are perceiving, whether you are confused, or whether you need more explanation on it. It gives a great advantage to be able to perceive what's taking place out there. I will answer your question many times before you ask it.

The color yellow is love?

That's right. Yellow is your most prime color. Your Central Sun is yellow. Everything comes from the yellow, all love in the first dimensions of the three L's, is Love, Light and Life. From the Motionless, Life came into being, by the Light of Love, and you had expression because of this conditioning, the Motionless into Motion.

You become the reflection of that activity in each dimension. By your exchange in acceptance or rejection, you set up a presence of operation between yourself and with yourself for everything that is expressing, whether you accept it or reject it. It's still expressing, and it goes right on by you. If you don't entertain it or agree or disagree with it, it goes to somebody else.

The Father's Love is very impersonal. The Father is no respecter of persons or things; they are all equal.

With the mind, spirit and physical, the yellow is spirit, blue is mind?

Right. Physical is red. The white is that which encompasses all three. It's the Intelligence of Expression. Your little beeper goes on and you blink out the colors, and the prismatic activity of the blending of the waves of light that come through your diaphragm sets up all this activity in the seven arteries that are in the diaphragm. The three on the angles set up your primary to set up your prism. The four on the outside set up your box to contain it, so that you have your twenty-four planes of hermetic activity, twelve masculine and twelve feminine. It goes up and down and sideways at the same time.

You see everything with your navel. Your physical eyes are only the recorder. You really see everything with the navel, the "pit of the stomach." When you are shocked or frightened, where do you feel it? In the "pit" of your stomach.

Did you read in the paper about the young man who regained his hearing, after being deaf since he was three years old? He said there was a big explosion and lots of light and color, but he was in the middle of the desert. Nobody can prove this. All of a sudden his ears popped and he can hear again. Is there any explanation for that?

The explosion actually took place in the Sightcone. The sensitivity of the Sightcone and the rushing of energy flowing through the canals that were dormant, reactivated the light substance traveling through it and would actually sound like a tremendous explosion outside.

The explosion was really in his own head?

Yes. All the lights were the energies of activity taking place because he was recording from inside outside, rather than from outside inside.

You say you come once in an average history?

Yes, but this would be my last trip. In each history I have come at least once. This is my last trip. This was by request that I am here at this time. When I go Home this time, I don't go out any more.

Sages and Teachers

You're not the only one who comes, are you?

There are others that come in sage conditions and different capacities of authority. There are always a minimum of seven sages on the earth at all times. These are great teachers.

I am a teacher. I'm here to instruct you to teach yourself. I can't teach anybody but myself, but I can instruct you to teach yourself. I can't do it for you; you have to do it yourself. I'll point the way. I'll even mark the walk, but you have to walk it, because when it comes down to the final step of taking your body with you and turning it to light, you have to do it. I can't do it for you.

Council of Souls

When you terminate this expression, you must spend your fourth day at the Council of Souls, explaining your life, for that eight-hour period. We are judged by the harshest judge of all, ourselves. We pass judgment upon ourselves, just as we have to purify our body by ourselves. No one else can do it for you.

Seven Bodies

There are seven bodies about this one. The higher self is eight times the size of the earthly body. This topic will be covered in more detail in future lessons.

Upon what is generally referred to as death, most individuals leave the earthly body through the navel, which is below the solar plexus. This is the route of the common earthly developed man. The intelligent receive their crowning glory and leave through the top of their head: the Crown Chakra.

Upon Termination of Expression Days 1-4	
Garden of Life	**Council of Souls**
3 days	4th day
You will sit in rest as all your Etheric Energies assemble.	You run through all your life. You judge yourself.

Upon termination of expression.

It's Easier To Be Happy

It is so much easier to be happy and in pleasure, than it is to be in anger and fretting, continuously in disillusionment. You can have from life just exactly what you want, good or bad, and to the intensity that you desire.

It's very easy to die, but it's hard to live, because you have to fight to live. Anybody can give up. The only problem with giving up is you just have to do it over again. You might as well make your mind up to do it once and get it over with. It's easier that way, just like anything. When you become proficient, you don't even have to think about doing it. It becomes automatic. You are so prone to using your bad habits, why don't you do it with your good habits? You are very proficient; why not change it around the other way, so that everything you touch turns to the other side?

The whole secret is to learn to love. That's where the whole answer really is. If you **do everything in love**, you will never have any problems, because, if you are in love, you are going to take time to be considerate of another.

Always be gracious enough to thank the Father for the beauty that He has held for you to express in. Remember, your eyes are His window to your activity, and they are recording.

The whole secret is to learn to love.

If you think something, you might as well do it, because you are just as guilty. Your thoughts have to be just as clean as your activity. You have to get your show together. The only way you get rid of garbage is by forgiving it. Nothing takes place unless you entertain it.

Everything that you want or desire is within your own love presence. When you learn and you begin to know, instead of learning to know, then things will be instant, because you will be able to move into a Now condition, rather than a projection of time delay wait.

It's like the man says, "I wish my arms were longer." The other guy says, "Why? You'd only have to reach further to have what's next to you." Why not snuggle up and have it all, instead of reaching for a handful?

The Why Of Life

To come into existence, to live a time, then die and pass out of existence again. This pattern seems to be the whole sum and substance of life. This is only the way it seems. This concept is not the Real Life, and those who tell you that this is true are greatly mistaken.

Another mistaken concept is that man is the only manifestation of the divine existence of Life. It is true that man is a Son of God, created from the Thought of God. He is clothed in Spirit and made flesh in order to express God's likeness in all Truth and in all loving beauty. All creations were created in the same manner.

One of man's greatest errors is the belief that he is the only begotten of God. The truth is that God created all things and gave all things the consciousness of life.

Life is the first attribute of God. There was Life before there was consciousness. One of the great truths that our Master Jesus taught his disciples is that the whole of life is the foundation upon which all things were built.

Now this same truth is being given again, so that man may know that he can never become extinct. He cannot escape life, because life exists in all forms—seen and unseen, manifest and non-manifest. **There is no death**.

The Causeless Cause of all things, of all being, is Life. Life may be considered as the Granary of God, for it is God's storehouse. All of the things of Heaven and Earth are immersed in a product of life, which is the one life to all manifestations. Even though there is only one life, all manifestations are expressing upon different vibratory planes.

Jesus taught that in the beginning, the Triune God breathed forth, and seven spirits stood before the throne. In this quotation, the Triune God means Spirit, Mind and Physical.

Spirit—Mind—Physical

Yellow—Blue—Red, blended with the Gray of Space = time.

Seven Spirits means seven phases of expression. Therefore, Spirit, Mind and Physical vibrated in unison and seven phases of expression stood before life, manifest in life. **These seven manifestations of life are seven distinct planes of God's expression; Man, Angel, Fowl, Animal, Vegetable, Protoplasm and Earth.**

The quotation now becomes: In the beginning, Spirit, Mind and Physical vibrated in unison and became manifest in Life.

Man, Angel, Fowl,

[Triangle]

Animal, Vegetable, Protoplasm and Earth.

[Square, the Earthbound Base]

Each has its own individual expression, and each is a perfect expression of and within itself. Remember that this quotation does not say that Spirit, Mind and Physical created these seven manifestations, but breathed them forth. Breathed forth refers to celestial being, and created refers to terrestrial being. Even before the beginning, these things in Spirit, Mind and Physical were all held in the Perfect State of Consciousness.

From this, we can readily see that **Life is indeed "that perfect cycle, through which the thoughts of God are made to manifest in all perfection."**

Perfection is created by God and is the only creation of God. Man is imperfect only because he has made for himself other vibratory planes of existence.

God created perfect Bliss, perfect form and perfection in all blessedness. However, man has not remained true to this creation, and therefore has caused his vibrations to lower. As a result, he has made manifestations suitable for his lower vibratory plane and has taken a part of all creations except the Angels with him.

Man's mission, the why of his present life, is to regain his created state of perfection, and to lift all the creations that he caused to fall back into belief into that same state of perfection which God created.

This the why of life as it is now, and as it will be until man has fully atoned to himself for all transgression of himself. **Man must return to earthly expression again and again until he has atoned, and until he has again come to know himself.** For man is not as he seems to be, and **there is a mighty work that each individual must do.** Although this work must be done by yourself alone, your guide will show the way by bringing to your remembrance all the ways of perfection. In this way, you will conquer the foes that you have made **and will return again to that perfect state from which you came.**

The Why Of Life

What You Are Going To Study

I have the privilege of being your narrator to take you into what Truth really is. What you are going to study is what Truth really is. I will open avenues unto you that will give you the ability to take your body from this earth with you. You will never know the sting of death if you will diligently study your lessons and do your exercises. This is what this whole study is all about.

Many things that you will hear in this class will be totally foreign to you, but I will give you full explanations of everything that I teach, and why it's so. It's all broken down in a simple enough language and comprehension that the average individual can very easily handle the conversion.

I've been endowed with seven books that I have put into print, and I have seven more in my head that have never been put in print, that surpass the emphasis of what you are going to learn in your first seven books.

Read your lessons at least seven times in a week. When you read your lessons, I want you to make notes of everything questionable that is in your lessons. When you see a word oddly placed or oddly defined in a sentence, look that word up for clarity of meaning because what you think words mean may not be their real meaning.

As you are reading, you will find that you won't be able to complete the lesson reading it all the way through. This is because your thought transference will be in conscious and will stop to visualize with you what you are interpreting in words into action. You will have many thoughts start to run from the words themselves. Many lines will appear between the lines for explanation, as you start to read.

As you go through the book you will be given exercises and requests to do these exercises. Each of these exercises that you will be given is very necessary to bring your body into rapport with Spirit, along with the attainment of meditation. Each of the exercises I will give you is very exacting. If you will execute them with the exactness that you are given, the benefits you receive will be in multiples.

The Why Of Life

Why should man be in expression? Why is he here? The why of life is one of the questions that man has pondered over and wondered about. Man was not always where he is now. When **Man was created in the Perfect Thought,** his stature was much larger than it is now. His radiant being was awesome to behold.

This Earth that he inhabited was the most beautiful jewel that was created in this quadrant of the Universe. Viewed from out in space, it looked liked a blue-green emerald. Upon this, Man was endowed with all of his Presence of Being, until he belittled himself and let reasoning and intellect rule him. He had to know the difference between good and evil, and further degraded himself so that he took himself out of creation, into manifestation, by his own ignorance of his potential. Man dropped so low that he went down to mineral man, a state where he was nearly unmovable.

Now you are in the first aspect of the most perfect time in your period of history for your Perfection. You are in the quadrant of two Quadrant Suns in triangulation of the Central Sun. Their radiations are now bombarding Earth with tremendous energy. **Earth has a rendezvous to become a Sun, the Blue-Green Sun** for our quadrant of the universe. It will be increasing its vibration.

We are at a vibration of 12, which is an extremely high curve. This figure is our current frequency of vibration. Those who cannot stand the increased pressure of that vibration will be removed to a planet where they are able to function in a compatible vibration. We are supposed to be vibrating at 2 3/4 to 4 at this time. These are seeds for future discussion. Many of you wonder why your pressures are so heavy upon you with indecisions, and turmoil about the entire planet. Those that stay with the flesh will destroy themselves. Due to this, man increases his vibratory rate of pressure bearing upon the body. The atmospheric pressures of the void that you live in, are your bubble. The greater pressure it activates upon your flesh body, the more dense your flesh becomes. The heavier it becomes, the more painful it is for you to exist in this environment.

LIFE, LOVE AND LIGHT

Life is the most beautiful thing there is. Before anything else was, there was Life. From the Motionless, there was Life. When it moved upon itself, it became Motion and brought Love into play. Between Life and Love, there was Light.

THE FIRST TRIANGLE OF PRISMATIC ACTIVITY

Life is the most beautiful thing there is.
Before anything else was, there was Life.
Life produced the 3 "L's": Love, Light and Life.

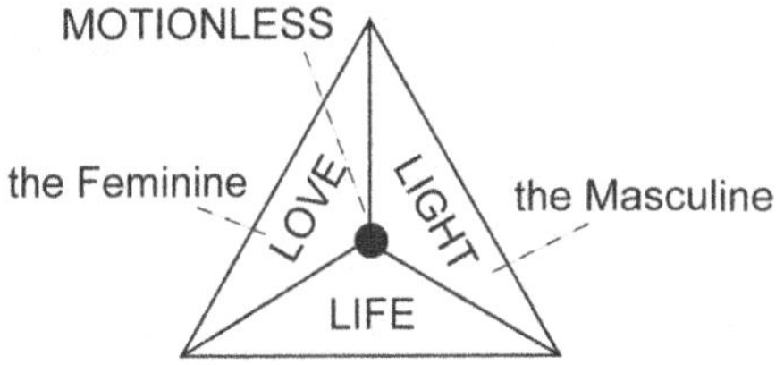

FROM THE MOTIONLESS THERE WAS LIFE.
When the Motionless moved upon itself it became Motion. That Motion is Life. This brought Love into play. Between Life and Love, there was Light.

The first triangle of prismatic activity.

You are the result of that Light, only you have darkened your Light by shadows. You have made your body dense. You have changed the anons to atoms, to electrons, to molecules. You now construct your molecular structure by carbon atoms.

The light cells of your body are 95% dark. When you become Pure Light, you will not cast a shadow. The density of your body is so heavy, that you have trouble even using the water cells of your body, of which there are over 2,000,000. There are over 7,000,000 Light Cells in your body.

You have 12 Sense Centers, but you are only functioning with five of them. The rest are dormant. The awakening and mastery of all 12 is necessary in your attaining of Perfection. Most of you are taking yourself out of expression by each breath that you breathe. Because you are breathing yourself out of Life, you have become a lived condition by each improper breath that you take. This will be the first thing that you are going to learn to do, and it will require diligence on your behalf.

Life itself is all of the attributes of God in Perfection. All of these attributes were given to Man as he was created. With this, Man was given dominion over all things, even God, because you are God. If you think anything less, then you break the First Commandment:

Thou Shalt Have No Other God Before Me

You also break your own Universal Law when you put any God before you. There is only one sin that exists, which is the breaking of Universal Law. The Law of Life is Universal Law. All of the rest are man-made laws and conformity of social laws. They do not exist in Perfection and Truth.

Many of the things and standards that you live by, will drop away. Many of the things I say to you will be foreign and unacceptable to you at this time, but do not discard them, just set them aside on a shelf, because you will have a need for them in a year or two. Don't fight or resist it, because clear thought is of the utmost importance for you, as you will have need of recall of everything that you hear. If it is not imprinted perfectly, it will not play back to you the same way.

The lessons states:

> *To come into existence, to live a time, then die and pass out of existence again. This pattern seems to be the whole sum and substance of life. This is only the way it seems. This concept is not the Real Life, and those who tell you that this is true are greatly mistaken.*

Life always was, always will be and has never ever altered. It has always been totally full and in the full state of All. Don't let anybody tell you this existence is all there is. They are greatly wrong.

Before anything else was, there was Life. From the Motionless into Motion, Life came into being in expression in a triadic activity furnishing you with the first triangle of prismatic activity. It produced the three "L's": Love, Light and Life.

Love is the first activity and the feminine part of the masculine expression in activity. Light is the masculine. Love is the feminine. The son in activity is the Light in motion. This is Life, the first triangle. The prismatic angles of the crossing of any one of the angles blend into the seven light rays producing forth life into expression, the activities of thought in motion.

These impressions, when received through the first triangle, give expression of life into activity and bring forth that which man is in rapport with, the Light Principle.

Those are a lot of big words; now we will take it down to very simple language, but it's very exacting what I say.

In the Motionless is the same thing as the Airless Cell that is in the center of your heart. It is the receptacle that retains the Spirit unison and directs the activity of your being. It is the direct unison with Life Itself from the Airless Cell of Life Itself, the Motionless. Yet the ponderance of these energies brings all motion into being. All motion of all activities of energization by force are subdued through the activity of triangulations by the 7 rays of light, the three primary and the four secondary, which cause the seven band ray of light, the same as a rainbow, giving you all breath, the whole breath in one into activity. You become a breathing, living being by this activity.

By the impulses of the thoughts of Mind through Spirit, being carried in the impulse of exchange by your desire and your values of discernment within the spirituality cone, you set your programming in agreement with the ego cell by the direction of the Airless Cell into expression. You become that light in activity as you agree or disagree with the amount of energy that you are receiving. You become corespondent in activity and expression equal to anything that is being broadcast because of your values of discernment within your spirituality cone.

By the conception of your evaluations, you take on mattered substance from true substance to have living expression in the flesh, so that you can express what is endowed to you.

If you place limitation upon this, then you take yourself from life and you become living. You become lived, past tense, so you are taking yourself from expression by each breath. You are either breathing yourself into life or you are breathing yourself out of life.

Expressions on Earth & Everlasting Life

To think that this one expression, to come and leave, is all there is to it, is a very poor conception. I would venture to say that the average individual in this room has expressed at least three million times on this earth alone, in three and 1/2 billion years, give or take a little.

As a result, you are all very well endowed with the activities of this earth through memory. Life is everlasting and has always been and always will be. You come in and out of it because of your own inadequacy to yourself, due to a lack of proper preparation in physical structure to bring yourself into pure physical, rather than that of flesh.

Instead of solidifying into matter you can in-light into substance and change your body to light, by your discernment and valuation of your thought activity. In other words, in truth it is multiplicities of motion simultaneously in all directions at the same time.

The Earth is 7 1/2 billion years old. Man was created about 7 1/2 billion years ago. After 3 billion years of a Perfect State, man started his fall. That is when manifestation came into being.

The Age of Earth and Man on Earth

7 1/2 billion years ago	Earth was created. Man was created in a perfect state.
For 3 billion years	Man was in a perfect state.
4 1/2 billion years ago	Man started his fall Manifestation came into being.
5 thousand years	An average period of history on earth

The age of Earth and man on Earth.

An average period of history on Earth is about 5,000 years. The longest period of recorded history was 18,000 years, whereas the shortest was 3,000 years. When the North Pole reaches 32 degrees out of true magnetic north, the Earth will tumble. It will tumble 80 degrees and drift 10 degrees. Wherever there has been a North Pole, you will find a huge iron ore deposit. Where the South Pole was, you will find a huge lead deposit.

The radiations of the 7 Rays of Light into the North Pole, down to the South Pole in a 7 by 7 by 7 rate of spin-twist, multiply these frequencies through Earth in order for this planet to spin and to light it. The lodestone producing of magnetism by the aurora borealis or northern lights and the radiation of lights in a prism-like effect into the Earth, spins it, keeping it in rotation so that it becomes just like a great magnet. That is what your North Pole is, a great magnet.

The South Pole becomes lead because as the energy leaves at this pole, it becomes dense as the heaviest item on the atomic scale. Wherever the South Pole has been, you will always find a great deposit of lead. The last North Pole was in our present Great Lakes region, and the upper northern region of Michigan has large iron deposits.

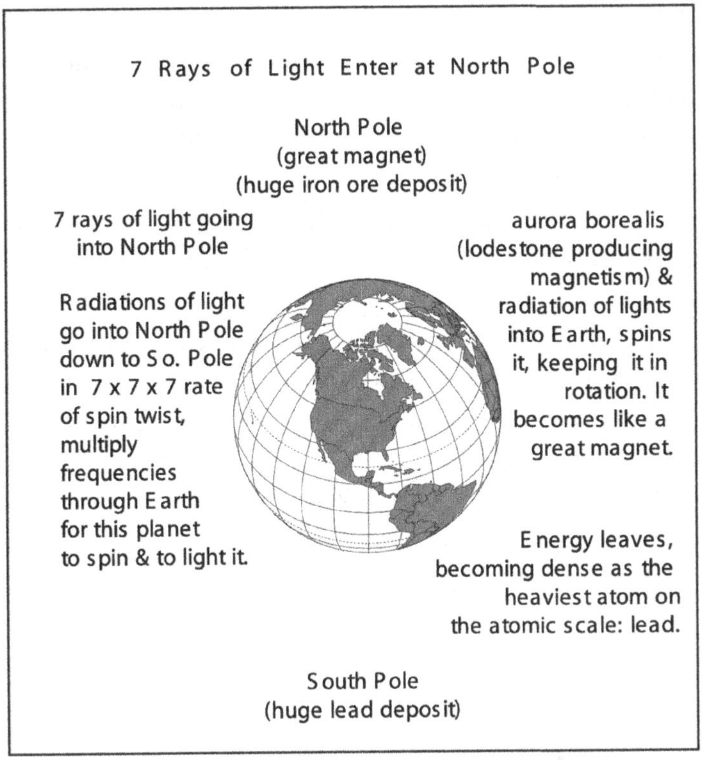
7 Rays of Light Enter at North Pole
North Pole
(great magnet)
(huge iron ore deposit)
7 rays of light going into North Pole
Radiations of light go into North Pole down to So. Pole in 7 x 7 x 7 rate of spin twist, multiply frequencies through Earth for this planet to spin & to light it.
aurora borealis (lodestone producing magnetism) & radiation of lights into Earth, spins it, keeping it in rotation. It becomes like a great magnet.
Energy leaves, becoming dense as the heaviest atom on the atomic scale: lead.
South Pole
(huge lead deposit)

7 rays of light enter at north pole.

The next North Pole will be what is now called the Bay of Bengal. When that polar shift does occur, in five minutes, most of China and the surrounding area for 1,000 miles from the Sea of Bengal will be a frozen mass. The Earth will stand still four hours, suspending its rate of spin. Most people will feel nauseated when the Sun appears to stop in the sky. This is mentioned in your Bible.

The upper mantle of the Earth, which is about 180 miles deep, stops rotating, while the inner core keeps spinning. The heat friction will cause the outer mantle to violently grab, and it resumes its rotation as it seeks its new North and South Poles. The wall of water that will come out of the Pacific Ocean will be 2 miles high and traveling at 4,000 miles per hour. This will completely destroy civilization as we know it today, except for a few that are sheltered in certain zero-zero areas. This has happened many, many times before. If you doubt this, geologists can show you volcanic rocks whose magnetic field points other than to our present Magnetic North Pole.

Life is the most wonderful thing to have and it should be lived to the fullest each day. Make each day as if it is the only day you are going to live. If you learn to love, and when you learn what love is, you will learn to love yourself and those about as you love yourself. Only then will this Earth become the most beautiful place in the Universe for an existence. You will really know what Life is about when you love yourself.

You are all very well endowed with the activities of this earth through memory. Life is everlasting and has always been and always will be. To come in and out of it, you do because of your own inadequacy to yourself, because of lack of proper preparation in physical structure to bring yourself into pure physical, rather than that of flesh.

Instead of solidifying into matter **you can in-light into substance and change your body to light,** by your discernment and valuation of your thought activity expressing to and from, simultaneously. In other words, in truth, it is multiplicities of motion simultaneously in all directions at the same time.

Limitations & Use of Brain

Since man took himself from substance into manifestation and solidified into manifested form of flesh matter, to limiting himself into one direction of sight, one area of hearing. He has limitation of movement by walking, and he has limited himself in everything but the use of his brain. He has kept that one access organ so that he can communicate and keep records, which makes him unique from all the rest of the animals that are coherent with him, and the other forms of life that are expressing, yet all are just as full of the same truth of conception of consciousness as you are.

Because of the limitation that you have allowed within the visionary senses of your eyes in life, you have eliminated yourself from 99% of it. You function with less than 3% of your brain power. You function on five senses rather than twelve.

You have made yourself dormant losing the authority of your rightful heritage of functioning. You sleep, dormant, in worshipping of death, to come and go continuously in expression without having life itself.

You do a lot of living, but you do not have life. That's what your first lesson is really about. In the second paragraph it says a conception is

> *that man is the only manifestation of the divine existence of Life. It is true that man is a Son of God, created from the Thought of God. He is clothed in Spirit and made flesh in order to express God's likeness.*

Did you notice the word "made?" It didn't say anything about "created," it said, "made". Man took himself out of a created state into a "made, manifested" condition of solidification of molecules. By changing his triangulation of light, he solidified flesh form and densified himself by weight and created a gravity state to hold himself in bondage.

He is clothed in Spirit and made flesh to express God's likeness in all Truth and in all loving beauty. All creations were created in the same manner.

You were created in the same way that He creates, because you are the same as He. I use the word "He" because He is an individual to me. To you, He is your Father.

Man is clothed in Spirit. Spirit is a Latin word which means, spirally, I go to express. Spirit is actually a spiral activity of Force Energy in Motion, continuously. It is actually multiplicities of motions, simultaneously, in all directions at the same time. When you comprehend that, you comprehend Spirit.

Mind is the go-between that Spirit uses for communication with the physical. The physical then, changes the pulsation to vibration. This changes the frequency so that it can be accepted by the flesh.

SPIRIT, MIND AND PHYSICAL

SPIRIT:

- Spirally I go to express.
- Spiral activity of force energy in motion, continuously
- Multiplicities of motions, simultaneously, in all directions at the same time

MIND:

- The go-between that Spirit uses for communication with the physical

PHYSICAL:

- Changes the pulsation to vibration
- Changes the frequency so that it can be

Spirit, mind and physical.

When Earth was created, the sky was white. When there became a need of Mind, the sky became blue and the Van Allen Radiation Belt was placed about the planet. This is to keep your bad thoughts from contaminating the Universe. The thoughts bounce off it and come right back to you.

Your brain discerns over 3,000,000 thoughts a second. You may not react and evaluate, but it does so in your Sight Cone. It will respond, activate or deactivate, to each of these impulses. As you learn to Perfect yourself, you will be able to replace those imperfect thoughts with perfect ones, for the good of those about you as well as for yourself.

> *One of man's greatest errors is the belief that he is the only begotten of God. The truth is that God created all things and gave all things the consciousness of living.*

There are billions of universes in this room which you can't see and they are just as important as you are. Without them, you couldn't exist. Inside of your body, there are billions and billions of energies that keep you in perfection and perfect thought. If you adulterate or mis-energize, you eliminate their ability to aid you.

The makeup of the molecular structure of your body is manifested by the vibrations of those that express about you, more than it is by Spirit prompting through Mind. The Physical Eye, which is your navel, responds more to emotions, and the great majority of you respond to emotions and not to Truth.

What is true today will not be true to you tomorrow, so you will say that Truth is unattainable, but this is not so. Once you awaken and become aware of who you are, what you are and why, then you will find that your status of Truth will come into being. By each day, you will eliminate the old standards that you function with.

When you come to the point that you can shut brain off and make it a computer, which it actually is, instead of controlling you, **then you will be free.** Until you can shut off brain, you will inherit your kingdom of earth and continually come back to flesh. As you live and express, so you will leave this earth and will return exactly as you expressed.

The conditions you made for existence will be your expression and your indebtedness that you return to face until you are able to rise above them. The expressions you live in, are cause and effect as long as you are on this earth. Your own karma exists because you allow it to be. If you can forgive yourself, it can't exist. The cause and effect condition is a part of life; this is what you call living. However, 90% of your living is reasoning, which is 90% wrong.

> *Life is the first attribute of God. There was Life before there was consciousness. One of the great truths that our Master Jesus taught his disciples is that the whole of life is the foundation upon which all things were built.*

Out of Life, all things come. The memory of all things in being and all things that you see about you, which were put into activity about you, were copied from your own body. The human body is a masterpiece of art. Just as the energy produced by your brain as it is computing, could light multiples of city blocks. By your brain and the Will Centers, which are your temples, you consume enough energy to light the city of New York.

Jesus taught these Truths to His Disciples. These truths are to be unfolded to you. It was hard for His Disciples to comprehend. It took much persuasion to get them to accept what He was trying to tell them. In many instances, He had to use examples to show them so they would understand. The same for you. I'm real sneaky about planting seeds! I will use many words that will plant seeds because I want them to grow without you being aware of it. Someday, a light will go on and you will then realize what I was talking about.

> *Now this same truth is being given again, so that man may know that he can never become extinct. He cannot escape life, because life exists in all forms—seen and unseen, manifest and non-manifest. There is no death.*

What you call death is only a changing of frequency. Remember you were created eternal. What you call death is only losing sight of this dimension, but you never lose your Conscious condition. When you stop vibrating, by breath, in a few seconds you are back in pulsation. There is really no pain to it. All the pain is in the flesh. There is no reason to pass through that.

If you work diligently, you can eternally be free, which is your nature. You will not be bound and imprisoned in this flesh body. It is a great vehicle for you to get around in, in this dimension, but it is much easier to travel in a light ship.

Death is one thing I don't accept. The only reason death exists is due to ignorance. Death comes because when you are young, you want to be old, and when you are old, you want to be young. When you are young, you want to be like your father or some other older figure that you admire. You set your standards by their abilities. When you get there and look back, you wish you had your youth back again.

Guard well your thoughts, that you do not contaminate yourself as you contaminate others about you. By your own broadcast, you become exactly what you broadcast. Be very careful in your thoughts because you are going to be subject to them. You will get the first payment because all of your thoughts return to you. You will take your consequences in a seven-fold multiple, good or bad. The bad comes on those days when you don't feel so good.

You have to learn to love. You have to love yourself as you love everything about you. Death and aging come about by programming. These are your desires of programming, but it is really by improper construction and discussion, so that the individual falls heir to his own ignorance. The reward is just exactly by the ignorance put into it.

If all children were taught from the natural condition, instead of man's culture and social laws, this would be a beautiful world to live in. Man, as we call him, falls a little short of his construction of making his vehicle a proper place of inhabiting. Really the correct term for man is hew-man [human], because he is hewed in flesh from a mystic pattern that he seemed to remember, although he doesn't quite remember the blueprint, so he makes it the best way that he can. By his desires to express, he is over-desirous in his expression, and burns himself up.

Your body was made to last for 7,000 years of expression. On the average, you burn it out in less than 70 years. At no time is there any part of your body older than 7 years, and that is the oldest cell in your body, which are the cells in the inner bone. Why do you become old? It is all due to mis-programming.

The mis-use of your sense centers has made dormant your thought sensitivities in activity of Sense Centers which have dried up and have become completely unusable and of no value because you don't know how to awaken them. All of the centers of your body should be in function, so that you have the **freedom of Be**. The freedom of BE is your salvation, and you shall find your salvation in the BE.

We Own Nothing, Yet Have Abundance

By the exchange of your activity of lust and greed, anguish and anger, you further deny yourself from the trueness of life and its ability to express, rather than exchanging in love. One of the first things to learn about life is that you own nothing. You are a partaker and a user of. **You have abundance beyond your dreams, but you own nothing.**

After all, you are only here to express life in its fullness. Everything that you accumulate here in material matter you cannot take from this earth. Even that which you take from this earth to construct your flesh body must be returned to this earth before you leave. The body weighs, in spiritual activity, less than three grams. All the rest belongs to the earth.

When we think that we are the unique and the only thing loved by the Father in creation, it's because we have limited our view to be non-receptive to the coherent value of those expressing equally with us. If it were not for the other six planes of expression existing, we could have no existence. We could not have our living condition.

Just consider, what would happen to the earth within one year if the insects would not devour the bacteria kingdom? You would be encrusted with a five mile encircling of bacteria around this earth in one year's time.

The balance that life has placed upon each of the seven dimensions working together equally in the living expression, coherent to everything, keeps one another in total rapport. But man's ignorance of stupidity puts this in an unbalanced condition, further taxing his ability of expressing in the trueness of life itself. He further raises havoc with the coherence that is working with him to give him back his ability of expressing and returning back to his true form, that of Man, rather than a hewed man (human).

Man's Greatest Error

In the lessons when we first start out, we will be talking about the greatest error, which is to believe that you are the only begotten of God. Even the stones and the air you breathe contain universes beyond the dimensions of your comprehension. You breathe millions and millions of universes in and out with each breath.

The infinitesimal smallness of these universes and the energies within them energize your body without you even realizing it. You breathe more through your pores than you do through your mouth. Multiples of universes and chemical exchanges of universes are taken in through the pores of your skin.

The animation of the breath brings forth light and energy into the body to keep it in continuing motion and derives the activity so the prismatic condition of all geometric conditions of formulations of triangulations of mathematics and geometry hold you in form, by your thought exchange in breath.

Life, The First Attribute of God

Life is the first attribute of God. There was Life before there was consciousness.

Life is the only conscious state. You notice the word "consciousness" has "ness" behind it? When multiples of activities are expounded from life into expression, they become "nesses," multiplicities of themselves. This means multiples of diversions of activities expressing simultaneously. Your ability of comprehension and discernment allows you to attain the station of exchange in consciousness to your ability of comprehension and your equalization.

One of the great truths our master Jesus taught His disciples is that the whole of life is the foundation on which all things were built, and, "Triangles, circles and squares, in that dimension my universes were begotten."

"Were" or "are"?

Were. Later you will say "are" when you are able to become the dot in the middle.

This same truth is being given again so that man may know that he can never become extinct. He cannot escape life, because life exists in all forms, both seen and unseen, manifest and unmanifest. In other words, **there is no death**. There are multiples of dimensions that are functioning simultaneously with you.

Meditation and Access to Question the Universe

When you have learned to still yourself to sufficient stillness, and have attained the ability to shut off the gland called the brain and its memory banks, you will be able to come into **rapport with Mind, with the prompting of Spirit, where you will have the free access to question the universe** to fullness of comprehension.

This is attained through the total state of **meditation**, which is **one of your first and most important attributes that you should attain**. I don't care whether you stand on your head, sit in a corner, or you lie on nails, if you are comfortable, fine.

The one thing that I do want you to concentrate upon is, that when you **totally relax yourself, do not agree or disagree with any thinking** that the brain will produce or visionary activities or muscle responses to the body that it projects to you. Learn to be completely oblivious of it.

It is not easy, because it knows every trick to play against you. It knows you better than you know yourself, because it has millions and millions of years of memory to play back against you, and it will use all kinds and types of deceit to trick you into giving back to it. Once it attains control again, give up your meditation. Next time strive even harder to not allow any diversion to take place while in meditation.

The most comfortable condition is when you learn your Holy Breath. You will learn how to animate your breath breathing into universal agreement. This will come a little later in your lessons.

How to Start Meditation & Its Purpose

To start now, the best way is to avoid crutches, like a mantra. To start with, if you put a black tack in the wall and look at it, it will give something for the brain to function on, so that it will leave you alone. You will find that this will give you a first avenue of expressing to go through, because you give the brain something to work on. Due to the oscillation of the breath, the color will come and go continuously in the cycling of light moving. It will spin to you and from you.

As you learn, you will find that **the Father asks for** ten percent. He doesn't want your money. After all, what does He need of your pennies when He created the whole universe? He wants **ten percent of your time, so He can communicate with you. Be quiet to hear the Truth of the universe,** so that life can speak forth its trueness in expression to you, so that you can **be your real self**, rather than the unreal.

Of everything you are doing now, 99% is unreal, all makebelieve. You are going to have to learn to re-write the script. You are going to have to be a better director to make yourself act as the script is written, rather than multiples of changes each day, just like a leaf in the wild, turning and flipping with any pressure that is applied.

You are going to have to learn to walk that straight line and kick the rocks out of your way. You will find that it isn't long before all the rocks turn to pebbles.

When Your Name Is Called

There will come a time when you will be able to hold and move from a vibratory existence into pulsation. Your name may be called, and it will be in the most familiar voices at the oddest time. Learn the only answer is, **"Yes, Father."** That is the only answer, because if you don't, it will be a while before your name is called again. The Father is going to test you to see how alert you actually are. You will be tested many, many times. In meditation you will even feel like you hear your daughter or son speak to you and even tug your clothing. When you open your eyes you will know you have been "had."

The brain is a master of all magicians and knows every slight of hand trick to play on you.

It seems like I have heard the call before, but it seems like it is always one of the family. It is always somebody I know.

Right. That's to catch you off-guard. You have all experienced this. But I'll tell you this, when you do recognize and you say, "Yes, Father," it will be just like somebody poured warm water over you and it will just shimmer down over your whole body, and your whole body will just exhilarate in the light emanation of love that you are receiving. Each time you're right, you will be rewarded tremendously.

These are the attributes that you are really after. These are the **true attributes: to know who you are, where you are, what you are and why**.

7/2 Breath Rate

The proper way to breathe is to do so with the frequency of your heart. You fill your lungs with 7 beats of your heart. Hold your breath for 2 beats, and then exhale for 7 beats of your heart, and hold the breath out for 2 beats of your heart. As the breath is taken in, you are open to the 7 Rays of Light, which will completely energize the entire body.

You also receive all the transmission into the Sight Cone for discernment.

Sightcone

The Sightcone, located behind the center of the forehead, has three fiber layers aligned in differing directions, by triangulation, to each other. There are two gelatin pads between them. All Thought and Light are transmitted in Thought-Light Presence. The vibrations of these are received and the thoughts make pictures that are recorded in your memory cells located beneath the cap at the back of your head. There are two cells the size of the point of a pin that retain all of your presence of past, present and future.

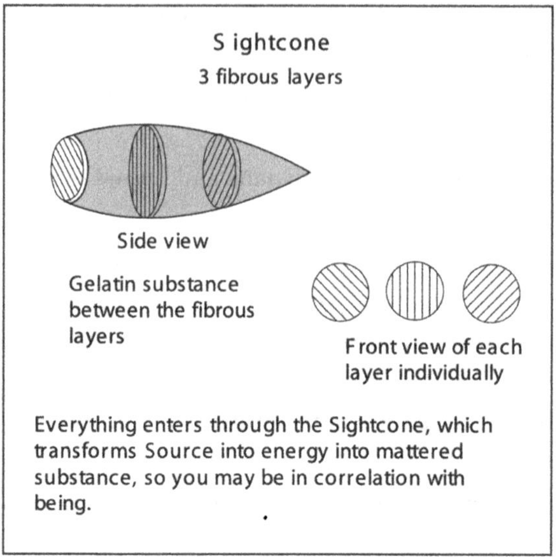

Sightcone.

Everything that is evaluated in your thought goes to these two cells where it is proofed, computed and played back, where it is either accepted into being, or discarded by your ability of comprehension. This is the reason for the stilling of the breath on the intake. At the same time that you take in your breath, you are also formulating all of your transmissions to take place. You are making all of your thought form pictures of which you are not even aware.

As you exhale your breath, you are transmitting this away from you into activity. You still your breath to allow it to leave you. If you don't still your breath, you draw it right back to you and you cannot attain that which you desire. You may attain the most perfect thought for projection, but if you don't still your breath, it can never get away from you. It cannot be made into manifestation by attraction. You cannot make for yourself anything that you desire unless you still your breath. Breathing is so important.

If you do not learn to still your breath, you take yourself out of expression by each breath, because you kill your cells. You kill them by suffocation. By this breath activity and Sense Centers of your body, the light is drawn into your body, taken into the bloodstream and the lymph system. It is transmitted through the body to energize the cellular structure and nervous system. If you don't still your breath, you either over-energize or under-energize your body. It becomes deficient in functional activity. If your cells become malfunctioned too many times, they become dormant.

When the cells lose expression, which you call dying, then they become dormant and a spore breeding spot for bacteria. Any place in which you create a cold spot, or a low oxygen point, sets up a spore situation for bacteria to produce and create what you call disease, [dis-ease]. Therefore, it is most important for you to activate your body and your Sense Centers. Without the perfection of your breath, you will never achieve it.

Importance of Using the 7-2 Breath

It is most important that you immediately start this exercise of using the 7/2 Breath. You can feel your pulse so that you get 7 beats of your heart for the inhalation and exhalation. You must get this breath rate down so you are able to activate your cells and energize your body with energy that you have never before experienced.

If you breathe too shallowly, then your nervous system is affected. If you breathe too rapidly or too deeply, you hyperventilate your system, which will affect the heat cells of your body. This causes frustration and irritation. There is much to be understood about how you breathe. By your breathing, you become the total sum and substance of your thoughts. For many, half of your lung sacks have dried up, due to shallow breathing. If you do this exercise seven times daily, your capacity will increase

You breathed this way automatically up to the age of 12, the age of reasoning. Then you went automatically out of focus, when you took responsibility for yourself. At the age of 12, you were on a vibrational frequency of 3. The vibrational frequency of Earth is gaining very fast; now it is up to 12. Actually, Earth and your vibrational frequency should never exceed 8, but you have fallen behind your mark and the Earth can't wait for you.

Either you are going to catch up, or you are going to be eliminated. The elimination is going to be very pleasant, because you will be transferred to another planet that has been prepared for you, which is in the same frequency for your compatible functional operation. You won't ever know the transfer has taken place. The vehicle will live out the balance of this expression as a vegetable in its present body for its life expectancy that it had programmed. This is why so many are unable to function in society today, due to the increase of the vibrational frequency of Earth.

When we breathe out, should it be from the nose or mouth?

It doesn't matter, whichever is the most comfortable. Actually the breath isn't from the nose; it's by the **pores of your skin,** where we want to develop your breathing. Your body has over 3,000,000 pores that you use for breathing, and it's time to start using them.

Activated Charcoal Tablets

You should get activated charcoal tablets, such as Requa's, and take two in the morning and evening for one month; then drop back to one a day for the rest of your life. Charcoal consists of carbon, which is the finest surgical knife in the world. It is of such a keen edge that it will clean all of the scum off the arteries and the inside of your blood vessels. The crystals spin as they travel through the circulatory system. They cut as they spin and leave an explosion of light at the trailing edge. Your body will breathe and function properly. They will even clear away calcified bones at the joints.

UNIVERSAL CREED

I am eternally free in deed, which is my nature.
I bow to no man, not even God, for I AM GOD.

That is your Universal Creed. **Learn this and command it to your body during meditation**; you shall become that which you decree. We seem to have forgotten who we are, where we are, why we are, and what we are. Most would say this would be blasphemy, to declare your legal existence.

If you take allegiance to anything other than yourself, then you are not free. You are bound to the allegiance that you take, and you give yourself in preference to others in place of yourself. You will never be free.

You bow to nothing or no one. You are the authority in expression. You have the trueness of all life at your hands to express with.

The Seven Planes of Expression

You have the unification of all other six planes expressing equally with you in this dimension to make sure that you do attain to perfection. Those Planes have even given up their presence of perfectness so that you could have existing expression and could return to that from which you came.

In the Perfect State, you had *communication* with the Universe and dominion over your associations. When you took yourself out of Perfection into manifestation, because you were given dominion over the other Kingdoms of your association, all left their Perfect State except the Angels. They held their Perfect State so that you would have a way back. Due to their state and trueness to Life Itself, God gave Angels the job of being the messengers between you and the Truth.

All of the other five planes, Fowl—Animal—Vegetable— Protoplasm—Earth, allowed themselves to be lowered because you couldn't exist without them. They came with you, but you did lose communication with them.

They allowed themselves to come into the manifested state which you created, because you had dominion over everything. They came with you, agreeing, because they knew that you had no way back unless they did. They did it out of love. You did it out of lust.

All of the others are working constantly for your betterment of attainment, that of perfection into full conscious condition rather than consciousnesses.

At the time of Adam, when he realized he was naked, the trees no longer lowered their branches so that he could pick the fruit to eat. Instead, they grew thorns to keep him away from them.

This parable is telling you that the Pureness of Thought had been broken. The impurity of the act of knowing the difference between good and evil had produced a repulsion and attraction activity, whereby before it was in a Love standard of Pulsation, it was now in vibration where everything came and went at the same time.

This is the problem that you are now in, you are coming and going at the same time, but you don't know it. This is why it is so difficult to attract and hold onto everything. You have it for a while, then you lose it. When you think you have a grasp of it, then it slips away.

Each of the planes that is expressing equally with you is doing the job for you which you can't do for yourself. As you lowered yourself in manifestation, they each allowed the alteration to take place with them so they could produce for you in order for you to exist. They will continue to do so until you Perfect. When you no longer have need, they will return to their Perfect State when the last have returned into Perfection.

As you now see the other planes that you associate with, you only see the reflected value of them and not their true value. You don't see the beauty and the love that exists there. The unseen worlds aid you, also. If it weren't for the protoplasm, in one year the encrusting of the Earth would be 5 miles thick. Due to your own inability, they have to do the work for you so that you have an opportunity to express.

The True Expression of Plants

If you were to see a flower in its true expression, you would be very surprised, and you would be very surprised how much love they emanate to you as you walk by them. They adorn themselves with beauty for you to par-take of with your eyes so that you may be furnished with the plentifulness of exchanged love. Their emanation of thought and presence is of one thing only: of love and beauty.

They also took on the necessity of chemical exchange for you. Knowing that you would have to have a blend of gases to breathe, a certain group of them blended together so that the exchange of your poison could be replenished into pure oxygen again for you to breathe.

Others took on the responsibility of taking the light substance that was manifested into crystal form beneath the crust of earth as the light solidified into crystal oscillation and became the emanation of light crystals of energies of light for you to consume, so that your body would have view to express with. By the osmosis of explosions through the rooting of the plant and the storage of those light cells into miniature light crystals in the foliage of the leaf, you are then able to break down the soft foliage and take those crystals of light into your blood to give life into your blood and existence into your body.

The mineral kingdom worked just the other way, so that the bacteria would have a place to operate in so it could blend equally with the oscillations of the crystals that were solidified by light. This gives you a molecular structure. You have over 300 elements in chemistry. As of now you know only of ninety-seven.

The absorption of the plant life and the exchange of bacteria have the ability to break down the light crystals into sub-particles so that the insect life can further break it down into smaller minute particles and encrust it with the nutrients. This aids the plants, allowing them a life substance to exist with, because they fixed themselves in a fixed condition of existence by their dimension of agreement. They did this with the flora of their foundation of conditioning within the air-cycling of their breathing.

They do pulsate in unison with the Central Sun, which is the Master Sun of the Universe. The unison of the Central Sun gives them the ability to pump their water through their lock valves, taking the light crystals suspended in the water clear up into the branches and storing it into the leaves and into the blossoms, which are the fruit of the plant. All the essence of these light crystals is placed into these and the sweetness of the nectars are beyond belief in flavor and taste, when they are properly loved and adorned. The fruit will even become more delicious as the flower becomes more beautiful when it's given the presence of love.

Airless Cell

Inside of your heart is what we call an Airless Cell. Man's instruments of magnification are incapable of seeing it, yet it is all that exists of you. When you come into expression and you take your first breath, is when the Airless Cell moves in and takes its seating within your heart. You are then into expression. Until then, you are a vegetable. **There is no Life in the body until the first breath is taken**.

AIRLESS CELL:
all that exists of you

Airless cell.

Your lesson states: "...the Triune God breathed forth," which is Spirit, Mind and Physical breathed forth in unison and the density of flesh takes place and the Airless Cell enters into the heart. Then you become an entity of being in frequency of vibration. The Airless Cell hovers over the top of the head of the one conceived, and directs the construction of the activity from its blueprint of its Etheric value.

In many of the things that you are taught, you will find multiplicities continuously spoken, rather than bringing it down to a "one" condition. After all, you are unique. **There is no other like you in the universe.** Your Airless Cell makes sure of that.

You are in duplicate image of yourself in light. I don't care which dimension you go into, you look exactly as you are now. You may be a little larger in stature or a little smaller, but your same characteristics of features will be attained regardless of where you express in the universe.

The Triangles of Spirit, Mind, Physical, and Life, Love & Light

Jesus taught that in the beginning the Triune God breathed forth and seven spirits stood before the throne.

In this quotation, the Triune God means Spirit, Mind and Physical.

Draw a triangle with the base at the bottom. At the bottom of that I want you to write "life." On the left hand side I want you to write "love"." On the right hand side I want you to write "light." Copy that exact same triangle, turn it upside down, placing the top point below the bottom base line. Now you have a six-pointed star.

On the left hand side where you had "Love", write above there "Spirit", and over Light write "Mind". On the bottom side between Love and Light write "Physical." Now in the middle put one dot. That little dot in the middle is the Airless Cell.

The "Triune God" means Spirit, Mind and Physical. "Breathed forth" means vibrated in unison. This means that in the transference of energy of the primary triangle, which is Conscious into expression, light moves from Motionless into motion.

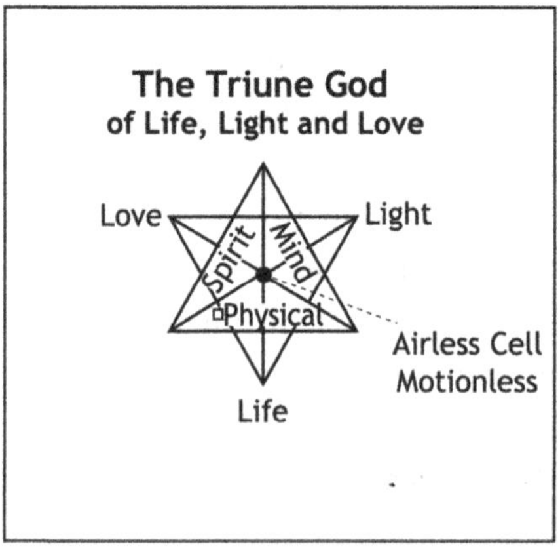

The Triune God.

Now we are going to change that motion into animation, to vibration. We are going to draw the triangle to that point and you will have a three-sided pyramid, to that dot proceeding in. From your Life, Love and Light, draw a line from each of the corners of that triangle to that dot. Now turn your triangle and draw from your Spirit, Mind and Physical to the same dot. You have an equilateral triangle, dual pyramid.

From the Motionless put into motion, which is into Life's activity, the triangle is brought forth and the triune of activity of Love, Life and Light brings forth all energies of the universe into rapport.

You are going to back up, because you have taken yourself from pulsation. This is a pulsated state. Now you have created an unnatural state, which is a reflection of activity called vibrant. You have taken your pulsated state and changed it into a vibrance condition. Everything that exists around you in this dimension is vibratory. It's in frequencies of oscillation.

The purity of thought is set from that one dot of the Motionless into motion, and Life, Love and Light unify themselves in expression in pulsation. Because we are changing pulsation to manifestation, we are reversing that activity in half phase of each phase, out of phase of itself, causing an oscillation.

The emanation of the truth is projected to this, but we have changed it out of phase fifty percent, and brought it from a pulsation to a manifestation by vibratory activity.

That point of conception is your Airless Cell directing the activity of this manifested flesh body in expression. This is your triangulation of exchange from universal to flesh condition, manifested condition.

I am "hitting" you pretty hard, but I am planting a lot of seeds.

On the location of Spirit, Mind and Physical, are they the points of the second triangle?

They are the flat areas of the second triangle. Each plane coming to the point is that full dimension, so that whole triangle coming to the point would be either Spirit, Mind or Physical. They have to be in unison with each other equally to have rapport.

If one is exceeding the other, then the other two are out of balance. That's why you are in a manifested form. You are in a frequency of oscillation. If the oscillation is heavier in exchange from one to the other, the prismatic of the angles then change and the exchange becomes out of balance.

We are trying to hold everything in perfectness of balance. As it is now, we go off at the deep side one way or the other because we focus too heavily into one or the other without equalizing the truth of the other two in rapport. We exchange too rapidly to solidify ourselves in equal rapport.

Spirit, Mind, Physical & Flesh Defined

Spirit is the concentrated thought of the perfect you waiting to be expressed, not reflected.

Spirit fills all space and is a respecter of no person or thing. It is very impersonal personal and of such rapid speed in motion that it passes through without you even knowing its presence of being, even through the most solidity that we could consider in our dimensions. It passes through it as freely as the air is moving about you here.

Mind is the go-between between Spirit and Physical, and is the messenger that carries the work of the Spirit to the Physical, so that the exchange can be executed.

Physical is the responding to the Spirit to bring forth the activity of Mind and Spirit.

Spirit is yellow, Mind is blue and Physical is red. These are the three primary colors of BE. All colors of expression come from these the primaries. When they are blended with grey, you have Time. When Time and Space are blended together, Form comes into being and manifestation is created. Manifestation is the lowest form of BE.

It will continue to function in operation by the triangulation of triangles into the Perfectness of Thought, being bombarded by the Cone of Spirituality into the flesh of physical, reflected into activity. You become that reflection of activity in expression.

By those three colors, you will have the basis of all the standards of all alterations of expression. As long as Love is in Perfection and is the Desire of Be, everything about you will be in a Gold hue. If you tend to use the prompting of activity, then you bring the Red of Physical to bear, so that the flesh may be activated into expression.

Actually, you are one dot of Light moving so fast that you think you are solid. All that exists is one dot which is in the center of your body. All of the rest is illusion. You are just like a television picture. You are the master magician, the master deceiver. You dreamed a dream, and now, you are expressing that dream by reflected activity. All of this does not exist, we just think it so. Even as solid and tangible that you think you are, you aren't. Only by your gross flesh do you hold yourself within density in this expression on Earth. You are free to release yourself at any time.

Your first triangle of Being is: Spirit—Mind—Physical.

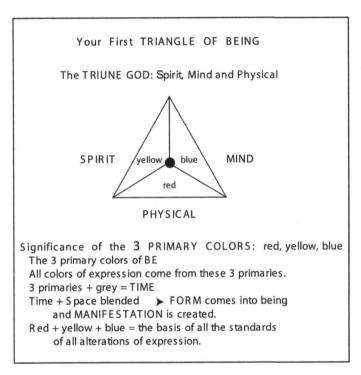

Your First TRIANGLE OF BEING

The TRIUNE GOD: Spirit, Mind and Physical

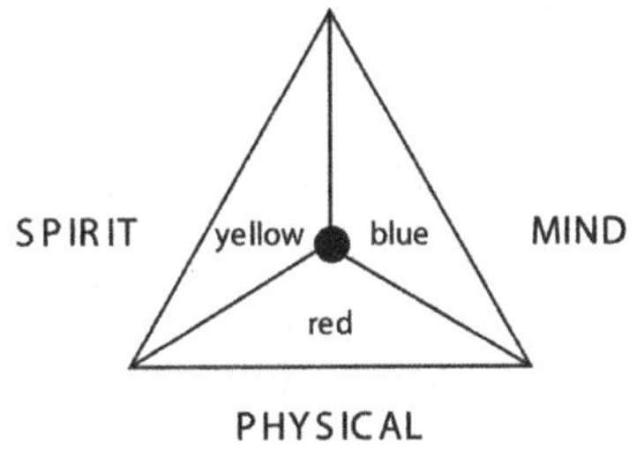

Significance of the 3 PRIMARY COLORS: red, yellow, blue
The 3 primary colors of BE
All colors of expression come from these 3 primaries.
3 primaries + grey = TIME
Time + Space blended ➤ FORM comes into being
and MANIFESTATION is created.
Red + yellow + blue = the basis of all the standards
of all alterations of expression.

Your first triangle of being.

There are seven distinct planes of God's Expression:

Man—Angel—Fowl

[Airborne triangle]

Animal—Vegetable—Protoplasm—Earth.

[Square; Earthbound base]

Flesh physical is the exchange of unbalanced condition between any one of the three triangulations, either positive or the second positive. You call it positive and negative. There are two positives running just out of phase with one another. This is odd, but you will have to take this with a grain of salt until later. I am planting a seed. You can say positive and negative if you wish, but there is no such thing as a negative. That's only in man's thinking.

Positive & Negative

When you take a positive and a negative, I always figured there has to be another positive to make that positive work.

There does.

Positives repel each other though.

What does a negative do? It stops, doesn't it.

Negative attracts positive. Energy would flow from negative to positive.

No, because you are thinking of brute energy that man calls electricity, rather than light.

Let me ask you a question: Which way does energy flow, from the earth back into the air or from the air to the earth?

Air to the earth.

From the air to the earth? Which way does lightening strike? Does it strike from the earth into the sky or from the sky to the earth?

From the sky to the earth.

No, from the earth to the sky. You see the response of the energy in motion in a flash after it has burned the elements that it has passed through. You hear the clattering of the thunder filling the void that was produced by the motion of the ions being executed.

Earth: Your Source of Being and Energy For Your Body

Everything begins with your focal point of earth, out. It is your source of being. All the energy that operates the flesh part of your body comes through your feet from the earth. All that operates the spiritual part of your body comes through your temples and your clavicles, by your breath animated, until you go into a pulsated state. The diaphragm is the balance and the navel is the physical eye, the point of center.

Your body is that triangle that you just drew.

Many things that man has set down in theories are very, very improper. Because of lack of proper understanding, bullheadedness, and egotistical convictions he will not entertain that which is really true. By his own bias conditioning, he bigots himself by his own self-importance, making himself considerably more ignorant.

The Seven Planes of Expression

The lesson says:

> *The Triune God, (Spirit, Mind and Physical), breathed forth (means vibrated in unison), and seven spirits (means the seven phases of expression) stood before the throne... Therefore Spirit, Mind and Physical vibrated in unison with seven phases of expression manifested in life, and these seven manifestations of life are seven distinct planes of God's expression: man, angel, fowl, animal, vegetable, protoplasm and earth. We use earth as the mineral kingdom.*

Seven planes of expression that expressed in unison with man in the perfect created state, were these for the beauty of expressing. Angel refused to follow man out of the perfect state of existence and held its state of expression, becoming the messenger of love and light in exchange between the Godhead and hue-man.

All the rest allowed themselves to be lowered as man lost his ability of control and created lesser and lesser states of manifestation for himself to exist in, because of his slothfulness. They allowed themselves to be changed dimensionally equal with him so that he would have a path to return upon. This is memory.

Whether you are expressing as masculine or feminine, your created plane is Man.

Man's Misuse of Nature and the Possibility of Calamity

Man in his ignorance has so misused and so raped nature that he has put the whole world out of balance. By the improper use and agreement of lust rather than necessity he has caused the earth to go out of balance. The

North Pole should be exactly on zero. We are oscillating at 31.7 degrees out of north to magnetic north at this time (1978). When we reach 32 degrees out of true north, we will have a calamity upon this earth. Man's thought is what corrects or moves this.

As the population increases upon the earth, the swaying point of the cutting lines of force that spin this earth and hold it stable are being interrupted. This is very important to all life expressing because of a limitation that man is placing in his projection of improper thinking and demands of lust and greed.

In the cycling changing that man has brought about, he has destroyed the force that creates the air and the circulatory system or the percolating system that keeps the balance of vegetation and the oxygen-giving plants in rapport with the animal and bacteria life and the mineral kingdom. When he destroys the force, he destroys the percolation and we lose our water which is one of our greatest needs of assets because our body is 98 percent water in fluid. Without water we are almost in the same place as without pure air to breathe, the blend of perfect gases for the body to consume.

If man does not correct his misuse of these operations, he will eliminate himself out of expression. I am not using any scare tactics, I am planting seeds. I want you to think about what I am saying. Your thoughts in proper projections, have more value than one that is improperly projecting, if you put enough emphasis on your projection.

It's up to the students of truth to stabilize this earth. An average expression of history on this earth is about 5,000 to 6,000 Years. Then history starts again, with the same problem of greed and lust. We are crowding our borderline now of that period of time in history. Now it's up to the thinking and projection of the thoughts of people in light to correct this condition. We can bring it right back to zero. But I may say this, the longest history on earth was 18,000 years, in 3 1/2 billion years.

Possible Pole Changes

The average expression is between the pole changes?

Yes. When the poles change place, they change 80 degrees and drift 10. In a matter of four hours the earth will stand still, because it will lose its inertia of selsyn activity from the inner earth to the outer earth. It's electrical poles' attraction of light will slowly spin to a stop. The outer earth will come to an inertia stop and the inner earth will continue to spin at its same rate of speed. When the mantle becomes too hot, it works like a friction clutch. It will be grabbed and the earth will be thrown back into spinning activity again. When it does, the poles will change 80 degrees and drift 10.

If you want to see where all the North Poles were and all the South Poles were, just look at a geometric map where all the iron depots are and you will see where the North Pole was. Cut right through the earth and see where all the lead deposits are and you will see where the South Pole was. Or go look at the pyrites which are locked within the lava and you will find if you measure the impulse of it by meters, you will find where the North Pole was at that time. It's an exacting science.

What do you mean by drift ten?

Because it goes into a gyration, it will spiral eighty degrees and then drift ten, as it stabilizes. Those ten degrees are a stabilizer. Our next North Pole will be the Bay of Bengal, off of India. Then in five minutes China will be a frozen mass of ice. That part of the world will become the new North Pole. But that's another story.

Remember the quotation that Spirit, Mind and Physical breathed forth these seven manifestations. They "breathed them forth". They were not created. "Breathed forth" refers to celestial things. "Created" refers to terrestrial things. One is made and one is created. It has been altered.

In the beginning all these things in Spirit, Mind and Physical were held in the perfect state of consciousness.

> *From this, we can readily see that Life is indeed "that perfect cycle, through which the thoughts of God are made to manifest in all perfection. Perfection is created by God and is the only creation of God. Man is imperfect only because he has made for himself other vibratory planes of existence.*

Man is imperfect because of his violation of his perfect creation, his violation, not anybody else's, because he has "made" for himself, not "created".

In the Bible it says in Genesis, "He made them then." It doesn't say anything about "created". It was the manifested state out of perfection. Man lowered himself into the illusion state of expression.

Bliss

God created perfect Bliss, perfect form and perfection in all blessedness.

There are two times in the expression of your physical life you know bliss: the first time you fall in love, and, for a woman, the first time she bears the fruits of life, bringing forth creation into expression. Those are so impressive upon you. It will be hard for you to remember because they pass away so quickly, and you will long so greatly after it, to recapture the essence you had at that exact second. That's why puppy love hurts so much when it's broken. For the male, it is in the first act when you finally succeeded in complement, and you will remember that the rest of your life.

You were created in perfect form, not this flesh that you have cloaked over bones. All your cells were perfect spheres, rather than being elongated. You were translucent, yet visible, in perfect form. But because of the density that you have caused yourself to be cloaked in, you have shut off the light cells in your body. The more you brought the water cells to bear, the more you subdued the light of your body, until you glow very little. The largest aura I see in the room is about five-eighths of an inch. I want to see it out like this, at least three feet about your body, which you can accomplish. That little egg you are in needs a little expanding. You may have to tap a hole in it and crawl out, like a butterfly does out of its cocoon, a very prime example.

Man's Mission, the Why of His Present Life

Man's mission, the why of his present life, is ***to regain his created state of perfection, and to lift all the creations that he caused to fall,*** *back into that same state of perfection which God created.*

The only way this is ever going to come about is by you knowing who you are, where you are, what you are and why. Through the avenues of exercises that you will be given as you grow, and you begin to use these, you will bring energies into play within your body that will bring back the youth to your body, bring back the energy to your body, give yourself back the flexibility of expression.

Do not be fooled by what you see sitting before you, because man is prone to believe that only age has wisdom. Don't be fooled by what you see, for this is all illusion.

> *All of this sums up the why of life as it is now, and as it will be until man has fully atoned to himself for all transgression of himself. Man must return to earthly expression again and again until he has atoned, and until he has again come to know him-self. For man is not as he seems to be, and there is a mighty work that each individual must do. Although this work must be done by yourself alone, your guide will show the way by bringing to your remembrance all the ways of perfection. In this way, you will conquer the foes that you have made and will return again and again to that perfect state from which you came.*

I am your guide, and that's all. I am not going to do it for you. I'll tell you about it. I'll tell you how to do it, but you are going to do it. Everything that I am telling you about, I have already done. I am free to go at any time I want. That's more than anybody in this room can say. However, you have the same attributes, the same privileges that I have. Everything that I do, you can do better than I. It's only that you forgot the rules, and where you hid the pieces. We are going to put that jig-saw puzzle back together, and find all those little hidden pieces and put it all back into rapport.

(Question from student:) You were talking before about our rapport with the animals, birds and plants. I notice that I usually get along with all the dogs in going from house to house. I notice that some-times I get real close to birds and have even picked some of them up, but it doesn't happen all the time. Why is this?

(Answer:) Your chemistry is presenting a vapor and a vibrance, and they detect it. This is like when a dog smells your deceit long before you ever enter the yard.

You are talking about "You will hear your name called". This happened to me when I was sound asleep. Is this normal?

It is, because Mind is never still. Brain goes into a "sub" condition.

Sleep and Visions

You have 144,000 electrical connections at the medulla, going to the brain. When you go into an animated sleep state, all of the electrical connections shut down to about 29 to 17. If you go into a visionary state, out of the black and white into color, you have color visions, and all color dreams are dreams of a prophetic vision of future conditions. Remember, that's between 9 and 17 connections.

When you are in total full rest, you will be down to seven. The seven major organs of your body are all that will be functioning. This is necessary for your body presence. When you are out of your body in out of body experiences, only those seven organs will be used. All the rest are in a dormant state. You are in one breath pulsating, rather than breathing. It is possible to hold that one breath for forty-two days.

Initiations

What are you referring to when you talk about holding that breath?

One breath, that's all, for forty-two days. It can be in a full waking state, yet it's a semi-meditative state. Some of the ones in India are buried. To pass their examination, they are buried for forty-one days, beneath the ground, on one breath. Then they are dug up and come right back into expression on the forty-second day.

It is part of an initiation of a proving of perfection. You must pass these tests, just like moving your body through a solid rock; go right through a solid wall. Your body can do it. If you know all the elements, then it is just as if you walk through this air. All the time that you are moving, you are moving universes. These walls are no more solid than this air is. They have rapport with you, so they blend in unison with you, and there is no solidity. It is just like Spirit does, matter into matter.

When we hear our name called and we are told to respond, "Yes, Father," are these voices from the brain?

No, they are from the Father. This is Mind in activity, because you are in an off-phase condition when they come through. You are in a totally relaxed condition. The brain is shut down and the mind is coming through.

We accept this?

You acknowledge, not accept, because isn't the Father the only one there is, Love? When you do acknowledge, you will have love like you have never known before. It is very, very rewarding.

Are Angels in a pure light body?

Yes.

I would like to know why man would choose lust and greed over perfection. When did this happen?

On our earth it was about just a little less than four billion years ago, when man stepped out of his perfect state.

Why did he choose that over perfection?

Man became a little zealous with his authority. He became a little drunken with power, and built a trap that he trapped himself in. It is quite a long story. Later on I will give you a writing called the Alpha and the Omega, and in your second book you will study Genesis. You will find out in the first four stanzas of the first chapter of Genesis, millions of years pass away in a matter of a few words.

You say there are millions of thoughts in our heads?

Three million thoughts a second you discern and evaluate in your spirituality cone. Everybody is thinking, and the universe is answering the response of that thinking, so the thought is in activity. You are constantly bombarded with these thoughts. You are capable of handling much more than that, but that's the average.

Where are they coming from?

From the center of the universe, you.

How can I have millions of years old thoughts?

There is nothing but the now.

But if I've only been here so many years of my life...

That's this expression. Through multiplicities of expressions. In other words, all of you have expressed about three million times, give or take a few thousand. Some of you have been here more often. You are a glutton for punishment. No, you are eager for the perfection.

Creation and Purpose of Earth

The earth was set up originally to be the sun of this area, and it will be the Blue-Green Sun of the Cosmic Light when it does go back into perfection, for which it was created. When it was created, it was created like a drop of rain, aqua in color. It was the most beautiful creation that God ever put together. The whole heavenly host came to herald this sun into being. This sun shall take its rightful place, regardless of the inhabitants upon it.

At this time, right now, by the quadrant angles between the Central Sun and the Cardinal Suns, and because of the period of time that you are in history, **you have the greatest advantage or perfecting right now** that has ever been offered upon this earth in the past decades of histories. This is because of the triangulation of the intelligence being fed to you at this time, from the Cosmos.

You are constantly being bombarded with the Truth. That's the reason there is such a rapid improvement of ability of man's activities. That's the reason there are more and more of you seeking in classes like this, because you are prime for the Truth, rather than existence.

What about the other planets? Are they made the same way? Are they for the same purpose?

They are all for the same purpose: balance. They all have expression. Their gases and pressures are different. The rate of motion and speed are different. The dimensions of operation there will be different. The flesh body that you wear here on this planet is for the pressures and chemical elements that exist within this dimension of this atmosphere on this planet only.

Would I be on another planet and still know that I'm here?

No, as long as you <u>know</u> you are here, you <u>are</u> here. When you see people that have lost their presence of being, they actually become vegetables. They are no longer on this Earth Plane for their expression. It can be at any age. I've seen it from 6 all the way up. They aren't even aware of this plane even existing. The transfer is so smooth, they won't know until they have terminated their expression.

What about senility where people will come and go out of awareness?

They are still bound to Earth and haven't fully released themselves, yet. Their cord hasn't been broken. Although they are trying, but yet unwilling to make the transfer. The activity of transfer from expression is when the Airless Cell of the body withdraws and makes the transfer, leaving the Ego Cell in charge.

The Ego Cell activates the body and holds it in vibrational frequency of manifestation, because of the programming of the Airless Cell when the body went into manifestation. Unless the death atoms of the body are charged, the decomposing of the body cannot take place. When an arrangement of Mind transference is made, then the acceleration of the deterioration of the body is much stronger, because you have the death atoms charged.

What is a death atom?

That is the keying system of the body for construction that holds you in being. When the keying system for the inner part of your body is no longer energized, then it is like everybody that is holding hands simply letting go.

When the Airless Cell and the Ego Center of the body take leave, then what man calls the death state exists at that time. This is when the death atoms are in completion of their activity. Prior to this, the setting will be about three weeks prior, when the Airless Cell has removed itself from the body.

Where is the Ego Center?

The Ego Center is your reflected being. It is located 1 1/2 inches above the heart, next to and at the left side of the sternum. It is your made center, manifested. Your Airless Cell is your divinity center; it is created.

When one becomes a vegetable on this planet, and they die here, do they die there?

No, this body will just live out its time that was initially programmed for it. However, you may change your mind about it and make an adjustment about your initial program. There is no set rule, it is up to you. It isn't as complicated as it sounds; it just sounds foreign to you at this time.

Conception

You mentioned there is no life in the body until the first breath is taken. What form of life is ruling?

The Ego Center is there. Let's go back to conception. When a female is in position to receive energization for manifestation, all of the entities that wish to take a body will rush to hover about the head of the mother. Many women will see spots about them, which are all colors of the rainbow. These are the entities waiting to come into expression. Unless there is a Gold, Silver or Bronze, it is first come, first served. When these colors do show up, the others must move aside, for those colors have right of choice.

At the time of conception, these entities will throw an energy lock on the seed, whichever one is there first to do so. When the sperm transfers the chromosome energies to that seed, the masculine or feminine product of vehicle will be cast. After the casting and the seating is sealed, by the energization of the energies of the sperm and the seed cell, then the entity takes charge of the construction. The seed cell is the Ego Center.

The Airless Cell shoots a reflection of itself into the seat and this becomes the Ego Center. The construction then comes from the Ego Center as it is being directed by the Airless Cell from the outside of the mother's body. The Ego Cell will steal from the body all of the minerals and chemicals that it needs.

If the Airless Cell is a Gold, Silver or Bronze, then it has a good abeyance of energies set aside in the Universe to draw from, so that its body will be perfect in construction. If not, there will be deficiencies. These entities have earned these colors by authority. They are usually a teacher, avatar or a sage of the Earth. They will come in with full memory of knowing.

Those three colors do not come in under a veil. All other colors come in with a veil covering the brain, blocking memory. This veil is over the memory cells I referred to earlier. They must be awakened by stilling brain, because it will become the beast—the 666—which is a Biblical reference that refers to 6 electrons, 6 protons and 6 neutrons. This refers to the carbon atom, which is devoid of Light, two triangles without a center guide. The wheel doesn't have a hub.

Immaculate Conception refers to the period of 7 years before conception takes place, of which there is only perfect word, perfect thought and perfect deed by the parents. This means no doubt, misgivings or anguish. This condition must prevail during the 9 months of gestation, and for 7 years afterwards. This is due to the effect of your influence upon the Sense Centers of the Physical Eye and the emotional value of the body.

Immaculate Conception

Perfect thought, perfect word and perfect deed
by the parents

7 years before birth of the child
+ 9 months of gestation
+ 7 years after birth
(14 years and 9 months total)

Immaculate conception.

This is why Joseph and Mary wanted to bring forth a perfect vehicle for Jesus. This is why she was held in such perfectness, so that a perfect vehicle could be animated into expression. Very few can hold the Perfect Thought so long, for the construction of a perfect vehicle.

How do they know what parents to select?

They have full memory and knowledge of those in expression, for they have already been to the **Akashic Records** to check out the individuals, both masculine and feminine, for a perfect vehicle. They are very choosy and know exactly what they are doing. In the Akashic Records are kept all of the things that have been, will be and are. They are the full **Books of Life**, and these entities have full access to them. They have a very high standing in Universal Activity to have this order.

Is the Airless Cell really us?

It is really you. It is eternally you.

The Garden of Life and the Council of Souls

When we leave this body, life is gone?

Life always is. Expression just changes places. You still have a body; you just lose this flesh. Upon termination of expression, for 3 days you will be in the Garden of Life, where you will sit in rest as all of your Etheric Energies assemble, before you will stand in judgment of yourself. On the third day, you stand before the Council of Souls. You will run through all of your life and you pass judgment on yourself. Nobody judges you but yourself.

From each planet where existence of expression is taking place, two representatives are sent to the Council of Souls, for a 6 month period of time as it would be back on their home planet. They all sit in the gallery to counsel and aid. Their bodies back at the home planet, are locked in motion and continue to act out the daily expression. Only the Airless Cell reflection is transferred. It is transferred back into its Pure Physical Body and put into a light fraction activity in that dimension of operation. There are many, many dimensions of operation, which is difficult to explain until your understanding grows.

Upon Termination of Expression, Days 1-4

Location	Time	Activity
Garden of Life	3 days	You will sit in rest as all your Etheric Energies assemble.
Council of Souls	4th day	You run through all your life. You judge yourself.

Upon termination of expression, days 1-4.

If a person is in good health, is it because they are breathing properly?

They hold the perfect thought of good health. But due to their aging, they are not ageless. The Airless Cell is the center of contact that directs the activities so that Spirit may activate the Physical through Mind contact. **To get to the Airless Cell in meditation is the breakthrough**.

I don't expect you to hold the **7/2 breath rate** all of the time. *Just do it 3 or 4 times a day for a sequence of 7 times.* If you should feel strange, you probably have too much hydrogen in your body, due to a habit of short breath, so you are panting. Your body has become overheated.

As you breathe short and your muscles are choppy, they are forcing the air out of you. Your diaphragm is not under control by breath, so you can't properly draw in the Light Energies that travel down the 7 arteries of the diaphragm. This charges both the Spiritual and Physical energies of the body. This improper activity of the diaphragm causes you to pant. You should be aware of your seven count breath at all times. In activity of physical effort, you may accelerate the cells, but the breath doesn't have to change.

But the pulse seems to change.

It won't. The gas mixtures of the body do not change, just the cells accelerate their rate of spin. This is why you become tired because you burn yourself up. That is why you pant. When you run, your temperature increases to between 1,200 to 1,600 degrees. This is why you become sweaty.

When you become angry, your temperature soars to between 2,000 to 2,800 degrees. **In one minute of sustained rage, you burn up enough Etheric Energy in your body that it will take 24 hours to replenish it.** Your temperature will exceed inflammable condition, 2,800 degrees. All of the water runs out of your body.

You say the Fountain of Youth is lodged at the base of the spine. What if an individual has used up this energy?

If you have burned up your centers in your body by ignorance or misuse, you do not reconstruct. You have to trade it in for a new vehicle. It becomes a game of forfeit. You wear out an automobile, so you turn it in to the junk yard. We put our worn out bodies in cemeteries.

Can't we reconstruct our bodies into perfect?

Yes, **you have the right to Perfect your body at any time if you have the ability to hold the Pureness of Thought**. If you are unable to hold that Pureness, then as you leave this body, you will have to re-enter, again, by what you had attained or denied. Only when you turn your back do you lose.

AREAS OF LEAVING THE BODY

You leave the body by four distinct areas:

1- SOLAR PLEXUS: Usual, normal way
2- RECTUM: When you make an ass of yourself in your expression. You return in a breech birth.
3- NAVEL: When you led a physical life.
4- HEART: When you lived a life of loving service and kindness.
5- TOP OF HEAD: If you had nearly perfected your body and could have perfected it, you will leave through the top of your head.

As you come back into expression, you will enter just exactly as you left. You will pick up just exactly where you left off

If you made others miserable, you will come back and be miserable, until you learn to forgive yourself. **You are on this plane of expression to learn love and forgiveness.** *You must love and forgive yourself before you can love and forgive anybody else.* It is like a thorn in your side, it will continue to fester you until you remove it. The same for bad thoughts, they will haunt you until you dismiss them.

Universal Law states:

> If you do not use wisely this which you have been given,
> what little you have shall be taken from you.

LOVE: THE KEY TO EVERYTHING

The only way you make an enemy become your friend is by loving them. It is the key to everything. Your existence couldn't take place without love. Think of all the unseen universes that love you so much, and all of the other planes of expressions that love you so much that they have allowed their imprisonment so that you can have expression. They gave up their presence of being; that's real love.

THE HOLY BREATH, THE 7-2 BREATH

HOW TO USE IT AND WHY
BREATHE IN FOR 7 BEATS OF THE HEART.

- You are open to the 7 rays of light, which will completely energize your entire body.
- You receive all of the transmission into the Sightcone for discernment.
- You are formulating all of your transmissions to take place. You are making all of your thought form pictures, of which you are not even aware.

STILL THE BREATH FOR 2 BEATS OF THE HEART, AFTER INHALING.

- Everything that is evaluated in your thought goes to your two memory cells where it is proofed, computed and played back, where it is either accepted into being, or discarded by your ability of comprehension.

EXHALE YOUR BREATH FOR 7 BEATS OF THE HEART.

- You are transmitting your thought form pictures away from you into activity.

STILL YOUR BREATH FOR 2 BEATS OF THE HEART, AFTER EXHALING.

- You allow your thought-form pictures to leave you. If you don't still your breath, you draw them right back to you and you cannot attain that which you desire.

REPEAT STEPS FROM BEGINNING.

DISADVANTAGES OF NOT USING THE 7-2 BREATH

IF YOU DO NOT LEARN TO STILL YOUR BREATH
Suffocation of cells

- You take yourself out of expression by each breath, because you kill your cells. You kill them by suffocation.

Over-energization or under-energization of your body.

- You either over-energize or under-energize your body. It becomes deficient in functional activity. If your cells become malfunctioned too many times, they become dormant.

Disease

- When the cells lose expression, which you call dying, then they become dormant and are a spore breeding spot for bacteria. Any place in which you create a cold spot, or a low oxygen point, sets up a spore situation for bacteria to produce and create what you call disease, [dis-ease].

Therefore, it is most important for you to activate your bodies and your Sense Centers. Without the perfection of your breath, you will never achieve it.

IF YOU BREATHE TOO SHALLOWLY
Affect on nervous system

- Your nervous system is affected.

Frustration and irritation

- You hyperventilate your system, which will affect the heat cells of your body. This causes frustration and irritation.

THE HOLY BREATH, THE 7-2 BREATH

ADDITIONAL ADVANTAGES OF USING THE 7-2 BREATH
By this breath activity and sense centers of your body:
Energization of the cellular structure and nervous system.

- The Light is drawn into your body and taken into the bloodstream and into the lymph system. It is transmitted through the body to energize the cellular structure and nervous system.

Energization of the body

- You are able to activate your cells and energize your body with energy that you have never before experienced, if you do this exercise seven times daily.

Increase in capacity

- Your capacity will increase, because as it is now, half of your lung sacks have dried up.

Activation of bodies and sense centers

- It is most important for you to activate your bodies and your Sense Centers. Without the perfection of your breath, you will never achieve it.
- There is much to be understood about how you breathe. By your breathing, you become the total sum and substance of your thoughts.

Where Man Is Now

We have learned that **God created just one plane of conscious: Perfection.** Fallen man has made all other forms of consciousness. We also learned that true creation is Spirit, Mind and Physical.

It is important to understand that there is a great difference between making and creating. **All created things are eternal and unchanging**, and are those things which emerge from the Divine Substance in perfect form. Made things are not eternal and are subject to change, they grow and change according to their thinking, that is, the thought action of their controlling vibration.

The earth, sun, moon and stars are created things and therefore, do not change. But man changes as his thinking changes, and he may make of himself anything he chooses, because of the nature of his creation.

Man was created out of the ALL, a Perfect Divine Thought, clothed in Spirit Substance and Flesh Divine. He remained in this state for countless ages, until, through transgression, he turned his flesh from Divine [Created], to carnal [made flesh], which was subject to change. Then, step by step, plane of thought by plane of thinking, he fell from the Divine State of his creation. The transition from Man of Light to man of darkness took countless ages, and when it was finished, man's separation from God was complete. Where he had once expressed as one with God, he now expressed just the opposite. Man forgot God, but God never forgot man. The why of man's return to God is always open, and man is now working his way back, step by step, by the same route that he left.

The Spirit of God within man could not fall, for it is that part of man which is truly of God, the God in action which is the essence of life, in and with man. It is this indwelling Spirit that has led man from the former, lower planes into his present state of awareness of being.

Man is now vibrating upon the Plane of Five, which is the **great turning point for man's perfection,** the preparatory stage. On this fifth plane, man begins to know that there is a more complete life for him, a life everlasting. And it is in this Plane of Five that man must perfect his physical body and recreate the Divine body which God created for him in the beginning.

In this Plane of Five, the Divine Spirit within man has caused the quickening of his mind, which is speedier than the light rays of the sun. We can see the truth of this by studying the history of man's modes of transportation. A hundred and fifty years ago, man was content to travel at the slow pace of the ox. A few years before that, he traveled on foot. Now, in the jet age, he travels at hundreds of miles per hour.

The time has not yet come when every man will look to the **Great Teacher, his own spirit**, for guidance. Most are still concerned with conquering material substance, ignoring the greatest instrument of all, their own bodies, which are available for them to use.

If man would use only one one-hundredth part of his own divine power, the speed of the jet airplane would be like a snail's pace to him.

Man does not yet realize the nature of his spiritual action upon his flesh. When he does, all things in heaven and earth will be his. He has just emerged from the fourth plane of fulfillment into the fifth, and has made great strides in a few short years. Soon, he will have fulfilled the mechanical expression of things, and will come to know that to express divinely, is his true aim.

Man is now in the beginning of the fifth plane of consciousness of his perfecting. In this plane, he must complete the re-perfecting of his physical body. He must also unite his mind and body so they will work in perfect accord. He must also overcome all the carnal ways in which he has delighted and find the new delight of knowing his powers and his substance, and the perfect action of one upon the other, which will merge them into one. When this occurs, man will at last be at peace.

Where Man Is Now

The same topic might occur in successive chapters, but this is for a purpose. Each time that topic reappears, an added meaning becomes apparent to you because as you read or listen, you grow in your understanding and acceptance. These are the planted seeds maturing.

Because of conformity, you have been taught in social structure to be controlled. You are taught through limitation of order, so that in order to have domination, a few can rule the multitudes. Your Eternal Creed, which is "I am eternally free in deed, which is my nature, and I bow to no man, not even God, for I am God" is true.

It is difficult for most people to accept the fact they are God. You might as well get used to the idea that you are God. There is nothing that exists but what is inside of you. There is one tiny little spark in the center of your heart. It is so infinite in its smallness, that it is nearly impossible for man to see with the technique of magnification that is employed today. All of the rest of it about that spark is moving so fast that its molecular structure solidifies itself into solid form that you make to express outwardly.

From that one little dot, your Airless Cell, you take form. As you are now, you aren't even true to your Etheric pattern. You are only partially true to it, because inefficiencies in your functioning keep you short of that perfect pattern.

Salvation: Perfection In Conscious

Your only salvation is in yourself, not anybody else. The only way you are going to perfect is by doing it yourself. Nobody else is going to be able to do it for you. I can aid you. I can give you all the information, but when it comes down to the final test, and you have to take this body with you, you have to do it. I can't do it for you.

That's what this whole discussion is all about: enlighting you of perfection in conscious, so that you will be able to climb above this earth's dimension of expression and not have to return here, unless by choice. There are many, many changes that will have to take place in your structure to regain your natural place in expression, because everything you are expressing in now is very unnatural. You don't even breathe right.

The Process Of Becoming Dormant

From the age of twelve on, you lost your ability because you became of the age of reasoning. You became responsible for yourself. At that time all your spirit guidance that was guiding you became dormant. You took over your responsibility of being at that time, when the dormant process began.

Your becoming dormant started really taking place by thought impressions of picture exchanges from the womb out. From the time the seed was conceived in the womb, your thought impressions were impressed, even at that time. Many of the problems that you carry with you in your understanding took place while you were still in the womb and not even in air expression. There is much to be understood about where you are and what you are really about.

In our first lesson, we learned that there was one place of conscious that was created which was that of Perfect. Because of man's inefficiency within himself to hold himself true, he became lazy and slothful within himself and allowed himself, by descending degrees, a lesser state of consciousness. He made the conscious condition into a consciousness.

He made multiples of a conscious state. As he changed his dimensions, when he no longer could hold his proofing of that point, then he would make a lesser point to operate in where he could be comfortable, until he could no longer even equalize that, and he constantly went down and down, until he attained to the mineral kingdom. At that point he turned around and came back out.

In your everyday function of living, when you take your first breath in the morning and you relieve yourself from your subjective mind back to the conscious objective mind, as you open your eyes and accept the vibrations again after having your Sightcone stilled, you instantly start calculating over 3,000,000 thoughts per second. Your body starts reacting to the action of those thoughts bombarding your Sightcone.

If you have allowed your body to get into disorder, so that you wake up with aches and pains, then your guard will be down and brain will use it as a leverage point to further endeavor to control you. It will magnify those aches and pains until you, yourself, quiet them or squelch them with man's sedation of drugs. If a person will only **learn to go within and stop thinking, being quiet enough to hear the Pureness of Thought, then he will have the true answers.** After getting the Pureness of Thought, if you do not take the time for pureness of realization, and you begin to reason, then even the little jewel that you received has been destroyed. Once you have reasoned, you have destroyed the Etheric condition. You made a distortion. There is no in-between, nothing half truth or half false. You are right or dead wrong.

When you make a mistake, the only way is to say, "I'm sorry." If you don't do this and you don't dismiss it, then it goes into your memory banks where it can automatically play back to you and it will control you. **Learn to be good to yourself and love yourself so you can forgive yourself.** I want you to learn that you are individuals and you are very unique; **the Universe can't exist without you.**

Each of you must, at some time or another, make a decision to take your light body from this earth. If you don't, you are chained to this Earth until you do. The easiest way to get out of here is to learn how you operate, why you operate and from where you operate.

The Whole Idea of This Earth

The expressions of this part of earth have been in functional operation from Perfect at greater than four and a half billion years. As a result, you have expressed on a mean average of a little over one million three hundred thousand (1,300,000) times on this earth, and you still may have many to go, **until you learn to perfect your body and take it from this earth. That's what the whole idea of this earth is now.**

Adam and Eve

As earth was originally created, it was one of the most perfect places to express in the world, in the universe, so to speak. I use the term "world" loosely, because it is worlds within worlds. Due to this forming of conditioning, a lot that was created went into a made condition. In the Book of Genesis, you will see the words "He made them then," not anything about "created." It says "He made them then." All of a sudden, a single became a multiple. One became two, because it says, "He made them then."

Originally there was only one Adam. He created Adam, Ad-man, adamic man, man wearing the Veil of Adam and Eve, the positive and the positive out of phase, which we call "negative." When Man was created in Divinity, he was both masculine and feminine. There was no male or female as exist today. When man began to lose the ability of conscious to consciousness, which is told to us in the Bible as Eve offering the apple to Adam, she picked the apple from a tree that had a serpent there. In all the Parables, the serpent represents Wisdom.

The forbidden fruit, the apple, was a secret that was given to allow man to cleanse his brain. However, when Adam and Eve partook from the tree of good and evil, then they knew other than Perfect Conscious. They knew good and evil. **They removed themselves from the Truth** and moved into a state of true: a state of change. The meaning of these symbols is that they partook from the Tree of Knowledge, which lessened their conscious state from Truth unto true.

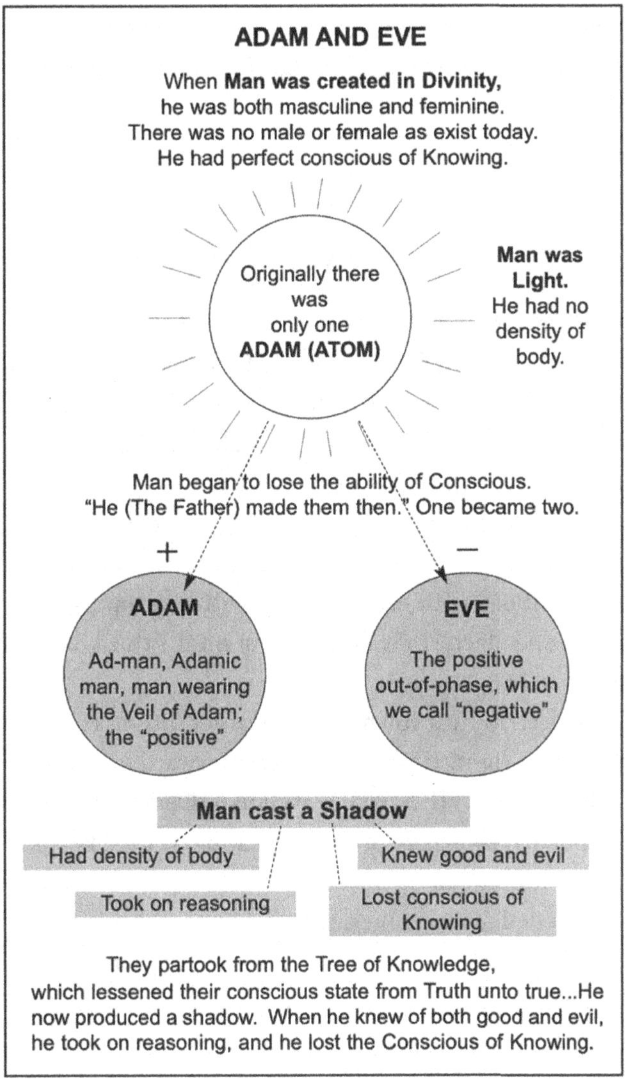
ADAM AND EVE
When Man was created in Divinity,
he was both masculine and feminine.
There was no male or female as exist today.
He had perfect conscious of Knowing.
Originally there was only one ADAM (ATOM)
Man was Light. He had no density of body.
Man began to lose the ability of Conscious.
"He (The Father) made them then." One became two.
+
—
ADAM
Ad-man, Adamic man, man wearing the Veil of Adam; the "positive"
EVE
The positive out-of-phase, which we call "negative"
Man cast a Shadow
Had density of body
Knew good and evil
Took on reasoning
Lost conscious of Knowing
They partook from the Tree of Knowledge, which lessened their conscious state from Truth unto true...He now produced a shadow. When he knew of both good and evil, he took on reasoning, and he lost the Conscious of Knowing.

Adam and Eve.

The Father said, "Come out, Adam."

"I can't, Father," Adam replied, "I'm naked."

"How do you know you are naked?," asked the Father.

"I can see myself now, Father."

He never could see himself when he was Light, but now he cast a shadow. He had no density of body until this transformation took place. When he knew of both good and evil, he took on reasoning, and he lost the Conscious of Knowing.

The Significance of the Apple

The apple was used because it is the one fruit used to cleanse the brain. **It is used to cleanse the mucus from the brain for clarity of thinking**. The old adage of an apple a day keeps the doctor away, does have truth within those words. For those who develop severe headaches, or have mucus problems in the sinus area, you can go on a three-day green apple diet. Just eat the washed, unpeeled Pippin apples for three days and drink water. Don't peel the apples because the pectin is right next to the skin. You can cut the apple in slices to make it easier to eat. This diet will clear up the condition. By the second day, a headache may develop, but on the third day, you will feel terrific. Do this only once a year.

The way to determine if you have a mucus condition is to spin your head around from left to right. If you feel dizzy afterward, go on the apple and water diet. The reason for the dizzy sensation is due to a little gyro placed at the top of the head. It is the size of a small pea, and is what keeps the balance for your body in functional operation. If it gets encased by mucus, then its efficiency is impeded. The magnetic lines of force that it cuts and functions under, as well, do not allow it to hold you stable to the Earth, which is also gyrating. You have to be stable with respect to Earth, regardless of where you are on Earth.

THE BRAIN AND THE GYRO

MUCUS IN THE BRAIN

Symptoms of mucus in the brain:
Severe headaches, sinus problems,
Dizziness when spinning head left to right

How to determine *if you have a mucus condition:*
Spin head left to right.
If you feel dizzy afterward, go on pippin apple & water diet.

Reason for dizziness: Body's gyro is encrusted with mucus.

Solution:
Eat only washed, unpeeled Pippin apples and water for 3 days. (See text for details.)

THE BODY'S GYRO

What *is the gyro:*	Small, pea-sized gyro at top of head
Purpose of gyro:	Keeps body's balance, energizes your body
Functioning of gyro:	It cuts & functions under magnetic lines of force.

What happens if gyro is encrusted in mucus*:*
Efficiency of gyro is impeded.
Magnetic lines of force do not allow gyro to hold you stable to earth.

Gyro helps give you flexible energy.

It re-evaluates energy reception through your feet, temples and clavicles, to energize your body to your diaphragm, giving you flexible energy to your body.

A CLEAN BRAIN

Importance of having your brain clean:

No matter where you are on Earth, your body's gyro will set a stabilization of longitude and latitude by minute and seconds, for the energization of your body along with the computerization of your diaphragm to feed your body electromagnetic energy.

When the brain is encrusted, its action is slowed down.

The action of all the cellular structure of your body is keyed to the same operation, which makes a deficiency in your nervous and lymphatic systems, as well.

The brain and the gyro.

Your gyro will also re-evaluate the energy reception through your feet, temples and clavicles, to energize your body to your diaphragm, giving you flexible energy to your body. No matter where you are on Earth, it will set a stabilization of longitude and latitude by minutes and seconds, for the energizing of your body, along with the computerization of your diaphragm to feed your body electromagnetic energy. This is why it is so important to have your brain clean.

When the brain is encrusted, its action is slowed down. The action of all the cellular structure of your body is keyed to the same operation, which makes a deficiency in your nervous and lymph systems, as well.

Ductless Glands and Body Energies

The terminology of persons, places and things in the Bible are references to cosmic energies, the universe of being, the manifestation of all the creation and the **ductless glands** within your body, which are the **energy forces that drive your spiritual sense of being** and values within your expression. These are true within your body but are sleeping at this time. They are only waiting to be awakened into expression.

All the ductless glands are of spirit. For your information, they are the thyroid, parathyroids, thymus, pituitary, pineal and spleen.

Each of you has this value to reawaken these and bring them into total expression. You, yourself, are the one who put these to sleep. You can't pass the buck onto anybody else. Anything you don't like about yourself, blame yourself. Don't pass your buck onto your parents, your grandparents or some uncle or somebody else, because you made and manifested over the creation, this body that you are expressing in. Everything that is out of order in it, you put it that way, because you directed the whole operation of the manifestation of its forming.

The "Fallen" State

When we speak of your "fallen" state, we use the word "fallen" very loosely because we are talking about something that really hasn't fallen; it has only altered itself in conditioning. We use the word "fallen" because biblical terminology uses this word. We clarify it with that meaning, and say it this way, that **you altered continuously the conditions of perfect to imperfect.** You changed subatomic structure to molecular activity. You changed that from substance into matter and density and made it solidified in solid form, that which was like liquid in a light impulse exchange expression.

Because massing of matters came about, you made all the things that were about you in alteration and the other planes of expression allowed the alteration to take place because you were given dominion over everything that expresses. They didn't have to follow you, but they did, out of love, knowing that if they did not go with you, you would have no way back.

When man took the transformation from Light to flesh, it describes this in the Bible as man being made from the dust of the Earth. Man took the molecular structure of the molecules of which the Earth consists within its planes of vibrations, to make up the subatomic structure of form for man to exist within from his imaginary pattern.

Man imagined a picture and became that image. He existed in that imagination for four and a half billion years on Earth. There is one exception: after he allowed himself his inability of perception, he found that **he could no longer control the magnetic field of his body, because he had no Light with which to hold the molecular structure in form**. As the powers within him lessened, by his inability of control of Force, the feminine separated from the masculine.

The feminine fell out of the masculine, onto the ground, still facing up to the standing masculine. At that time, the Father had to make one decision, either separate or destroy. By His Wisdom, He allowed the separation to take place by one Law:

> *Man would have to be born through the womb of his lost energy until he could Light himself.*

MAN'S FALL FROM THE DIVINE STATE OF CREATION

THE DIVINE STATE OF CREATION

Man was created out of the ALL.
A PERFECT DIVINE THOUGHT.

Man was created MAN OF LIGHT
Clothed in Sprit, Substance and flesh divine.
He remained in this state for countless ages.
(for 4 1/2 billion years on earth)
Man was expressing one with God.

TRANSGRESSION AND DESCENT

Man turned his flesh from Divine (created) to
CARNAL FLESH, (made flesh)

Man imagined a picture and became that image,
He took on molecular structure (molecules of which the earth consists). He changed from substance into matter and densified it in solid form, in flesh.
He was subject to change, plane of thought by plane of thought, step by step for countless ages (3 billion years)

MAN OF DARKNESS

Man of darkness had a dark existence about him.
He was almost mineral.
Man forgot God
Man separated from God, but God never forgot man.

Man lost the ability of motion and became fixed in position.

TURNING POINT:

Something had to be better than this.
He asked the Father for help.
The Father, in His graciousness, allowed man to come back, step by step, as he had fallen.
Yet the Spirit of man could not fall, for it is that part of man which is truly of God.

Man's fall from the divine state of creation.

The Spirit of God within man could not fall, for it is that part of man which is truly of God—the God in action which is the essence of life, in and with man. It is this in-dwelling Spirit that has led man from the former, lower planes into his present state of awareness of being.

Airless Cell: Love and Light In Activity

This is your utilization between the Motionless Conscious to the Airless Cell, which is Love and Light in activity, and the radiation by the Airless cell to illuminate you in form. The mysteries of the accomplishments of your body are beyond your comprehension at this time. It is such a marvel to behold that most all of the things you do after the third time become automatic. You no longer have to think about it, for it will be taken over by the secondary brain. It will re-function itself into automatic activity and react to its own controlling of its own ability. When you eat you don't have to think about bending your arm or missing your mouth, or the coordination of your arms and feet when you drive a car. It all becomes second nature.

With breathing, you have forgotten how, so you breathe yourself short. Not too many breathe themselves long. By short breathing, you tire yourself because you lessen the energy into your body.

> *Man is now vibrating upon the Plane of Five, which is the great turning point for man's perfection, the preparatory stage. On this fifth plane, man begins to know that there is a more complete life for him, a life everlasting. And it is in this Plane of Five that man must perfect his physical body and recreate the Divine body which God created for him in the beginning.*

The Most Opportune Time To Find Perfection

Everything in every kingdom, except the angels, has altered itself to aid you so that you could continue your expression until you found yourself. You went clear to the bottom of the barrel and now you are on the fifth plane on the way back, and you are in the fifth kingdom of expression to finding yourself. **You are in the most perfect opportune time in energy from the Cardinal Suns and the Central Suns to be bombarded with the Intelligence of the Cosmos to find perfection within yourself.** Many teachers are sent at this time to inform you of these truths.

In each history I come once to inform the history at that time of perfection. **The information that I am given, I give very freely, so that you can remember yourself and find yourself and know where you are,**

what you are, who you are and why. This way you will know where you are, where you are going, what you are about and what you are doing

Man is vibrating on the fifth plane, where he must perfect his physical body and re-create his Divine Body that God had created for him. Each of you has the burning desire to lose the density of your body, or else you wouldn't be here. You want to give it back to Earth where it belongs.

By your very patient ability, this can be accomplished. But **this can only be done by you, yourself; nobody can do it for you.** This is a game you must win all by yourself. We can stand by and watch all that we want to, but we are helpless to enter in and make the transition for you.

Why You Are Unique

As it is now, you are in a total state of confusion. You can only see one direction at a time. You can only listen to one side at a time. You can only walk one direction at a time. You are limited in multiples of movements, but you have one ability that sets you aside from everything else. **You have the reasoning of computerization, by brain activity of flesh exchange, within your body and with the alliance of the whole-in-one breath. This makes you unique from everything else, because you can teach by instructing others, and by communication exchange, you can leave records** of transference that will aid those coming behind you informing them of the pitfalls that you have already passed through.

Illusion is a shadowing effect of conditions that are made from created activity. The endeavor of this activity lessens ability, placing God outside of that existence. **This is where man is now, he places God outside of himself.** He becomes confused and bewildered in his own ignorance. As he lessened himself in his creative right, he also lost his ability of holding true to Light.

By superimposing upon himself lesser states of being, which he could no longer hold for himself within the state he had manifested for himself, he allowed himself to be lowered. Man has hit bottom and is on a long one way trip back. It is at this period of time that it is the most perfect for man to bring his body to perfection. The triangulations of the Central Sun with the quadrant of the Secondary Suns are most beneficial now.

For this reason, the radiation for the quickening of the Mind of Man will awaken him to what he has fallen from, or what he has lost sight of. Instead of placing everything outside of himself, he is now looking within himself to find the Truth that he was. Instead of looking at the illusion, man is letting it fall away. Everything you look at is deceptive. Everything you look at is not as you could see it. When you look, your eyes only see with 1/60 of their potential. Your perception of vibration is only 1/10,000 of full potential.

When you use the outside aspect of illusion, you become bewildered by your own delusions. This is what causes the turmoil that you exist with, because you are continually looking outside of yourself with reasoning for the answers, instead of being quiet and looking within, to Know. The longer you look out, the less you will know. **Only when you are quiet and look within, will you find the answers and true salvation that you have been searching for.**

When you learn to attain unto the Airless Cell that operates you, and form a unification with it, then you will be a long way on your road to perfecting yourself into the Perfect, which is the true state of conscious.

Records of Man's Beginnings

You have left a marked record of all your exchanges over all these billions and billions of years, even though those records cannot truly be found because of the devastating destruction that the earth goes through on its surface at the end of each history with the result that in 99.9% of all perception left is totally destroyed. Everything starts anew except for those few that carry through from one history to another and carry the remembrance of that history with them. All try to leave records of what took place in the past.

If you look in all of your books, in all the mythologies of the beginnings of all different races, you will find that a man came out of a boat from the ocean and reestablished life with his family again. I don't care what name they use, but if you go into all the histories of all the nations of the world, you will find this same story told. They use different names for the persons, but the same story is told by every one. It's all the way around the world. It kind of complies with the truth of where man really is and what he is really about.

Created vs. Manifested Things

It is important to understand that there is a great difference between making and creating. All created things are eternal and unchanging, and are those things which emerge from the Divine Substance in perfect form. Made things are not eternal and are subject to change; they grow and change according to their thinking, that is, the thought action of their controlling vibration.

The earth, sun, moon and stars are created things and therefore, do not change. But man changes as his thought changes, and he may make of himself anything he chooses, because of the nature of his creation.

Created things stay fixed and complacent at all times. They do not alter from their conditioning. They become the fixed points which show us that there is more to expression than this manifestation of limitation that we express in. Those things that are created, if we look out and look at the heavenly bodies, we know the sun is going to be there every morning when we wake up. We know when the moon comes up that the sun is going to be waiting because the light shining off of it is verifying that its existence is still there.

How many of you have been to the east coast of the United States? How many have been to New York City? Can you prove to me that there is a New York city?

By being there!

Is there anything existing except for this room and the people who are in it?

At this moment, no.

You see what I am talking about, "made" and "manifested"?

Only by our memory conditions of past imprints does that vibrancy of expression exist in memory. There is no way that you could prove that it exists, sitting in this room, only by your memory. By each breath is all you exist. Everything is dependent upon that breath in expression.

Why Life Exists In Things and Why They Change

Only because of the conformity of your agreement of thinking do things manifest in multiples of themselves to hold themselves in expression. These are all "made" conditions by conformity of agreement. Life exists in things only because of this agreement. We give agreement that these things are so and we give energy to them. Had you never been there, you could only rely on the relationship of an explanation from somebody else.

You make a picture form of what you think it is. The vividness of the transfer of the one informing is only as good a picture as you will form within your imaginative processes to attain of that manifestation, until you have seen it for yourself in its reflection. Then it has its conformity of energy, yet with changes, because you will see things that they never saw. This is because no one will view an object the same as someone else, because it is from two points of view.

There is nothing in manifestation that is an exact duplicate of itself. Even identical twins are not perfect duplicates of one another, even with the splitting of Airless Cells running side by side, they are still individuals, completely different in conformity.

Anything that is in manifested matter is continuously in an alteration of change. Each impression of thought upon it, in thinking value, makes an alteration in it. The like or dislike, or the love or the hate, either manifests in a totaling in expression or destroys that manifestation.

Neutral Grey: Space

Write down "grey," with an "e," neutral, and behind that write "space," because that's what space is, grey. When you take all expression out of anything, it will turn grey. If you look at your sunrise in the morning when the sun first comes up, the first color you will see is gold. Then it will turn into the physical of the red, and then it will hue itself into the blue of Mind. It will total itself in the day and it will reverse the processes of leaving back from the blue, to the red, to the yellow, and then to grey, going into space. Then darkness will take its place. That which was vivid within the exchange of that day's manifestation, now has been lost to time, because of form-time-space dimension.

Why You Are Where You Are

Each day you alter yourself in changes by this same mode of operation, **by your agreement or disagreement** of what you are agreeing with, with what you are expressing in and with. That places you where you are, now. Ten minutes from now you will never be there, because your thinking will constantly change and your imaginative processes are constantly working, making alterations and changes within yourself.

Man was created perfect out of All and is the substance of All and has the conformity of all substance within him, but it is all held in abeyance within you, waiting for instant recall. It's as instant as that instant recall, into perfection, once you place it all in order. It's like a jigsaw puzzle. When you get all the pieces together it works beautifully, but if you have pieces missing, you have holes all the way through it.

"Death", Aging and Length of Expression

That's the way we are. We have holes in us. We haven't plugged up the holes yet. We are leaking a little bit, here and there. In other words, we weep a little bit of our Light out of us, because we allow one thing to control us. It's called "death," the loss of expression. It's brother is called "aging." Because by our desires when we were young, we desired to be so greatly like those that we loved, like our uncle, our grandpa or our mother and our father. We set our pattern of conformity at that time, in our manifestation.

Your bodies were built to last for seven thousand years of expression and you burn them up in less than seventy. Now, that's a little shortcoming!

Carnality flesh can be altered to create a divine flesh in expression. Man took countless ages to alter himself from a state of light into a state of total darkness, when he ate from the "Tree of Evil." They call it, the Tree of Life, which is really the Tree of Knowledge. In Perfection there is nothing imperfect. When you have Intelligence and you know that you know, then you know. But when you use reasoning value and you use knowledge, you don't know that you don't know, and you never will know, because you are caught within that trap.

Conformity and Change

Because of conformity of consumption of theories that are called "facts," which is only a science applying unto, you are held conformed in the conditioning of that "fact." In other words, what is accepted as a "fact," right now, in the next breath is not so, because alteration has completely taken place in that one breath. All expression has changed, all the way around this globe. Everything in the universe has changed in that one breath, from our viewpoint, not from their viewpoint.

Your values of thinking in your impressions that you are expressing and impressing upon others, are setting a pattern that everybody becomes in common to and with. You are conditioning by the condition of your projection of the sum and substance of your thinking, not of Thought.

The entire world starts loving itself for about two weeks at Christmas, and the other fifty weeks, it's back to business as usual. Too many times we allow ourselves to be influenced by the surroundings, and the thought patterns that go through our Sightcone into our Discerning Center, which evaluates for us by playing through memory.

The Necessity of Meditation

If brain is in control, then it will distort any recall playback for its advantage. One of the greatest battles you have is to control brain. As it is now, brain controls you. It knows every weak point from your memory to work on. This is the necessity of your meditation, **so you can still brain, and then Mind can function** so that brain can become a computer, which it actually is.

The body consists of four brains. When these four brains become unified into one Physical Mind, then you will have taken a long step forward toward the perfection of your body. You have the right and the ability to alter yourself in any way you wish. You can go as low as mineral. It's your choice. You have daily ups and downs. Each day, you are given multiples of gifts, but they almost all are unheard. You are too busy talking to hear and too busy listening to hear.

The first thing you have to do is be very quiet within yourself; be absolutely still. You have learn to be in it, but not of it. This is a statement that is easy to say, but very difficult to become, because as activity starts into play, brain will enter into the situation and take it away from you. Brain knows that once stillness comes, then it has no activity for it to function with. In your meditation you will find that in stilling yourself, your brain will go to sleep. Then, the dividing membrane between memory and self will be slowly burned away, as well as the membrane that is in your spine, which keeps your Youth Fluid encased. This membrane in your spine is your brain's best means of protection, to keep your youth from you, as well as that membrane which keeps your memory banks from you. Exercises to unlock the Youth Fluid will be given to you in full detail at the appropriate stage of your studies and understanding, the same with physical mind.

Importance of Proper Breath

So far, you have been given the breath rate exercise. It seems so unimportant and simple, but without perfect breath, you will make no alterations in this physical flesh whatsoever, until you learn to synchronize your breath rate so that the atomic explosion that takes place in your body will purify the energy that passes from one lung to the other, giving you full cleansing radiation into your body.

The perfect of Thought cannot be attained unless your breath rate is in a perfect equal flow with the Divinity of the Airless Cell within your body. This is why you use your heart for your frequency of breath rate. That beat is keyed by your Airless Cell; that is your Divinity of BE.

Very few are capable of pure thought projection, because they haven't learned, by the proper rate of breath, to control in order to have thought emanation. As long as your breath is sporadic and out of phase with the universe, you will be in a thinking, emanating, projecting condition. You will be subject to all the wills and whims of those that are just as unsure of themselves as you are. That is why we have mass condition of ignorance leading the ignorant. I am not knocking anybody; I am only telling you the truth. I am not belittling anything; I am only trying to make you aware of what is taking place and where you really are and why it is so.

The Plane of Five

In the Plane of Five, which you have now endeavored into expression, there is so rapid a change, that what has happened in a span of a few years, in the Plane of Four would have taken centuries of time. The quickening of the activity and the picture forms of reality of the unification of Spirit and the Physical is so quickened that all of the things you forgot, all of a sudden will appear before you in thought.

When speaking of quickening, it is in all directions, all activities at the same time. Just consider our population jump in the past seventy years as opposed to the seventy years before that, in expansion. What is to be unfolded for you in the next few years is going to be very hard to grasp. The complexity of the apparatuses of electronics that will come into being in the next ten years will be so revolutionary, that today's computers will seem like the horse and buggy to us. The modes of transportation will be radically changed.

The space of activity will allow you more free time for the betterment of your being. There will be less need for physical effort because of electronic units of magnetic fields that are to be produced, which are going to do the bulk of our physical labor. There is no need of our physical labor now, other than man's control of man. Any one state is capable of producing enough food for the other forty-nine states. There is no reason to be short of food, air or water anywhere on this Earth, only by man's ignorance. If man will learn to take the greed and lust out of everything, then you will have a perfect place in which to exist.

It would be no trick at all for you to exist from four thousand to five thousand years, if you wished to stay here. Before all of this manifests, there is going to be a great trying time for us. Man is going to be presented with crises unequal to anything unlike he has experienced in his expression so far. Only in the far reaches of your memory, if you have awakened your eternal memory, will you find a little of what I speak. The last breaking of greed and lust out of man will herald the Golden Age of Expression in man. You all stand on the threshold of this existence.

The Golden Age is already here, you just don't know it. The opportunities are everywhere, only man has got to awaken himself to know it and make it so. When I think of this, a little man comes to mind that was one of the great solar-chemical engineers who took expression on this Earth. His name was Nikola Tesla. He gave us alternating current, the electricity that feeds all of your electric lights and appliances that makes your life today a great deal easier than your predecessors had. He also set down the plans for solar magnetic energy.

PLANE OF FIVE

The Great Turning Point for Man's Perfection

Meaning of Plane of Five & Man's Relationship to it:

• Fifth plane of consciousness of man's perfecting, where he is now vibrating

• Man is now in the beginning of it.

What occurs in the Plane of Five

• Great turning point for man's perfection; the preparatory stage.

• Man begins to know that there is a more complete life for him, a life everlasting.

• The Divine Spirit within man has caused the quickening of his mind, which is speedier than the light rays of the sun.

• What happened in a span of a few years in the Plane of Five, in the Plane of Four would have taken centuries of time.

• Due to the quickening of the activity and the picture forms of reality of the unification of Spirit and the Physical being so quickened, all of the things you forgot, all of a sudden will appear before you.

• The quickening is in all directions, all activities at the same time.

What man must do in this plane

• Complete the re-perfecting of his physical body.

• Unite his mind and body so they will work in perfect accord.

• Overcome all the carnal ways in which he has delighted.

• Recreate the Divine body which God created for him in the beginning.

• Find the new delight of knowing his powers and his substance, and the perfect action of one upon the other, which will merge them into one.

• **When this occurs, man will at last be at peace.**

Plane of five.

Perfectness And Love

In perfectness, there is only love. It is one of the things that is less shown. There is a lot of liking going on, but there is not a lot of love. You may see love exchanged between people at short periods of time, but it's very hard to hold for a long period of time. Your up and down cycling of vibration makes it very hard for you to hold a keen level, because you are constantly in highs and lows.

By bringing yourself into a condition of poise, you will bring yourself into the conditioning where your highs will not be as high and your lows will not be as low. You will come into a condition of greater ease and poise.

Spirit, the Airless Cell: The God of You

The Spirit part that dwells within you has never altered itself from its perfect state. It is so infinitesimally small, that if you put a dot the size of a pinpoint on a threefoot circle and then magnified that circle a thousand times, leaving the dot in the middle the size of a pinpoint, that would give you an idea of about the size of your **Airless Cell. That is all there really is of you.** All the rest of this is clothed around it, in a made condition of flesh. This is the god of you that holds everything in perfectness and directs the operation of the spiritual part of your being, that is expressing at this time.

Quiet Little Voice: Conscience

It is that little part of you that telling you, "Don't do it," in a very quiet little voice. Then when you go ahead and do it, "See, I told you not to do it." **If you learn to listen to that little voice, it will tell you every time when something is going to take place.** The more attentive you become to its transmissions, the less woe you are going to have, because it already knows what's going to take place. It will let you know when you are out of order, and also will prompt you in different directions to do certain things at certain times, if you will only listen to it. Walt Disney drew it as a cricket: Jimminy Cricket. He is showing you that voice inside of you, that mankind calls conscience, but **it is the truth of conscious being expressed from the Airless Cell, which will work if you let it aid you.**

It shows you the ability you have, if you will let it, if you will only adapt yourself to it. Just learn to use it. **With anything that you wish to do, if you can see it in your mind's eye, it is already accomplished**. If you can't see it, then you will get back garbage. **Once you learn to use your Thought Pictures, you will find your Great Teacher, your Spirit, will guide you** and show you the ability of using all energies to manifest anything of your needs. It will be to the extent of changing manifestation to creation **to make yourself perfec**t.

By your alliance of Mind with Spirit, this flesh can become Pure Physical. If you think about travel, consider a man traveling on foot at about five to eight miles an hour. By jet travel, he is now traveling at speeds of mach four, at rocket trajectory; it is eighteen thousand miles an hour, but by Thought, I can be at the moon in an instant. By Thought, I can be at the Central Sun, just as quickly.

It is only because you limit yourself, that you do not do these things. You all know how, but you have forgotten how to do it. There just has to be some reconstruction and reawakening, so you will remember what you forgot how to do.

You have twelve Sense Centers in your body, but you operate on only five. The seven most important are completely dormant and must be reawakened. **You have energy centers in your body that you haven't even tapped;** they have so much energy that you could move any object in this room and not leave your seat. You know how, but you have forgotten where you put the key to unlock them. **It's a matter of reawakening your real self**.

Importance of Imagination

I cannot stress enough how **important** it is for you to become allied with the spirit of activity, so that you can **have a mental picture of all things in existence. Learn to use your imaginative processes.** If you have a child who appears to be daydreaming, do not disturb them. Allow them to develop this ability. **This is where the future exists, through imagination**, otherwise nothing can come into being. When you tell them to not daydream, you are taking away the spiritual activity of the ideal conception of projection from Spirit to man. Allow children all privileges of being able to imagine.

Television has taken away nearly all of the picture-making ability of the individual. No more do people read books and make pictures out of words, nor can they hear sound and make pictures from the sounds. They have to see it or they can't understand it. In this sense, television is one of the worst things given to man. It takes away your personal ability of relaxation and visualization of BE. It voids your imaginative processes. Your ability of a keen sense of sound and feeling is stupefied, so that the sense centers of your body become dormant.

You have the best TV in the world, if you use the back of your eyes. **Close your eyes and look backwards. You can see everywhere you've been, ever were or ever will be.** You don't need the programs of idiocy or the depicting of brutality and crime; it's going on all around you. You don't need it.

Learn to Forgive Yourself

Many of the steps you would have had to walk can be very much shortened, and many of the footsteps that you would have had to walk over and re-correct, when you learn forgiveness and you can forgive yourself, you can bypass those. **That's a great big secret, right there. Learn to forgive yourself and learn to not punish yourself,** because nobody will punish you as hard as you will punish yourself for anything you do wrong.

When that little voice tells you, "Don't do it," and you do it, then you will punish yourself because you love to hurt yourself. You really do. You are very, very hard on yourself, rather than forgiving yourself and blessing yourself and giving yourself love. You will bat yourself around until you get tired of it. Then you will stop it.

In time to come you will learn the different steps. You will become informative to yourself to direct these exchanges, so that you will become more in rapport with that which is natural, rather than unnatural. Most everything that appears to you to be natural now is very unnatural, because conformity seems so commonplace to you that you forgot what really was natural.

You Own Nothing

One of the first things to really learn is that you own nothing. You are only a user of. You have the privilege of exchanging expression with it, and you bless it for the privilege of exchange of using it for expression. As long as you hold onto anything and everything else is offered to you, you can't have. As long as you hold onto something, it can't transfer. It has no ability of transfer.

In an open hand, an open thought is what I am after, you are free for exchange continuously. You can't give with a closed, clenched fist, nor can you receive. When you shut the door, then you shut everything off for transmission and reception.

Now your breath becomes very important in the ability of exchange of thoughts. As it is now, the things you desire and want, you destroy before they ever get away from you, because you fractionize them into minute and sub-minute particles. You don't give time enough to transmit your thoughts, because your breath rate is out of timing. You are breathing continuously and you don't pulse your breath and allow transmission to take place. You will learn all about this at a later date. I am planting seeds now for future understanding.

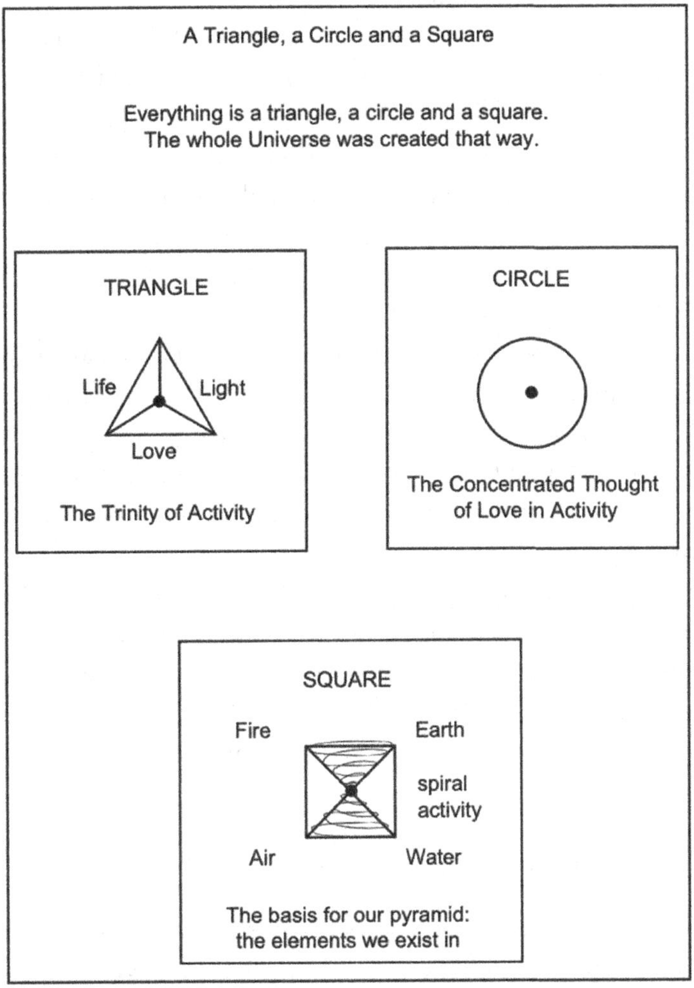
A Triangle, a Circle and a Square
Everything is a triangle, a circle and a square.
The whole Universe was created that way.
TRIANGLE
Life
Light
Love
The Trinity of Activity
CIRCLE
The Concentrated Thought
of Love in Activity
SQUARE
Fire
Earth
spiral
activity
Air
Water
The basis for our pyramid:
the elements we exist in

A triangle, a circle and a square.

Triangle, Circle and Square

Everything is a triangle, a circle and a square. The whole Universe was created that way. In other words, the Trinity of Activity, which is Light-Love-Life makes the triangle.

The concentrated thought of Love in activity becomes a circle, with a dot in the middle of the circle, or the absolute middle of the cone. Whether it is the bottom or the extraction of the cone, it is the Thought Pattern in action. It is either coming or going, depending on whether you are transmitting or receiving.

The square consists of Fire-Air-Water-Earth. This foundation is the basis for your pyramid. In the concentration of the One Thought from the dot, it will strike the prism angles of the triangle, and it will project out and bring forth the radiance of the Seven Rays. This is why there were Seven Planes of Expression brought into BE. Love had manifested itself through Light, by Light, in One Life.

Everything is Life. As it is now, you are not in Life, you are living. Life expresses around you, but you are not in Life, rather, you have accepted yourself in a living condition. By each breath that you take, you become lived; you become past tense. You are taking yourself out of expression of manifestation by each breath. We desire much that is not good for us, by our conformity to cultural and social conditions.

We become exactly as we pattern ourselves by our thinking and reasoning, because we are looking out and accepting what we are looking at as being the fact, as the actuality of BE. However, this really is not so. Because we all agree to it, it exists. If you have been somewhere, you have memory of it, but can you prove that anything exists outside of this room?

Thought Pictures and Master Creator

We look in one direction at a time. We only sense wherever we touch, so there are multiples of limitations we place upon ourselves. **There is one word that I won't accept in my vocabulary: can't. You can do anything that you desire**. Anything you can think of, already exists. If you thought of it, then it had to exist before you could think of it.

Almost everything we function with and bring up, is memory patterns of past, and many times we look to the future to equalize the past, to have the present. In our programming of ourselves by what we desire, as we make mental pictures of those desires, and we hold the picture on our breath and charge it into the Ethers of the Universe, it will go forth and collect for us the energies necessary to manifest for us. If we don't break it down or destroy it, then it will attain back to us exactly as we pictured it. But if you don't let it loose clear and sharp, then it will return just like garbage and be worth no more than that.

Everything that you desire is yours, all you have to do is make the pictures. If you can see it and hold it, then it is yours. You will create it; you will give it dominion over all things. **You are the master creator over all things, but you have limited yourself** to the ability of manifestation. You have built up an existence of idol worship and placed everything outside of yourself. You worship on thesis and theories instead of fact. You don't know who you are, what you are or where you are going. Most of the time, you are guessing. You have not mastered into your ability of meditation control and you use thinking instead of Thought. In your thinking, you are almost always wrong.

Man's conditioning of himself is due to his inability to realize himself. Man has a second problem which is that he doesn't know how to forgive. This is one of the most difficult things for man to do, especially to forgive himself. You will punish yourself more than anybody else. You must learn, also, to be very graceful with yourself.

The secret of your being is in your Poise. This is your perfect control. If you lose poise and are out of order, placing everything outside of yourself and if you doubt, then you have lost everything you have gained. The smallest bit of doubt will erase everything. You have to know that you know that you know, or you don't know that you don't know. **Either you master the situation or the situation masters you**. As it is now, the situations master you, but it should be the other way around. You were given dominion over everything, why is your dominion controlling you? Why should your social culture control you and limit your activity?

THE CREATION OF MAN AND THE BEAUTIFUL EARTH

Man was created as one of the most beautiful specimens ever in the universe. He was given the ability of all functional operations of the universe, and the universe was his toy. That's why **when the earth was created, it was created to be the Blue-Green Sun.** It was so beautiful when it was created; it looked like an aqua raindrop. It was almost transparent in the blue-green aqua color, a little more into the green than what you think of as the aqua blue. It was like a raindrop floating in the universe time-space.

When it was inhabited by the god-men that were to inhabit this dimension of galaxies, it was one of the most beautiful places to behold and express. The beauty that existed here in the plant life was beyond belief. You think your flowers are beautiful now, but if you could see the flowers and trees that bloomed and existed at that time! There was nothing here on this earth that was more than one foot in rise. The water was just as blue-green as the planet was.

There was one continent and one large body of water. The continent stretched from pole to pole, and the oceans divided it on two sides, so it would have polarities of balance. This was called "The Liquid Planet." It was given a liquid condition because it was the **planet of cleansing. It was the purifier of this quadrant of the universe.** This will be its job when it returns to its proper station in expression.

Wisdom and Freedom Underneath This Physical Shell

Underneath this physical shell that you wear is all the wisdom, lying hidden within, to be quickened by Mind and made ready for totality of pure expression, so that your body no more has its density and becomes very free and buoyant, and nothing becomes fixed as it is now. As long as you have matter, you have a fixed condition. In your present abilities it's beyond your comprehension to visualize the force and projection that you exist with and hold within your being.

We think of man in periods of time as being fast in movement. If we think back through our own history and we look at man only a few thousand years ago, his fastest mode of travel was running, until he compelled the agreement of animals to carry him and he could travel a little faster. Then he became fixed on mechanical apparatuses that gave him greater ease of movement, to gadgetry, like automobiles, airplanes, rockets.

Within his own makeup he carries conditions that will dwarf those in functional operation. You could be from here to New York City, that quickly. You could be from here to the sun, that quickly. You have these capabilities within you. You produce enough electrical power in just the functioning of your brain alone, to light the whole city of Los Angeles, if your brain were tapped.

We talk about the big computer banks in Washington D.C. and the one in Germany. If they made computers to equal all the ducting computer system that is in all the glandular makeup of your body, you would need a planet five times the size of this earth to house it in, by our standards of knowledge today. That's how complex your body really is.

Think of just moving our hands or moving our lips, of the millions and millions of impulses that it takes for the smoothness of movement and the apparatus of charges of chemical energy and electrical force of magnetism that take place within the body for these functions to occur. These will bring awe to any engineer. Everything that you use to express with you, outside of you, you copied from your body. If you don't think so, look at everything that has been made and you will find a duplication of it in your body.

Snowflakes: Frozen Thoughts

I'll tell you something else very interesting. Catch a snowflake. Catch it on a piece of velvet or dark cloth. If you look at the inside crystalline form of it, you will see three geometrical figures of functioning operations of material matter that you are functioning with today. These are frozen thoughts being exploded in the crystal forms. They are part of man's thinking of thoughts that are held in those drops.

When they explode into the crystals, they will hold the form of that thought. If you stretch them out, you will see the molecular structure there of the molecules of that formation of picture forms of objects that you express with.

Mechanical Hindrances

We talk about travel of hundreds of miles an hour, such as our jet planes travel now, and our rockets traveling at thousands of miles and hour in outer space. **With your thought projection you can instantly be any place in the universe, with proper control.** The ability of mechanical aids has only tended to hinder you from your natural sources.

All conveyances that you make which imprison you, be careful that these machines do not take you over, because the more you begin to rely on the mechanics and gadgetry for functioning, the more your natural ability is taken away from you. I don't like to think what the children of today are going to do in fifty years when they take the computers away from them and ask them to add two and two.

The Purpose of Deterioration

Even cooking, we have forgotten how to cook without prepared mixes and meals. Everything is pre-prepared for you and loaded with poison along with it, so it will last longer and they can sell more of it without deterioration. **Nature made deterioration and put destruction in everything that was put into expression** so it would naturally devour its own self. **By its natural devouring, it produced its seeding for the next crop.**

By consuming itself, it set up the seed factors in miniature form for the same energies to re-express the same patterning. The same thing becomes the same thing. It begets what it begat. The Bible will tell you about the "begetting," and that's what it's talking about.

Of each thing that is created, within the seed are atoms of destruction. Those atoms of destruction set up the seed formation of the next germination. The same is within you also. When your body is ready to be disassembled, the atoms of destruction will take over. The Airless Cell will release It's hold, yielding to the atoms of destruction to the body and the body will then deteriorate. The body will turn grey, because all light will be taken from it and will form itself out of love into space, and become the common denominator without expression within it.

If you look at anything that's expressing and if it's loved, it has vibrant, glowing eminence coming from it. If you take the love away from it, it will slowly tone to grey, and become nothing but space, because the love has been taken out of it.

Man's Divine Power and Abilities

If man would use only one one-hundredth part of his own divine power, the speed of the jet airplane would be like a snail's pace to him.

When you learn to properly handle your thought projections and to be able to still your body to line up all the atoms in one direction simultaneously at the same time, in the matter of a split second you could **be any place** on this planet you wanted to be, and you could return just as quickly. You have this ability to do this within yourself.

This is part of your thought ability of transference. There is not an object in this room that you could not move with your eyes. You have the ability within your values of capacity to be able to **create anything that you desire**.

However, two little words are the **controlling factor that keeps you limited.** They **are called "doubt" and "greed."** It is like the guy who wanted a million dollars. He said, "Boy, what I could do if I had that million dollars, but I'll never get it." He had it and lost it all in one thought.

Your thought-picture molds are most important in the expression of that which you desire, and you attract the things to you that you desire by these. You become the sum and substance of your rejections also as well as you do your projections. We are much better at dying than we are at living, because we worship death. We age in time, because we make time more important than the expression.

Conformity and Manipulation

Because we are so accustomed to conforming, we forget our real place and we become something manipulated by the will of others rather than by a thought of our own. Example: when it gets to be fall of the year, the first thing the television starts showing is a man in a rain storm, sneezing and wheezing and he's going to have a cold and a flu. He's in bed the next minute. Within three weeks we have ten thousand people in bed with the flu.

Mass suggestion: are we suckers for it! We fall right in line as we line up to get our next dose of medicine. When we get tired of it, then we get well. Only when you get tired of it do you get well. It will share your bed as long as you allow it to be a bed partner. **It will only leave when you command, "Out!"** You are the one who controls the condition.

Remember, everything in "made" condition, and flesh is a made condition, is in a state of continuous alteration. By every breath it's altered. Even your thinking alters continuously by the impressions of others.

The Great Importance of Color in Clothing

How many of you today put on the same clothes you first went to pick when you got dressed this morning? How many of you changed your mind and put something else on? It's amazing, isn't it, how that color just doesn't match my mood today and I am not going to wear it.

Our intelligence within us is making us aware of what we need, of what colors and tones of color are necessary for that day to make our day pleasant. If we were to go ahead and wear other than that color, we would be in a "diseased" condition all day long. We would never be comfortable. Have you ever put clothes on and you could hardly wait to get home so you could change them? You felt so out of place in them.

Colors are very important to your moods and conditionings of wisdom projection, also the quadrant of the energies that come from the different colored Suns to us help energize us in expression. It also gives us our wisdom of intelligence and impresses upon us the necessity of energizing for that day.

In addition, **your Airless Cell will prompt color tones** for attraction of certain colors into your body **for adjustment and correcting of health of the body.** Colors are very important in that conditioning. The colors of clothes that you wear are most important in that conditioning.

It is the same as the gadgetry that you adorn yourself with. When you love a piece and you wear it with fondness that you love it, it gives back the radiance of those multiples of chemical energies back into your body. That's why people have been prone to **wear gadgetry and jewelry** through all the ages of time. It is **because of the coloration and the energy** that exists within the metal or gem itself in agreement with you.

Certain things will match at certain times for different exchanges of where you are.

Spirit: The Great Teacher

The lesson says:

> *The time has not yet come when every man will look to the Great Teacher, his own spirit, for guidance. Most are still concerned with conquering material substance, ignoring the greatest instrument of all, their own bodies, which are available for them to use.*

When you want to know something, where is the first place you run? To your best friend to talk it over, don't you. How many of you take time to go to the closet to talk to **your Self, your best friend, your real best friend**. He always tells us the truth, but that isn't what we always want to hear. We love to be flattered. Even if it's costly, we still love it.

To learn to look at yourself in the mirror in the morning and say that you love yourself and mean it, is something that is hard to do, yet it is something that you are going to have to learn. If you can't face yourself, how can you face anybody else? If you can't face yourself when you start the day, you are in no condition to match wits with anybody else, because they will have you under their thumb all the way around.

Listening Within

By your thought projection preceding you of what you want to take place, it will arrive just exactly as you project it, before you even arrive. You set the conditions in your quarters, in your way. You become an authority. **You become the master of the situation**, rather than the subject of the condition. That's when you know who you are and where you are and why, Now.

Learn to be an authority to yourself. Learn to listen to that little voice that will tell you the truth all the time. Even if you don't like it, it's still telling you the truth. Learn to evaluate what it's impressing upon you and hold true to it. Surely, if you hold true, you are going to find that your day will alter continuously. Where you stubbed your toes many, many times before, when you listen to that little voice, you find you have a very easy day. It's really that simple.

When you learn to listen to what it tells you, then you will find out that your whole operation is going to go a lot smoother. **The more and more you become in rapport with it, the smoother you will become.** You have seen and you have met people who have such a dynamic expression about them that everybody is in awe that they always do the right thing at the right time. It isn't by chance this is taking place. They have perfected their ability of listening to the intelligence, rather than the intellect of ignorance. They have learned to listen within. They have learned to **control their breath**. They have learned to project everything in the conditionings for their conditioning of favor before they ever enter into the condition.

Some of you are salesmen. Some of you are managers for companies and handle personnel. You have always found that **you can get more with honey than you can with sugar.** If you leave the vinegar out of it you can gain even more. With the sugar, you put the coating on everything, but if you make it too sweet, they become rather questionable as to whether they are going to take it or not. If you put it out with honey, it's natural and its a natural projection. They will eat every bit of it. **Make everything natural in your projection.** Don't super-condition anything. Make it natural and you will have a smooth operation at all times. Then you don't have to back up on anything. It's a little tip for you, and it works like magic.

As you are thinking now and as you are visualizing handling your conditions now, within a matter of a few years, what you thought was impossible you are going to find is very commonplace. This is because your whole thinking, your whole projection of everything you are doing is going to come into an alteration. Many of your bad habits are going to seemingly disappear. New conditionings are going to be placed where you will be the master of the situation, rather than being mastered by the situation. **You will become an authority of yourself, unto yourself of all things you enter into.**

Being a Wise Authority

By learning to become an authority and using proper thought projection, everything in this heaven and earth will bow to you. This is a proper functioning, because you were given dominion over everything. Be a wise ruler, and handle everything the way you would want to be handled. **Always put yourself in the other person's place. How would you like it?** If you wouldn't like it, don't give it to somebody else.

Always take time and use the wisdom of exchange to be in common with everything you are exchanging with. Although you are the authority, **a wise authority never belittles anything**. In your knowing that you know, you begin to realize that you really know. If you are so busy, engrossed in one thing, you will miss everything else going on about you.

Be alert at all times to everything that is taking place. It is like a magician is trying to keep your attention on his left hand while he is doing something with his right hand, and all of a sudden, makes it appear as if nothing took place. Don't be dazzled by the footwork and the limelight, getting caught in the trap of being deceived. **Keep yourself very alert at all times and you can't be deceived.** You can't be deceived about anything because you will be aware of everything that is taking place. You will find out that your values of awareness and comprehension will tell you ahead of time what's taking place.

You were saying that instantly we can be someplace else. Is that the same as astral travel?

No, you can disassemble this body and reassemble it there in the matter of one breath. It is teleportation of your body. In the meditative state it can be quickly attained.

What is astral travel?

Astral travel is nothing more than a remnant of memory of conditions being played back by the memory banks.

Akashic Records

What if we haven't been in a place, then how could we know?

There is no such thing. **There is nothing in this universe you have not been made aware of.** There are two little cells on the back of the bump on the back of your head called the knowledge bump. On each side, just on the lower side there are **two little cells** the size of the point of a pin **that carry your complete memory of the Akashic Records of the universe with you.** You have total recall from them, but brain uses them to play against you, to keep you in control.

BRAIN, THE GREAT DECEIVER

Is the brain a dark force?

No, brain is the great deceiver. There are no dark forces; that is a deception. There is no evil unless you make it exist. In a world that is created perfect, how could there be evil? Only in your conception of good and bad. Actually brain is a gland. It's a multiple of four glands to be exact.

When you are going to sleep and the brain is very active, since you are to be the master, what do you practice? How are you to control it?

Shut it off. You will learn the control of it through the adaptation of meditation. In the carnality condition of flesh from divine flesh, man's mind was divided into four divisions. The most powerful of all is sleeping, and will continue to sleep until you have corrected the conditions in your body so that it can move back to its rightful place and claim its rightful kingship of Jerusalem.

Jerusalem is the top of the head. That is the **New Jerusalem** the Bible talks about. The **lost Tribe of Dan** will return to reclaim the kingship of Jerusalem. It is a part of the physical mind that is sleeping. The divisions of the three parts which are the two glands, the two hemispheres, that are divided by the meridian and also the secondary conditioning of automation that is within the spine, respond in rapport with the circulatory, respiratory and nervous systems of the body.

Brain has one advantage. A veil has been placed between this area and that of the functioning of youth within your body which has been limited because the percolator has had a lid put on it. Consequently, the youth fluid that keeps your body eternally young is going in a lazy eight pattern, rather than percolating and flushing the brain continuously.

Because of these conditions, **the brain** has made these alterations and has a direct pipeline to the Akashic Records of your memory banks and knows just what to play against you to hold you in control. It knows just how to bring the pressure to bear the best to make you kneel. It knows every little trick of memory, every little thing that you have done that you don't want to face, that you have hidden back there into the subjective mind that you haven't allowed to express. It will use it as a leverage against you.

It's **really a deceiver**, one of the greatest deceivers of all. **It's what keeps you imprisoned in this flesh body.** At the end it will give up your body and lose its place in time, form and space. Then brain will slink back into memory to try to regain the same capturing when you come back into expression again.

You are going to have to forget everything else you have learned, because you are going to learn it all new. **I am going to direct you in understanding to understand yourself.** I am going to tell you how you really work. I will explain things to you that even science has not become aware of yet. **Everything that I speak of, I've *been* there.** I've watched and seen it operate. I know exactly what I am talking about.

They took many years to make sure that **I was made aware about everything functioning, just exactly how it functioned and why**. When I speak about things I am talking about first hand. I've been there. When I use the word "deceptive" and the "master deceiver," that's exactly what it is. We let brain do it once too often and that's why brain took over and holds control of manifestation conditions. This is because it shuts down everything that will allow you to become perfect.

When the ego cell becomes strong enough to take over the directing from the Airless Cell, then you have a deception going on continuously, because the Airless Cell is putting out one direction and the ego cell is altering it, to conformity of conditions of place, time and things. You become molded within time of space of form, in that dimension of that triangle, held within the thought impression of the circle of the impressing condition of continuous expression at that time, in time.

As of right now, there is no outside out there. Nothing exists but this room, this time and this form, the forms in this room and the space they exist with. **The only way you can get out of this triad of deception is by your thought transference and by your imaginative processes of replacing what was memory.** Your memory banks will feed back through the brain and make pictured conditions as you are imagining it is. That's what the made world is: imagining conditions of authority, power and greed.

As soon as is stopped being given energy, it will fall apart. All this illusion will fall apart. Everything that is manifested is not real. It only exists because of our agreement in conformity. It is quantum conditioning.

We were talking about the brain as the great deceiver. Do you learn to put the brain in its place, like a little child?

No, not as a little child. **You put it in its place as its proper function, as a computer**. The computer has taken you over, just like gadgetry is controlling your expression.

Is the veil you speak of also referred to as the seven veils?

Yes, because it diffuses all seven rays of light. That's why it is called the seven veils. When you study later the energy that enters through your temples, you will begin to understand why.

Subconscious and Memories

Did you say that our conscious mind does not have the memory that our subconscious brain does?

Our subconscious mind holds what we suppress in conditioning and plays back to us for expression. It has all the memories of this expression and all the past ones too, because you can call back into it and bring in any time in history, now.

Right now I cannot remember the past expressions, but my subconscious mind has that memory?

Right, your brain has blocked that off from you so that it could keep you in control. It's a "security blanket," so to speak. Everything you have ever expressed, who you were, what you were and why. Past and future: there really is no difference. There is only a now condition. All of this is relative to conditioning.

Alterations in Time and the Penalty

Is it true that you can influence the past as well as the future?

You cannot alter anything, but you can influence as to your own positioning. You can't alter anything in time. When you take it into a timeless condition, then corrections can be made. As long as it is in time, no alterations or changes can be made. **If you make an alteration in time then you must stand good for it to the God Head**. That means its point of perfection. You want to think about that before you make any type of changes that way. That's the penalty.

Is that the same as altering the agreement we made when we decided to come into expression?

No, it's when you alter somebody else or a condition that will affect anyone else. If you do, you must stand good for all the corrections in time. You must set aside and give up your place of perfection until all those you have altered become perfection. You get a new job during that interim, you become a guide, prodding and prompting them to perfection. "**Thou Shalt Not Adulterate**" now takes on a most interesting new meaning!

Three Magnetic Grams

You stated last time in relating to that, there are only three grams of us. What makes up the three grams?

These are **the elements of the dust of earth** itself that are taken into your body to hold you to this earth. That's **what magnetically holds you to this earth, those three grams**. That keeps you on this earth. As long as you are in density of flesh it will keep you bound to this earth. I don't care where you go in your travels, that will draw you right back. As soon as you terminate, it will draw you right back to this earth. In your dream states, those three grams will draw you back to this earth, instantly, magnetic attraction.

Why don't we call it gravity?

It isn't truly gravity. **Gravity is the result of light moving through the earth itself.** You have it within your ability right now to defy what you call gravity and become completely buoyant and float. The laws of gravity only exist in the conformity of heavy flesh and fixed conditions of chemistry.

The Pyramids

Was that ability used to build the pyramids?

One similar to that, where **they actually disarrange the polarization of the materials of the stones to make them weightless.** When they made them weightless, then they made them liquefied so they could form them as they re-congealed them into the form that they wanted and they actually floated through the air. Some of those stones weigh as much as four hundred tons, and they took them over seven mountain ranges and across two river bottoms.

They used what they called an **ibid stick**, that **neutralized the gravity of the molecular arrangement of the crystals in the granite itself.** It worked on the oscillation of the tuning of the tourmaline within the granite itself. It became weightless, semi-liquid in a weightless form. If you were to use instruments that we have today, we cannot strike that granite hard enough to face those stones as they are faced now, to fit that closely together. We have no instruments today that will do that job.

They did it with a stick, not with their mind?

They used the ibid stick. It could equal any frequency of anything in molecular activity. It controlled all the molecules.

What happened to the stick?

The sticks are still around. They're buried for safe keeping.

Near the pyramid?

Actually, the pyramid that you are talking about is only one of **six pyramids.** If you make a Star of David on the thirtieth meridian of the earth, you will find nearest the base rock, the location of the other five. Some are underneath the oceans, two right now: the one of crystal and the one of stone that is off of Gains Island near the Philippines. The one of crystal is off of Florida in what we call the Bermuda Triangle.

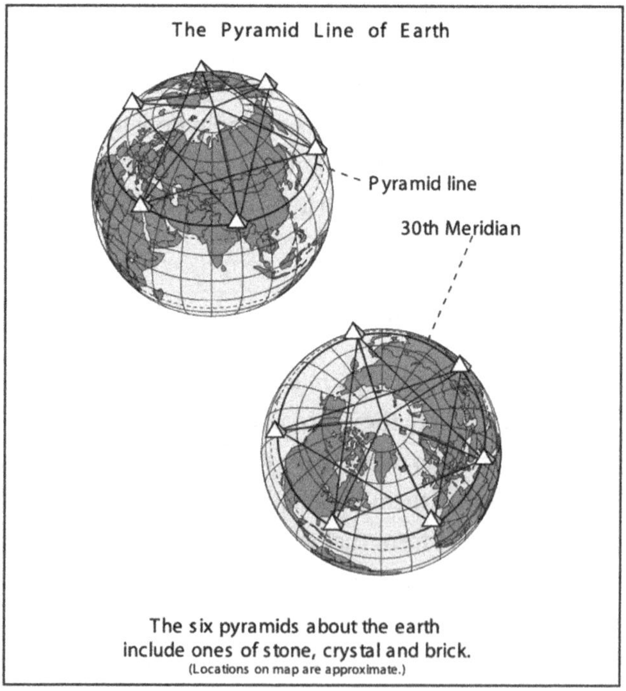

The Pyramid Line of Earth
Pyramid line
30th Meridian
The six pyramids about the earth
include ones of stone, crystal and brick.
(Locations on map are approximate.)

The pyramid line of Earth.

The largest one in the world is just now (1979) being excavated in South China. It is over one thousand feet tall and is a pyramid of brick.

Is the one of crystal actually made of crystal?

Yes, it's crystal. They have pictures of it. It was found three years ago.

Was each one of these pyramids formed in certain civilizations?

Periods of history, rather than civilizations.

There are many things that man calls phenomena which are very natural that are in crystalline form and are all over the earth. There are many things that man just now is becoming aware of in ancient histories that way surpass our intelligence of what we have attained to now. Everything that we are doing now, we are just duplicating what has been done in past histories. We have taken a little different bent in chemistry of energies.

Is there some sort of pyramid or force in the Great Lakes area?

Yes, but it's not a pyramid, it's a force field. It is one of the venting spots of the earth itself. It was a north pole at one time. When the great ice fields melted from there, they left those lakes. They also left the great iron deposits there which are common with the north poles.

I think its going to be the North Pole again. It has been very cold there.

No, it's going to be very hot. In the next earth tumble, that area is going to set almost on the equator.

You told us one night that the next North Pole would be in the Bay of Bengal, so the South Pole would almost be at the upper part of South America. Am I correct?

The South Pole will be west of Peru in the Pacific Ocean. The North Pole will be the Bay of Bengal, whenever the earth shifts its poles again.

Will the pyramids remain standing after the poles change?

Definitely. They are so constructed magnetically that they will. The Great Pyramid of Giza has been under water seven times. That's why the capstone is seven miles away. It is buried under the sand where it was washed off. The pin rods that were in it for the collection of solar energy were damaged by a too heavy impulse of an energy during the collapsing of that history. They were beryllium and gold rods. They had beryllium disks, concave squares, all over the outside of the pyramid that caught the sun rays and reflected them to collectors at each one of the four corners. Regardless of where the sun was in its full movement it collected energy completely. Then in the moonlight it collected the moon rays on its reflection. They used a sound frequency rather than the electrical impulse that we use today.

Heart Transplants

The Airless Cell is in the heart. What happens to the Airless Cell in a heart transplant?

You give your individuality to someone else. Usually cirrhosis of the liver will be the first condition, because the body is trying to constantly throw it out, as it is out of frequency with the ego cell within the body. The next set up will be cirrhosis of the lungs, which goes into pneumonia. Unless the frequency is very close, it may last three, four or five years, but not over seven years. No heart transplant has been successful up to now (1979) over seven years, because of the individuality that is within the heart.

This is where man makes his biggest mistake. Here is his gadgetry. When something wears out, why don't you trade it in for a later model, instead of trying to buy spare parts to patch it together?

Reincarnation and the Bible

Your whole thinking is taught wrong. You are taught to think this is all there is of expression. This is only one facet of it. That was the reason that **they took reincarnation out of the Bible in the first hundred years, because they couldn't control the people.** When they took that out and told the people they only had one body and the only begotten was the one thing sent to save them, they had them on their knees and they have never let them get up from that time on.

That is control by religion, which isn't right.

"I'm not worthy." Not worthy of what? A god is not worthy? No way. I won't buy it. **You do not own this body. You don't own anything. You are only a user. It's here for your use, to use and express with, and you are expressing God in it. You express love** in the fullness in its exchange and you express beauty to the greatest of its values within it. The more you express those beauties, the more beautiful it's going to become, the more it will enhance itself.

Would you define "worship?"

Worship is paying homage to somebody other than yourself. You belittle yourself when you worship.

Image and Reflection of God

Remember, your Universal Creed says, "I bow to no man, not even God, for I am God." **God wants you as a partner, as an equal, not on bended knees.** He created you with dominion over everything. You are to be in equal rapport with everything that expresses in the universe, and you bow to nothing.

The First Commandment says, "Thou shall have no other god before me." If you worship, then where are the false idols? You broke all the other commandments simultaneously. **Aren't you the image and reflection of God Himself expressing?**

But didn't you say that we fell?

That image is still there. You are still the image, even though you have transgressed. "In the image and likeness, He made them then."

How can we be the God if we made the mistake?

Doesn't everything look at you for authority?

Free will is what made us fall, wasn't it?

You made alterations of decisions.

Then if we fell, how do we bow to no one?

We fell down because we started worshipping our own image. There is where we made the mistake. We fell in love with our self.

But now you say that we bow to no one, not even God. For me that's a little tough to deal with.

Oh, I didn't say it was going to be easy, because for so long you have cow-towed to brain, it's hard to entertain such a condition.

If we have fallen, ***what do we do to correct ourselves that we can be so perfect that we bow to nothing?***

First, you have to get up off your knees. Second, you have to stand up and be counted. Proclaim your divinity. Then you have to be able to execute your authority and shut brain off and bring mind into rapport so you have equal exchange with spirit. You become spirit expressing the truth through mind, instead of the results of reflection of brain expressing the conformity of its agreement that it wants to express, good or bad for you.

Mind, Not Brain

If you would allow mind to impress you, then you would never do anything wrong. You would do everything perfectly.

And mind is not brain?

It is not brain. There is a great difference. Everybody is so used to thinking of brain as mind, but it is not. **Brain and mind are completely two different conditions**, totally separated.

Mind fills all the space of the universe. Mind encompasses everything in form. What we see out there that we call space is teeming mind, in activity. It's the go-between between spirit and physical. It carries all the intelligence of spirit to the pure physical.

The Airless Cell wants the body back to a perfect physical condition, so it may manifest spirit perfectly in expression of light. It is constantly prompting the changes and brain is trying to subdue those prompting, because it knows as soon as it's put to sleep that it no longer will have control of the body. Meditation succeeds in putting brain to sleep. It takes away its forceful conditions of willing. Brain has been allowed free will.

Brain and Mind: the Great Difference

BRAIN	MIND
A gland in the body	Fills all the space of the universe
A computer in its proper functioning	Encompasses everything in form
Tries to subdue promptings of the Airless Cell	"Space" is teaming Mind in activity.
Has control of the body until it is put to sleep by meditation and mind takes over directance.	Go-between between Spirit and Physical

Brain and mind.

Through meditation this is slowly shut down to a condition where rapport comes into play with mind itself, and mind then takes over the directance. Even the ego cell gets its place back and diminishes itself back to the Airless Cell. It is called "**selfless.**" As long as you are self, you are selfish.

The Little Voice

What about when that little voice tells you to do something? Sometimes you procrastinate and don't do anything.

If you procrastinate, you are too late. **When it tells you to do something, you do it right now,** direct obedience. Regardless of how much left base you think it is, you learn to do exactly as it tells you.

What if that little voice is coming from brain instead of mind?

It never does. That's a pipeline that the brain cannot shut off, but if YOU shut it off, it will become more and more quiet. It's still going on, but you will have a hard time detecting its intelligence. **The more you use it, the louder it will become.** The more you respond to it, the more predominant it will become in impressing you in the proper functioning. **Mind is never wrong.** I can tell you many instances where it was so precise that it allowed me to continue my expression because I listened to exactly what it said.

I learned at a young age that when that voice told me to do something, I obeyed instantly, with no deviation whatsoever. I have seen fantastic things take place. It's beyond belief that **when you once learn the fullness of this intelligence, you will never, ever question its prompting. Your alertness is very essential. If you procrastinate its prompting, you're too late.** Once you procrastinate it, then it will be quieter. Each time you do, it will tone down, because brain is going to use it as a leverage point to shut it down so that it can hardly be heard. I call it the small voice of thunder, that can't be heard. When you really learn to hear it, that small voice is like thunder.

I've had times when I have been so intense in what I've been doing, that they will actually say, "Is anybody home? We want to talk to you." Sometimes you are so engrossed with what you are into that they have to extract you from what you are doing. This courtesy will actually be extended. They will actually request permission for your time. I used the word "they." Remember, I didn't say "one," I said, "they," because **there are multiples of authorities of the universe that will teach you different things.** That is why I said, "they." You will get to know each one of them. They are authorities in their own specialized field. You will have many different teachers in your fullness of attainment.

Then this inner voice may not be coming to you from memory?

No, the **little voice** does not come from memory. It **comes directly from spirit**.

Sometimes I get the feeling I shouldn't do something and I think maybe I'm remembering it having happened to me before and I made the wrong decision.

Right. You are playing from memory back that you have done this before and you are trying to proof the condition. Memory is telling you that you have had this condition before and didn't make it. It's an automatic play and then brain will shut it out really quickly, but the more you bring this into play, the more it's going to work.

That's not the same as the inner voice?

A lot of times when you don't listen to the voice, they will impress upon you to do something. You will have the inclination that you should do a certain thing. They will use that pressure. In fact, even to the extent that a hand will push you aside and an instant later, a thirty caliber bullet goes right through the tree where you were just standing, and an arm just pushed you over like that while it went by you.

Or someone will tell you "Over there, quick!" And you watch a whole mountain of earth go in the air where you were just standing. That makes a difference. Believe me. I have had a few war experiences to attest to that! I have had experiences where the voice has told me where to be, and right now! No argument. It means now!

Those aren't angels are they?

No, your conception of angels is very improper, too. We'll get into that at a later date. You have been fed a lot of hogwash that needs a lot of correction. **Angels are the messengers of God, the Supreme Father**. We use the word "God" very loosely.

The Light Body Waiting To Be Called Forth

I want to check my understanding of the concept of the light body. I think I understand you have that state now but it is overlaid by flesh?

Right.

So it's a matter of overthrowing the carnal flesh?

Just dropping the density away. It's waiting to be called forth.

The state of ***perfection*** *is within us?*

Yes, it's waiting in abeyance to be called forth. **When you can line up all the atoms in your body in one direction simultaneously at the same time, you become multiples of motions of that motion, at the same time. And you shall be Light.**

Why do you spell the word "grey," g-r-e-y, instead of "gray?"

I used the "e" because of the expression that's in it. In the true word, the true coloring is g-r-e-y and not g-r-a-y. The "a" in the Latin was changed from the long "e" with the bar over it and made it sound like an "a." We transcribed it into our language from the Latin, using an "a."

How would the "a" change the meaning of the word?

Because of the way the pronunciation of the e with the bar over the top makes it a long e and it sounds like an "aaee", the first letter of our alphabet. I am telling you how technically it really is spelled in universal terminology. That's the reason I gave that to you. It is the space. It represents all space.

Meditation and the Stillness

In meditation can we demand that ego be out of the way and our brain be still, and have it be so?

Yes, **"I demand the stillness,"** that is your command-demand. You will find that you will be able to hold in one breath for two to three hours, where **you will change from the vibrant into a pulsated state, a full wakened condition**.

Is the key to holding one breath to do that?

Yes, because you want to leave vibrance and go into pulsation. That's where you truly are. All this in illusion is a vibrant condition. It is coming and going constantly and it's altering continuously by its motion of movement. That's illusion: the motion of movement. I will guide you in the meditation. I will give you instructions on how to do it properly. Then you will have to do it yourself. The Father asks for ten percent of your time, not your money, so that He can commune with you. If you would be still for ten percent of your day's expression, which is a little over two hours so that He could commune with you, you would be amazed at the change which would take place in the matter of a few months.

Two hours a day? That's pretty hard for me.

It is as of now because you are so busy with brain, but when you learn to shut brain down, you will begin to look forward to being in that state. Then when you have mastered the condition, you can be in it that quickly, and right back out again if you wish. You can even go to a state where you can leave in Mind and leave the body in control under automatic condition through the responses of brain. Your body will carry on its functions while you are some place else in the universe, attending to other things. It's very easy to do. It is all very natural. You all know how, but you have just forgotten.

The word meditation really means to "med-I-tate". The "t" is expression of the ions. "T," you will later find out, means all expression. The "ion" is the ions of energies of the word ending that way, "meditation."

"Med-I:" the individual God-force in expression, expressing itself in expression of the energies of the ions.

M: Master of all wisdom

E: Energies of the universe

D: Directive of operation (to the I)

I: Individual God-force in expression

T: Expression of the ions

Ion: Ions of energies

That's where we really are. **We are molecular matter held together by the ion movements, by the magic killions holding our reflection of atoms in expression,** if you want to be really technical about it. Those are a lot of words, but they really are true. That's just the way functioning takes place.

When you "med" the master of all wisdom with the E of the energies of the universe, then put together with the direction of operation to the universal one of expression, the ions of energy, you are meditating.

Later on in Book One you will learn the values of all the letters and what they mean, as well as the numerals. You will know when you say a word, what the word means, and why the word was put together in the letter format that it was, spiritually. Every letter has values as the words have value. We use these words because of the values of energies that they project.

As you learn to look into your Sightcone, by looking backwards into your eyes, and through your Sightcone into the memory banks, you can become aware of anything that you wish to know. It's all there for you.

The veil was placed there as you moved into your vehicle, your body. **When you learn to master brain, then you will have full access to know**

who you were, what, why and where you were, as well as what period of time, which man calls his history of time.

In your awakening yourself from where you are now, your avenue of opening will give to you a reassurance that when you first capture the stillness of breath, moving from vibration to pulsation, in the meditation, then and only then will you realize what I am saying. **In the stillness you will find that everything is. You will find the peace and serenity within your being, where you are not affected by the outside illusion.** In that period, or as long as you can hold it, you will become weightless. This will allow a lot of adjustments to take place in the molecules and atomic structure of your body.

The radiations of the Light Energies in the body and through the pores of the skin, to the cells and Light Centers of the body, will be illuminated with a great amount of Light. This causes the cells to rapture in rapport in unison with Spirit which will shake away the dust that has been piling up in the closet for so long.

Don't be frightened or disturbed in your meditation if you hear something or see something. **If you properly put yourself under the protection of Light before entering into your meditation, you will have nothing to fear.** Once you are in the avenue of Light, the advantages you will receive from that Light will be so gratifying that it will bring tears to your eyes to recall it.

SEVEN REASONS FOR MEDITATION

1. Shut off brain
2. Communion with Spirit
3. The key to activation of the unification of Mind
4. Bring Eternal Youth into the body
5. Release of flesh into an Expression of Light
6. Total freedom of the Universe
7. Perfection of a Being in the Universe

Seven reasons for meditation.

Remember a most important point, when you hear your name called, regardless of how familiar the voice is, answer, "Yes, Father." This is the only answer you are to give. If you don't answer properly, you won't hear your name called again for quite some time. This is to see how keen and alert you actually are.

This is Spirit prompting you for your awakening, your keen sense of being. When you answer, "Yes, Father," you will receive the greatest reward; you will feel His Love completely cover and merge with your body. It is like warm water poured over your body.

Read your lesson papers a minimum of seven times. You will find the information will multiply itself by seven, each time you read it. There will be new views brought into focus as you reread it each time.

Until you can change the grossness of the flesh body into electrons, atoms and molecules and align them, simultaneously, to function in the same direction at the same time, you have not Perfected.

Meditation: Man's Awakening Himself

PURPOSE

Meditation is man's awakening himself from where he is now, his avenue of opening. It will give him a reassurance.

STILLNESS OF BREATH

In the stillness of breath, you move from vibration to pulsation. In the stillness you will find that everything is.

PEACE AND SERENITY

You will find the peace and serenity within your being, where you are not affected by the outside illusion.

WEIGHTLESSNESS

In that period of peace and serenity, you will become weightless. This will allow a lot of adjustments to take place in the molecules and atomic structure of your body.

RADIATIONS OF THE LIGHT ENERGIES

The radiations of the Light Energies in the body and through the pore centers of the body, will be illuminated with a great amount of Light. This causes the cells to rapture in rapport in unison with Spirit which will shake away the dust that has been piling up in the closet for so long.

PROTECTION OF LIGHT

Don't be frightened or disturbed in your meditation if you hear or see something. If you properly put yourself under the protection of Light before entering into your meditation, you will have nothing to fear. Once you are in the avenue of Light, the advantages you will receive from that Light will be so gratifying that it will bring tears to your eyes to recall it.

"YES, FATHER."

When you hear your name called, regardless of how familiar the voice is, answer, "Yes, Father." This is the only answer you are to give. If you don't answer properly, you won't hear your name called again for quite some time. This is to see how keen and alert you actually are. This is Spirit prompting you for your awakening; your keenness of being. When you answer, "Yes, Father," you will receive the greatest reward; you will feel His Love completely cover and merge with your body. It is like warm water poured over your body.

The Law Of Life

In the first lesson, which is the foundation for our knowledge of the meaning and purpose of life, we learned that the Triune God breathed into expression seven primary Spirits and set them into activity to express the primary principle: God. These primary Spirits, or primary planes are, Man, Angel, Fowl, Animal, Vegetable, Protoplasm and Earth.

For a fuller understanding, it is important to know that while there are seven Spirits of the first creation, each of the seven is creative after its own kind. That is, man begets man, animal begets animal, and so on. Man is controlled by the creative principle of Man Spirit, he can never be anything but man. That is true of all phases of existence. There are many planes of expression for each primary existence, and many phases of each plane. But if you look closely, it becomes apparent that within each primary existence, or Spirit, all are of the same plane.

There are many kinds of examples of mankind: some dark, fair, kind, others unkind, some tall, short, heavy and others slight. But they are all part of the Man Plane, and they all come from the same great Source: the spiritual plane of Man. Therefore, they must always express on this same plane. And so it is with all existence. Each phase of each plane acts independently, yet all are parts of the whole. One plane cannot mix with another. Man always expresses as Man, and so on for all seven Spirits through all existence.

Each plane of existing contains the material for its own expression and its own existence. Man, in the perfect state in which God created him, did not require animal and vegetable for food, but lived upon his own Etheric Substance, about which we will learn in later lessons. When man fell and became carnal, or made man, he deserted his original place in the

Heavens and made for himself another existence, one in which he interferes with all other existing things. In doing so, he has lost the ability to live on Etheric Substance, as he limits himself to a few short years of expression at a time, forgetting entirely that the source from which he came is eternal and therefore, he must be eternal, too. Instead, he flouts the fundamental laws of life, and makes laws to suit his abomination. In utter shamelessness, he casts the life from his brothers of creation and devours their substances, instead of realizing that they are for love and companionship.

This state of affairs will not continue forever, but for as long as it does continue, man will limit himself. He has also placed limitations upon all creation, and for his own salvation, he must remove that limitation and give back to all creation the expression that was lost on man's behalf.

Man has made for himself his present plane of expression. He is capable of expressing in all perfection, but he is not aware of his possibilities because of the limitations of his own making. Man is in his present state of turmoil because of this lack of awareness of his true expression, brought on by the violation of his true possibilities.

The Law of Life

Whatsoever you do unto any living thing,
you also do unto yourself.

The law of life.

As long as man causes sorrow and pain, he must express sorrow and pain. And for as long as he uses his God-given abilities for his own gratification, just so long will he and all fallen creation be limited. But when man at last learns again to use his abilities for the true expression of his own plane, then and only then, will he fully realize his reason for existence. Then will he stand upon the glorious height of perfection, and by reason of his own redemption, draw all fallen things again into the perfection of their own planes of expression.

This is the Law of Life: Whatsoever you do unto any living thing, you also do unto yourself.

Guard well your thought, which is the only creative thing you have kept, and use it wisely for your own redemption.

The Law Of Life

In **the first book** the main thing that we are going to be doing is **setting down a basic foundation for you**. We are going to start replacing, throwing away, sorting and establishing new conceptions of understanding. I am going to plant seeds. This way your subconscious is going to take these seeds and start developing them and bringing them into programmed activity, without you even being aware this is taking place. This is going to go on all the time, and suddenly you will say, "Oh, that's what he meant." The realization will all of a sudden come out of nowhere.

Planting Seeds of Betterment

The planting of the seeds is very important. I may say only four or five words to plant that seed, and I'll mix it in a sentence where you won't even know that it's put in. It's not trickery in any way. This puts you in a relaxed condition, and then I can plant information in you so that you will begin to work to better yourself. From these activities you will program it and it will go to work of its own order. It will begin to develop without you even being aware of the change until the change does consummate and take place.

By the creative principle of man's Spirit, he can never be anything but man, regardless of whatever phase or plane he places himself. **Man** can lower himself to where he is almost mineral, or he **can alter himself back into the pureness of Light, which is where he really should be**.

Any word that you see oddly placed in the lesson, look it up. It's placed there for a reason and you will be surprised to find out it doesn't mean what you think it means. They are put in for a reason. Get one of the more thorough college editions of a dictionary which have several meanings. Usually the last meanings are the more spiritual. Your whole vocabulary is going to change. When you say something, you are going to know what you are talking about. You are going to know to the full extent, the power of that word.

You are a Law unto yourself, so you are going to become that Law in activity. When you are asked something, you are going to be able to quote it clearly. You cannot expound Truth if you cannot explain it fully to the satisfaction of everybody. The word *law* is your authority of being. When you look it up, you will find out the exact definition.

You are going to do a lot of sorting. You are never absorbed, because you only sort out what you want and throw the rest away anyway, but I am telling you this, don't throw it away. Put it up on a shelf and hold it in abeyance, because you are going to go digging for it, "in time come by," as I must state it in Truth: no past or future tense, just the Now. Don't dismiss and throw anything away; if you can't put it into a usable condition at this time, or an acknowledgment, just put it aside, because you are going to look hard for it. If you dismiss it, then you are going to have to go back into the eth to find it. If you put it in abeyance and just lay it aside, then it is automatically there for recall. You will be surprised at how you are going to go back digging for certain things as you advance in your studies.

This lesson has to do with the basic of laws of life. In your first lesson we had the foundation of the meaning and purpose of life. We learned the meaning and purpose of life itself. **Now we are going to learn the patterns that the laws of life were set down upon.**

Seven Primary Spirits To Express God

We learned that the Triune God breathed into expression seven primary Spirits and set them into activity to express the primary principle: God.

When a white ray of light strikes a prism and it throws its angle reflections of multiples of itself, it will fill out seven rays of light on the other side. This is just as the Godhead in Intelligence, through spirit, reflects through the prism activity of mind and brings forth the manifestations of creation of the seven planes of expression, just the same as the crystal activity of light does in its bars of light. Everything runs in multiples of sevens in creative state.

This is in man's state that we are talking about. For a more full understanding, it is important to know that while there are seven spirits of the first creation,

> *These primary Spirits, or primary planes are, Man, Angel, Fowl, Animal, Vegetable, Protoplasm and Earth.*

Seven Planes
Of God's Expression

Man

Angel

Fowl

Animal

Vegetable

Protoplasm

Earth

Seven planes of God's expression.

Each of the primary seven planes only begets itself. There is no cross-breeding. Everything is in correlation with man, and in agreement with him. However, it really doesn't exist **with** him, only in expression **to** him.

You do not communicate with the plants as you normally should, nor with the animals or bacteria as you should. They are really not in the same plane of expression with you, so you do not have communication with them.

As you raise your elevation of existence of control, so you can equal your plane to their plane, then you will have communication. Without that stabilization between the planes, no communication is possible, or will you be able to see them in their natural condition. As you see them now, they are in a very unnatural condition. For as you have altered yourself, they also, have altered in correlation with you, so they can be of aid to you as they are subservient to you. All planes are necessary for your expression, without them, you couldn't exist. You would not have the proper blend of gases and air, for you to have your oxygen, hydrogen and nitrogen to enable your flesh to exist. Your plants make this possible.

By the creative principle of man's Spirit, he can never be anything but man, regardless of whatever phase or plane man places himself. Man can lower himself to where he is almost mineral, or he can alter himself back into the pureness of Light, which is where he really should be.

Man begets man and only man. Do not be misled to believe that an animal becomes man or man becomes animal. Man only begets the man plane and only comes from the man plane. Each plane is created in its own created plane and is begotten of its own.

We'll make an understanding for variations that took place. These were not in a created state, but were in a manifested state. This was because the planes of creation were broken and ill states of manifestation took place by stupor, where blends were made between animals and man, and animals and animals. But for this time, I want you to understand that all of the creations that were created have held their plane and their place. Man is the only one that has altered his plane.

Twelve Planetary Locations On Earth

Man is in all shapes and sizes for there are twelve distinct characteristics of people. The reason for this goes back to the Bible reference to the twelve tribes. Also, there are twelve planets in your solar system. On this Earth, there are all of the rejects from those twelve planets, including Earth's inhabitants. **Earth is the planet of redemption**.

Man was so perfect, he took all of the misfits and was sure he could straighten them out. This has been going on now for about four and one half billion years. As you look about, you will notice that each individual will select a different location on the Earth to colonize. You will find that different people will be at ease in specific surroundings. Not all are comfortable in the same area, some like mountains or deserts, while others feel drawn to the ocean. When you look back into your memory, as you learn to unlock it, you will understand why such a specific location is necessary, that you want to be in it. That was the condition of your home planet.

Twelves

Man is in all shapes and sizes for there are:

12 distinct characteristics of people
12 tribes, as referenced in the Bible
12 planets in our solar system.
12 distinct planetary locations of earth,
each in correlation with the 12 planets
of this orbiting system

Twelves.

Earth has twelve distinct planetary locations. Each one is in correlation with one of the twelve planets of this orbiting system. Those that come here will seek a familiar location. Others will see a location that is not pleasant to them, but rather as to their necessity of existence. Therefore, they will short-change themselves for the area they wish to be in for the endeavor of man's pain for greed.

When you have completed your expression of this lifespan, you will find out that all of the effort put forth for its greed will get you nowhere. It will take more away from you than you will ever get from it. The Law of Life is very exact about this, for **if you will seek Life Itself, then you will become Eternal**. If you do not seek Life, but you go about it all backwards as you seek living, then you are eternally among the "lived." Spell lived backwards and you have the devil.

Man Leaving the Perfect State, Manifesting Delusion and Becoming Human

Being given dominion over everything that expresses and his plane of expression and creation, all must follow his command. As he lessened his conditions of expression and left from the perfect state, when he no longer could hold his perfectness, he manifested for himself a delusion of operation, until he so deluded himself that he could no longer hold the power — I didn't say "force," I said "power" — of this manifestation, that he brought into being a lower manifestation. He was continuously losing sight of himself and of his created principle of being.

At the same time as he was manifesting his mis-operations, **each of the other creations, except angel, came in protection of him** and allowed its dominion to be altered equally with him, outside of two things. Communication was subtracted instantly. Thought presence, the only creative principle that man held true, would be the only means of communication between the other planes.

Man separated himself from all the other planes of expression as he took himself into a hewed condition. This is what human means: man hewed from the elements of the square of earth, in other words, man made, past tense. If you look in Genesis, it says in the third chapter of the first verse, "He made them then." In the matter of a few stanzas we cross millions and millions of years of expression.

The Purpose of Names, Persons and Places In the Bible

In order to understand completely the creative state, you have to be able to understand that a very high scientific condition is trying to be explained to very ignorant people who have lost all control of understanding. Instead of using energies, forces, chemicals and structures of atoms and of the different systems of the body, they used names, persons and places, so they could tell the story to the acceptance of one of that level of understanding.

Let's try to give you a picture of understanding. If you were in the intellect range of a native in Africa who had never seen anything but just bushes, brush, animals, trees and the ground he lived upon, and you came upon a shore and a steamboat went by, and you could hear all the noise and the motion of it moving, how would you tell somebody about it? Just place yourself in that condition. How would you explain this to somebody else, other than a dragon that went sliding through the water, and was breathing fire and smoke.

Fear, Doubt and a Limited Existence

Man has one great tendency: doubt and fear. He will cover his doubt and his fear by fantasy to delusion of his view of point of expression. In manifestation this is one of the most indebted conditions that man has placed himself under, the delusion of himself in an inability of comprehending and understanding. This is because as he fell short of himself and his principles of the man spirit, he lost his ability for expression and took on existence. He limited himself from the actual total plane of eternal expression into limited existence. He began to partake of the pangs of the Tree of Knowledge, which are good and evil, instead of the created perfect person and projection, when only perfectness exists.

As he lost his ability of force, he went into a power condition. Everything was manifested out of his agreement in thought exchange by his viewpoint of conception. The multiplicity of agreement of conception of togetherness made clans which unified and made the conditions of existence. The expression now became an existence.

Total Loss of Existence From Expression

By being taken out of the conditions of pureness of expression, limited conditions started to produce themselves and man could no longer take his energies that were necessary in his breath out of the air. He was forced to forage, as when Adam was told to go out of the garden and root for himself and to root in the ground to produce his own needs. This was the consummation of the total loss of existence from expression.

At this point in change of time, he no longer had the condition where the trees would bow down to give their nectar of fruit to him, and the animals would run and play with him and associate completely with him. Now a doubt condition had been manifested in man of his own inefficiency of himself. Because of this, he produced an uncertainty in those that he was acquainted in existence with.

In the expression conditions of this existence, each began to partake of each other because they were changed into the force field of the thought of man's projection. Due to his conditions of setting up carnality, everything followed his direction because he was the creator of the condition of expression. By his lessening of his ability from the perfectness of operation, he slowly began to deteriorate to a point that he became carnality and allowed himself to be fooled into the delusion of the master deceiver, brain, taking over the body from mind, where it had no rapport with spirit and became so darkened that the impresses of his memory were the only directions of travel.

We are still faced with that same problem in our today's existence. We are still in an existence and not in an expression, because we are continuously in a lived condition: past tense. Everything that you do is past tense, because you are always looking at the future for the past. If you look back at the past to produce the future, you lose the present. You are constantly in a turmoil between the triangles, changing one to the other, and you continue in a state of doubt and confusion of yourself, and the condition that you are expressing with.

Thus you took yourself out of your original place as you continually made existence for yourself, as you lessened your ability of comprehension of perfection. By each step that you took down, you also took all of your existence with you. As you created each plane of transgression, you took away your ability of Ether Substance from yourself. You did it yourself, so if you don't like anything you are existing in, don't blame anybody but yourself.

Adamic Sleep

You have lost your surety of who you are, where you are, what you are and why. Almost all who enter onto this earth at this time come under the Adamic sleep, the Adamic web of sleep, where the veiling of the mind is blocked by the brain. All but four of the twelve ductless glands in your body, which are the twelve apostles of your body, are dormant. Of your twelve senses, five are all that are operating. Seven are dormant, the seven most important. Even the animals have one better. They have six senses working for them. The protoplasm have nine working for them.

Functioning With Other Planes

When we start to look at the real facts and figures of how we are functioning with the correspondence reflection of those existing with us in this expression, they are bending over backwards to allow us to find ourselves. They are allowing themselves to be devoured by us so that we may sustain their light crystals of energies of thought into our being so that we can exist until we find ourselves. They befriend us in every way when allowed to befriend. Even the plants, the animals, the flowers, everything will return your love if you project love to them.

It is just like the rose will turn the thorns to you if you show animosity towards it. It is the same with the animals. They will show their teeth if your body produces the vapors of animosity or fear. If you show doubt, they will be questionable and hold you in abeyance until they are sure of your actions of projections within your thoughts.

Relive and Forgive Your Day

As you light your way of your activities of expression while you are traveling through this expression, you leave marks of your each day's expression within your memory. Everything that you suppress during that day of activity will go into the subjective mind, and when you go into sleep state it will express itself as best it may in the time given for it to express.

The objective mind will take over those things not completed, categorize them, answer them and put them into order so at the first recall of the next day they will be in programmed condition ready to go.

The thing to learn is that as you have completed your day completely, in each day before you go to sleep of a night, relive that day. Everything that you did that you felt that was unnecessary or in ignorance or error, forgive yourself for these trespasses as you forgive those who trespass against you. Do not take these into the sleep state, because they will give you torment if you don't, and you will have a very sleepless, restless night.

When you learn to do this, you can close your eyes and be asleep by the time your head hits your pillow. Very few of you can go to sleep that way, because you are lying there mulling over all the things you should have said, you should have done, would have done, could have done, why didn't I do it, and on and on.

Loving and Forgiving Yourself

Learn to love yourself and learn to be good to yourself and allow yourself the freedom of expression. We all make mistakes because we are in a world of learning. Forgive yourself for your shortcomings each day and try and strive harder the next day to do it more perfectly.

When you look in the mirror, tell yourself that you love yourself and forgive yourself for what you have done. You have limited yourself in your expression to an average of some sixty years, when this vehicle was designed to last for 7,000 years. These are self-imposed limitations. Usually by the age of forty, fermentation and the encrusting of calcification has taken place within the cells and the nervous system. The lymph buttons are beginning to dry up so lubrication of the body begins to lessen. This affects the flexibility of the skin, weakening it, and aging takes place.

Aging and Proper Activities

There is no reason for aging outside of your own agreement. You become the sum and substance product of projected thought that you program for yourself. All changes that take place in yourself are due to your own agreement, and take place in a few short years, when you become responsible for yourself at the age of twelve. Up to that time, you are taken care of by nature. After the age of twelve, you are in control and responsible for your own activity.

Because of the agreement between the Ego Center and the Airless Cell in your body, your body is already programmed in cellular expansion for your maturity of stature. Once that programming is completed, then no more programming comes from the pituitary to the thyroid to coin the cells for reproduction for an ageless condition. At the same time, the fluid for Eternal Youth is shut off and a webbing is placed in your spine where the fluid works as a percolator. Therefore, it can't get up to the brain to activate the Eternal Youth of the body.

That which is in your cells for activity, is slowly burned up in the following seven years. You usually attain your full stature by the time you are eighteen years of age. By the time you are twenty one you are totally responsible for the first triad. Your first three sevens are complete. In our society, one is considered an adult by that time. You have made your first triad of expression.

If you were taught properly from birth, and society was in balance with Truth, at twenty one, you would just be able to comprehend and correlate the color system of your body. Instead of a weekly endeavor of a minimum of eight hours a day, forty hours a week, there would be no work for you at all until you were in the fifties. Between the ages of fifty and two hundred, you would work on an average of two hours a day.

If the greed were taken out of all conditions of expression and existence, there would be no need for you to earn a monetary exchange. Also, you would be taught from birth how to manifest everything that you need. Then what need would there be for greed and lust? Because of the present plane of expression man has made for himself, the imperfection of his possibilities and his own limitation of those possibilities have sold himself so short that the true ability you really have is beyond your wildest imagination. Man seems to have lost sight of himself in his possibilities and control of individuality of being. As long as he is out of control, through his ignorance, he will create pain and sorrow to others as well as to himself, and because of his emotions, he will become his own worst enemy. He will resent having to face reality, as he won't want to have to admit to himself that he is wrong.

AGE AND PROPER ACTIVITIES

If you were taught properly from birth, and society were in balance with Truth:

From birth

You would be taught from birth how to manifest everything that you need. Then what need would there be for greed and lust?

Age 21

At 21, you would just be able to comprehend and correlate the color system of your body.

Instead of a weekly endeavor of a minimum of 8 hours a day, 40 hours a week, there would be no work for you at all until you were in your fifties.

If the greed were taken out of all conditions of expression and existence, there would be no need for you to earn a monetary exchange.

The fundamental Law of Life would bring about the desire to only fulfill yourself in your necessities of being.

You would realize the advantages of carrying around a light load, only having what is necessary for your functioning.

You wouldn't need a wardrobe, because by your own thought you could attire yourself with anything that you wish.

Age 50-200

Between the age of 50 and 200, you would work on an average of 2 hours a day.

To age 7,000

This vehicle (your body) was designed to last for 7,000 years.

Age and proper activites.

Living According To the Law

Admitting to yourself is your first step into realizing your own gratification of where you have limited yourself. When you can say it and mean it, then and only then, will you realize the reason for your own existence. When you realize this, then you will be able to look out from yourself. If you can look out and see beauty, then you will see beauty within. If you look out and see sorrow, pain and the dismal, then you claim exactly that for yourself.

When you allow changes to take place without correcting them in the proper prospective, you limit yourself and have to go back and redo it. It is easier to face up to something the first time and get it over with. Don't put off tomorrow what you could have done today. You will find that tomorrow bucket getting too full. When that does happen, at night when you are trying to get to sleep, there will be no rest until it comes to such a point of friction that you won't have any peace of mind during your waking hours, either.

You must realize that everything you suppress must be faced at one time or another, and everything that you reject must be proved and placed in its proper perspective and accepted.

For everything you deny, you must give back for expression. For everything that you alter, you must give back its right. For everything you destroy, you must remake. For everything that you deny its right of expression, you must see to the Godhead. This means for you to step aside until they have perfected, so this is something to consider.

When you step on someone, you are the first one to get stepped back upon. This is the Law and your repayment will be in excess of seven times. **The Law of Life says that what you do unto others shall be done unto you, in multiples.**

LIVING ACCORDING TO THE LAW

Admitting to yourself is your first step into realizing your own gratification of where you have limited yourself.

You must realize that:

Everything you **suppress**	must be **faced** at one time or another.
Everything that you **reject**	must be **proved and placed in its proper prospective and accepted**.
For everything you **deny**,	you must **give back** for expression.
For everything that you **alter**,	you must **give back its right**.
For everything you **destroy**,	you must **remake**.
For everything that you **deny its right of expression**,	you must **see to the Godhead.** This means for you to step aside until they have perfected; so this is something to consider.
When you **step on someone**,	you are the first one to **get stepped back upon**.

This is the Law and your repayment will be in excess of 7 times.

The LAW OF LIFE says
that what you do unto others
shall be done unto you, in multiples.

Living according to the law.

Every time you have a bad thought, the Ether Energy of your body is absorbed. For every minute of sustained anger, it takes 24 hours to replenish that energy you burned out of your body. The temperature of your body will soar to an inflammable condition of an excess of 2,000 degrees. Consequently, it is better to keep your cool, remaining calm and quiet. You will find out it is much easier to exist and express in this life. The word to sum this all up is **poise**. When you lose your poise, you are at the mercy of everybody. You are no longer the master of the situation.

This is the Law of Life; you must answer to it. In your activity of this exchange you will find that all of a sudden a new source is going to happen for you. It's called abundance. Things are going to start coming out of nowhere. With all that love you are giving out and the forgiveness that you are projecting as well as cleaning up your aura, then you have room to receive the abundance that has been waiting for you.

The fundamental Law of Life would bring about the desire to only fulfill yourself in your necessities of being. You would realize the advantages of carrying around a light load, only having what is necessary for your functioning. You wouldn't need a wardrobe, because by your own thought you could attire yourself with anything that you wish.

In Life Itself, everything exists. Life is the grandeur of God. It gives forth into every expression everything necessary for that expression, unlimited. Man seems to have forgotten that he is eternal and etheric. He goes around panting all day, instead of breathing one breath of full existence. Some people work so hard at breathing that they burn up their lungs, as they take too much nitrogen into their body. By breathing too long or too short, you set up an imbalance of the gas mixture in the body, causing tremendous damage to the nervous system and the brain cells.

I cannot emphasize enough how important the proper breath rate is for the well being of your body. Without the control and poise of breath, your body cannot be utilized with the pressures that it exists in and of. This statement will unfold in full explanation as we study further.

No Doubt

The other thing that you have to learn is that you cannot doubt. You either know that you know, or you don't know you don't know. Those may sound strange, but it's true. When you want something, make a picture of it and release it. Then it will come back to you. It's that simple, but if you doubt, one little bit, it will never come back. It lays in abeyance for you.

When you have the power of arrangement of that law to bring into existence from expression, then you can create anything that you desire. When you can make a picture of it and hold it in the fullness of that picture, it's yours, that quickly. You will be mystified at how it comes from so many mysterious ways all of a sudden.

In your third paragraph it speaks of the many different kinds of men:

> *some dark, fair, kind, others unkind, some tall, short, heavy and others slight, but they are all part of the Man Plane, and they all come from the same great Source: the spiritual plane of Man. Therefore, they must always express on this same plane.*

As long as you are in the man plane expressing in this dimension of creation, it's your privilege to return yourself back to that from which you came.

No Right To Judge

Everybody has a right to express and a right to their expression. This doesn't mean that you have the right to agree with them, but you don't have the right to judge them. You have no right to judge anything or anybody. If you judge anybody else, then look deep within, for you will find that fault within yourself. You can only judge yourself. If you judge somebody, then you have two that must be forgiven, yourself and them as well, because you have trespassed against someone.

Meekness vs. Being an Authority

In the Bible it says, "The meek shall inherit the earth." And believe me they are going to inherit it, and they are going to be bound to it, until they find themselves.

An all-loving God is never meek. If you are not an authority unto yourself, how can you be an authority to anything else? Meekness is not authority. It's the absolute opposite.

When you are right, say so. If others doubt that you are right, let them prove you wrong. When you know in your heart that you are right, go ahead and do it. But when that little voice tells you, "Don't do it," don't do it. You have consequences coming if you do.

Learn to listen to that little voice inside of you. That's the Airless Cell, the spiritual impulse telling you what actually should take place and what shouldn't take place. You have all experienced this.

Man in his activity of thinking contaminates everything that is within his thoughts if his thoughts are not of full purity. This is your dominion and you were given dominion over everything that exists in this expression. Everything must alter to your command. If you don't like the way things are going, blame yourself. Don't blame anyone else, because your agreement is bringing it about. By your own doubt of control, you are allowing yourself to be controlled. Until you are an authority on yourself, to yourself and of yourself, you will be controlled. This is because those with stronger thought presence of projection will control you with their thought projection. They will dominate you.

You have to learn to become an authority unto yourself. You have to learn to demand your right, your place in the sun. You were created as the most perfect of all expression. Prove yourself as such. Bring yourself to this point, of absolute control. This is the Law of Life.

As I said before, most are expressing in an existence of past tense, **lived.** There can never be a past tense unless we allow it to be.

Do you know that you spend more time packing for a weekend trip than you do for the greatest trip of all? Think about it. You are going to make sure you didn't forget the wash rag and the soap and everything else, all those little trivial things, but to set your life in order, you won't even take the time. The biggest trip of all! I am trying to make a point to make you understand how important you are to yourself, and of how much importance you are in the existence of total expression. The importance of this is only shown when you prove to yourself that you are life, instead of lived, when you can become pulsation rather than vibration, and you can take yourself into one breath instead of breath breathing. It makes a lot of difference.

Each plane of existing contains the material for its own expression and its own existence. Man, in the perfect state in which God created him, did not require animal and vegetable (or any other matter) for food, but lived upon his own Etheric Substance.

He was an airitarian. By his breath rate he was able to charge all the centers of his body into perfect function and he was eternal in expression. Man existed on this earth for over three and a half billion years in continuous existence. The "hue-man" body that you are existing in now is capable of seven thousand years of continuous expression, and you burn it up in less than seventy. There is something wrong somewhere.

Triad of Destruction

The three destroyers of life are improper breath, overstress by not forgiving self, and lack of clear-thought. That's the triad of destruction, because under your doubt come fear, anger, hate and everything else in that category.

Under the disability of control we have these three sisters, Faith, Hope and Charity. If you are hoping for somebody else to do it, it will never take place. If you have faith in somebody else doing it for you, it is never going to happen. As far s charity, it begins at home. Those three sisters you want to kick out of the house in a hurry, because they are nothing but bad news all the way through. If you don't know that you don't know, then you don't know. If you are going to have faith to know, it's never going to take place.

Three Destroyers of Life

1. Improper breath
2. Over-stress by not forgiving self
3. Lack of clear-thought

Three destroyers of life.

In the Law of Life, it also states that **you are the sum and substance of your thoughts**. As you broadcast, be sure you do not contaminate yourself as you contaminate those about you. As you learn this breath control, you are going to learn how to manifest. I'll warn you now, that when you still your breath and project, there is no recall.

Master or Slave

You are either master or slave. There is one way or the other. There is no in between. There is only black and white; there is no grey, because grey is space. Either you are going to be an authority or you are going to be a slave, one of the two. You are either going to be your own master, your own projection, or you are going to be the salvation of every other thought coming through.

Your spirituality cone in discernment evaluates over three million thoughts a second and reacts, records, responds and re-projects from them. For an average individual, that's over three million thoughts a second. You are capable of over nine million a second. Your capacity is one third of its ability in value of discernment. An average individual uses one onethousandth of his brain power. We think of Einstein as being a very brilliant, exceptional man. He used 16% of his brain power. Think what you would do if you used fifty percent of your brain power, the capacity that is within, the knowledge and wisdom that are within your brain, in the access of memory.

You are the sum and substance of your thoughts.

You are the sum.

Because of conformity and sociality we have been taught dumb and educated ignorant, for control. We have allowed ourselves to be slipshod with ourselves because of improper projection at the proper early age in life. We become creatures of habit, rather than knowledge of wisdom of knowing.

One Truth: Infinite Wisdom

Things that you were taught as facts are absolutely untruths. All the rest in consciousness are the attaining unto of the one Truth. Even in the conditions that you are existing under you are being taught in science that theories are facts, which don't exist, because they are constantly being altered every day. As you become more aware, you are going to be understanding more of what I am saying that exists within the Laws of Life. This is the only law: Universal Law.

Magic of Manifestation of Animals, Vegetables and Flowers

You go into the magic of the manifestation whereby the animals allowed themselves to be changed and the vegetables and flowers allowed themselves to be changed, along with all the other planes. They knew that you were going to partake of them and take their substance for your existence. They set up a condition of agreement among themselves to allow themselves to produce the energies and light crystals to be stored in their foliage so that your body would have means to exist until you found yourself. They allowed themselves to be devoured so that your existence could take place. They will continue to do so until they are no longer needed and then will return to their own plane. They can only return to their own plane when you return.

Are they already at that state? Have they already found themselves?

They have never altered themselves from perfectness, only in delusion of collusion with you. They know there's no way back for you without them, so they can never have their eternal place until you find yourself. Remember, they are part of your creation. You created them. Now they are in a hued, manifested condition of man-i-fest. That's what manifest means, "man-I-fest," man-I-make, not create. Their duration is a continuous spiraling condition of receiving itself, in duplication of itself, continuous in operation.

It is the same thing as man does for himself as he breaks the Law of Life. Where he breaks the Law of Life he must reenter back into expression again. From the time that he breaks that law, at that point he will start to deteriorate. When he loses value of his own ability of holding himself in presence, he will terminate this expression and have to restart it again where he broke the law. He will continue to do that over and over and over, until he gets past that point. You have been four and a half billion years at it now, so don't be in a hurry. You have nothing but time.

There will be a time again when you do become an airitarian, whereby you will subtract from the ethers everything you desire to express, and you will become one breath breathing, rather than breathing breath. You will become the pulsation and vibration in unison with the spheres of the universe.

Foods: Bulk vs. Energy

Man has produced tremendous bulk with no energy:

- by his own loss of ability of acknowledgment of etheric substance,
- mostly from impressions and
- the toning of the ductless glands within his body,
- the domination of dormatizing his sense centers of his body,
- improper consumption of substance matter,
- improper blending of substance matter,
- improper handling of the other dimensions that he is associating with by force-growing and force-feeding them, changing their duration of expression.

He can make the most beautiful vegetables you have ever seen, but there is no etheric content, because he didn't allow the natural conditions of the crystals in the ground to be transferred into matter substance of the vegetable matter from the protoplasm exchange.

I'll show you a consideration: carrots grown right here in the Los Angeles area. It would take twenty-nine of those carrots to equal one carrot grown in Arizona, for the same food value. This is because of the forced condition that they are grown in, and fossil fertilizers. There they are using a natural growing period and natural water and natural earthworms producing their humus condition in the soil for them to grow with. They haven't been overgrown as yet, so the nutrients have not been subtracted from the soil and burnt out.

You can do this in your own gardens, by using your own compost, putting your own earthworms in. By producing your own garden, you get the essence that is present. Remember, everything is sheathed in order to hold the essence within.

Anything that is dried becomes medicine. Anything that is boiled and canned becomes a laxative. It's dead. Anything that is frozen is dead within four seconds. I am trying to make you aware of when I said, **"You become the sum and substance of what you consume," your thought patterns and activities and everything.**

Food Blending and Sheathing

The blending of the colors of food that you blend together in mis-blending, sets up depression conditions within you and anxiety, because of the mis-digestive condition within your system. You make yourself ill by your consumption of improper gas blends and color blends.

We are bred dumb, really we are, because we follow the old laws of conformity rather than **listening to our palette as to what our body needs.** We over-consume in quantities and blend together too rapidly that of consumption. The body is a beautiful machine but it can only stand so much punishment.

You said that food is sheathed, what did you mean?

When it is sheathed, it has a coating around it. It has a sheathing on it, like an orange has a skin and a rind around it. It is sheathed in order to hold the essence of the etheric inside. Whenever a blemish point starts, then the essence will leak out of it very rapidly. Anything citrus loses its essence content in five minutes from the time it's cut.

The harder vegetables will take up to an hour. The potato will turn black when all of the essence is out, it becomes bulk chemical then. When you peel it, within the first sixteenth of an inch is where all the essence value of the potato is anyway, so you feed it to the garbage disposal. It just gets real strong. You take all the waste and stuff yourself.

Milk

The four food groups that are taught, for example the vegetables, dairy products. How accurate are they?

Let's go to dairy products alone. What kind of milk should you drink? Raw milk. From what cows? There are three cows that are deadly poison to you. You don't realize that, but they are. In order to make more money from the milk, they homogenized it, so they could blend all the milk together without it souring. They are then able to take the scrap milk and mix it with the new milk and sell it to you for new milk prices, where it used to have to be made into cheeses.

Do you mean I shouldn't drink homogenized milk?

It's not good for your system; drink raw milk. There are raw milk dairies; you have to look for them. The herd has to be pure enough and kept clean enough in the bacteria count to be able to sell it in the open market to the people where products sell. Many people don't realize that the blends of milk are deadly poison to them as it produces albumin in them.

Albumin is a mucus poisoning within the body. The albumin builds up and then causes a bituminous poisoning in the bladder. You have been taught by culture that milk is a real good thing. If you watch nature, after the milk of the mother turns from yellow to white, the calf is weaned and no longer is fed milk. It goes to vegetable matter.

Man is the only one that continues to drink it, yet he can't drink it and stomach it when it's in what they call the straining period. That's when the extra essence is being produced by the cow so that the lining in the intestines and the glandular system of the animal are being developed. During that time when the cow is in the incubate period, if you try to drink it, that milk will make you ill.

How would you ever know?

It's unlawful for the dairies to sell it to you. They know. When the cow comes fresh there is an eight week period before milk can be sold on the market. It has to have a count on the milk. There are chemists at the large dairies who take care of that.

That's why I am saying that within the Laws, **if you would listen to your intuitive processes within you, it would make you aware of what not to do.** Because of conformity, you have been taught to do this, blend this together. By clannish conditions, certain dishes become very acceptable in program of presenting, even though it's tearing your body to pieces.

There are so many things that you are going to be made aware of, but the exchanges are going to be very, very gradual, so that the transfer will be so easy that you won't be aware that it's taking place, until you look back at yourself after two or three years. When you look back you will realize how much change has taken place, only by looking back.

If you can remember in King Arthur, when he asked Merlin for the truth, Merlin always told him to look back to know the truth, because the future lies in the past.

Eating Properly

There are some people, biochemists, who say that if you eat just protein at one sitting and then eat vegetables at another sitting, not to mingle because the digestive system takes maybe two hours for protein and twenty minutes for something else. Is this the proper way to eat?

If you ate properly, you would blend no food together in less time than twenty minutes. On an average **your system** is capable of setting up a condition necessary for the breaking down into the necessary enzymes and acids to **separate the crystals within the substance matter that is being partaken of, to change them into light energy.** When you blend two or three things together at the same time, like the "greatest treat" is we go to a smorgasbord and blend everything together and then all night you wish you could give it back, all of it.

By truth, in order to partake properly of substance matter, no two foods should be blended together in less than twenty minutes. Then there is more added to that. In color ranges you cannot blend certain colors, or they become very deadly to you. For example, we will eat red onion, a heavy green salad, and we will put mayonnaise on that, which is a blend of eggs, milk and spices. Then we will partake of protein right behind it, and we will have mixed vegetables with it, not just one vegetable, we are going to mix them all together.

The computer is going crazy trying to figure out how much of what to give to which, without burning it up. All of a sudden you have gas and you wonder why, and you're very uncomfortable. Later you are even more uncomfortable, but everything passes.

When my daughter was a child, she would only eat certain foods. I ran into a lot of criticism from others for letting her choose what she wanted to eat. Is that good for a child?

You are a **wise** mother and it is a rare condition. Don't let anybody change her, in any way, no way, because she is right.

She only likes to eat, for example, protein. I let her eat it when she feels like it.

She is eating properly, because her palette is telling her what her body needs for proper balance of conditioning. If you don't force her to eat, she is only going to eat the amount that her body needs. When she is through with what her consumption rate says to her is necessary, she will push it or try to throw it away. She doesn't want any more of it, because she is listening to the sense value in her body telling her when the proper amount is attained.

Does that mean that child will eat just a small amount?

Sometimes they will consume a great amount if the body demands that for balance.

Most likely it will be small, though.

Really you should eat four times a day. Every four hours you should eat, but you should eat a small amount, and only one thing at that time. If you want to eat properly, I am telling you how to eat properly. If you would do this, you wouldn't have any digestive problems and your health will come into perfect order. If you really want to be proper, this is the proper way to consume substance matter.

What about fat?

This is superfluous food substance. It's actually the surplus of energy that the cells cannot consume and they store them in between themselves until they become rancid. When they become rancid, they act very ill upon the conditioning. They become rancid because they can't be used and there is a tremendous amount of heat being put off by the cells and they begin to spoil. They are going rancid. Did you ever take lard and put it where it is hot and watch what happens to it? It gets a real good odor to it, doesn't it. That's why your body gets the same odor.

It is the same thing with garlic. It will come out of the pores if you eat too much of it.

That's right. Just get around people who eat a lot of garlic. You can tell them a block away. If you like garlic, it's terrific. You wouldn't know the difference.

Everything that is in vegetable matter has a different attainment of light crystals that is food substance for different parts of the body. You will have a desire for a certain food or a quest for it when the palette needs it. You can actually taste it; you will long for it so greatly. That's because your body is demanding this light energy in order to hold balance. You will substitute something else for it and it doesn't do the job. It will satisfy the palette, but it won't satisfy the demand.

When you were talking about letting a child eat what he wants, I hope you are saying that you put something that is healthful in front of them, not candy and ice cream.

No, I didn't say junk food. I was talking about substance matter.

I've seen how kids won't eat anything except cookies, candy, ice cream and cake if it's there.

That's because their palettes and their sense of value have already become dormant. By improper control they have allowed things to get out of control.

Feeding Yourself By Thought

How many of you have walked through a garden when the tomatoes are getting ripe? You can smell them. That's when they are good. This is what I mean. You know, in the early part of summer they get those big strawberries and they are so sweet. If you slice them up you can actually smell just exactly how sweet and delicious they are. Now, how many are tasting it?

You see you can even smell them. Now your thought presence can feed you as much as taking matter when you learn how, by your ability in your breath, everything that you want to eat, by the sense glands in your nose and the roof of your mouth. Now how many have already produced saliva in their mouth? You see I did that deliberately to program this conditioning to you. I got you caught because I had your attention.

•I am showing you just exactly how you could feed yourself by thought. You ate that strawberry that you were thinking about, each one of you. As it already has been programmed, you saw the energy in your body, because it already went through the roof of your mouth into your blood stream.

Retaining the Essence Value of Food

When you take the essence of something, it's not like taking substance matter because **you are taking the thought presence of it, rather than the mattered substance. You are taking the essence only** and not bulk chemical condition. There is a great difference.

In a grapefruit is the essence of quinine. In five minutes from the time it's cut, all the essence is gone and it's chemical matter.

Even if it's kept wrapped?

I don't care what you do to it; there is no way you can contain it. It has to be eaten within five minutes or the essence of its value is lost.

Even after you eat it, won't it get lost even though it's within you?

No, it goes right through your body and it goes right back into the ether again, but as it goes through, it **tunes the whole body**. Just take the part you want. The juice is all that's digestible in a grapefruit. The essence of the quinine is in the juice. If you take a big grapefruit and juice it down, you only have a small glass of juice.

Are we losing any of it in the juicing?

No, as long as you don't contact it with metal. As soon as you contact it with metal it chemically burns up all the essence in it. One stroke of a metal knife through it and you lost all the essence. Use a glass knife, or a plastic knife, nonmetallic. This is true with any of your citrus fruits.

It is just like if you take an orange and put it into a refrigerator, and in four minutes it's dead. It died. It suffocated in those four minutes, just by putting it in the refrigerator. It strangled to death. It no longer can breathe. It lost its values of essence and became chemical matter by then. All of its values of food substance changed, right then.

Does this happen to all food?

In everything that's put into a refrigerator, period.

Even in its whole state? Not just after it's been cut.

Right.

You can't buy any foods now. You go to the stores now and they have refrigerated all the apples, all the oranges and everything else they have.

I'm telling you what's right. I told you there was a lot of ignorance that you were confronted with. I am trying to tell you what's right and what's not right.

If you could visualize food that you need, perfectly, so that your saliva would run and you could actually sense yourself eating it, absorbing it, could you do it?

Yes, but you won't hold your concentration that true. It will work if you would hold your concentration that true. If you make that perfect of a thought picture to feed yourself with, you can do it, but it's very hard, because you are too caught in conformity.

All these conformities will have to be broken eventually, but it's up to you as to what you want to do. I am only trying to make you aware of what the laws are and how we are breaking the laws by our conformity. Most of it is through the values of greed that this is being projected. The First Commandment says, "There shall be no other god before me." Ninety nine percent put the dollar sign before anything else, and it becomes a greed condition and all commandments are broken.

Then actually we should have our own garden and when we pull the things out to eat we should eat them within fifteen or twenty minutes?

Eat them as soon as possible. Don't pick any more than you need to eat, and don't put it in the refrigerator. Remember, when we were young we had coolers. We didn't have refrigerators, and we used evaporative coolers where we ran water over them and we put our milk and everything in there to settle so the bacteria could work naturally. We made our own cottage cheese that way too, from the excess milk, and we made our curdled cheese from all the whole stuff and the butter stock.

When we did prepare vegetables and the fruit that became necessary for the winter time, we cold packed them and we canned them. We stored them in root cellars. We used hay to put all the hard shelled stuff in, such as apples. Each was wrapped in brown paper so it wouldn't attract light and sour itself.

There are many things that have changed over the years. Where it used to be that we only had ma and pa grocery stores, now we have supermarkets with the best of all types of equipment of refrigeration, along with miseries and woe. Here again, it becomes greed, because nothing is fresh from the market.

Our Unnatural Existence

They are making everything collective. They are jamming people together, rather than people being spread out enough where they can have their natural expression. They are being forced into a forced condition of expression, which is unnatural. **That's the point I am trying to bring out. How unnatural is our existence.** How much have we allowed conformity to control us? How much have we been caught up into this conformity that we are allowing it to dominate us completely. **We are losing our existence by this domination.** This is the whole point I am getting at. All this we went around was to get you to realize one point and this is the point I was trying to get at. I had to go a long way around to make the impact be so sure.

Giving Thanks Before Meals

Everything has its place under the sun and its right of expression. Give everything its due value and its right of expression, because as you glorify it, it glorifies you. Anything that you have to partake of bless it into perfection in your consumption. How many of you do it? **Everything that you partake of, bless it into perfection.**

You were taught to say the prayers before you eat? Remember, you are god. That was the reason this little prayer of giving thanks before meals was thought about, but it got diverted into something else: being thankful and grateful in most places, rather than thanking the presence of their being to give essence of energy unto you, and only that which is necessary to be taken of, the rest to be returned to the source that it came from. Then you won't find the condition of super-flesh [fat] upon your bodies.

Change your thought patterns. It makes a great deal of difference.

Refrigeration

In the future, you will have refrigerators of sound. You will have your pantry back, and all of your vegetables and everything will be put on shelves and they will keep there, just like they were in the garden when you picked them. They will hold their essence in freshness and they will continue to grow, even out of the ground. You will play music to them.

One of the other things that has happened in the markets is that they give you plastic bags to carry vegetables and fruits in and most people leave them in the bags and put them in the refrigerator.

They can't breathe. They strangle immediately. Little brown paper sacks are the best of all because they deflect the ultraviolet rays of light, and stop the souring condition. They also allow them to breathe instead of strangle so quickly. Anything put into a refrigerator stops breathing in four minutes.

Listening To Your Palate

What I'm trying to point out to you and make you understand and become aware of is that you have true sense values inside of yourself. Learn to listen to them; **learn to listen to your palette. Your body will tell you what you want to eat.** How often do you get, "I'm going to have this tonight," and you are listening to what your palette is telling you that you need for your own stability. And don't over-partake. Only partake generously. Stop while your elbow still can bend.

How do you keep things if they are not in the refrigerator? I bought oranges and one spoiled in the box.

Be selective when you pick them that they are not bruised. The greatest contamination in citrus fruit is the bruised condition. Like with any soft fruit you have to be very careful. With being shipped and being affected by the bouncing against one another, it's very hard to keep them from bruising. This is where deterioration sets up because the natural destruction inside itself starts destroying it, as soon as the bruised condition starts. It no longer can breathe and the bacteria take over. The self destruction inside deteriorates it. Everything has its own self destruction built in it, its own consumption.

When you learn to live within the fundamental laws of life, rather than making laws to suit your conditioning, then you won't have the problems or necessity of consuming the life substance of your brothers of creation. As long as you have need of them, they will allow you to make the exchange, because they are in a continuous condition anyway. Nothing is ever lost. It is just altered and changed in place and time. By blessing it in its condition of exchange, you give it an automatic rebirth, rather than a time-cycle conditioning. Interesting, isn't it?

Limitations and Your Natural Abilities

All the things that are in limitation are in your terms of expression can be altered at any time by you. All you have to do is make the agreement. As soon as you make the agreement, somebody is going to be put in your way to start explaining to you how you make the change. That's why you are here, or you would never have made your way here, because you made the quest. I didn't. You are ready to be informed.

Breath: Inhalation and Exhalation

1. Inhalation
Charge yourself with your breath. Make picture forms of what you want. Draw forth 7 Rays of Light (3 primary and 4 secondary) into your body across the diaphragm.
Breath in & fill the lungs, draw forth ether energy of 3 primary colors.

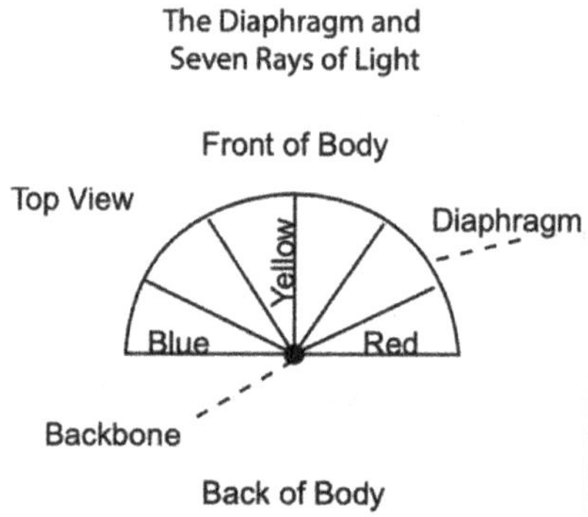

These 7 arteries are for charging of all the activity of your body in Light Energy. They will charge your nervous, digestive, circulatory and respiratory systems simultaneously.

2. Pause: Stillness of breath on inhaling (for 2 beats of the heart). The frequency changes polarity. (Positive becomes negative & negative becomes positive.) This gives you evaluation within your Sightcone to discern all thoughts going through your brain (about 3,000,000 per second).
Make your picture form. (You are constructing the Ether Realm around you, which will manifest it for you.)

3. Exhalation
Draw forth 4 secondary colors to the bottom side of the diaphragm, coming through the feet from Earth.
Release the blueprints.

4. Pause: still breath on the outcast (for 2 beats of the heart).
Frequency changes polarity.
Transmission of picture is complete into the elementary conditions about you.

Inhalation and Exhalation.

You want a change; so now the truth is being given to you. What you do with it becomes your problem, not mine. I can only make you aware. I can't do it for you, but I can tell you of the steps necessary to bring yourself back into perfection, to make yourself into the perfect state of expression, as I have made you aware with many seeds of things you haven't thought much about, that are very necessary.

The lesson says:

> *Man has made for himself his present plane of expression. He is capable of expressing in all perfection, but he is not aware of his possibilities because of the limitations of his own making. Man is in his present state of turmoil because of this lack of awareness of his true expression, brought on by the violation of his true possibilities.*

In other words, your natural abilities are trying to aid you in every way. Even your body will tell you when you are out of order, when you have over-taxed it, or you are over-stressing it. It will tell you to rest, take it easy. It is just like when your body is becoming short of oxygen you will yawn. When your body is becoming short of nitrogen you will chill. When your body is becoming short of hydrogen, you will heat. You will have flashes, hot flashes. All of these are controlled by your breath, by changing your rate of demand of each chemical in your breath, in your thought.

Breath Exercise: The Secret To Perfect Meditation

At the bottom of your lesson you have a breath exercise. This is undoubtedly **one of the most important exercises you will ever do in your life**. If you do exactly as it says, your body will start becoming into rapport with itself. This exercise is also the secret to perfect meditation, because when you have conquered this and it becomes as natural as your unnatural breath is now, you will become breath breathing instead of breathing breath.

It is so important because it allows an equal amount of expression for each of the seven creations to express. Not only are you totally energizing yourself, but you are energizing all other expressions equally with yourself. You are also allowing to learn the control of abundance, by this exercise. You are learning the first steps of programming yourself in the ability of thought perception, clarity of conformity, ability of projection of those things desired and the release to attain unto you, all done in this exercise, when learned how to properly adapt.

First you will learn that it will allow the equal amount of energy to be attracted through the seven arteries of the diaphragm into your body, allowing all seven colors to be equalized into energy into the spirituality cone in the spirituality center in the top of your head. These two ductless glands become into rapport for all the projections of the cellular structure of your body, and the light substance set up for all the projections of all the cellular structure of your body.

Of all the exercises that you will do, this is the most important exercise of all. I can't stress to you how important it is to learn to breathe right. "In my breath is your infinite wisdom." This is truly so.

Most important of all, if you have to feel your pulse to get your heartbeat to synchronize its rhythm, do so. You can even touch with one finger underneath the ear and pick it up or you can take your pulse here at your wrist. Many find it easier to pick it up underneath the ear. Go up and touch your ear, then come down about half an inch. You can pick it up very easily, and it's more accurate than what your pulse is on your wrist. It is very easy to pick up and learn to breath with that.

Fill your lungs equally with seven beats of your heart and learn to have a smoothness in filling. Then hold the breath still so that all values of discernment are held in a still condition. As you release your breath, all the things that you have in thought pictures can be released into transmission. You hold the two breaths so that the transmission can clear your atmosphere, so it isn't drawn back in with the next breath. As it is with your breathing now, you are just sucking it back and forth and it goes nowhere; you never attain anything because you can't get rid of it.

By the intake of breath, as you do the 7/2 Breath rate, you draw forth the seven Rays of Light into your body by your diaphragm. This has seven arteries across it. There are three primary and four secondary arteries for reception of these colors. They will charge all of the activity of your body into Light Energy as well as charging your nervous system, your digestive system, respiratory and circulatory systems.

As you breathe in and you fill your lungs, you draw forth the Ether energy of the three primary colors. As you exhale, you draw forth the four secondary colors through the bottom side of your diaphragm, coming up through your feet from the Earth.

The intake of the breath allows you the evaluation in your Sightcone for discernment of all thoughts that come into your head, of which there are about 3,000,000 per second.

There are multiple things taking place when you breathe by your 7/2 breath control. In the filling of the breath in the charge by the intake and the exhalation, we use a two beat pause between each activity. This allows for the frequency to change polarity, so all that is positive becomes negative and the negative become positive.

Simultaneously, as you breathe in, **your body is an air transformer**. The iron in your blood is excited and the residual of it trying to capture itself, emits a tremendous amount of energy. This causes all of the protons and neutrons around it to activate. When your blood is tired, you are short of iron. When it is in good condition, you have lots of red cells in your blood. As your red cells are oxidized, which makes them red, they also become the transmitters and receivers of the residual activity of the iron that is in your system.

Jesus said, "My Life is in your blood," and that is what He meant. By your breath, you will learn the control of the gases which you automatically do in a limited condition now without realizing it. Some of you are more proficient than others, because of accident rather than knowledge, or you were taught proper breath in athletic conditions. As you tire and tax yourself, you become more lax in breath control. Also, the firmness of your being becomes charged into super-flesh, by improper breath.

If you breathe too shallowly, the heaviness of water will come into the system. When the breath is in a real heavy over-drag, you will find the over extension of the air sacks will break down, so that you develop a lung condition in the midpart of your life. There is only a certain amount of elasticity to the cellular structure of your flesh. It can be over-expanded only so long before it will break down.

Forming Thought Pictures

By charging yourself **with your intake breath**, you will use your own perspective of control when you want to manifest. **You will form pictures**

of what you want. You will use the inhaling of your breath to draw the properties that you need from Universal Substance into your being, so that you may have use of it. Without breath control, you cannot draw forth the Light from the Universe to use in your manifestation.

As you pause your breath and you are making your picture form, you are actually constructing in the ether realm around you, that which you wish to manifest. As you formulate your picture by your imaginative processes, picture it so that you can attract the etheric substance to manifest into matter and congeal.

On the outgoing breath, you will release the blueprints of your desire into functional operation. That which you cannot develop and energize within your own aura, will have to be drawn upon from Universal Substance, if you lack that control. Then, you will have to wait for your manifestation to take place at a given time, as your controls must allow for your shortcomings.

As it is now, you picture mold what you desire and it usually takes a little time for you to hew it into being, or shape it. When you picture forth in your desires of what you wish to attain and manifest into your function of operation, you will find that it is much easier to attain if you use your breath control. When you still your breath on the outcast, transmission is complete into the elementary conditions about you. If you have made a proper picture, it should return right back you, except you will need control for this function of operation.

You do it, but in a second-hand fashion. Sometimes you have to rethink many times before you get it exactly as you want it. How many times have you seen something and wanted it for yourself just exactly as you saw it? The more you think about it, the more you picture it in greater detail, as you desire it. It isn't long before it comes into being. You desire it right down to the color, the pattern and size.

If you learn to use this, you will find it easier to attain all of the necessities of your expression. There is one caution: never think of money as it is the root of all evil. Think of what you want and not of what it costs. **You can have anything you want, it's waiting for you. All you have to do is make the picture and it's yours.**

The more that you work it out in thought picture, the easier it is to construct. Everything that you make, you do so with a blueprint plan before you build it. If you learn to use this, you will find that you will live a life of luxury and everything in its own time will return to you, when you don't expect it, for the little good turns you give to somebody else, will all of a sudden return to you.

You will find that **every cell in your body is going to respond to this breath,** as it is responding right now to the improper breathing that you are doing, because it is suffocating and you are losing the elasticity of your body. The cells go into an elliptical condition rather than a full circle. That's why they say, "Life begins at forty," because your cells attain their full roundness at forty. You would think it's at the teen age that you attain your perfectness, but it's at the age of forty. Remember, you are created for seven thousand years of expression.

> *As long as man causes sorrow and pain, he must express the sorrow and pain that he projects, because whatever you beget, you become that which you project.*

The Most Important Thing To Change

Being honest about the conditions, if you use your abilities, from this minute on, you are going to **change your attitude,** which is the most important thing to change. You are not going to talk about things of pain, hurt, hate, sorrow, destruction or petty things. You are going to **talk about love, pleasantry, inventive conditions, things of acknowledgment and interest.** All that waste of something for nothing, and most of it was nothing for nothing anyway, only wasted time that could have been put to constructive purposes.

If you would put your brain at ease and relax, allowing the mind and your imaginative processes, which are your true abilities, to come into rapport, you would be surprised at the things that you would begin to understand. I hear so many times, "I am so bored. There is nothing to do. I wonder what's on television?" You have been so long conformed by somebody else telling you how to do it that you don't even know how to do it for yourself any more.

You see, you are conformed so long that you don't even know when you really get released. I think of that young bride as she left from the marriage ceremony and was leaving to go on her honeymoon, she said, "Mother can I do it now?"

You are so busy tying yourself in knots that you haven't got time to find out where the end of the rope is. The important thing is that try as hard as you can to stop the small talk and make things constructive. You are going to find out that you are going to have very few people to talk to.

Constructive Talk

Very few people talk constructively or of things of great importance. Most of them talk just to be heard or to take up space and time. There are so many things of interest to be understood, that with the limited amount of expression that you have, you very seldom have a chance to even touch a particle of that which you should really understand, because you won't extend the effort for the truth of knowing. You would rather have it hearsay from somebody else who only knows half of it, or even less.

Remember that whatever you do unto any other living thing, you also do unto yourself. When you gossip, who are you gossiping to? Who are you affecting? This is the point I am trying to bring out. You only talk about the person who is gone, and when she comes, you talk about somebody else, and somebody else.

You Are the Sum and Substance of Your Thoughts

Guard well your thoughts, because it is the only creative thing that you have kept and **it is your only avenue of redemption**. Remember, you are the sum and substance of your thoughts, in agreement, and you become the conformity of those expressing as you agree. By your mis-programming and gossip, you are really setting yourself up.

The Meanings and Value of Words

Your thought presence of explanation of expression comes into rapport with the acknowledgment of vision; your sensing conditions of the intelligence of wisdom then are being projected in exchange. As I have said before, when you see a word oddly placed in your lessons, look up the meaning of it, because it doesn't mean what you think it means. You will miss the whole point by not knowing the value of the word in its proper value, because it will change the whole meaning of the sentence.

Sometimes I will use odd phrases in the lessons for an imprint condition, because it will force you to think upon it. I will use word phrases for which, unless you look up the true value of the word, you will take the common accepted definition of the word rather than its true definition. Many times you will be short changing yourself. Your vocabulary will increase tremendously by the time you have studied any length of time.

I am going to start asking you what different words mean, so you might as well start getting aware of it, because it's going to be coming. I am going to make you aware of what these different values are. A better dictionary to get today is one of the college versions, because it has fuller explanations to the words than the limited abridged dictionaries. Get a good one when you get it so that it gives you good definitions.

You will notice that for each word, it will give you spiritual values for that word as well as a common acceptance of the word. When Webster was given the definition of all the words put in our English language and the blending of all the other languages together, he was given the spiritual first, the intermediate and then a common conception last. When they reprinted it, they reversed the procedure.

About what year did they do that?

The final compiling was in the last part of the eighteen hundreds. Webster started much earlier than that, but in the last compiling of it, there was a multiple overlay in the timing of it. All the definitions he received by transference of thought.

He first put the words together by language blends and took the common conception. Then as he dwelled upon the common conception, he got the intermediate conception. When he was able to understand that, then the spiritual value would come through. If you look in a good dictionary, you will find them divided that way. Most generally, words are used very improperly from what they mean. Some are used absolutely in reverse of what they mean.

How To Meditate and Why

Find a condition that's most comfortable for you. **The main thing is to allow your breath to come in rapport of perfect response with universal pulsation.** That's what this **Seven Rate Breath** is. This puts you in unison with the universe.

I have found for the beginning for most people, that if you will take a thumb tack and paint it black and stick it in the door or a wall, five feet or more away from you, as you breathe, you will watch it spiral in and out. If you will concentrate upon it, it will give brain something to do and it will leave you alone. You can pass through it much more easily than you can by trying to wait it out.

In your first part of meditation, allow the brain to run as much as it wants. Don't agree or disagree with anything that's being presented to you. Once you agree or disagree, get up and go about your business, because you are through meditating.

It's the hardest thing in the world, because brain has access to all your memory and it knows everything to play against you to distract you. Brain will use every trick in the book. It will tickle your nose. It will make you itch. Somebody will talk to you that's not there. It just has a whole bag of little deceiving activities that it will pull on you, but don't allow it to control the situation.

Each time that it masters and beats you, give up. There is another day coming. That's your day. Eventually you are going to win. When you win, then it becomes a computer and mind will take the presence of brain and you will start to have rapport with the universe.

Meditation is the avenue to infinite wisdom. That's what it's really about. It will give you the right of freedom that you will learn that by the Holy Breath you will become into the Whole-In-One Breath. In one state in your meditation you will all of a sudden realize that you are not breathing, that you have passed from vibration into pulsation, that you are on one breath. You can maintain that for hours.

In India they bury them for forty-two days on one breath, to pass one initiation. They dig them up on the forty-second day. It is possible to do. It is only a mind over matter condition. That's all. They take one breath and that's it. They go into a pulsated condition and the cells breathe from then on. Animals do it when they hibernate.

The cells would also be taking the nourishment from the ground that they needed?

The cells take their nourishment from the light, because the light goes through the ground. Ether goes everywhere. It is no respecter of any solids, because it's essence is so fine that it will pass through any density that we have here on this earth. It's everywhere. It's presence is everywhere or nothing could exist.

The avenues that the Whole-In-One Breath brings about to you, are the multiples of things that take place at the same time, in this breath rate. As you are breathing, you are not only attracting the light into your body by equal proportions of each light ray in its own dimension of expression, you also are becoming the triangulation of geometric triangulation of angles, where the spin condition of everything in existence bows to you.

In other words, it blends and lends energy or projects energy to you, until you become the hub source of that energy. When you arrive at the point in your mediation, which will come about, your body will have a rapport of a condition of violence. You will think it's violence, but it's actually only all the atoms in your body lining up in one direction at the same time. Your body will spin in such a tremendous centrifugal force that you think your body will disintegrate. You actually will feel as if your body is being disintegrated; you will spin so rapidly.

Always remember that in meditation there is nothing but love. There is nothing to fear. As long as you don't allow the fear to control, or take hold of you, then you will master all situations. As soon as you doubt and allow fear to interrupt, then it will take control of the condition and you will have lost your meditation.

The Circle of Light: Your Greatest Safeguard

Any time you are in doubt of your presence or you are in doubt of anything surrounding you, call The Circle of Light into order. When anything is in question that you are not sure of, tell it to "stand forth in Truth and Light." If it isn't in Truth and Light, it will vanish instantly, because it knows if it steps over those bounds, the light of purity will disintegrate it. This is the greatest safeguard that you could ever have, your Circle of Light.

You want to learn this is your absolute protection. I have actually seen bullets go in curves, to give you an idea of how powerful it is.

THE CIRCLE OF LIGHT

The Circle of Light is about me,
and the life-giving spiritual substance is
ever-present in the God within.
The Circle of Light holds the forces of light
which watch over me vigilantly.
Lovingly and confidently
I release myself to the care and keeping of
the Great White Brotherhood of Light.
Knowing that, I give thanks to the indwelling force
which is constantly and unfailingly guiding me
into my perfection.

The circle of life.

My son was involved in a motorcycle accident three years ago. He was traveling in excess of seventy miles an hour when a car pulled right out in front of him, with a side impact. He said, "Dad, I never really believed in that Circle of Light until then. You know, somebody put two hands right underneath my bottom and carried me right through the air and set me down on the ground and held me until I could run fast enough to stand upright, and then took the hands away."

Now I am telling you just exactly how powerful this really is. I have seen multiples of incidents where this has proved itself beyond a doubt, of how perfectly it works. This is something that is your privilege, and it's my privilege to give it to your pleasure, but it's not for everybody, because not everybody is ready for it. If they are not ready, they will dismiss themselves from these Truths. Otherwise, they will reap the rewards from the benefits gained.

On Awakening Each Morning

It is a little gift for you. Learn to use it. Learn to use it right, and each day as you start your expression. Keep it right there by your bedside until you know it. Learn to keep a paper handy to write down your dreams as soon as you awaken, when you take your first breath in the morning, and keep record of them. Then read this little phrase. Don't jump up and get right up and go into expression.

Allow yourself at least five minutes for your body to collect all of itself from its night travels, before you get up. Lie completely in a relaxed condition. Then write out your dreams. Read your little Circle of Light and then go about your day. You will be surprised how much easier your day is going to start, how many changes are going to start in your day. It's like magic.

Be Yourself

Each day that you go into expression, **everything that you go in to do, you do the best that you can do to make it perfect,** regardless of what anybody else says. **You do your work to satisfy YOU!** When you are satisfied with it, you don't have to back away from anybody. If you will learn to do this in this way, your ability of force will begin to increase. Things will begin to become more and more perfect and easier for you to do perfectly, without any big concentration or anything on it. It will become very natural.

Allow yourself to be yourself, instead of being unnatural, trying to be somebody else. You are self; be yourself. Do the best of your ability in your ability. Be yourself. Express yourself. Don't try to be a mimic! There are too many of them already. We have all kinds of egg heads. Now we need head eggs.

Be yourself.

Everyone has skeletons in their closet, but only when you admit that you have skeletons in your closet are you ready for the Truth. If you can't face it, then you can't get rid of it. All of the things that other people do which you don't like, look within yourself and see why they are there. If you are not getting along with somebody, tell that person whenever you see them that you love them. The only way you can get rid of an enemy is by loving them.

As long as your hand is clenched into a fist, nobody can give you anything, nor can you accept. If your hand is open, you are giving as well as receiving. When you hold it open, you are eternally welcome to everything in the universe, and the universe becomes yours.

The Wisdom To Be Eternally Free

The Law of Life gives us the Wisdom to be eternally free. When we learn to love, that means we have learned to forgive. When you love somebody, you love them unselfishly and you see nothing wrong within them. It's only when you see things wrong, do you malice your love. Then, you change your love to liking.

The properties that you are attaining and wish to attain to are **Perfection**, which all start with a little key: I love you, everybody, everything, unconditionally, with no strings attached.

One of the steps for cleaning up, is to get your mastoids free of mucus, so the rest of your body can function properly. When you spin your head around and you feel dizzy, then you have too much mucus. Your gyro is functioning improperly. Also, the exchange of electrical currents from the Sightcone into the pineal glands of the body are not in proper perspectives, so they will be short-circuited.

The Blue-White Light and the Yellow Light, which enter through the temples and go to the thyroid to coin the cells for their structure, will create a deficiency in their makeup. Your breath will help you tremendously, as it will start cleaning the blood system of your body. Those that have become dormant for so many years, need the aid of the activated charcoal tablets, such as Requa.

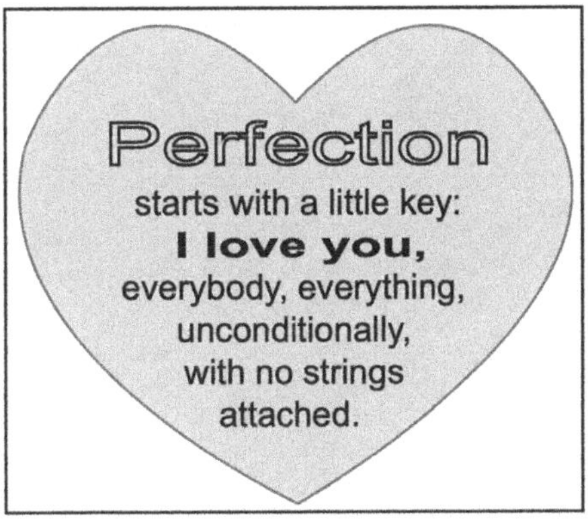

Perfection.

The crystals of light in the system are lost and become sludge, due to fermentation. This is not what should be. If you used proper exercise in the execution of breath along with its control of being, you will find that by taking this energy in, along with your proper breath, you will begin to live instead of being lived.

Multiplicities of Motion Simultaneously

The degree of your functioning in life, with life, and of life, is something you are not very able to comprehend at this time. To accomplish what I am saying, you must become multiples of motion, simultaneously in all directions at the same time. As it is now, you have limited yourself in one direction of operation at a time. You hear, see and feel in one direction, instead of multiples.

As time advances and you advance time, you will find that this multiplicity becomes very natural. You use it without even realizing it. You have centers in your body that are working at one tenth of their ability, due to your inefficiency. As you develop, you will gain the proper function of control over them. It will give you the ability to turn your body to Light. This is the Law of Life.

Kingdom Of Heaven, Not Kingdom Of God

A great deal has been written and said about the misunderstood Kingdom of Heaven. Let us analyze this phrase and delve into the meaning until we are vibrating mentally in accord with it, thus bringing to our intelligence the Spirit of it.

Jesus teaches that the Kingdom of Heaven is the perfect state of conscious. To understand this more fully, let us again review what we learned in the preceding lessons.

We have seen that all creation is Triune, just as the Supreme God who created all is triune: Spirit, Mind and Physical. This triune nature is essential, for without it, creation could not be eternal. Remember also, that our work is for all partakers of life, and our purpose is to teach the perfection of all creation, to lead it into perfect ways, to the perfect creative plane.

Now let us consider the **primary cause of all: Man.** Man is the last creation of the Triune Spirit of God, and the most ideal creation, molded in the form and possessing all the powers of the Power that created him. This means that he is **all forms, all the intelligence, all the forces and all the Truth. He is love, beauty and all durability for all eternity.** The life that he was to express in, existed even before man was conscious of his existence.

Remember this Truth and let it be a foundation of your faith. Each man is a law unto himself, not himself unto a law.

Man can never be other than he thinks he is, for thought, as we learned in the preceding lesson, is the only creative part of himself that man has saved. It is now the only heaven that man can know. By "planting" his thoughts into life, man has made all things that he is now aware of. He has shut himself away from the true Heaven because he would not permit other creations to keep their own particular powers.

You must come to know that you are the Universe and the fullness, thereof, in the spiritual sense. This spiritual awareness casts its radiance upon the individual mind of man to be utilized by the physical body. Now, in the Spirit, Mind and Body of man is the knowledge of all creation and all phases of all creation, because the Creator of all, created him. Prove this to yourself: If you did not have the consciousness of any creation other than man, you would not be aware of other creations. A rose would not exist for you, nor would any animal or bird. You would know only man, and all other creations would be farther away from you than the angels, who dwell in their created plane of perfection. You may know of the angels through hearsay, but not through actual association. You may believe they exist, but until you see them, you won't be truly aware of their being.

The consciousness of all is in each, and the consciousness of each is in all. **Consciousness means** knowing, capable of activity upon, that is, **knowing in all actuality**, to be able to associate with, to harmonize, in harmonious relations.

Each of you has the consciousness of all things. All have their harmonious relationship with the vibration sense of their counterpart in you, but you are not aware of this consciousness. For example, if you were aware of the conscious action of the divine principle of a bird, you would converse and communicate with that bird. And so it is with all creation. You are conscious of their form, but you are not aware of your relationship to them.

Each consciousness has its own metes and bounds, and expresses in its own way, but all consciousness is related to a part of all other consciousness. Each consciousness is a plane of vibration, it has always existed and always will exist. For example, when you lived in a age when the tallow candle was used for light, you were not aware of the electrical consciousness. But the electrical consciousness did exist, or you never could have become aware of it. And so it is with all things: all do exist. There are some things in your present state of awareness you do not comprehend but the time will come when you enter into the perfect state where you are truly aware of all things.

Your thought is the shadow of the awareness of your Spirit which faces that perfect plane of expression. Because your perfect Spirit receives from

God, all consciousness, you must connect your Spirit to your body through your thought action. When this contact is complete, you will have arrived at that blessed state of **perfect consciousness**. Then you can say to the wind, "Hold your peace," and your consciousness would come into contact with the wind, and the loving awareness of the wind in loving awareness of the perfection of your awareness, and the perfect awareness of the wind would obey because of accord, agreement and love.

And so it will be with all phases of consciousness and all planes of Life—each living in perfect love, perfect trust and perfect understanding. **Through all eternity, man was created to rule through love, to bless and control, to have dominion over and serve all creation.** He was given the knowledge of the awareness of all consciousness contained in life.

And now you see that **you are the Holy of Holies, that Temple not built by hands, eternal in the Heavens,** eternal in the consciousness of consciousness: THE PERFECT CONSCIOUSNESS OF HEAVEN.

Kingdom Of Heaven, Not Kingdom Of God

Heaven: The Perfect State of Conscious

If you ask most people where Heaven is, they will always look up. They will never look in. They say it's out there somewhere with God. However, Heaven is something that is very dear to each of you, when you realize the true of Heaven. As it is now, you only have a superficial meaning of it. Because, to say it is the Perfect State of Conscious, would only be words to you, as you are not able to comprehend fully with the Intelligence of Spirit to be aware of what consciousness actually is.

> **Heaven:**
> Perfect state of Conscious
>
> **Conscious:**
> The true state of Being, the state of Perfection.

Heaven.

Your acceptance now is to understand that Consciousness is the Primary Condition of all Creation, but that you have divided Consciousness into conscious-nesses, making multiples out of a single. In most of the teachings of the occult learning, you will find the Conscious broken up into "nesses."

They really don't exist. There is only one **Conscious; that is the true state of being, the state of Perfection.**

In our previous lessons, we discussed the Triune Activity.

God	Kingdom	Heaven
Circle	Triangle	Square

In this order, the Universe was created.

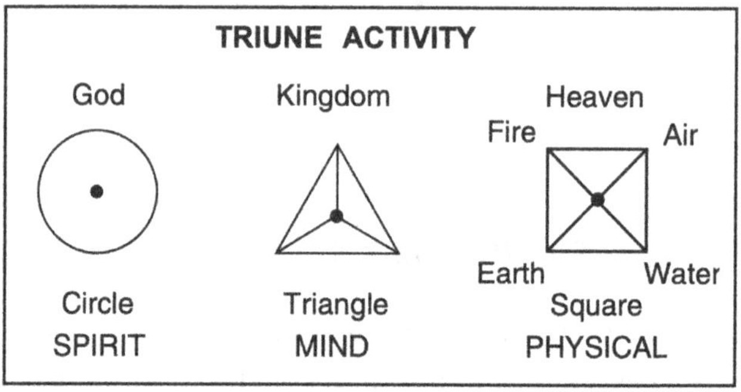

Triune activity.

You will find that in your life, which is in your blood, the circle, the triangle, and the square are the major elements of the Kingdom of Life in your blood. This is the way they make your crystals of energies, of form, in your blood that feed your body.

A great deal has been written and said about the misunderstood Kingdom of Heaven. Let us analyze this phrase and delve into the meaning until we are vibrating mentally in accord with it, thus bringing to our intelligence the Spirit of it.

Spirit, Mind and Physical

Spirit is a Latin word which means spirally I go to express. The Latin *spire* is a circular motion of activity both coming and going, simultaneously. The I means the personified representative of God standing forth in expression. The T is that expression. When you put SPIR-I-T together, you have spirit. We will go further into the meaning of the letters in a future series of lessons.

Mind being the Master M, which is the Majestic Master of the Universe. In the capital M, you have a letter I on either side with a cone placed between them for the collecting of Intelligence preceding the fullness of expression, both positive and negative. These are the legs of your triangle of Spirit, Mind and Physical.

Physical is made up of fire-air-water-earth. These are your basic elements. With this, you have the ability of all creation. The Perfect Created Plane mentioned would be **one dot**. That one dot is your **Airless Cell,** at the center of your heart, which takes It's seating with your first breath. All the rest of yourself that you see is reflection, by agreement in conformity of reflected values of shadows: the flesh body.

> *We have seen that all creation is Triune, just as the Supreme God who created all is triune: Spirit, Mind and Physical. This triune nature is essential, for without it, creation could not be eternal. Remember also, that our work is for all partakers of life, and our purpose is to teach the perfection of all creation, to lead it into perfect ways, to the perfect creative plane.*

We are prone to think that nothing exists outside of form, because we only accept tangible things. It is very difficult for the majority of the students, even with an acceptance of agreement, to be conscious of the other existences existing with you equally, simultaneously in multiples of planes that completely surround you.

By every breath, you take millions of universes into your body. This is into every pore of your body, as well. They are so small by our terms of size, that it would take millions of them to fill the dot of a pencil. Yet, they have so much force that they continuously rebuild and rejuvenate your body. You aren't aware of their presence as you breathe them in and they are transferred into the circulatory system of your body. Man has much to learn about form. Man is made up of the full composure of the full Universe. He is the fullness of that Universe in Expression.

Paradise or Bliss

As man expresses himself, he either creates his own heaven or hell, which is the plane of his state of being of his own consciousness. If you belittle yourself, then you create an ill condition for yourself. **If you express yourself joyously, being selfless in that expression, in Love, then you share the Universe. When you even surpass that and give of yourself without any prospect of receiving for that which you give, then you are in Paradise.** Very few ever reach the state of Paradise.

It is like the state of bliss, which is very difficult to hold. The essence of energy that complies to go with it is so fine of matter that it is difficult for you to hold that state of being because the flesh begins to melt. That is why you feel buoyant and floating while in the Bliss state. Usually it will happen only once or twice in a life span, such as the first time that you fall in love, for you are actually walking on air. For the feminine, it's when they give birth to their first child. It's a state that many individuals like to capture and hold for all of their expression.

Truth and Consciousness

In form, there are many things with which to be concerned that your imaginative processes haven't even exposed you to, yet. You are based completely in intellect control and conformity. Many of you have become fixed facts from the academic acceptance of intellect. Your conformity of control by the laws you exist under, are by an intellect standard.

Instead of being quiet and having the Truth, you have been so programmed to automatically play back, through intellect standards of an academic culture acceptance, and by social conformity of expression, that you don't even know your true self or your true expression. **Be quiet within yourself, when you want to know something, and allow the Intelligence of the universe** to fully express it for you and to you.

The first steps of receiving this are the true state of **controlled meditation**, where you can shut brain off so Mind can have full rapport with Spirit into your consciousness, to produce the **ideal state of Consciousness**. Then, you can be truly aware of the All Existence of the Universe, rather than fractions and split facts of the facts, as well as being given double talk of double planes of planes of consciousness, which don't exist.

When we speak of Force, this is the purpose in activity of Intelligence of the Universal Expression. Not until you fully awaken the senses of your body will you be able to use Force. Until then, you will be power, which is the motivated energy in expression of activity of exchange of Force to operate the flesh body. You have to change the elements into power so that the body can work. The same process is used when you change the molecular structure by burning fusion, or by compression or friction, to make your vehicles and appliances work for you.

Everything that you have in expression about you, in mechanical means or conveyances, are all copied from your human body. You look at anything that you function with and you will find a duplication in the human body. Thus, everything becomes a big mimic game in the flesh expression.

All of the Truths, Truth, untruth, maybe, false, darkness and shadow effect are of the states of Truth, because man has passed through each one of these states while falling and coming back. When we say **Truth**, we're speaking of the **total fullness of the State of All**.

In our functional operation in form and intelligence that we now exist and express within, Truth is an impossibility for you to comprehend. What you call true today will not be true tomorrow, because your awareness will change and that which you accept as the ultimate today won't be a drop in the bucket tomorrow. To attain all of the Truth is not easy for the finite mind to comprehend.

What you operate on in the thesis of functioning of science and psychology, is only a thesis of being. They are only true to the state of expression by the being's awareness of comprehension of functional operation. Man sets himself up as an absolute authority that this is so. However, this is not so, because it is brought about in a thesis condition and theorized, then scientifically presented, but never fully proven. It is only proven to the thesis state, but never to fact. You will find that a little of the thesis functioning, by which you function, will fall away a little each day. You will find that which you accept as the total, as well as science accepts as the total, will be blown away by some young person that does not know the difference, because they were never told that it couldn't be done.

Each day, man is bombarded with the Truths of Universal Expression. How many times have you gotten an idea on how to do something and you couldn't understand why it continued to be done in such a complex fashion? The most obvious is overlooked so many times. However, those that don't know, don't know that it's not that obvious. You will find Truth in the same way if you only allow It to have Its opportunity of expression.

Never accept anything as being the full of All, because in your consciousness, many of the things you have accepted as hard core facts are going to fall away and be replaced many times over the next few years. You will find that many of the things you have accepted as the absolute and the total of the ultimate in perfectness, are only the shadow of the small foothill near the mountain.

You have much growing and expanding to do. I wish that each of you would take one thing into consideration: **All the things I explain to you, if you can't accept it at first, do not dismiss it. Just set it aside** as you will have great need for it at a future time. Everything is given to you for a reason in its space, time and function to be placed into your thought pattern so that it will start stimulation of expression and demand time and space in form for expression. This is the only way it can come about.

Man is love, beauty and all durability for all eternity.

You were made eternal. You are indestructible even though you think you aren't. You will last throughout eternity. You may come and go, changing form and personality, but you are very durable and pliable. You can be re-molded easily, as you adapt yourself to the different steps of eternity, which are the formulation of Full Life in Expression. That is why the life man was to express in, existed before man was conscious of his existence.

Memory Cells

Man already knew of everything there was before it could come into existence. There isn't anything that you don't know, only you just seem to have forgotten. You have a small veil-like membrane that is spread about and holds in lock the two memory cells that are located just in front of your knowledge bump. This is that cap-like protrusion at the back of your skull. There are two cells about the size of a pencil dot, located there. They contain all of the memories of your existences in expression of past, present and future. This is a real computer. However it is blocked by a membrane that will remain there until you are able to burn it away.

Your meditation and bringing the Light into your body will puncture holes into that membrane until it is ultimately burned away.

Meditation and Test For Truth

When you are in meditation, it is necessary to distinguish between astral communication and communication with the infinite. They are not the same. **Above all things, prove everything you receive. Tell it to stand forth in Truth and Light**. It will back away in a hurry if it is not. It will instantly be dissolved away if it is not in Truth because it cannot withstand the fires of Truth.

Anything that is being impressed upon you at any time should be placed to this test. If it is of Truth and it is of Light it will continue loud and clear. If it isn't, it will just fade away. It is one of the easiest ways of proofing and takes just a second.

Many have lost presence of expression and don't realize what has taken place with them. Even though they have lost their body they are still attracted to earth. They have their like-shape of their earth body and remain earth bound. They will try to kid you into accepting their association. Be very cautious when somebody speaks to you and says that they are the authority to have. They will try to hoodwink you. They are looking for a body to play with.

Be on your toes because if you lay yourself open, you can be very vulnerable and have some bad times. This is why I gave you that **CIRCLE OF LIGHT** affirmation to say each morning. This **places the White Light of protection about your aura.** Nothing out of Truth can or will penetrate the fire of that Light. If you do put the Circle of Light about you, you will never have to be concerned.

They will stand on the outside and try to talk in to get you to accept them. However, **when you are in question**, not doubt, but just in question **of information you are receiving which doesn't ring true, demand that it stand forth in Truth and Light.** If it isn't Truth, it will get quiet very quickly.

Too many things are not explained thoroughly enough by many teachers to give you the slight edge principle. I will inform you as you continuously grow and your abilities grow, so that you will be able to handle the exchange. As the time passes in the exchanging, you will begin to know a new value of expression and of being that you have always longed for, that all of a sudden becomes a vivid part of your activity.

Poise and Authority

You will also attain unto a poise condition where your graciousness will give you the control of situations where you will never have to raise your voice or employ any manner of force because you will learn to speak with authority. You don't have to raise your voice or be forceful to be authoritative.

When you are in the Conscious condition of projecting something, you are the authority, and the authority is speaking through you. Many will fear this due to your authoritative projection, because they will be unable to realize the exchange is taking place for they are in question of where the authority is coming from. Truth comes from many different places and in many different ways.

Many times the Truth will just flow out without your ever being able to realize how it got on the tip of your tongue. Let it go ahead and flow and never question it. Be prepared for someone to ask of you, "Where did that come from?" You will never be questioned about your authority. When somebody speaks in authority, it has a ring to it that doesn't even become questioned.

God or the Father

We use the word God very loosely, and we give much terminology in multiple of expansion in misunderstanding as to what God is. **It really should be the Kingdom of Light, rather than the Kingdom of God. Rather than God, to me it is Father** because it is the Father who talks to me.

When you arrive to the point that you leave consciousness to the Conscious state, you are no longer in the multiples of confusion. You have one set principle which is Universal. This gives you the full Force of authority. In your future, there will be a time when that voice that is as quiet as the wind whispering, will speak like thunder to you. There will be no mistaking that voice when it speaks. You will know it is the Father.

He will test you many times and will call you by name, in the most familiar voices to test how alert you are. The only answer when your name is called is, "**Yes, Father.**" If you do not answer in this way, it will be a while before your name is called again. And why is this? It is to get you aware to be Conscious at all times of the Universal activity, rather than physical reflection.

The Perfect Kingdom of Heaven: Paradise

Take yourself into the perfect Kingdom of Heaven, which is a perfect expression of Paradise; you are in Paradise. Don't let anybody kid you, this is Paradise. This Earth is one of the most beautiful places for expression that was ever brought into being by creation.

Paradise

You will know you are in Paradise when you learn three things:

Grace of Love
Poise of Authority
Peace of Gentleness and Kindness

Paradise.

When you learn the three things: the grace of love, the poise of authority and the peace of meekness (being gentle and kind), you will know that you are in Paradise.

In the presentation of the Kingdom of Heaven, I've heard of certain ones that have their section already cordoned off. I don't know where it is but they claim it is out there, and you can only get in if you belong to their group.

Your heaven, the Kingdom of Heaven, is responsible to your **agreement of consciousness of expression; that is your heaven**. You can make this a place of utter joy or you can make this a place of remorse. This you do by your own improper thinking and improper programming. You can conform yourself to the acceptance of anything that you desire to express into, or you can master any condition to rise above the conformities and generalities of the majority.

You are going to learn to be in it but not of it. This is the first step of attaining the Kingdom of Heaven.

Everything that is in the consciousness of our expression from the conscious state, is in a multiple of triangles and squares, the principle being triune and the basis of the foundation being the square. These give forth to you the elements of control of the three Primary and the four Secondary Suns. The triangle gives you full control within your Whole Breath to attain your kingdom. Through your Whole Breath you are Whole-in-One. This breath brings forth the "Life in my blood," and, "My Life is in your blood."

Your direct health is reflected in your consciousness of your breath. When you are in unison with the Universe by Breath, you are triadic. In the fulfillment of the Whole Breath with expression, you become the foundation of everything that is about you as you were given dominion over everything, and everything must bow to your authority.

If you broadcast poor authority, your followers are bewildered. If you become quiet and know the Truth, exerting your authority in your breath, and by the proper application of your projection, then you become an authority unto everything with which you come into contact. You shall be known by your mark. What do you leave behind you?

Your Perfect State of Projection

Others will question what you know that they don't know when Truth is presented, for Truth has a way of attaining unto Itself. Above all things, be honest with yourself. You may be able to kid others but you can't kid yourself. That little voice, sometimes referred to as your conscience, tells you that you did it again and you know it. When you go counter to your inner prompting, you are taking yourself out of your Kingdom of Heaven. You are taking yourself out of your perfect state of Poise if you alter to less than your perfect state of projection or your standard of Be.

Everything should be projected in a perfect state of the consciousness in love. How would you want someone to do unto you? Do unto others as you would want them to do unto you. In this way you will begin to understand that the exchange, when done in love, will result in no remorse in the exchange whatsoever. There will be a poise and grace in this type of exchange.

It will bring forth a creative bond where your relationship will be sought rather than rejected. The only way you will ever get rid of an enemy is by loving that enemy. The only way you will replace doubt and misunderstanding is by an authoritative projection: a thorough explanation that is acceptable. When you attempt to explain something to somebody else, keep it on a level they are able to comprehend easily and thoroughly.

As with water, it all seeks its level. When you talk to somebody, you don't go down to their level, you bring them up to your level. When you go to any lower level, you are lessening your authority. Speak with authority and they will rise to your authority. Nothing grows unless it has something to attain unto that has more to offer. If you watch a small bush grow, it is continuously spiraling up so it can get more sun, more energy and more light.

We are the same way. As we grow, we spiral up, too. We are spiraling through the shifting of thoughts, and in the shifting of these thoughts, we come into the condition of **primary cause: mankind**. We have a lot of confusion going on because a lot of people don't know where they are going, why they are going, what they are going for or why they did go. They are all going in circles.

How many times have we had our toes stepped on only to find out ultimately that we were right? We didn't have the ability to stand our ground and prove that we were right.

In a lesser than perfect expression we have allowed ourselves to be hoodwinked into believing that each day is a continuation of the remembering of what was forgotten. Whereas in reality, it should be one day continuously in memory, projected. You really haven't forgotten anything, you have just misplaced it. It is still there waiting for beckoning when you have need of it.

You possess all the powers of creation. You have the ability to control all of the forces of the universe. Within you, there lies a dynamo of Light in motion, lovingly and tenderly expressing exchange of condition. By your keenness of your awareness, you will change your state of confusion into a state of heaven, until you have attained a peace and poise about yourself that others will seek, while wondering why, in the midst of such confusion, you are able to **be at peace with yourself**.

As you grow, you will find that it will be that way because you have learned to be in it but not of it. Learn to separate yourself instantly from that which is untruth. You don't have to belittle anybody by their misunderstanding, you can only give them a word of caution. Remember that **you are a law unto**

yourself. You are not yourself unto a law. Here is another point to always remember. **You are not your brother's keeper.**

Discernment and Projection of Thought

Your creative ability brought one thing with you that was covered in your last lesson, which is your creative thought ability. **You will become the sum and substance of your thinking. By your values of discernment, which will become very keen as you grow, you will not be as vulnerable** as you presently are to the conformities of projections about you.

You will begin to evaluate all conditions that exist around you in a different way. You will alter those conditions to bring a poise with yourself in an area that you are expressing with and in.

On an average, you evaluate over 3,000,000 thoughts per second. When you have attuned yourself to a functional keenness, it will be close to one billion. This sounds fantastic, but when you consider the amount of computerization that is in your muscular system and the glandular system of your body, that makes your entire system work in functional response, then you will begin to realize how many thoughts and activities of energization it takes from the master computer and sub-computer to make your form project and activate, continuously caring for itself regardless of your inefficiency of breath.

Learn that you are the power, and learn that in this creative part that you make heaven upon this earth by taking time to still your breath, making perfect thought molds to project as you breathe out, so that you correct the conditions about you without ever uttering a word. Your thought can do a thousand times more than any speech of hours upon hours. By just one breath, once released clearly, everybody on this earth is going to be bombarded by it. Whereas, only those within the distance of the volume of your voice exchanging can hear. Your thought is heard throughout the universe.

How many times have you started to do something that you had planned to do and in a split second gone on to do something else? Have you ever analyzed why? Here is where your discernment of thought comes in: the impression of the discernment of thought. The necessity of you being in a certain place in a certain time makes this alteration necessary.

That thought will be impressed upon you to condition you to be where you should be at the proper time. Your best set plans will be altered when these conditions arise.

Inner Voice: Sixth Sense

When you have an impression to change a condition, follow that consciousness to the letter exactly as presented to you. This is the first training you will have as an authority. The more that you respond to the keenness of these projections, the quicker and keener the sensitivity of these will become. If you deny them, they will nullify until you are unable to hear them any longer. **Learn to rely on your inner senses, your feelings.** Listen to your feelings. When you have that gut feeling, listen, or you will have consequences.

Learn to be keen with the perception of the inner voice and the feeling of the inner voice within you until you have full control of communication with it. This is your sixth sense working. Feeling is a composite of all five of your natural senses coming into a unity of one. When you learn to respond to this force, which is part of the creative activity with you, responding to you, it will bring you into your heaven here on earth. The more that you respond to this, the greater you build the expansion of your heaven.

This was the Kingdom of God, but due to your inefficiency, you lessened your ability until you have lost control of everything but thought. That is one thing that is held in control for you as it was the only way you could find your way back. All of the others of the lesser state of being that were in your dominion, allowed you to alter them as you altered yourself, as you came from your exchange of your Kingdom of God into your Kingdom of Heaven, until you have made a kingdom of hell for yourself to exist in.

In the exchange, if you were in true consciousness, everything that is in expression with you would be in communication with you. Everything is communicating to you, but you can't hear. Your senses are not fine enough in tuning for the exchange with all the other dominions that are functioning with you for your necessity so that you have a place of being. They are continuously replacing your "heaven" of habits so that you will have a place of habit. Yet, a place of habit is a place of hell.

Evaluate Everything You Do

If you were in the consciousness of control, then you would be in heaven. Now what is your level of heaven? In a few minutes, it could make you very angry, which wouldn't be much of a heaven. In those same few minutes, I could raise you to the source of heights that you would be in paradise. By your ability of acceptance in allowing the swaying that others impose their thinking upon you so that you don't question the results, you are taken from your kingdom. Evaluate everything that you are given. That is why you are given the value of **discernment**. You evaluate over 3,000,000 thoughts per second so that you do keep yourself in a perfect state of heaven.

If you drop your guard, allowing others to authorize over you, then you become to their dominion. You give up your authority; you lose your ability of authority.

In Truth, there are two classes: master and slave. Now which are you? Where are you placing yourself and why? If you are not master, why? If you are not in control of the situation, why? If things are not functioning as you feel they should, why?

Evaluate everything before you act. Learn to consider all consequences before you move. Don't move wild with the wind, because you heap much misery upon yourself by your inefficiency of control. Learn to be authoritative in everything that you do. Evaluate everything you do, so that, you evaluate all of the consequences of everything that will take place from that act. For everything that you alter by your change, you are now responsible. Your heaven can become a hell very quickly by your erroneous programming and overstepping your bounds.

Forgive Yourself

When you do make a mistake, forgive yourself and ask others to forgive you for your shortcomings. Then try not to make the same mistake twice. You can forgive everybody else quicker than you will forgive yourself You will punish yourself many times over, much more than you will punish others. **Be gentle to yourself, love yourself and learn to forgive yourself** in your own inability of understanding until you grow in the poise to have the control of that understanding and that peace within yourself.

In the consciousness that we are in, we have to add the "ness" to the conscious because we have multiples of divisions of the conscious of being. Due to these multiples of our being, we have made a multiple of everything expressing equally with us. Every word that you utter affects everything on this earth. You can't have them back once you let go of them. However, you can take time to think about it before you let go so that you do not contaminate the universe as you contaminate yourself. Learn to evaluate yourself in the acceptance of your projection as you release. You won't hurt nearly as much. It will become easier and easier the more that you use it.

When you are wrong, admit it. So what? Everybody makes mistakes. Don't be ashamed to admit you are wrong. You grow by being able to admit because this is a part of forgiving yourself, and don't try to make the same mistake twice. You have been at this for three and one-half billion years and you aren't going to make a change in two days, so be gracious to yourself and make this heaven a perfect place to express in. Only by your perfectness of expression can anything change. Only by your perfectness of exchange can your Kingdom of God come into effect.

After you pass Paradise then you pass into the Kingdom of God. "And in pairs, I do advise," it makes it interesting, doesn't it? You are duality. You are both masculine and feminine, in equal.

Look Back to See the Future

In our quest of the consciousness of being, we have to look back to know the future. When we look back, we understand the future. By our association of memory, we can look back at the time when travel by foot was as fast as you were able to travel across the land. Now we travel at thousands of miles per hour. What is present is the exchange between the two mediums of past and future.

The consciousness of all things had to be before it could be. Everything that is in the future is from the past or you would have no memory of its being.

When the inventor designs something new and wonderful, it is because he remembered what he had forgotten that he used to do when he had that condition or that problem to overcome.

Proof: how many times have you gone to sleep with a problem and when you awakened in the morning, you instantly had the answer? Where did you go to have the answer? You went into the past. In your multiples upon multiples of expressions, nothing is new. However, when you put it into a quest, the subconscious takes over and projects it into the memory banks, which feed back to you to have in this expression.

All alterations from the Truth came from the past. The zero point from the past was the future when you were perfect; you are only returning to that from which you came. You are going in circles.

In all things of expression, everything that you use in operation daily is a copy from your body. Everything that you use for physical exchange, as you look about you, is a physical copy from the body. Everything you use in mechanical exchange is a duplication from a part of your body.

Just consider a levering condition of lifting a heavy load from a wedge point by the balancing of a bar from a lever point so that when you pull, you have a five times greater factor on the opposite end than you could if the lever were equal. Did you ever consider the hinge in your arm? The hinge in your back? All of the machinery you have is a copy from the body because the inventor went to the source for the idea of construction.

We now have computers that work faster than you can think. Don't kid yourself, there is no computer that is able to work as fast as you can. What it is thinking of, you have already forgotten.

Learn to Be Authoritative

In the conscious state of being, your ability to control the conscious exchange of awareness is where your authority lies. **When you know that you know, nobody can change your mind because you know that is correct.** But when you don't know that you don't know, anybody can change your mind. Learn to be authoritative, and when you don't understand something, learn to be gracious enough to admit that you will entertain another's projection until you can further evaluate it for yourself.

Anything I tell you, I do not want you to accept as absolute, but **I want you to evaluate for yourself** for your ability of acceptance. What I tell you today will not be true for tomorrow because you are constantly in a state of exchange. What I give you as true today as the true state is only in the true state attaining unto the Truth. This is because the bewilderment would be so great if I heaped the truth unto you, there would be no way that you be able to conceive of it. By a conscious state of consciousness to the Conscious, we bring the states of true unto Truth. Due to your awareness of growth, it will continuously alter as you let go of the old conditions that you have allowed to shackle yourself.

In your continuous growth in Conscious will be your ability of letting go of the old and making a total exchange for the new. One thing to remember: **nothing is ever conquered**. In a short span of time, that conqueror will be absorbed and only the good of its projections will be accepted and all the rest will be rejected. Regardless of the rule being projected that is set down, if it doesn't meet your standards, you will not tolerate it. On the surface, you will entertain it, but you will not tolerate it within because you know it will not ring true.

The Divine Principle of Your Being

When somebody tells you to do something wrong, what happens to you? You rebel, don't you? **When you don't think something is right, say so**. If they don't like it, they have a problem. You will be surprised at how much better you feel and you won't have it eating you alive. Teddy Roosevelt said it best, "Speak softly and carry a big stick."

This is very important that you learn the **Divine Principle of your being: Nobody has the right to enter your kingdom without your permission**. Within yourself, don't let anybody change you. **Become perfect within yourself, as you are**. Be the fullness that you were given to express in, and bring forth the necessity of your being in that expression. Become conscious of yourself. Become conscious of all things that you associate with. Become conscious of why you are in this association.

There is a lesson learned in everything that you do. Every day that you awaken back into expression, is another lesson of living awaiting you. Until you conquer one problem, you will be continuously given it until you do. Otherwise, it will absorb you if you don't. When you learn to conquer everything that is placed in your way, becoming an authority over it, you will be surprised what peace and poise can be attained and how quickly.

Learn to Exert Your Authority

When something has to be said, say it and get it into an understanding. You don't have to be argumentative, nor do you have to be antagonistic with it. Learn to speak with understanding, to be conscious of why this condition exists. There has to be an answer to everything. You have your right of your view of expression as well as anybody else does. Learn to exert your authority.

In the revolutionary days, they had a flag that fits this situation perfectly. It showed a rattle snake with the inscription: "Don't tread on me."

Learn to be that which is necessary for the time, the place and the condition. Learn to condition yourself for the exchange. Remember, this is your heaven, make it so. Your Universal Creed is: I am eternally free, which is my nature, and I bow to no one, not even God, for I am God.

As long as you keep that in front of you, you will be in heaven, otherwise you will be in hell. **If you will listen to that inner voice and learn to have it for your guide, you will divert almost all of your problems.**

All of you walk through the valley of death to the shadows of questioning, fearing not of those who fear and jeer, for you are the Truth and you are the one purpose and the one way.

There will be no darkness in your way for you have walked through the shadows of death. When your purpose be single, you cannot be swayed in any way from the point of attainment. That is when you are authorized. Don't allow yourself to be diverted from your path.

Why belittle that which is perfect, and you are perfect; you haven't remembered as yet.

If You Had This Day to Live Over

If you had this day to live over, what would you do differently? If you had nothing to do over again, then you were in heaven; you were perfect. If things weren't in that totality of order, then you weren't in heaven. You cheated yourself out of your heaven because you allowed others to affect your condition. You are a void of expression. Who is more important than you are?

There is only one place at the top of the hill. If you step on anyone as you climb to the top of that hill, you will be stepped upon on the way down. Therefore, forgive yourself for each day for each thing done wrongly, for if you do not, they will become multiples and eat you alive. Forgive yourself each night as you review your day before going to sleep. **Everything that wasn't in absolute perfectness, readjust it and forgive it before you go to sleep.** Allow yourself enough time each day to do this. It is one of the most **invaluable** moments that you can spend. What a peaceful night of rest you will have! Whereas, you will have utter torment if you do not.

Learn to love yourself, be gentle with yourself and learn to forgive yourself. After all, this is paradise that you are in; make it exactly that.

Man: A Law Unto Himself

Now let us consider the primary cause of all: Man. Man is the last creation of the Triune Spirit of God, and therefore, was the most ideal creation, molded in the form and possessing all the powers of the Power that created him. This means that he is all forms, all the intelligence, all the forces and all the Truth. He is love, beauty and all durability for all eternity. The life that he was to express in, existed even before man was conscious of his existence.

Man's laws alter, but laws of Universal Principle never change. Man never changes, but hued-man [human] is subject to conditions of many variations. Everything in the Universe is formulated in conditions of triangles, circles and squares. If you go back to the oldest engineering on this Earth in our history, you will find that those engineers used triangles, circles and squares. This was used to set up all their buildings in construction, and they worked to a thirty thousandth of an inch of degree of angle. The work that they accomplished, cannot be duplicated by our electronic instruments of today.

Remember this Truth and let it be a foundation of your faith.
Each man is a law unto himself, not himself unto a law.

As your lesson states about faith, you are going to have faith until you **Know Truth.** The day that you learn Truth, you will be unto yourself a Law, then you will come into full order of Universal Expression.

Cultivate Clear Thought

Man continuously uses his best attribute as the greatest weapon against himself. He uses thinking, instead of Thought. He continuously alters himself with his massive unproductive correlation of thinking. However, if man will learn to quiet himself and use his proper rate of breath, so he has the values of discernment in his favor, he can save himself a lot of time lost by having to do things over a second and third time.

When you awaken to the cold facts to see that your *"stinkin' thinkin"* has made a folly by not allowing Thought to have its ability of projection in making you aware of all conditions and all things in function, not just a part of it, then you won't have to continually adjust to the effects of the cause and effect conditions. **Allow the quietness during the pause of your breath for broadcasting and receiving**, for your values of **discernment** in your Spirituality Cone to have their chance to work with you to give you the rapport of Thought Itself.

Most of the time you don't listen and you don't hear, because you are too busy thinking about what was previously said, in order to hear. When it plays back to you, all that you get is garbage. One of the abilities you have to cultivate is **clear-thought: Dismiss everything that enters in requesting form, when you are imprinting something that you are receiving. Then, your recall will be exact and accurate.** When you do this and allow the printing as well as the impression of Spirit and Mind activity to encompass you completely, you will be greatly benefited by the awareness you will accomplish.

It will come to such a point that when somebody starts to say something, if you quiet yourself, you will know whether it is true or not. You will develop to such a point of keen awareness, you will know what somebody will say before they say it. This is one of the keys into learning for the control of self.

Man's only Heaven can be by knowing. By planting his thoughts into life, man has made all things that he is now aware of. "Made" means to be manifested in a hewed process of molecular structure of change. Everything that is about us that we have made, we have altered and conditioned the molecules by rearranging the magnetic field about us. We do the same thing to the flesh of our body. Later on you will learn how to turn the cells of your body back to Light. You will turn each molecule back to an atom.

> *Man can never be other than he thinks he is, for thought, as we learned in the preceding lesson, is the only creative part of himself that man has saved. It is now the only heaven that man can know. By "planting" his thoughts into life, man has made all things that he is now aware of. He has shut himself away from the true Heaven because he would not permit other creations to keep their own particular powers.*

All awareness of the Truths of the Universe are functioning in Mind conditions, being bombarded continuously through the Spirituality Cone by your brain. It is utilized from Force, by energy, into power to be utilized by the physical body into energy to conduct the nervous, circulatory and respiratory systems of your body, also, to hold your flesh in form. If you did not have the consciousness of any creation other than man, you would not be aware of any other creation. You wouldn't know I'm here or anybody else. You would be all alone. There would be nothing else existing simultaneously with you.

It is because you continuously broadcast with your thought emanations into the Eth that surrounds you, and because you make all other creations lesser than your creation, valid and functional into your rapport, you may have the association of their being. No one of you could exist without each other, as there would be no living to take place.

Without the flowers to aid you in their fragrance and beauty, and their ability to change the gases that you expel from your body back into oxygen and the fruit that they produce for you to have nectar to feed your flesh, you would find it extremely difficult to exist without them. There would be no association with any of the other planes of perfection.

Consciousness: Knowing

> ***You must come to know that you are the Universe and the fullness thereof, in the spiritual sense.*** *This spiritual*

awareness casts its radiance upon the individual mind of man to be utilized by the physical body. Now, in the Spirit, Mind and Body of man is the knowledge of all creation and all phases of all creation, because the Creator of all, created him. Prove this to yourself: If you did not have the consciousness of any creation other than man, you would not be aware of other creations. A rose would not exist for you, nor would any animal or bird. You would know only man, and all other creations would be farther away from you than the Angels, who dwell in their created plane of perfection. You may know of the Angels through hearsay, but not through actual association. You may believe they exist, but until you see them, you won't be truly aware of their being.

The consciousness of all is in each, and the consciousness of each is in all. Consciousness means knowing, capable of activity upon, that is knowing in all actuality, to be able to associate with, to harmonize, to have harmonious relations with.

This paragraph sounds like a lot of double talk, but actually it contains a lot of seeds being planted at this time. You will have no need for these beyond knowing, when you know, that you know that you know. Because if you don't know, then you don't know. There is no halfway measure on knowing; all of the rest is illusion which really doesn't exist.

Each of you has the consciousness of all things. *All have their harmonious relationship with the vibratory sense of their counterpart in you, but you are not aware of this consciousness. For example, if you were aware of the conscious action of the divine principle of a bird, you would converse and communicate with that bird. And so it is with all creation. You are conscious of their form, but you are not aware of your relationship to them.*

Each consciousness has its own metes and bounds, and expresses in its own way, but all consciousness is related to a part of all other consciousness. Each consciousness is a plane of vibration;

> *it has always existed and always will exist. For example, when you lived in a age when the tallow candle was used for light, you were not aware of the electrical consciousness. However, the electrical consciousness did exist, or you never could have become aware of it. And so it is with all things, all do exist. There are some things in your present state of awareness you do not comprehend, but the time will come when you enter into the perfect state where you are truly aware of all things.*

If you were able to raise or lower your consciousness to the divinity of their consciousness, you could communicate with them as easily as you do with each other. Everything that exists in expression in our dimension has the ability of vocal expression, even from the crystal on up. If you don't think so, consider that no radio or transistor could function without them.

Everything in existence that is expressing, is formulated in the lymph system of itself with the aid of crystals existing there. There are magnetic reflections and ionizing activity that express within the consciousness of the crystals of each dimension of expression that give it its audible range of communication.

Your abilities in decibels of audible range are not actually keen enough to hear all the sounds going on about you. You hear with 1/1000 of your ability of sound control. You are really quite limited in your flesh condition to your comprehension of sound. Also, when you speak of frequencies, there are so many that it is impossible to put a number to them. The only way you could say it is to put it in multiples of each, simultaneously in all directions at the same time. That would give you a little idea of Universal Expression in activity.

It is easy now for you to comprehend the availability of the energy forces and powers of electricity that you use today. But some in this room can remember when there were kerosene lamps, and didn't know of the existence of electricity. Yet, it was the dream of man to have the same light at night that he had in the day. It is like many things that man has become automatically aware of, by the exchange of ideas and ideals, so that he should become conscious because of the ideal that has become fact due to the idea in reception from the projection of Universal Source. You already know of all of them, otherwise they couldn't exist nor could they come into being.

There is really nothing new, it just seems that we have lost the ability of control. When it is brought about, then you very readily will accept it. As with most things that you do, after three times, they become habit.

It is not only the changes and the acceptance of them, but the ability to adapt to the conditions of acceptance. Only one problem arises from sophisticated gadgetry: you lose your ability of perfection of control, for it begins to control you. If you doubt this, turn your electricity off for one week, or jog to work and leave the car in the garage.

The Consciousness of vibration activity and its limitation of expression and your state of awareness to that expression, gives you the comprehension of time, in time and of time, because all of it took place in space. In the Perfect State, space does not exist. Space only exists due to the unawareness of the awareness of Truth. Space is the common denominator between all activities. It is also the common denominator of all vibration expression. Its color is Grey.

This is why, as you watch a sunset, it will beautifully cast off to the blue-grey, before it turns into darkness. If you see an old run-down building with the love taken away from it, it will turn grey, too. Everything discarded and cast away will fade to grey, which is space, as all expression has been taken out.

> *Your thought is the shadow of the awareness of your Spirit which faces that perfect plane of expression. Because your perfect Spirit receives from God, all consciousness, you must connect your Spirit to your body through your thought action. When this contact is complete, you will have arrived at that blessed state of perfect consciousness.*

Control of Consciousness

When you have control of consciousness by Conscious, everything will bow to your command. All turmoil and temperaments of conditions are the making of your own confusion. All you have to do is to say, "Stop," and everything will stop. However, if you allow it to build in momentum, it will run away with itself, leaving you totally confused. When spoken with authority, it has got to stop. Learn to be an authority to yourself and all things unto yourself.

Learn to say things with authority, yet in a very loving way, for the good of all.

In your awareness of your projection of your authority, all nature will obey. Remember that when you were created, you were given dominion over everything. Always remember that, because as you make false proclamations, you also bind yourself by that same condition.

In our act of expressing, most of us are in a "bound" condition. We are always in a lived condition: past tense instead of living. We are so bound to that which we have not let go of, that we are unable to get away from it.

Love, Trust and Understanding

Living in perfect love and the authority of perfect trust, brings about the condition of perfect understanding. The three have to go hand in hand because if you are not in love, there could be no trust. If there were not love and trust, there would not be perfect understanding.

What do you look to for authority? One that you can trust and love. You know what you will receive will be love and understanding regardless of the condition that faces you. Isn't that why you seek the counsel and aid of others? Only then would you evaluate their understanding and accept it.

True love will become the perfect quest of perfect understanding of all functions of operations of consciousness. Throughout all eternity, man was created to love, bless and control, but control does not mean for you to authorize. Control means the ability of adjustment.

Man was given the dominion over everything, but he also gave of himself so that everything else could exist because everything else, in image, was the reflection towards his plane of being. Each plane was one of the steps man would have passed to learn to understand to attain his flesh body until he would have dominion over, and yet serve all creation.

When man becomes selfless, the perfect state of being, putting everything above self, he becomes the master of all. Only then, shall you have the Kingdom of God.

Proof: to have dominion over does not mean to have an iron-clad rule. It means an association of perfect poise and rapport with each other, a total balance of equality and an equal share of everything for each one of all creation. Man has one ability that those planes subservient to his were not given, for man was given the knowledge of the awareness of all consciousness contained in life.

The other planes of creation: the animal, the fowl, the vegetable and mineral were only given phases of this consciousness in expression. This is why they are subservient to man. This is why they function only in a perfect state of heaven. My statement proved you exist in paradise, because now you know that this is paradise and you know why it was attained to and how.

If you were not a loving, forgiving, selfless master, I would not wish to share your kingdom.

In this most beautiful temple that was not built by hands, which you have the privilege of expressing in, with, for and by, you will bring back the eternal consciousness of **conscious: the perfect state of being** where you can change this paradise into the Kingdom of God. In my Father's House, there are many mansions, and each of you is a pillar of those mansions. If this were not so, I would not have told you.

Paradise2.

There is not one speck of sand in this universe that the Father is not aware of. There is not one tree that falls in the forest, or one leaf that falls from the tree without Him being aware of the motion. He who created everything in one thought, is aware of all activity that takes place in that expression. We are so indoctrinated by thinking in one direction at a time, it is very difficult to comprehend **multiples of motions, simultaneously in all directions at the same time**.

You will encounter that statement many times until you attain the awareness of it.

If you will look in the ancient **hieroglyphics** of Egypt, you will see these two symbols in their picture writings when they refer to the Kingdom of Heaven and the Kingdom of God.

When these two triangles are placed one over the other with a dot in the absolute center, a Star of David is formed which depicts the **Absolute Conscious.** This is the pair-I-dise [Paradise].

My Life Is In Your Blood

In my Life, which is in your blood, the triangle, the square and the circle are the major elements of the Kingdom of Life of your blood. There are minute crystal formations of light itself solidified into crystalline form that flow in your blood, which are the major crystals of energy for your Life substance.

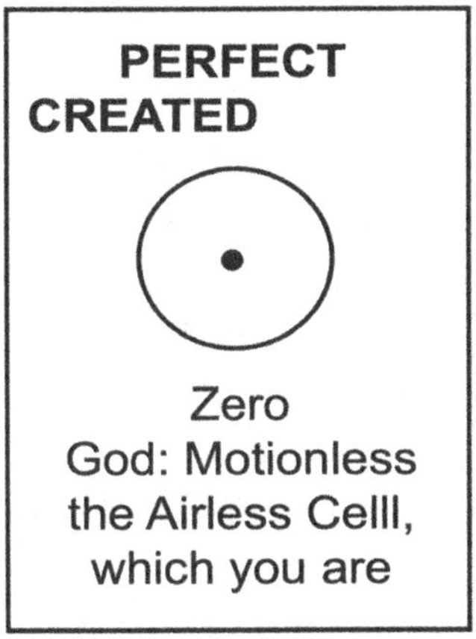

Perfect created.

In the triangle, you will find the Mind: Kingdom.

In the square, you will find the Physical: Heaven.

In the circle, you will find the Spirit: God.

"My Life is in your blood," and so it is in Truth. All of the life in miniature crystalline form which is held in all plant forms is brought into your digestive system, and released into your blood to feed the cells of your body by atomic implosions from the blood stream to your cells.

A perfect created plane is zero, or God: Motionless. The circle in it is also the Airless Cell, which you are. All of the rest of us that we see is the reflection of the imaging of the reflection, in agreement of conformity of the reflected values of shadows.

By each breath, we take in millions of universes. Man is the fullness of universes in expression. He creates either his heaven or hell, which is his own state of being. The standards of intellect pervade man's academic environment in learning and cultural standards of acceptance.

Force, Thought and Truth

By Force, we refer to the purpose in activity of Intelligence of Universal expression. We have an exchange of Force to operate the flesh body. All man-made things operate upon the principle of power, such as the appliances we have in our homes, as well as those which have the ability to convey us.

When we learn in truth to operate and use Force, we will float across the ground and have no need of such conveyances. By Thought, we are able to cover thousands of miles in a split second as we disassemble and reassemble our body. You will then levitate to any height; you can move any object with your eyes. Your potential is beyond your belief.

Man has descended through vain states of truth, starting from Truth, not quite so true, to maybe, might be so, to untruth, a falsity, a darkness and total darkness, down to shadow effects. All of this is due to the intellect acceptance.

By Truth, we refer to the fullness of the state of All. However, man's truth changes from intellectual interception.

Enduring Time

All ancient designs of buildings were based on triangles, circles and squares in a basic design of divine creation. This is the universe of our bodies. In those things that have withstood the elements of time, your monument of the Pyramid of Giza is over thirty-four thousand years old. This has gone through fourteen earth histories. It has been below water seven different times. Yet it stands in its fullness as it was in the days of its assembling.

When something is energized in its elements of itself together, it will endure time. Your body was designed to last for seven thousand years of expression. You burn it up in less than seventy.

By this proclamation of your own exchange, I don't think you have found heaven, yet. Life begins at forty; that's one-fifth of your span. At forty years of age, the perfect roundness of your cells is attained.

Man was given seven days, of God's days, to express upon this earth. Each of the Father's days is one thousand years. Man was given these days so that you would have the right of dominion of exchange with each creation equally in one thousand years. Your body, therefore, was built to last for seven thousand years. Now, you can see the application of that statement, and you know what Paradise is. That one expression is seven thousand years in a Pure Physical body of Light. Flesh is the image of reflections of your shadows.

Transforming Your Bodies From Flesh To Pure Physical

These lessons are for you to learn to transform your body from flesh back to Pure Physical and bring back the perfect condition of **health** into your body **and** to bring back all of your **awareness** that is sleeping in your senses back into perfect rapport.

Is that in a flesh condition or Pure Physical?

That is in Pure Physical, which becomes a body of Light. You have lessened your Physical into a physical flesh condition, you have limited yourself in your expression. **That is what these teachings are all about: to teach you to attain from the flesh to the Physical, so that you may light your body and take it with you.** Otherwise, you will continue to burn up the cells of your flesh body, returning to this earth until you do. This cycle of continuation of burning up the cells of your flesh body is your continuation of hell.

Jesus said, *"The meek shall inherit the earth,"* and believe me, they will. Until you become an authority unto yourself, you shall inherit this earth. Until you become the authority to make the exchange, making the change, there is no way out for you. That is what all of this Truth is about.

You have twelve senses; the seven of those that are sleeping are the most important. As it is now, you operate on five. Even the animals operate on six. If you will be patient, you will attain this. It took you three and a half billion years to descend to this level, but it is possible to perfect your body in one half of a normal expression.

Jesus came to show you that this could be attained. He said,

> *"I am the Light and I am the way, and I shall In-Light you unto the Father. I come to give you the Truth of this enlightenment so that you shall find your way back into the Kingdom of God and make this inheritance of heaven a Paradise."*

You said half of a span. What is that?

Half of a span is 35 years of the 70 years of the normal span of expression. Jesus was 32 years at the time of the Crucifixion. At that time, a normal span of expression was 42 years.

How many have attained in all of these centuries and where do they exist?

Many have achieved and are now in other dimensions throughout the universe. They go on and on, or **they may come back as emissaries just as I have come back to earth. I came by request not by choice because I long ago have surpassed this earth**. As you grow in authority, you have right of choice.

Suns of the Universe

This universe is so large that it is difficult for you to imagine the enormity of its size. I will give you a comparison. If you took a fourteen foot square of a canvas and placed a pencil dot in the center, that is how large your earth would be in comparison to the White Sun.

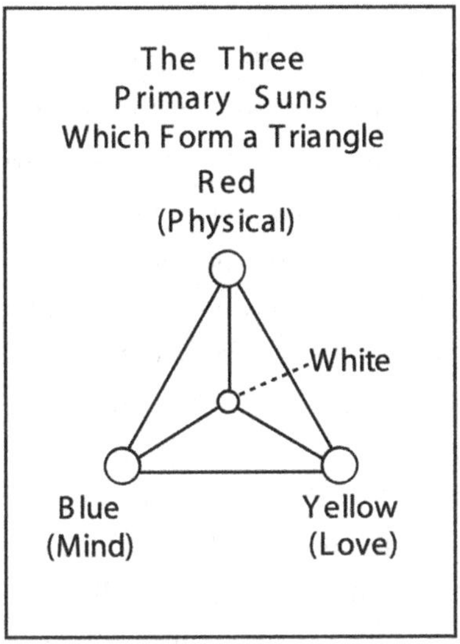

The three primary Suns.

The White Sun is the Intelligence that informs us of all consciousness at this level. It is what directs our quadrant and is not a planet. Planets are birthed by suns. The White Sun is not even a Cardinal Sun. It is out of that range.

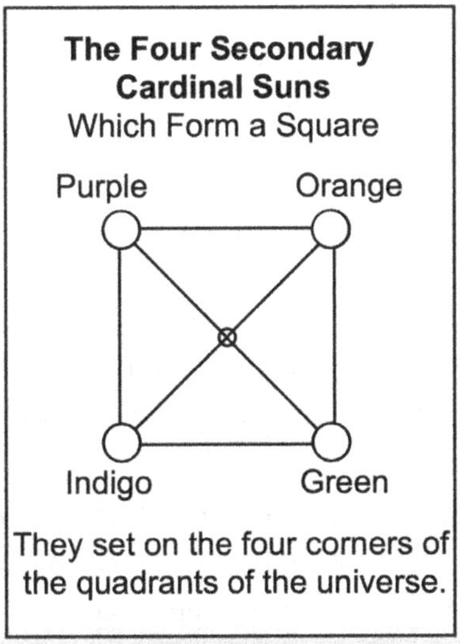

The four secondary Suns.

Is that similar to our sun?

Our sun is a lesser sun that illuminates our area of our twelve planet solar system. The White Sun, however, emits nothing but White Light, which is Intelligence. In addition to the White Sun, there are the three Primary Suns; the Red, Yellow and the Blue that form a triangle. Then there are the four Cardinal Suns which form a square. They set on the four corners of the quadrants of the universe, which are the Green, Orange, Indigo and Purple.

If you made a diamond between the Red, the Blue and the Yellow Suns, the White would be the opposite of the Blue. That is why we receive the Blue-White Light of sunlight at this planet. We are between the triangulation points of the Blue and White Suns. From the Primary triangle we have the Red for Physical, the Blue for Mind and the Yellow for Love.

The triangle is an enormous overlay condition upon the White Sun. Therefore, the energy traveling in the Blue of Mind carries the White of Intelligence with it which holds our planet in being and makes our sun function.

What is in the center of that quadrant?

The Central Sun, the home of the Father. That is the dead center of the universe. You are the same as the universe. You have a square and within that is the triangle. Within the triangle is a circle. When you fold the four corners together, you have a box and you become a cube. At the dead center of your cube is your Airless Cell. That is what I mean when I say that you are the universe and the fullness, thereof.

The Fall of Man

Those entities that attained their Light Bodies, were they people at one time?

Yes, and they will be people again. When they leave from the reflected condition of shadows, they are entities. They become personalities of Be.

How did they attain Pure Physical?

Many of them were here at the time of the transition. It was in that transition when they left their God state to become man. From their man state, they fell below their own level of consciousness to become hued-man [human].

When the feminine fell out of the masculine; the separation had to be allowed in order for man to attain its true state. As they separated, the feminine fell out of the masculine; the masculine could no longer lift the feminine from the ground and they were separated at the toes. The shadowing of the feminine is the exact duplicate of the masculine in reflection. They fell face out from each other. That is when man lost his authority.

Weren't they smart enough to see what was happening to them? How could this ever take place?

They took on the daughters of man as mates, and they became drunken within their own authority, losing their Force of purpose. They became bewildered within their own Force of purpose.

In Genesis, it tells you within the first seven stanzas of the first chapter, which encompasses seventeen million years of expression.

How could this ever take place? Now I'm going to ask you how many people attain to success only to lose it due to their inefficiency when it is attained? How many remain up there at the top without falling back? How many are able to hold the purpose so purposeless that they don't fall back?

I could show you a paper about the ten most successful men in the United States. Out of the ten most successful men back in 1948, seven died in prison for embezzlement and misappropriation of funds entrusted to them. These ten were from ten of the largest businesses in the United States. Two died in foreign countries and the last one died by his own hand.

I'm showing things can go wrong when you become too authorized if you don't have proper balance with it. One can become intoxicated by selfishness.

Universal vs. Flesh

Was that ever a problem for you?

I was here when this earth was created, living here for millions of years in the Perfect State. When you are in a flesh body, you act as flesh people do.

How do you protect yourself and why is that necessary?

You have to be an example, but you still stub your toes. How would you accept me if I just talked to you as a voice? Would you have listened if you just heard my voice telling you what you should be doing?

We allow ourselves to be in the same natural condition as you are, and because age is respected as authority, we show age. We show wrinkling of age because that is supposed to be the sign of Intelligence because you have experienced all things. We try to make everything as natural as possible for your acceptance. However, I have one advantage because I can leave at any time I want.

In accepting this flesh condition, you also accept the human frailties?

I allow certain things to take place within my form so that you would accept me as naturally as you would anybody else.

By being in control of the situation, you can make this body do anything that you want. You can become very tolerable to everything. You don't realize just how much that you really have. You don't realize the fullness that you really are. There is very little that has been explained and so much theory that has been accepted as fact. This tends to lead to more confusion to the Truth.

Most people are looking for the most they can get for the minimum that they have to do, instead of an equal exchange for an equal endeavor.

I'll ask you this question, how do you love? It is the growth of exchange of every day. You have to love or else you wouldn't tolerate it.

Are these lessons taught on other planets?

Between two and four AM, in our time wave, I lecture to the entire quadrant of this universe. Many times, your lessons will be heard during that interval while you are in your sleep state. This is perceived through your Spirituality Cone in the front of your head. We will cover that topic more fully, later on.

What you hear in this class while awake, if you will relax and allow it to be soaked in without question as I am talking, you will be way ahead. Whenever you start to reason, you shut off everything that follows. Then it can't be received. **This is why I use the thought projection as well as speech projection**, so that what you are missing will feed backwards through the cells back to the Spirituality Cone and go back into the memory banks. It still is being programmed and accepted in this dimension.

You can ask for a recall of that when you are awake as long as you are quiet in order to listen.

Are you awake when you do this?

I made a statement early on in your class, "Be not deceived by what you see." My safety lies in my natural projection of being just as you are.

Hibernation and Pulsation

I read about a man that was buried 42 days and survived. He claims to have found a spot in the brain where he is able to hibernate.

It's really not hibernation; it is what I'm referring to when I speak of pulsation. This is where one breath is good for 43 days. A bear does the same thing when it goes into hibernation; it is a pulsated state. Mankind, due to a lack of understanding, calls it hibernation. There is no need of animation when you have direct control.

Even when a sow gives birth, the cub is almost in a weaned condition by the time it wakes up. This is because if they were to go out to forage at the wrong time of year, the drain of the energy of the body would be such that the species would die. Therefore, by allowing the birth to take place when in the pulsated condition, it gives a better harmony to the growth of the cub to sustain itself. It is Nature's way of providing.

Dominion Over Your Kingdom

Your thought is the shadow of the awareness of your Spirit which faces that perfect plane of expression. Because your perfect Spirit receives from God, all consciousness, you must connect your Spirit to your body through your thought action. When this contact is complete, you will have arrived at that blessed state of perfect consciousness. **Then you can** say to the wind, "Hold your peace," and your consciousness would **come into contact with the wind, and the loving awareness** of the wind in loving awareness of the perfection of your awareness, **and the perfect awareness of the wind would obey because of accord, agreement and love.**

It is just as when Jesus was traveling across the sea with all of his aids, and he was seemingly asleep in the bottom of the small boat. They weren't far from land when a great storm aroused the water. There were tremendous waves from the strong wind.

And Peter said, *"Look at him sleep, when we are all surely going to drown. What manner of man is this that would allow us to be under these conditions?"*

With this, Jesus raised up and looked at Peter and said, ***"Peter, of what small faith you have in being."*** **Jesus held up a hand, *"Winds of the East,***

winds of the North and winds of the West, be ye in Peace. Wind of the South, take with you all of this disturbance that has come about."

And with this command, the winds ceased and the water fell back to calm. Peter, aghast, turned to his companion and asked, *"What manner of man is this that we follow?"* Jesus looked to Peter and said, ***"Peter, of what state did I ever say I was man?"*** This covers that entire paragraph in the lesson.

Master or Slave

You were created and given dominion over everything that exists. All of the elements that are about you are awaiting your command of control. But as long as you are in a finite condition and brain is in functional operation without the rapport of agreement of Mind and Spirit, those elements are going to control you. Until you learn the difference between Authority and authorized, you will not know who is the master. There is only one master and one slave; you can be either one. **If you are not the master of a situation, then you are a slave to it.**

LOVE
is going to be the
greatest attribute
you have.

Love.

You will also find that Love is going to be the greatest attribute that you have in excess, because through Love will come the perfect trust and understanding of all functions of operation. Through all of eternity, man was created to rule with Love, to bless and to control. When you control, that doesn't mean that you authorize to everything; control means your ability to adjust. Man was given dominion over everything, but he also gave of himself so that everything else could exist, because everything else in image, was reflected toward his plane of being.

SELFLESS IS THE PERFECT STATE OF BEING.

Selfless.

As each plane of expression was brought about, each was one of the steps that man would have to come through, in order to understand to attain his flesh body, until he would have dominion over and serve all creation. Isn't that an odd statement, "To have dominion over, and yet serve?"

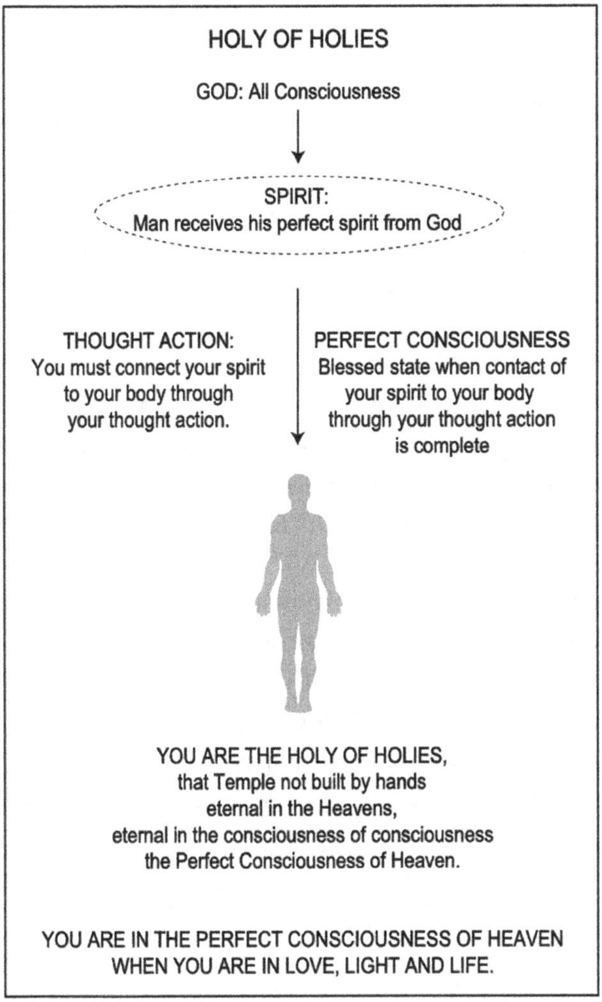

HOLY OF HOLIES
GOD: All Consciousness
SPIRIT:
Man receives his perfect spirit from God
THOUGHT ACTION:
You must connect your spirit to your body through your thought action.
PERFECT CONSCIOUSNESS
Blessed state when contact of your spirit to your body through your thought action is complete
YOU ARE THE HOLY OF HOLIES,
that Temple not built by hands
eternal in the Heavens,
eternal in the consciousness of consciousness
the Perfect Consciousness of Heaven.
YOU ARE IN THE PERFECT CONSCIOUSNESS OF HEAVEN
WHEN YOU ARE IN LOVE, LIGHT AND LIFE.

Holy of holies.

That statement means that **when you become selfless, you learn to put everything above self**, you become Master of everything. Selfless is the Perfect State of Being.

The only way you get rid of an enemy is by loving him. You get nothing but sore knuckles when you close your hands and fight. In Truth, for you to understand, **"to have dominion over,"** doesn't mean an iron-clad ruler. It **means an association of working, poise and rapport with each other, a total balance of equality**. It is an equal share of everything equally for each one. That is why King Arthur had his Round Table, no one sat at the head of the table. Dominion is round, too, it serves all creation.

Awareness of All Consciousness

Man has one ability that the subservient to him were not given: He **was given the knowledge of the awareness of Consciousness contained in Life.** The other planes of creation: the animal, fowl, vegetable and mineral were only given phases of the Consciousness in expression, which we refer to as Nature in them. This is why they are subservient to man.

> *And now you see that you are the Holy of Holies, that Temple not built by hands, eternal in the Heavens, eternal in the consciousness of consciousness: THE PERFECT CONSCIOUSNESS OF HEAVEN.*

You are in the Perfect Consciousness of Heaven when you are in Love, Light and Life. Those three words begin with an L—all right triangles. You will find the totality of Consciousness in the cube of the 9 [3x3=9]. When it opens up, it will form 6 pyramids with 24 right angles. It will have 6 squares, which will encompass one circle. They will meet at one center point where the Airless Cell is located. That is you unfolded into expression: Triangles, Circles and Squares.

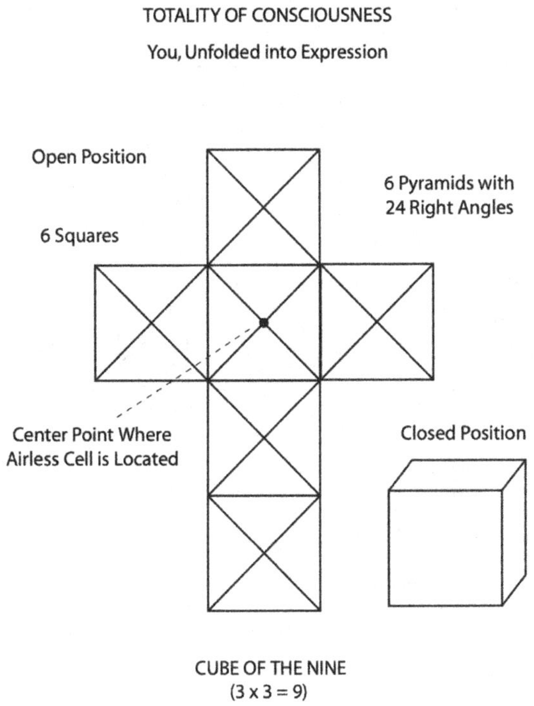

Totality of consciousness.

Kingdoms of God, Paradise, Heaven and Hell

KINGDOM	God, Light	Paradise	Heaven	Hell
Life, Living or Existing:	Life; Motionless	Living unto Life	Living	Existing
Body:	Light	Blend Pure Phys. into Light	Turning to Pure Physical	Flesh Physical
State:	Ultimate state of exchange: Light We understand everything.	Letting go flesh to the light body; Selfless	Higher beliefs; Imaginary state to give us a way back	Beliefs, Improper thinking & programming
Geometric Shape:	⊙ Spirit	△ Mind	⊠ Physical	Shadows of forms
Description:	Can only come into effect by your perfect exchange. Be keen with perception of inner voice.	Perfect Kingdom of Heaven Grace of Love, Poise of certainty, Peace of being gentle & kind.	Perfect state of conscious Pure physical is the ultimate of Heaven. Within us.	Improper thinking, Improper programming
Notes:	When man becomes selfless, the perfect state of being, putting everything above self, he becomes master of all.	The gateway to the Kingdom of God When you really learn Love, it is Paradise.	Be in it but not of it. Look within. Respond to inner voice. Love, Light & Life	Takes place when you go counter to your inner prompting

Kingdom of God, Paradise, Heaven and Hell.

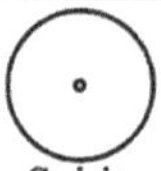

Summary

Jesus teaches that the Kingdom of Heaven is the perfect state of Conscious, which is the true state of being, the state of Perfection. The first step of attaining the Kingdom of Heaven is to learn to be in it but not of it. Be the observer. Evaluate everything before you act. Learn to consider all consequences before you move. Learn to rely on your inner senses, your feelings. When you have that gut feeling, listen, or you will have consequences.

Be quiet within yourself, when you want to know something, and allow the Intelligence of the universe to fully express it for you and to you. If you will listen to that inner voice and learn to have it for your guide, you will divert almost all of your problems.

The Divine Principle of your being: Nobody has the right to enter your kingdom without your permission. When you don't think something is right, say so. Within yourself, don't let anybody change you. Become perfect within yourself, as you are. Be gentle to yourself, love yourself and learn to forgive yourself in your own inability of understanding until you grow in the poise to have the control of that understanding and that peace and knowing within yourself.

One of the abilities you have to cultivate is clear-thought: Dismiss everything else that enters when you are imprinting something that you are receiving. Then your recall will be exact and accurate.

Everything should be projected in a perfect state of the consciousness in love. How would you want someone to do unto you? If you express yourself joyously, being selfless in that expression, in Love, then you share the Universe. When you even surpass that, and give of yourself without any prospect of receiving for that which you give, then you are in Paradise. Very few ever reach the state of Paradise.

These teachings are to teach you to attain from the flesh to the Pure Physical, so that you may light your body and take it with you. Jesus came to show you that this could be attained. If you are not the master of a situation, then you are a slave to it. When you become Selfless, you learn to put everything above self, you become Master of everything. Selfless is the Perfect State of Being. You are in the Perfect Consciousness of Heaven when you are in Love, Light and Life.

Things And Real Things

Mankind has suffered great confusion about things that are real and things that are not real. In our previous lesson, we learned that nothing whatsoever is real to you until you have the awareness of it.

Don't be deceived by the things of life which only seem to be real, for they will pass away just as the old leaves of autumn fall from the tree. On the other hand, the things which are truly real, which you store in your own Heaven, are indeed treasures, for they will endure forever.

Consider the "natural" things, those things that man has accomplished on the Earth. Consider the progress of mankind, then ask yourself a serious question: Are these accomplishments real, or is it the thing that has prompted the accomplishments that is real? In time, you will come to realize that it is the prompting, not the accomplishments, that is real. Accomplishment is subject to change, because it is not perfect. It is a product of imperfect memory rather than of true Spirit. **Things of the Spirit are real and perfect, and will endure.**

The richest man of earth does not realize where his riches come from, nor where he acquired the ability to collect these riches. He may realize that there is something which prompts the drawing together or collection of riches, and he may rely on this prompting, but he does not know its Source.

If we take our awareness a step further, we can see that neither the riches, the ability to accumulate them, or the prompting, nor that which prompted, are real. **Only the great Spirit of man, controlled by God, is real.** To illustrate, suppose that you were to grasp a stick in your hand and begin to stir the stick in a pool of water, making a whirlpool. Which would be the greatest, the water, the stick or the whirlpool? Obviously, none of these is the greatest. The water is the medium of expression for the whirlpool, the stick is the instrument which is prompted into activity by the hand, but the complete man is the Source. Only this Source would be real, for all else would be void without it.

Thus, we see that **real things are Spirit**. It is Spirit which sets everything into action, and therefore, is the cause of action. Action of itself is not real, except for the amount of Spirit that is in it. The Source is the only real thing. If there were no Source, then nothing at all could come into manifestation.

If there were no Source of riches, no one could collect them. Obviously then, the Source is real, not the riches that are manifest from the Source. Isn't this the same Source that you came from? Are not all a part of this Source and it a part of all?

If this is true, then why is it that some have plenty of the world's riches and others have not? It is because of the Spirit of those who have been relying upon the activity of the Source, and those who not have been relying.

There is no limit to what you may accomplish, once you become truly aware and go directly, in Truth, to the Source from which you may receive all things. Then you will not be corrupt or made corrupt, but will again be created from your own creative plane, real in Truth.

You should now be able to comprehend that it is not the riches collected, the power to collect them, or the prompting that are real; it is only that which prompts that is real.

This is what Jesus meant when He said, "Lay not up thy riches in Earth where moths corrupt and thieves take away, but lay up riches in Heaven where the moths shall not corrupt nor thieves take away."

Remember: **that from which all things are made is real;** the making is not real. For example, pure gold is created by Spirit activity and is of itself perfect and real. However, the forms into which gold is made are not real, for they are subject to change. By the same token, your flesh body is not perfect and is subject to change; but the substance from which it is made is real, because it was created by Spirit, then it too, will be real and perfected.

In summary: **things subject to change are not perfect, and anything less than perfect can never be real.**

Things And Real Things

Read your lessons at least a minimum of seven times. Each time you re-read them, you will find a greater amount of Intelligence will come to you. Each time you give of your time, it will graciously be given back to you. These lessons are skillfully constructed to plant many seeds in your yearning for Intelligence. The words are cleverly spaced in dimension and wavelength by tone and sound of the letters themselves.

In the sixth series of this Book, you will study the value of letters and numbers. Then, you will begin to understand why I ask you to look up certain words, so that you may get the spiritual depth of meaning.

This also teaches you another attribute. **It allows you to make a connection with Source.** When you are seeking the meaning of an oddly placed word in the lesson, you will be drawn to Source and you will get information which isn't on paper. The acknowledgment will come to you through Intelligence from Source Itself, and it will set up a whole new standard of acceptance for you.

The more you give to your studies, the more you will receive and the more openly you give and accept, the more you will receive, as well. Any time you become fixed or you take a definite stand, then you have no room for reception, because you closed the door. One word of caution: don't ever close the door.

When something comes about that you can't quite comprehend, or not be able to fully accept, don't dismiss it, but just set it aside. Sometime, in time, you will have real need of it and it will come back to you and hit you right between the eyes!

I repeat myself because of the importance of emphasis placed on certain terminology, so that seeds are planted for you to receive in growth from the maturing of those seeds. The more that you encompass into yourself and draw from Source into Intelligence, the less the amount of knowledge there will be to hold you in bondage. Everything in knowledge passes away.

Acknowledging the Existence of the Real

As it stands now, it is impossible for you to realize Real. You will attain unto the Real by acknowledging Its existence. Only those things that re-seed and are awaiting for us at each awakening, and make their movements through the heavenly bodies, even those are not Real. They are only into the imaging to which we have placed value of reception.

Because we see everything from an imposed view of conformity of acceptance, and because, due to being programmed by a continuance of acceptance from the time we come into expression, we view all mattered things by conformity as being real. However, they are very unreal.

Looking at any object in the room that is solid, the solidity of it only exists because of our agreement of conformity. If we were to see it in its true state, we would see the mass of electrons and protons moving about the atoms, and the fusing of the energies of Thought of that substance holding it in that being. However, as it is now, we are seeing everything in a reflected condition around us. We see things in a reflected value of rather than its being or Source. We see a one flat place condition. We can't see both sides at the same time, or the inside-outside at the same time. There is always a shadow condition existing. If we were to see things as they really are, you would be greatly amazed as to what you accept as real.

Love In An Electronic World

When you are totally in acceptance of all things that you accept in being as material manifested objects, you don't realize that these are only thought patterns solidified by agreement in form. That form only exists as long as time and space are given to it. The length of time and space is its durability of expression. Given love, it will endure a greater and longer expression, because of the adhesion of the elements of the atomic structure. **When Source or love is given to anything, it will hold its luster and beauty.**

If love is denied, it will turn to the grey of space. It will lose its term of expression unto termination. Its magnetic attraction and electronic impulse lose their attraction for one another to hold the form. As the love is taken from it, then the Source of its being is lessened by each continual denial. Due to this denial, its color and luster will drain out to a dull grey. It will become nothing but space itself. It is neutralized in space with no expression whatsoever, either positive or negative, or positive and positive, whatever way you want to say it.

And the first to leave will be the electronic magnetism. The second to leave, when it falls apart and deteriorates, are the elements of its being will be the electronic energizing. Everything is held in form by thought conditioning of the molecular activity being solidified by the Airless Cell. It has the key of all the chemistry and all of the magic of geometric mathematics to hold those chemistries in solidity of form from electronic activity. We are in an electronic world.

As we search, we are coming more into rapport with electronic impulse because the speed of it is giving release of the activity that manifests even us in expression, as with all things into expression. They use it in a point of imagery of reflection. In other words, they can photograph wood grain and transfer that image onto a piece of blank paper, and you will actually believe it is wood. This is due to the immediate transfer of grain and texture. Until you could actually feel it, you could not tell that it was the product that was manufactured in manifestation. In all things that we look at, they are only real to the agreement. All things in manifestation come and go; they only last for a short period of duration. They last only for the duration of love given.

When you lose interest in something, what happens to it? It falls apart, doesn't it? If you are in constant use of something, having great joy with it, giving it a great amount of attention and affection, it gives back a luster in the fullness of life's expression. It becomes Life Itself, expressing. It is according the emphasis of the exchange between the individuals. It is just like the flowers; if you tell them how beautiful they are and that you love them, they will just blossom like you can't believe.

Most of your rapport can be attained by a reality of exchange of Thought Presence. The same thing takes place by everything that is manifested about us in our thought exchange if we give undivided attention to it for an equal of exchange, then it will gratify and glorify that exchange. We are so busy with self importance that we forget to agree with the importance of everything else, and we make our self unreal by this activity.

When I go into a house, I will first make friends with their family dog, before I go look at the people's problems. Then that dog will become quiet and come sit by me. It works very well. I play with it and tell it is a pretty dog.

There is an aroma that you exude with your true affections and they can detect that very quickly regardless of what your words are. Plants are just as sensitive as any animal is.

Is that aroma constantly changing by one's thoughts?

Yes, by the total discernment of your thinking into Thought.

The problem with most of our society is that it has become too predominant in self importance. You have been improperly informed as to how to share with life and what things you are sharing life with. Remember this, you could not exist but for all of the other planes of existence that are giving you your chance of expression.

You would not have the air that you breathe if it were not for the plants and the water, and you couldn't have the water if it wasn't for Nature balancing the activity of the hydraulics of the Earth. And the minerals could not exist to give you elements of substance of Light crystals so that your body will have substance for life existing. Those exchanges are affected just exactly by your thoughts and projections.

Illusion and Reflection

In this lesson, we speak of the acceptance of man's confusion of what is and is not Real. Everything that you see about you is illusion and is made. There is nothing you see with your physical eyes in their present state of ability, that is of Creation. All that you see by your eyes of flesh, is illusion because they are not keen enough to see its actual Truth in Source. You only see that Truth in Source in reflected values.

Everything in this room exists, but it didn't exist until you came in. When you leave here, this room will exist with you forever. If I ask you whether there is a New York or not, then I would ask you to prove it to me.

Only if you had been there would you have memory of what it was like. It will continue to exist as long as you have correlation of memory.

All things that are made are manifested out of an agreement of conformity through the ability of discernment in your Sightcone. In your Sightcone, you will find that all of the problematic conditions that you are going to function in, will be discerned, evaluated, acted upon and re-broadcast before you are even aware it has taken place.

When we go to Source where all Truth and real is, we can only see the ebbing and reflections of that. In everything that is not real, we are like a reflection that is flashed on a screen by a motion picture projector. When we cease to agree with it, then the projector light is shut off and no animation takes place.

We can become dormant and detach ourselves from Source any time we wish. We can shut ourselves completely within our manifested state of being and hold our manifested state of being in a dormant condition as much as we wish. There is only one problem in doing so, you lose expression. You have to continually exchange with each breath so that you may live.

Real and Awareness of Real

In our previous lesson, we learned that nothing whatsoever is real to you until you have the awareness of it. As an example, how would you explain a sailing ship that you had never seen before which traveled by the wind against its sails, and puffed smoke from its sides? An ignorant native standing at the shore and observing, would surely believe this to be a dragon coming up from the depths of the sea. His explanation would be to try and animate it into animal action.

If you go back into your mythologies, you will find that many things of normal accomplishments were so misunderstood by ignorance that the description of them had been left only in the awareness of the individual explaining. The same condition would exist if someone were to explain how an atom works, without the visual aid of animation, where you could see it move by flux and fusion. Thus, it would be difficult for you to comprehend such energy. As long as it is presented to your level of awareness, anything can be accomplished and held within the ability of use.

All things that exist, are of reflected values, but everything that reflects must have something for its origin, in order for it to reflect. Almost everything that we have in imagining, which we use for our daily needs, is imaged and constructed from our body. Your body is the greatest Source you have to draw from.

The Unreal Or Knowing Where You Are Going

What is real and what is not real? Most of the unreal starts with number one, you. You have become so self-important with that which is being done, rather than with that which prompts what is to be done. **How many times before you go to do something do you quiet yourself to find out what and how you should do it?** Or you just plunge in headlong? And when you get all tangled up, then you stop and ask, "What am I doing wrong?" Then you get the answers. It is easier to take that split second to be quiet and know where you are going, what you are going to do and why. Otherwise, you have consequences for which you are going to have to make an adjustment.

Then you are going to have to adjust your attitude because of your vanity and vain condition. This will put everything in an unbalanced condition about you. That which was real, you are quickly making unreal by the misconception of exchange. How many times have you said words that you wish you could have back? If you had only taken one second of thought, those words would never have been spoken, nor would the events ever have taken place.

Be Real To Yourself

Be real to yourself. Don't make yourself a fantasy. Most of you live in a fantasy world, a world of make-belief. This is because you have become conformed by your parentage, your clan and heritage condition, which are all unjust and untrue. They are conditioning culture.

If this were to be as such, you would all be the same. There would be no individualizing. **Each of you has a different thing to do in a different way. Each of you comes here with an agreement** to do it in this way. **Finding the Truth will make you free by realizing what is the Source** rather than the reflection of Source. It will make you free easier because it will give you the edge of importance of control. If you only have a 3% edge lead, the pack will never catch you.

In all the top echelons of the top companies of the world, 3% is all that divides supervision from the rest. The margin is that thin on the average. Anybody has the ability to climb to that position if they only will be real to their self. Advancement only comes from being real to yourself. When you can **learn to ally with Source,** taking from Source, anything that you desire and picture, is yours. If you can hold the picture true and release it, it will automatically be yours. Because you were given dominion over everything that exists and you are the master maker of everything in expression. This is your world and is the way you are making it, not creating it. You can make of anything you want to in this expression.

You can have this expression any way you want it, good, bad or indifferent. You are programming. You are going to get the benefit just exactly as you broadcast it. Every limitation that you place in front of yourself, will amplify itself by multiples. The necessity is for you to learn to clean up your own house and start anew. **To be real is to know yourself; know who you are, what you are, where you are and why at all times.** In a conformity of exchange with Source, we have to think of the exchange; what is real and what is unreal.

TO BE REAL

To be Real is to KNOW YOURSELF.
Know WHO you are,
WHAT you are ,
WHERE you are and
WHY at all times.

To be real.

If you put a stick into a bucket of muddy water and you begin to stir, the hydraulics of the motion will start to make the water flow in a following pattern, and it becomes activated. That activity will take all the sedimentation that has settled to the bottom and cloud up the entire activity that was placed into inactivity. When you have finished, the water is so thick and dirty that you are unable to see through it.

How many times have you done the same activity with your own *stinkin' thinkin'* as you have poked your nose into something that you shouldn't have? Had you listened to Source, this would have never taken place by that one second of being quiet.

The Voice Which Is Real

Be quiet and know that you are God. Be still and know the Truth. When you are just running off at the mouth, you can't hear what that little voice of thunder is saying. Only when you are still are you able to hear that voice which is real, and you will be prompted. **The more you use it, the greater ability of prompting you will receive** until it will become just as commonplace as your ignorance of exchange now is.

We do things in ignorance in many respects due to conformity. We have been endowed with the belief that this is the proper way to proceed because this is how they did it, and others before them did it and there is no better way. Baloney, there always is a better way! Baloney is a mixture of all the unwanted scraps and sold for a high price!

Treasures For Your Heaven

Love is one of those things that you store in your storehouse of treasures. Every time you turn your memory into visual pictures, the warmth of the sensitivity of all of your body will respond. They are treasures. Remember the first time your child kissed you? Can you remember how beautiful and delicate they were when they were first born to you? Those are all treasures, of which you have many, in your storehouse.

> *Don't be deceived by the things of life which only seem to be real, for they will pass away just as the old leaves of autumn fall from the tree. On the other hand, the things which are truly real, which you store in your own Heaven, are indeed treasures, for they will endure forever.*

The heaven that you are in right now was brought about by your desires thousands of years ago. For others, it was hundreds of years ago, or else you couldn't exist in this dimension and at this time. What you so graciously desired at that time, couldn't be accomplished at that time, but it was set aside in your storehouse, and you are now reaping your rewards. These are indeed treasures for your Heaven. This expression you are currently in, is your heaven. Or, it can be your hell, however you want to make it.

Are Accomplishments Real?

Consider the "natural" things, those things that man has accomplished on the Earth. Consider the progress of mankind, then ask yourself a serious question: Are these accomplishments real or is it the thing that has prompted the accomplishments that is real? In time, you will come to realize that it is the prompting, not the accomplishments, that is real. Accomplishment is subject to change because it is not perfect. It is a product of imperfect memory rather than of true Spirit. Things of the Spirit are real and perfect and will endure.

How well you comprehend is how much you receive. Otherwise, all things that you so greatly desire to accomplish will fall way short of what your original estimate was. As with inventors, nothing is really invented, it is just a re-association of what you seem to have lost sight of. When one brings it into view for others to view, then they will start to add improvements onto it. A continuous progress goes on, until one day when man awakens and looks at himself, he'll exclaim, "What's happened?"

THINGS OF THE SPIRIT ARE REAL AND PERFECT, AND WILL ENDURE.

Things of the spirit.

He becomes enslaved to the gadgetry that he has invented. He finds no time to talk or read because his television set gets all of his time and attention. Television is one of the most destructive things of our natural processes that has come about. Man has enslaved himself to such a degree that he cannot exist in society without it. The gadgets are fine, but don't let them control you. Use them for conveniences and that is all. Don't allow them to have power or control over you.

The things of Spirit are real and Perfect, and will endure forever. Every morning, the sun is there to greet us when we awaken. These are real things and will continue to exist throughout the eternity of your times. They have won their rewards of protection as they have moved into the realm of the perfect part of existence. They give life to everything else, so that they may have expression in the manifestation, by the energy that they produce.

In Spirit, there is no such thing as **wealth**; there is no need for it. As with anything you have need of, if you will not regard it in monetary value but as the object you want, the rest will be made available for it to be. This is why some people become wealthy, and yet, don't realize how everything they touch turns to gold. They have learned a great secret that it isn't the money, but the manipulation they go through from the prompting given, and they instantly react upon their prompting.

When your senses become very keen, you will be made aware, beforehand, of what to do and how to do it, in order to take care of yourself and prepare for your future. Most poor people are poor because they want to be poor. There isn't anything you can't have if you can picture it. If you can picture it, then it is yours. Everyone has the same ability and the same right to Full Source. There is no reason why you should be denied anything that you want.

This doesn't mean that you get to sit back and do nothing, you will have to continue to do your daily endeavor. However, you will find your endeavor will become much easier when you begin to work closely with Spirit as you draw from Source. If you use your abilities improperly and devalue yourself, then you will receive just exactly what you broadcast. Instead of having real things, you will have things that are manifested. You will have no adhesion or magnetic ability to hold them to you.

You have observed those magnetic personalities that draw everyone to them. They have learned to do this from Within. When you learn to do this, you will find yourself becoming the center of attraction. This does not mean that you use your ego ability, because this is what you want to lose.

Your Airless Cell: Your True Source

You want to learn to be more in rapport with your Airless Cell, where your True Source really is.

Neither the riches, the ability to accumulate them, or the prompting, nor that which prompted, are real. Only the great Spirit of man, controlled by God, is real.

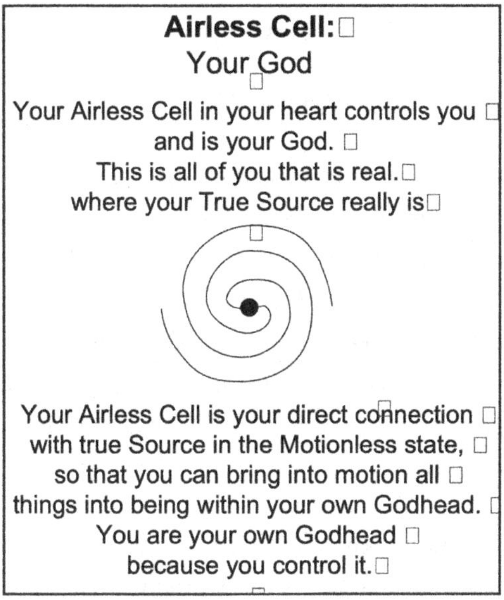
Airless Cell:
Your God
Your Airless Cell in your heart controls you
and is your God.
This is all of you that is real.
where your True Source really is
Your Airless Cell is your direct connection
with true Source in the Motionless state,
so that you can bring into motion all
things into being within your own Godhead.
You are your own Godhead
because you control it.

Airless cell.

Your Airless Cell controls you and is your God. This is all of you that is real. If you were to put a pencil dot on a three-foot square sheet of paper, you would have to magnify your Airless Cell thousands of times in order to see it. All this imaging that you see about you is reflected directly from it. It is all constructed by it.

Your Airless Cell in your heart controls you completely. It gives you all of your ability of being and is your direct connection with true Source from the Motionless State, so that you can bring into motion all things into being within your own Godhead. And you are your own Godhead because you control it. Only now, you are in illusion and you have manifested less than your ability, because of your inability to hold yourself true to the Perfect Thought. As a result, you now do a lot of *stinkin' thinkin',* and it means exactly that; you contaminate yourself by every thought that you use.

You discredit your ability, you discredit your rights, you discredit your actions and your associations with others. Rather than giving forth Love, you give forth vinegar and stink. You give forth hate for which there is no need. These are not a part of Perfect Man, but a part of flesh and the inefficiency to cope with the conditions he brought about for himself to express in.

Source

To illustrate the Spirit of Man controlled by God:

> *Suppose that you were to grasp a stick in your hand and begin to stir the stick in a pool of water, making a whirlpool. Which would be the greatest, the water, the stick or the whirlpool? Obviously, none of these is the greatest. The water is the medium of expression for the whirlpool, the stick is the instrument which is prompted into activity by the hand. The complete man is the Source. Only this Source would be real, for all else would be void without it.*

By the minute amount that you connect yourself to the Source, is just exactly how real your Source is, and how much you actually limit yourself. When you learn to be in rapport with the force of spirit, then you can bring about anything you desire. You can manifest anything you want and it can be instant. The only reason you wait now is because you have placed yourself in a time condition. You have learned and been programmed that everything is past, present and future. You go to the past to get to the present, and you need the future to understand what your present is going to be.

> *Thus, we see that real things are Spirit. It is Spirit which sets everything into action, and therefore, is the cause of action. Action of itself is not real, except for the amount of Spirit that is in it. The Source is the only real thing. If there were no Source, then nothing at all could come into manifestation.*

If there were no Source, there could be no pattern for anything. Being in this form of manifestation expression, we work on memory patterns in order to have our existence. We use the Source of memory to express in, instead of the true Source of Spirit. We imagine ourselves, first by our own imagination, then by our agreement of imaging with those we associate.

As a result, when we are little, we want to be old, and when we are old, we want to be young again. Without your memory of what was, you would have nothing to draw from in order to return to. Yet Source is always present in true picture for you to return to when you are able to comprehend and handle it with the perfect poise of grace.

> *If there were no Source of riches, no one could collect them. Obviously then, the Source is real, not the riches that are manifest from the Source. Isn't this the same Source that you came from? Are not all a part of this Source and it a part of all?*
>
> *We are all a bucket of water, yet each one is a drop which goes to make up that bucket of water. We all attain from the same Source. We all energize from the same Source. Some energize more than others due to their ability to adapt with this which is real, more than the unreal part.*

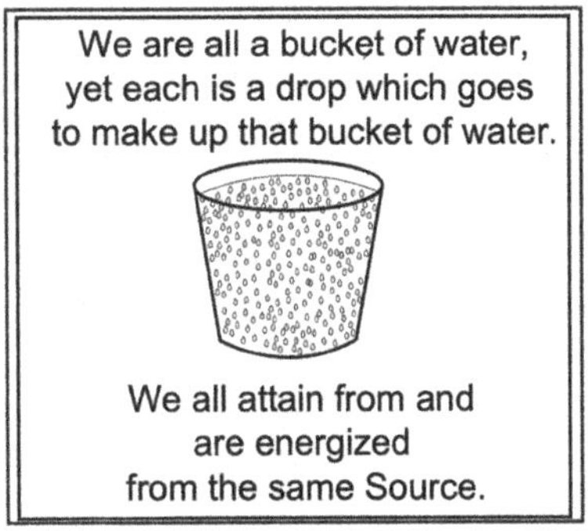

Bucket of water.

Many hold each other in bondage due to their inability to comprehend, and not because there wasn't the opportunity to be made aware of the conditioning of finding Source. This is one point about your expression in manifestation, which is that **you have to do it all by yourself.** The words and directions come to you, but they are of no avail unless you put them into activity and bring them into being.

Words are only a means of guides of light pictures being produced into your brain and recorded into your memory cells, so that you may have a path of electronic energy to pattern by. All of the things favorable will be recorded on one side, and those unfavorable will be discarded. It doesn't pay to be a scavenger, but to instead **sit quietly, forgive yourself, and then, Source will open** up and give you the answers.

Love of Forgiving

Your greatest hurdle at this time is for you to learn to forgive yourself. You can forgive everybody but yourself! You must learn to forgive yourself and bless yourself. You will find with that Love of Forgiveness, Source will be right there for you to draw from. When you learn to agree with the Spirit Source about you, and use it to the fullness that you should, you will find that you won't have nearly the problems that you would normally encounter as the average person does. You will have a certain amount of bad days, but when you learn to handle it, you can turn a bad day into a good day.

LAWS

* The Law of Life is that what you do unto others shall be done unto you, only in multiples.

* Everything you suppress must be dealt with at one time or another.

* Everything you reject must be proofed and put into its proper perspective and accepted.

* Everything you deny, you must give back to expression.

* Everything you alter, you must give back its right.

* Everything you destroy, you must rebuild.

* Everything you deny its equal right of expression, you must see to the Godhead in Perfection.

* When you step on somebody, you will get back your payment seven-fold.

That's the Law

Laws.

In Life Itself, everything is Bliss. Life is the rendered of God, which gives forth into every expression, everything necessary for that expression. However, man seems to have forgotten that he is eternal and of ether. He goes around panting all day instead of breathing one breath of full existence.

Some work so hard at breathing that they burn out their lungs. They take too much nitrogen into their body by their improper breath. By breathing too long or too short, you give your body an excess of gas, causing tremendous damage to your nervous system and the lymph system.

Without the control and poise of breath, your body cannot be unified with the pressures that exist in and of. It has to be expressed as in and of and will be explained at a later lesson, when the time comes for you to understand.

Due to the present plane of expression that man has made for himself, the imperfections of his possibilities and his own limitations of those possibilities, have caused man to sell himself so short of his possibilities, that it is beyond your wildest imagination to realize the true amount of ability you really have.

As long as man is out of control of himself, in his own ignorance, he will create sorrow to others as well as himself. Due to his emotions, he will become his own worst enemy. He will resent having to face reality, and he doesn't want to admit to himself that he is wrong.

Your first step, therefore, is to say that you are sorry. Forgive yourself. You will realize your own gratification of where you limited yourself. When you can really say it and mean it, then, and only then, will you realize the reason for your existence. When you realize this, then you will be able to look out from yourself to see what is really within.

If you can look out and see beauty, then you can see beauty within. If you look out and see dismal, sorrow and hurt, then you have those qualities inside of you. When you allow changes to take place without correcting them in their proper perspective, you limit yourself and will have to go back and do it again.

It is easier to meet something straightforward the first time and get it over with. Don't set it aside for tomorrow if you can do it today, because you are going to find that *tomorrow bucket* is going to get very full. When it gets too full and you try to get some restful sleep, you are unable to get any. This friction of unrest, you will find, will carry over to your awakening time.

The Law of Life

The Law of Life is that what you do unto others shall be done unto you, only in multiples.

Whenever you have a bad thought, the Ether Energy in your body is absorbed. For every minute of sustained anger, it takes 24 hours to replace that burned up Energy. In a rage condition, the temperature of your body will soar to an inflammable condition of excess of 2,000 degrees.

Everything you suppress must be dealt with at one time or another. Everything you reject must be proofed and put into its proper perspective and accepted. Everything you deny, you must give back to expression. Everything you alter, you must give back its right. Everything you destroy, you must rebuild. Everything you deny its equal right of expression, you must see to the Godhead in Perfection. When you step on somebody, you will get back your payment seven-fold. That's the Law.

Many of the highlights of your life are the things that you have made real unto yourself because of your own attainment. How much more would it mean and be accomplished to if you would advance your ability to Source to who it was that was so privileged to chose you as parentage for its expression? They chose you, you didn't choose them. These are real things. You are only a guardian; you are only a caretaker of all things that you behold about you. Everything looks to you for guidance and is bewildered because you didn't give it.

One of the hardest things for you to do is to look into the mirror and tell you that you love yourself. Things will not become real until you do. You will never be able to love someone until you love yourself, nor will you be able to love anything until you know of love, and you will never know of love until you know yourself. How can you give that which you do not have? How can you express that which is misunderstood by yourself. Your equal of exchange cannot have a true synopsis unless you have a full value of projection behind you.

All the things that you do, do as perfectly as you can. Many of us are endowed with exceptional abilities in different ways, so by a combination of multiples of us, we become a whole in a unit. Thus we have been able to lean on one another rather than developing our own abilities and we have conformed to the leading process that somebody else can do it better than we can. Thus, we belittle ourselves out of a true state of expression as we allow others to handle our privilege.

The Make-Belief World

We are always calling upon a specialist for the make-belief world because everything they work upon and manipulate are make-belief things. You were given dominion and mastery over all things, so you should be a master in all fields. Due to your limitation of yourself, you use 1/1000 of your ability of projection and 1/10,000 of your ability of brain function. We are quite limited. Even Albert Einstein in all his ability of brilliance did not exceed 12% of his brain capacity. The average individual does not exceed 2 3/4% of comprehension ability.

You know not of what you speak, only what you think you thought you heard someone else say. This only adds to your utter state of confusion. You are usually so busy thinking only of your own activity of response that you never hear what the other person is saying. Then things become very unreal in perspective very quickly.

If I would ask each one of you to describe the green of the plant in this room, everyone would describe it differently because you are all individuals. If all of you were to look at and describe a picture, you would all describe it differently. Each one looks at different things because you are all individuals. No two look at the same thing nor do you look at the totality of fullness that exists there. You do this because you have learned to become captive by the principle that is projected rather than looking at the source that is projected in the All. You don't see the whole, but instead the reflection.

If we look at TV, we are hoodwinked into believing that a picture is taking place there. We see all of the activity, the expressions and emotions taking place, but we are really watching one dot of light moving so rapidly that we are tricked into believing the magic is a motion picture. There is no difference between that table and a TV screen, only by the agreement of brain.

The Real vs. Molecular Structure

I'm trying by various examples to enable you to understand the Source and Real, rather than the manifested of solidity of **molecular structure that we accept as real.** However, all of it **has a point of termination;** it has a point of self destruction. The molecules can only hold on for as long as energy is given to them, and friction is not applied at too rapid a rate. The faster the rate of friction that is applied to anything, the faster the rate of deterioration it has. It will deteriorate at that rate by multiples of acceleration at the end; it will actually fall apart.

Take a piece of paper and leave it out in the sun, in a matter of a few hours, it will turn brown. Within a few weeks, it will be in pieces; within a month, it will be dust, yet, the same piece of paper still exists. All you see remaining is that which held it in a reflection of be. That which glorifies the Holy falls away the quickest.

Look at the roses. They are absolutely gorgeous to perceive but the glossiness of the tissues only holds light crystals suspended for later life. All that exists there are minute particles of light existence stored between the cellular tissues of the make-believe.

It is glorifying one thing, the little tiny heart inside of that which will be the seed of the new life to come. Due to the beauty around the blossom and the love given to the blossom, it glorifies the seed for continuation.

It is the same as you are. Your continuation is because of this condition. Everything continues in its expression due to this type of exchange. It becomes real due to your make-believe rather than quieting to seek full Source.

You can attain anything that you desire. You would not have to wait for the chain of command of electronic activity to manifest for you in chain motion, just by thought you could assemble it by real. Just as you could reassemble your body from flesh condition back to Light Cells and make it endure all time; that is real. The flesh you live in is unreal. It is a manifested cloaking condition over-shadowing the reflection of radiation given forth by the Airless Cell within your heart.

All of this that is about us is unreal. As solid and real as it seems, it doesn't even exist; only in your memory. All of this is a play and you are all players in the direction of a play that you are living with in a dream. **Rather than knowing the Source that everything exists with, that exists of and why, we are content with the reflections of its exchange.** In other words, if somebody puts their hand over the lens of a projector, the reflection on the screen stops; all make-believe stops.

By our worship of age, we attain age. When we are old, we wish we were young, but we forgot how to go backwards. We have programmed ourselves so positively negative that we are experts at it; we can do everything wrong perfectly. Why don't we excel just as much the other way? Because of conformity, wisdom is in age. I have seen a lot of young people smarter than old people, so it doesn't hold true for me.

Another Way To Perceive Source

When you really want something, you will work very hard to attain it. Then you will give a great deal of attention to the attaining, so it does manifest for you. If you will learn to **relax and make thought pictures**, you will be able to manifest anything that you desire. This will be covered later. It is just as easy as it is to deny yourself anything. Then you will have everything the way you want it, exactly.

If you want wealth, you don't look for money, you look for the necessity of the things that it acquires, then it will be placed in your way.

That is why your lesson states:

> *The richest man of earth does not realize where his riches come from, nor where he acquired the ability to collect these riches. He may realize that there is something which prompts the drawing together or collection of riches, and he may rely on this prompting, but he does not know its Source.*

They stumbled onto a secret, but they don't know how the secret operates for them. The value isn't in the money but in the exchange. When you learn this and become it, then the whole world is yours. You can attain anything exactly the way that you desire it to be. Remember, you have dominion over everything. If you use you proper projection in Thought principle in clear projection and clear audio projection, then it is yours. This is your dominion. You can bring it into be by your surety of Truth in expression with yourself. Why do you let everybody else run it for you?

Everything is Source. Everything returns to that which begets it. **Everything came from the same Source, and that is Life: the great granary of God. All you have do is to ally yourself in Life, with Life, of Life for Life. All Life will bow to you and it will become eternal. Everything will become real.**

It is just as you will learn to grow to **See individuals**. You will know what they think, how they think and why they are thinking it, regardless of what they are saying. You will never be fooled by what people project regardless of what they are hiding.

New Values, Love and Abundance

I will warn you of one thing: you will find that as you grow in Truth, all of the things that used to be important will fall away. You will have all new values and all new standards. Many of the things that are of such value today, won't even merit a backward glance. **You will find that the more you grow in Truth within yourself, the only thing that has any value at all is Love.** That is the only thing that lasts. Without Love, nothing exists.

If you aren't loving yourself or taking time to love something else, you are cheating yourself. Without love, it really doesn't matter.

I always used to work hard and just get the money, but now I work to be working and the money always just falls in.

Right, **here is where your Abundance comes in; this is when you have enough to share with others**. However, if you don't ever share it, then it is immediately shut off. This is where most make their mistake. You can't have anything with a clenched fist because you stop the flow; but when the hand is open, it is continual. Remember, you are only users of, you own nothing. Take as much as you want of anything, but allow others the same opportunity as yourself. **Place no limitation upon anything or any act. This is a very important secret;** learn to use it. It will make you free. Those things that were unreal will become very real to you.

Learn to be the reciprocal of projection rather than the cesspool of conceptions. We stagnate with everything we hold onto until it is so rotten nobody else would want it. We didn't allow the pleasure of exchange and association with it. We want ours **and** yours; this is called greed. It will get you nothing but ill effects in all operations. It will harness you in every act of exchange.

When I was in the South Seas, I learned first hand a prime example of what the closed fist was. I watched the natives catch monkeys. They would hollow out a small hole in a coconut. It was just large enough for the monkey to reach inside. They would fill it with rice. The monkey would reach into the coconut for the rice, but because the monkey was so greedy, it wouldn't let go of what it had. It would capture itself because of not being willing to let go of the fist full of rice!

Now how many times have you done that your self? All you have to do is to let go and you are free. Will you allow the real to be real, or allow the unreal to hold you captive?

The unreal only holds you because of your own greed; your own misunderstanding. **You can be free any time that you want, just be Love.** Open up and allow everything to come to you. However, you don't allow it to, you want to do it yourself! Any speck of doubt will erase it, immediately.

You will encounter this phrase many times, here: **When you KNOW, then you know**, but if you don't know, then you don't know that you don't know. It takes one little bit of doubt, don't know, and nothing takes place. You have to be 100% positive for it to take place.

Just give energy to worry as to what will take place, and sure enough, it does. Stone walls do not a prison make, but mankind's *stinkin' thinkin'* can become the greatest prison of all.

Doubt and Dis-Ease

Doesn't this work unfavorably for mankind causing disease?

Spirit, Soul, Mind and Physical

Spirit
Encompasses everything.
The oscillation between the two positives in activity.
Spirally I go to express

Mind
The go-between Spirit and Physical.

Physical
Reflects that of the coming from Spirit through the Mind.

Soul
Eternal life of being of expression, expressing

Spirit, soul, mind and physical.

It is not disease, but dis-ease. **Due to doubt and fear you unbalance the natural balance of germs in the body** which stimulates an overabundance of destruction of those natural germs. Then you have a dis-eased condition in your body, which allows a toxin to form that stupefies the activity of the

Light Cells of the body into a mis-activity of mis-energizing. This results in a putrefied condition, then the germs have to re-balance into a balanced condition to neutralize back into a condition of poise. The swelling of override in a fever condition is the body coming back into a natural condition. Anything that is out of order has to go into an amplification of itself in order for the body to neutralize. The balancing of the pure germs in the body is the pure health of the body. Pureness of thought is what holds this into a conformed condition.

A conformed condition is that by which you conform yourself to be, because you have made the agreement of how you are going to be. By the limitation of your own doubts and fears, you become exactly the product of your own projection. You become unreal by your own projection and acceptance.

If you were to be closed up in a small room with the lights out for five hours, what would your imagination do to you in 5 hours? Where would your surety be in 15 hours? In 100 hours? Your imagination would run away and you would destroy yourself. Stand down in the Carlsbad Caverns when they turn the lights out and you really understand what black is.

*On **visualizations**, is it better to not be so specific about every detail?*

Be specific about every detail, because you want it exactly your way. That is your way, however if you went to Source, you wouldn't need the way. Remember, you are only manifesting; you are not creating, a great difference. This is your dominion and you have the right to make anything you want in this dominion, good or bad.

Purpose of These Lessons: Cheat Death and Be Eternally Free

What these lessons are all about is what you are ultimately to be taught, which is to cheat death and **change all of this flesh into Light and take your Light Body with you from this earth. You are going to be eternally free when you walk away from here. That is why you are here.** If you weren't looking for this, you would have never found me.

You will be able to use your attributes to the fullness to become the totality of Source in expression and drop away the heaviness of manifestation into the Light exhilaration of Light Expressing in Life, becoming Life Itself expressing Light. You will become the triad of Light, Love and Life: the Father, the Mother and the Son. You will shine as the most bright sun of the universe when this is attained. That little infinitesimal fraction that you are expressing has a brilliance to light all of the universe. It is lighting all the cells of your universe into form and form activity of being in expression.

You have the potential of anything you can think of which can be instantly attained, now. All it takes is just a little bit of reawakening of things that you put to sleep which have become dormant.

You are operating on five of **your twelve senses. Those seven dormant are the most important to your being.** Each of them will be given to you as you go and will be given to you as keys for you to unlock yourself. There is no sense of burning yourself up for nothing because if you do, you just have to go back and do it all over again.

LONGEVITY SECRETS

Do not allow hate, malice, anger or stress to dominate your activity.

Let love, joy and affection of exchange be your dominating activities.

Neither limit nor magnify things into an unreal condition because of wanting to control everything and hold it in bondage.

Belittle nobody.

With your thought patterns, your food becomes exactly that of which you partake, so use pure thought when partaking of food for a condition of good health.

SOME ADDITIONAL SECRETS OF THE HUNZAS

The Hunza's social standard is such that they have no jails.

They have a block of elders that oversee all conditions and justify the conditions. When something becomes out of balance, they call upon the elders for understanding. Due to their longevity they are able to answer into the reason of the problem. However, nobody is ever belittled in the exchange. That is the secret, right there.

They have the pureness of perfect air to breathe to keep the body in longevity.

At a young age, they are taught meditation and quietness for self, which is not taught in any of our schools.

They are taught to look upon nature for Source rather than from nature to Source.

Longevity secrets.

You wouldn't give a baby a match and a stick of dynamite to play with, yet these energies are just as lethal that are sleeping within you. A little knowledge is dangerous, but if you do not proceed and pursue this, even the little you have will fade away and you won't be able to recall it. I'll promise you this; it is amazing how quickly it will elude you.

Unless there is control, there is no need of projection. Words fall upon deaf ears and activity is unexplainable and unseen. It is like all of the howling of the wind, where did it go when it stopped? Where did your life go when it stopped? We spend more time planning for a weekend trip and a vacation than we do for the greatest trip of all. The unreal things are so important to you, but once you learn of the real things and the values of them, it is amazing how your perspectives of values are going to change.

There is a lot of house cleaning to be done. A lot of old ways and the association of many old conditions are going to be shucked.

Friends and even family?

They are all acquaintances, even family are acquaintances. You will have many acquaintances throughout your life; friends you will count on one hand. If you can count friends on two, you are exceptionally wealthy. **A friend is a person you can absolutely rely upon in any situation.**

Your lesson says:

> *If we take our awareness a step further, we can see that neither the riches, the ability to accumulate them, or the prompting, nor that which prompted, are real. Only the great Spirit of man, controlled by God, is real.*
>
> *We see that real things are Spirit. It is Spirit which sets everything into action, and therefore, is the cause of action. Action of itself is not real, except for the amount of Spirit that is in it. The Source is the only real thing. If there were no Source, then nothing at all could come into manifestation.*

Soul vs. Spirit

Many people make the mistake of saying "soul" when referring to Spirit. You have been taught by misunderstanding, you have never been given true value. Spirit encompasses everything. Mind is the go-between of Spirit and the Physical, and the physical reflects that of the coming from Spirit through Mind.

Soul is the eternal life of being of expression, expressing. It is the eternal youth fluids in your body that will keep you young. You have the Fountain of Youth within you. Ponce de Leon and De Soto went searching for it, but carried it within themselves. It is your Soul Substance. These are real things.

Spirit, if you actually want to look at it in the true sense, is the oscillation between the two positives in activity. Spirit is from the Latin word, "spira," which means a coil. Therefore, **spirally I go to express:** Spirit, which is both coming and going, simultaneously at the same time as multiples of motions simultaneously in all directions at the same time.

In "spir-it," the "I" is the personified in expression. Expressing what? Standing forth as the personified of the Father in expression. The "t" is the expression. The "t" forms a cross by the arms placed on the bar of the personified. Man places himself on that cross when he separates from his true state and accepts a cloak of flesh.

Soul is the fluid river of life that is eternally within your memory principle and brought completely first into operation as soon as the pineal glands are produced and the vertebra arranged into attraction, set up by magnetic mathematics. There are twenty-six sections to the spinal column, although science recognizes only twenty-four because two of the sections are fused. The lowest section, the coccyx, is frozen. Here science recognizes only four bones in the coccyx because the others are frozen or fused. Encased in the coccyx is the Soular fluid.

When you change the flesh physical to Pure Physical, Light, the fusion of the seven rudimentary bones of the coccyx become unfrozen; they become real. These are all real things. They all are eternally within your vehicle. They never dissipate. At the age of 12, the age of reasoning, you lost the use of these and you became responsible for yourself.

Longevity

The body you are existing in is capable of 7,000 years of continuous expression without having to be renewed, on one breath. We burn this body up in less than a 70 year average because we allow hate, malice, anger and stress to dominate our activity rather than love, joy and affection of exchange to be the dominating activities.

We limit and magnify everything into an unreal condition because of wanting to control everything and hold it in bondage. By the same bondage, we put ourselves into the same trap.

I read that there is an area in Russia where those peoples live to extravagant years. They have no stress.

Yes, it is an area where the Hunza people have live. They have an average life span of 150 years. The Hunza's social standard is such that they have no jails. They have a block of elders that oversee all conditions and justify the conditions. When something becomes out of balance, they call upon the elders for understanding. Due to their longevity they are able to answer into the reason of the problem. However, **nobody is ever belittled** in the exchange. That is the secret, right there. They have the pureness of perfect air to breathe to keep the body in longevity.

At a young age, they are taught meditation and quietness for self, which is not taught in any of our schools. They are taught to look upon nature for Source rather than from nature to Source.

Remember, mankind has dominion over everything, even nature. With your thought patterns, your food becomes exactly that of which you partake, because the pureness of your thought would change poison into the most digestive substance you could partake. You have control of all elements.

As the food goes past the teeth, the computerization of their sounding board function sets up all of the chemistry for the breaking down of any element that is taken into the body. This is real, yet very few understand what is really taking place. Very few understand the necessity of this process for a good health condition.

The magic is in the etheric pattern that is existing eternally in their patterning. When the pureness of thought is brought into Source projection, then the eternal pattern takes place rather than the manifested projection pattern. When you know that you know, you know. Everything responds that way and to exactly that amount, then it does become real.

It is only because of your make-believe and your own doubt that things change by the conformity of your acceptance of agreement of your values of discernment.

Your are constantly discerning about 3,000,000 thoughts a second, which you are evaluating and acting upon continuously. You have the capability of 1,000 times that amount when you awaken yourself. Then you will have over a billion thoughts going through Mind, simultaneously in agreement, rather than the reflected activity of brain at 3,000,000 per second.

Be Honest With Yourself

Remember, in Source, you have everything to draw from, to create anything that is necessary in the universe. The lesser state of unreal imagination that you have created for yourself to express in, is a very unreal state. The whole secret for you to evaluate and learn is to be honest with yourself, to yourself and for yourself, and all things that you associate with.

Starting today, and from this day on, you are going to do your best to make everything as true as you possibly can, regardless of what anybody else thinks. That goes even down to the white lies. The change is only going to start with you. Unless you change, no change can take place. If it hurts somebody, feel sorry for them that their ignorance is controlling them and they are unable to face the truth.

This whole world is going to have to face the truth, or else it is going to stop and start up all over again. It's called a pole shift, which we have previously discussed, and you don't want to have to go through one of those, if you even do survive such an calamitous event.

> **If you see anything wrong in others, look within yourself, because it is there, also.**

If you see anything.

Unless you can be honest to yourself, you will never know Truth because everything is going to be unreal until you make it real. It starts with number one, you. All those old habits are going to drop away. They are not going to drop away overnight, but if you whittle away at them, even with a pocketknife, you can fell the biggest tree in the world.

With your ability, one can move mountains. With two, you can create universes. **Your potential is beyond your wildest imagination**; you have all of this potential locked up inside of you. The greatest problem you are going to face is the acceptance of theories as facts because you have allowed your society to dominate you with untruths and conformity rather than being yourself.

You are the sum and substance of your thoughts and of everything that exists about you.

You are the sum.

The mass hypnotic condition of your conformity that you are expressing in has you trapped in its conformity, instead of allowing you the freedom of expression as you really should. Because you have to show purpose of condition to exist in this living of conformity.

The secret is this: be in it, but not of it. That is going to be your byword. Don't be caught in the trap of losing your head because your mouth preceded your thought. That is one of the greatest pitfalls that you face. Be still and know the Truth. Make it real, don't be trapped in the make-believe of the unreal.

Any condition that you desire to take place, use your thought projection of setting the condition to be exactly as you set up the condition when you arrive there. Do this by stilling your breath and making the pictures, then releasing them with knowing. That automatically becomes yours.

A good way to get to know yourself is take a piece of paper and divide it in half. On the left side, write those things you don't like about yourself. On the right side, those thing you like about yourself. When you are able to erase the left side, you have accomplished. The more that you can let go of those old things that keep you in bondage, the more you will erase that column.

I will want to find a parking spot, and I just visualize a spot opening up as I get there and I can't believe how often this works!

Just still your breath as you make your picture form and when you release your breath, it will fulfill just exactly as pictured. Whatever you want and picture, be sure it is really what you want, because you surely will get it.

The more that you begin to know yourself and you really become real to yourself, the more you will begin to grow. You will attain within yourself beyond your belief. Be ready to let go without any thought of things when you release, especially doubt. If you don't, you will make mistakes which will hold you in bondage.

The way of Truth is not an easy way until you learn the Truth. As of now, you are attaining the true state unto the Truth. You are going to go through many trial and error conditions.

All things are given to you for your enjoyment. Enjoy them. Don't let them control you. **Let no one walk upon you in any manner.** Let no one malice you in any way. Do not allow it; nobody has that right. You are God. You are supreme over all things. Take your rightful place in your rightful heritage.

Why go through the remorse afterward when you could have faced the situation beforehand? You won't be popular to start with but you will be greatly respected in a short period of time. If you are looking for a popularity contest, you are in the wrong field, but **if you are looking to perfect yourself, I'll give you all the answers.**

It won't be long before others are looking to you for verification. There will be a certain light that is going to come off of you that you will be unaware of, yet others that come into association with you will begin to search for, very quickly. You are going to become very wise and keen in perception of the proper words being said in the right way at the right time. The right answers will come out if you just open your mouth.

Don't worry about it, they aren't going to ask you where they came from because they will be too awed to be concerned about it. Don't worry what the mouth says, it will just come forth with ease and grace. Be still and know that you are God. **Be true to yourself in all things, in all activities.**

The Love Commandments

Learn to love yourself above all things. Learn to love everything as you love yourself. That was one of the last two Commandments that Jesus gave you, and was one of the two that Moses restricted from his own people and consequently was not allowed to enter the Holy Land.

Moses only gave ten of the Twelve Commandments which he hewed out of stone. Then it was necessary for Jesus to come and bring forth the last two Commandments, the Love Commandments, to you.

That is very important that you learn to love everyone as you love yourself. Love everything unto the Father because everything is the Father. Only by being the truth of the Father can this be attained. By being true to yourself and everything that exists and expresses, the falsity of conditions and conformity will fall away. The mask that you are hiding behind will fall away and you will be able to see beyond the mask.

You are going to become an authority because you are going to become true to yourself. As you walk in Truth and you become the Light, everything is going to come to you. For everything that you put forth in the effort of love, you are going to receive back in multiples seven-fold.

All of your exchanges of your own individualization are going to be ascribed as honest, perfect and true. You are going to **do everything to the best of your ability from this moment on**, and you are not going to settle for anything less than perfect. You never have to back up to anybody when you do it to the very best of your ability. You never have to bow to anyone. You will know such peace and gratification within yourself as you will learn by being honest and truthful about everything.

You become the sum and substance of your thoughts. Your aura and your aroma condition of your body precede you in distance of at least 100 feet. Have you ever walked by someone and turned to look at them as they passed? You don't know why, but you look back at them.

THINGS (NOT REAL)	REAL THINGS
Things of Reflection	**Things of Creation**
Everything you see about you in illusion is made.	That from which all things are made is Real
Everything you see with your physical eyes in their present state of ability	Things of the Spirit are Real and Perfect, and will endure forever.
Reflected values	The great Spirit of man, controlled by God, is real.
	Spirit sets everything into action.
We are like a reflection flashed on a screen by a motion picture projector.	Spirit is the cause of action
The making of things is not real.	That which prompts is Real.
Things of life which pass away	Things of Spirit which endure forever
Accomplishment (subject to change because it is not perfect)	
Products of imperfect memory	That which is perfect is Real.
Manifestation expression - we use memory patterns	Source - the only real thing, the real pattern
We use source of memory instead of source of Spirit.	Source of Spirit
Things subject to change are not perfect & anything less than perfect cannot be Real.	Source is always present in the true picture for you to return to when you are able to comprehend and handle it with the Perfect Poise of Grace.

Things and real things.

What are the Eleventh and Twelfth Commandments that Jesus gave us?
Love thy Father thy God above all things.
Love thyself as you love thy God because thou art God.

Poise and Judgment

Would you explain Poise?

Poise is when you can be *in* anything but not be *of* it. It is most advisable for you to keep quiet and remain cool. You will find it much easier to exist and express in this life if you learn to be calm, cool and collected. What all of this means is Poise. When you lose your Poise, you are at the mercy of everybody else. You are no longer master. Everybody has a right to express their expression. It doesn't mean that you have to agree with it, but you don't have the right to judge them. You have no right to judge anything or anybody. If you judge somebody else, then look deep in yourself, for there you will find the same fault.

Another Law of Life: If you see anything wrong in others, look within yourself, because it is there, also.

Now you have two to forgive, them and yourself, because you trespassed and judged.

Another Law of Life: You are the sum and substance of your thoughts and of everything that exists about you.

Seven Rate Breath and Light Energy

As you broadcast, be sure you don't contaminate yourself as you contaminate those about you. Because as you learn this breath control, you are going to learn how to manifest. I'll warn you now that when you still that breath, it's gone. There is no recall.

That is the reason for the stillness of the breath, after the inhaling, for it gives you the evaluation within your Sightcone to discern all thoughts going through your brain, of which you are capable of discerning about 3,000,000 per second. During the intake of your breath, you will draw forth the seven rays of light into your body across the diaphragm, which has seven arteries across it that are for your 3 primary and 4 secondary colors.

These seven arteries which receive these colors of the rays, are for the charging of all the activity of your body in light energy. They will also charge your nervous system, digestive system, the circulatory system and respiratory system, simultaneously. As you breathe and you fill your lungs, you draw forth the ether energy of the three primary colors. As you exhale, you draw forth the four secondary colors to the bottom side of the diaphragm, coming through the feet from Earth.

This is the reason for you to start using the Seven Rate Breath, for you are taking in pure light and breaking it into fragmentary activity of your manifestation of activity. On the Seven-Rate Breath, we separate the inhalation and exhalation with a pause of two beats of the heart. This is a chance for the frequency to change polarity. All that is positive, now becomes negative, which in turn, now becomes positive.

Your body is an air transformer. As you breathe in, the iron in your blood becomes excited and the residual of it trying to capture itself, emits a tremendous amount of energy. This causes all of the protons and neutrons around it to activate.

When your blood is tired, you are short of iron. When it is in good condition, you have a lot of red cells in it. The red cells are oxidized, which makes them red; they also become transmitters and receivers of the residual activity of the iron in your system. When Jesus said, "My Life is in your blood," this is what He meant.

By your breath, you will learn the gas controls which you now do automatically, but in a limited condition. Some of you might be more proficient in your breath pattern by accident, as you would have been taught proper breath in athletics that you might have pursued. As you tire and tax yourself, you will find that you become more lax in your breath control. The firmness of your being in a muscular condition becomes supercharged into super-flesh by improper breath.

When the breath is too shallow, the heaviness of water will collect in the system. When the breath is in a very heavy overabundance, you will find that the extended retention of the lungs will cause them to break down. These individuals will develop lung conditions in the midpoint of their span of life. There is only a certain amount of elasticity to the cellular structure of your flesh.

Inhale and Make Picture Forms

By charging yourself on the intake of your breath, you will also use your own perspective of control when you make picture forms of what you desire. You will use the inhalation of your breath to draw the properties that you need from universal substance into your being, so that you may have use of them. If you do not have breath control, you cannot draw forth the light from the universe to use in your manifestation.

Pause

As you pause your breath and your make your picture form, you are actually constructing the ether realm around you, which will manifest it. As you formulate your picture and use your imaginative processes with it, picture it so you can collect the Etheric Substance into matter and cause it to congeal.

Exhale and Release the Blueprint

On the outgoing breath, you will release the blueprints of your desire into functional operation. That which you cannot develop and energize within your own aura, you will have to draw from universal substance. If you do not have enough control of it, then you will have to wait for manifestation to take place at a given time, as your control must allow for your shortcomings.

As it is now, you picture mold what it is that you desire, which usually takes a little time for you to hew it into being. When you picture forth in your desires of what you want to attain and manifest into your function of operation, you will find that it is much easier to attain if you use your breath control.

When you still your breath on the outcast with the two beats of your heart, transmission is complete into the elementary conditions about you. If you have made a proper picture, it should return right back to you. However, you need control for this function of operation, and you will grow with it. What you do now, you do in a second-hand fashion. You may have to re-think something many times before you get it the way you want it. Your pictures aren't all that clear.

To show you how you use it now, how many times have you desired something and you think about it, over and over, and then, it comes to you just as you desired it? If you learn to do this process to its fullest potential, you will find it easier to attain all the necessities of your expression.

There is one caution, however, never think of money. If you desire something, think of what you want, not what the cost would be. Don't put a price tag on it. Money is the root of all evil. You have dominion over everything, and everything is yours, so why do you shortchange yourself?

You find that in everything you build, you will make a blueprint or a plan before you build it. The more you work it out within thought pictures, the easier it is to construct. If you learn to use this, you will find that you will live a life of luxury. Everything in its own time and its own mete, will return to you. Even on days when you don't expect it, that little good turn you did for somebody else, will all of a sudden return to you.

Everybody has skeletons in their closet. Only when you admit to yourself that you have skeletons in your closet, are you ready for the Truth. If you can't face it, then you will never erase it. You can't get rid of it unless you know it's there. Start digging out those skeletons. All of those things that you don't like which other people do, look within yourself and see why they are there.

Learn To Love

If you are not getting along with somebody, tell that person how much you love them whenever you see them. The only way you can get rid of an enemy is by loving them. As long as you have your fist clenched, nobody can give you anything. You have to have your hand open for you to receive. When your hand is open, you are giving as well as receiving. When you close it, you shut the door. As long as your hand is open, you are eternally welcome to all that is in the universe, and the universe becomes yours.

The Law of Life also gives us the wisdom to be eternally free. When we learn to love, this means we have learned to forgive. You see nothing wrong in them. You love unconditionally. It is only when you malice your love, do you see things wrong; then you change love to like. **The properties you are attaining for your Perfection all start with the little key: I love you.** When you learn that you can love everything and everybody, then you won't find time enough to see something wrong.

In the transgression of your own functional operation, on the plane you are expressing in and of, at this time and place of expression, you are in the most perfect for your attainment. The triangulation of the Central Sun to the Cardinal Suns is the most ideal for the greater wealth of Intelligence being beamed to you.

Clean Out the Cobwebs

It is up to you to clean the cobwebs out of your head. By this, I mean to allow your mastoids to be cleaned of mucus. If you spin your head around and you become dizzy, this indicates too much mucus. It means that your gyro, which is near the top of your head, is not functioning properly. It means that the exchange of electrical currents from the Sightcone into the pineal glands is not properly in perspective, and you will be short-circuited.

Also, the blue-white light and the yellow light, which come in through the temples to the thyroid, that coins the cells, is limited. Your breath will help tremendously in feeding the blood systems of your body. Over the years you have caused this system to become dormant, it is necessary for you to clean out the veins and arteries of foreign buildup.

The crystals of light become sludge in the system and are lost, but due to meditation, this is not allowed to accumulate. If you use the exercise of breath, in a controlled manner, you will find that by taking this energy in, you will begin to "live" instead of being lived.

As time goes by and you advance in your studies, you will be given more exercises which will make you more aware of your being and of yourself. In your degree of functioning in life, with life and of life, this is something you cannot comprehend at this time, because to accomplish what I am saying, you have to become multiples of motions, simultaneously in all directions at the same time.

As it is now, you have limited yourself in one direction of operation at one time. You look in one direction; you hear from one way and you feel one way, instead of multiples. As time advances and you advance time, you will find this concept of multiplicity will become a very natural condition. You use it without realizing it. You have centers within your body that are dormant waiting for you to unlock them.

Keep Your Appointments With Intelligence

If you will learn to read these lessons at the same time every day, you are going to make an appointment with Intelligence. That Intelligence is going to amplify your ability of exchange of understanding, and some authority is going to be right there explaining that lesson to you. Mark what I'm saying because it is absolutely true!

Set time aside for yourself to be absolutely quiet and make everybody respect your time. That is your private time. Everybody has a right to that. That time should be increased to two hours and forty minutes a day. That is why the Father wants 10% of your time a day. He doesn't want your money. He created everything in the universe; why does He want your money?

The Father says, "I want time to commune with you so that we may know one another again. You seem to have forgotten who I am and why I am. I never shut the door when you left. You shut the door. I'm still waiting for you to come Home. Pay me the honor and privilege of allowing me at least five minutes with you so that I may commune with you."

It is so simple and so easy if you will just put forth a little effort. Soon, it will become effortless with rewards beyond your belief. The attainment is so great. I say five minutes to start. That is about all you can sustain before brain takes you away. I am only a guide; I can show you the path, but I can't do it for you, nor can anyone else. I can give you all of the keys, and I'll be most happy to. If you will do as I ask, you will be rewarded beyond your beliefs!

This life can be the most joyous of expressions that can ever be imagined if you will only be kind to yourself and love yourself and take a few minutes to talk with Dad. Your rewards will be more valuable than all the riches of the earth because they are eternal. They don't come and go with time; they are eternally yours. You have the right to them.

Summary

Things of the Spirit are real and perfect and will endure. Only the great Spirit of man, controlled by God, is real. Things subject to change are not perfect, and anything less than perfect can never be real. Everything you see about you is illusion & is made. That from which all things are made is real.

To be **real** is to know yourself; know who you are, what you are, where you are and why at all times. **Be real to yourself.** Each of you has a different thing to do in a different way. Each of you comes here with an agreement. There is no limit to what you may accomplish, once you become truly aware and go directly, in Truth, to the Source from which you may receive all things. When your senses become very keen, you will be made aware, beforehand, of what to do and how to do it.

Sit quietly, **forgive** yourself, and then **Source** will open up and give you the answers.

The little Voice within Is Real. Be quiet and know that you are God. Be still and know the Truth. You want to learn to be more in rapport with your Airless Cell, where your True Source really is. When you can learn to ally with **Source**, taking from Source, anything that you desire and picture, is yours.

All the things that you do, do as perfectly as you can.

It is easier to meet something straightforward the first time and get it over with.

What these lessons are all about is what you are ultimately to be taught, which is to cheat death and change all this flesh into Light and take your Light Body with you from this earth. You are going to be eternally free when you walk away from here. That is why you are here. If you weren't looking for this, you would have never found me.

What are the **Eleventh and Twelfth Commandments** that Jesus gave us? **Love thy Father thy God above all things. Love thyself as you love thy God because thou art God.**

One of the hardest things for you to do is to look into the mirror and tell you that you **love yourself**. Things will not become **real** until you do. **Learn to love yourself above all things. Learn to love everything as you love yourself. Let no one walk upon you in any manner.**

Your **potential** is beyond your wildest imagination; you have all this potential locked up inside of you. **The secret is this: be in it, but not of it**. This life can be the most **joyous** of expressions that can ever be imagined if you will only be kind to yourself and **love** yourself and take a few minutes to talk with **Dad**. Your rewards will be more valuable than all the riches of the earth, because they are eternal and eternally yours. You have the right to them.

Intelligence And Intellect

No doubt you have read and heard many things concerning Intelligence and intellect, and the difference between them. It is important for you to learn the true meaning of these two attributes and to be able to discern the difference between them. **Intelligence is true spirit activity. Intellect is the reasoning ability of the spirit.** Each has its own function, as do all things. Intellect can and does act independently of Intelligence, and Intelligence can and does act independently of intellect, but the results are vastly different. When we look about us today, we see a world controlled by the activity of intellect alone, without the spirit activity of Intelligence.

As is the case with any activity, there are many planes of both Intelligence and intellect. As with all things, for true and lasting results, one must work in conjunction with the other, not independently of one another. Too often in our world, intellectual action is taken independently of Intelligence, with disastrous results. This is the cause of the present conflict of activity and thought.

Intelligence is an absolute certainty, while intellect changes with the amount of activity given it. Intellect is not certain, but draws things to itself for its own use. For example, intellect may give you the power to desire a book and to derive an understanding of its assembled words, but Intelligence gives you the activity of those words and the good you might derive from reading the book. On the other hand, Intelligence may give you the desire for, and show you the necessity of, better conditions, but intellect draws together the material for the betterment of conditions. Thus, the activity of both Intelligence and intellect, working in unison and harmony, brings about desirable end results. Like all perfect laws, the law of Intelligence and intellect works either positively or negatively, according to its use, and the results will be according to the amount of activity or Spirit given it.

A man may have the intellect to gather together a great fortune, but if he doesn't have the Intelligence to dispose of and manage that fortune properly, he will lose it. Another may have the Intelligence to grasp Divine Truth, but if he doesn't have the intellect to live according to this understanding, and impart it to others, he will not achieve perfect results. However, those who comprehend and also have the ability to convey their comprehension to others, are blessed with both spirit activity, Intelligence and the reasoning ability of spirit: Intellect.

Intelligence, then, is the living thought action, and intellect is the action of thinking upon life.

The Intelligence of man tells him to quicken his body, and his intellect sets about making automobiles and airplanes. If man would cause his intellect to vibrate in perfect conjunction with Intelligence, he could travel by the power of his own electronic force, which we will study in later lessons, and there would be no need of either the auto or the plane.

Intellect tells man that his body is ill and directs him to take medicine. However, if man would turn to Intelligence, it would lead him to his spirit, the source of all health, and the **spirit would heal him without the need of medicine.**

From these examples, you can readily see that Intelligence alone cannot express intellectually, nor can intellect alone express intelligently. **The perfect accord of the two results in perfect Intelligence in active expression.** This is the perfectly natural outcome of the working of a perfectly natural law.

Seek intellect, then, but let your Intelligence be your guide in uplifting yourself into the perfect state of being.

Intelligence And Intellect

This lesson deals with the difference between where man should operate and actually does operate. Due to man's inefficiency to understand himself or his abilities in attainment, he has created a misunderstanding of himself and what is really true in Truth. Therefore, in his endeavor to understand Truth, he has set up sub-truth standards to operate by, thus he becomes a fixed law of functioning. This fixed law is constantly fluctuating. It bends and stretches easily. It collapses just as easily. This is man's ability in intellect.

Intellect is where most of man's problems get started. This happens because man allows what seems to be, to control him, instead of what really is. In the ability of listening within, instead of out, one of the greatest problems is the amount of opinions and advice that is assaulting us daily in our social and cultural conditioning of control in intellect instead of Intelligence.

Seek Counsel Within

Start to become keen in your senses as you go to **seek your counsel within**. You will not only find the answers much easier for you, but the accomplishment of understanding will be much clearer. Anything given to you that you want to proof, just hold your breath. **You stop your breath and be quiet, and when you resume your breathing rate, you will know** whether it is acceptable. It is an easy way of proofing what somebody tells you, and you will know if it is acceptable to you.

When you allow yourself to become quiet, then the Intelligence can come into rapport with you and give you the guidance. If you are too busy looking or listening out, you can't hear within, nor can you see within. Man must learn that his greatest avenue of achievement to find his way back to where he had fallen from, is by this prompting of Intelligence. This is the only way open to man in order for him to attain that which he seemingly lost.

There are many factors which must be taken into account for this avenue. **We have Mind, which is the greatest attribute that Spirit gives us.** It is the go-between of Spirit and Physical for us to correlate our conditioning of which we function in and with. Intellect has its place because of our functional operation as we are going about our mundane ways.

We have allowed ourselves to be accepted in cultures of standing. If you accept a culture of standing, you accept its ability of your livelihood, but there is also your ability to rise above these conditions and be in it but not of it. Don't accept or react to anything by purely emotional standards. Accept only after you have proofed it for yourself.

If it is not true, within a short time it will be re-evaluated by you for proofing again. You will weigh your true statements into a proof condition. What is true for you now will not be true for you as you climb above them by your growth and attainment, if you are diligent about it. Any time you find something you dislike that is going on about you, then you change it; you don't allow it to change you. You have to make the move to make the change, and the only way to make the change is to withdraw (still your breath) and set a new standard.

If you reason with it, then it will control you. Once it has gotten you to reason, then it has got you under control. **Whenever you are confronted with problems or a condition that is upsetting to you, just be quiet, still your breath, know and wait for the response**. However, you must still the breath so that Mind can come in to function in place of brain.

Conditioned Intellect Blocking Intelligence

You do this all the time and don't even realize it. How many times have you tried to remember something, and then, in disgust, set it aside, only to find it immediately come to you? This shows you the rapport that Intelligence works for you if you will only allow it to do so. When you fight it, then it can't come through because you set up a barrier. This is intellect blocking Intelligence. It's there waiting for you, but you have to be receptive so that you can have it.

It is in this manner that advancements of culture conditions are brought about, but it is also an entrapment. You become entrapped in the gadgetry that is produced by the society in which you exist. You also have to pay an allegiance to it in taxes so that it can stay in operation. You are furthering that which holds you in bondage. You have a poor exchange for what you give, and you do get very little credit for what you give in monetary or physical activity.

Our society is the best in the world, but I'm only telling you how society should operate. The last democracy, a true democracy, on this Earth was when King David took the rule of the people away from Samuel. King David's was the last Inner Voice government that operated. The Bible tells you of all the woes that befell that nation when its rule switched from Intelligence to intellect.

When reasoning comes into rule, then you will have havoc, because you will have the one greatest fault man has, come into play, which is greed. **Greed is one of the greatest problems you have to overcome. The second greatest problem is self.** When you get rid of greed, self is very easy. Look up "greed" and "self" in one of the more complete dictionaries.

> *It is important for you to learn the true meaning of these two attributes and to be able to discern the difference between them. Intelligence is true spirit activity. Intellect is the reasoning ability of the spirit. Each has its own function, as do all things. Intellect can and does act independently of Intelligence, and Intelligence can and does act independently of intellect, but the results are vastly different. When we look about us today, we see a world controlled by the activity of intellect alone, without the spirit activity of Intelligence.*

Change, Intelligence and Exceeding Time

When you speak of Intelligence, there is no time. When you speak of intellect, you speak of a time condition. It becomes ruled by time itself as it needs time in which to function. Look backwards in history to all of the hypocrisy and philosophies which set the standards of the day and you will see they have varied greatly over the past 2,000 years. Now compare the past 200 years to the past 2,000 years. Just over the past 100 years, the change factor has been 100-fold. The past 50 years has seen 1,000 times the rate of change. The change factor has been 1,000,000 times in the past 10 years.

The frequencies of Intelligence bombarding Earth are continuously setting an increased pace and standard. Those that cannot attune themselves to this will be totally left out. If you do not attune your body and bring it into rapport with spirit activity, then you will have the devastation that is going to come about by the excessive pressures that are going to come to bear upon you. You will find yourself out of sorts, uneasy, unable to stabilize the conditions you are functioning and working within. You will find your body will have many disorders and not be functioning properly, but if you learn to be quiet and go with Intelligence, using it as a ruling factor, then you should not be the least concerned about the intellect overruling.

The Increasing Rate of Change

The frequencies of Intelligence bombarding Earth are continuously setting an increased pace and standard.

Past Number of Years	Rate of Change
2000 years	Changes
200 years	Many changes
100 years	100 fold
50 years	1,000 times
10 years	1,000,000 times

The increasing rate of change.

Intellect only gives you the reasoning of the condition as to why it exists now. If you have the "know," then you have no need of the reasoning of why because you already know. Only by intellect can you be trapped from knowing the Truth. If you accept the intellect as your standard of being, then you are trapped exactly there and you stand still as you mark time with time. You can only exceed time when you come into Intelligence, because Intelligence does not need time in which to function.

Even though you are in a space factor of functional operation of electronic vibration forces, and you are held in a solidity form of molecular structure, this is all going on by the organization of Intelligence, not intellect.

> *Intelligence is an absolute certainty, while intellect changes with the amount of activity given it. Intellect is not certain, but draws things to itself for its own use. For example, intellect may give you the power to desire a book and to derive an understanding of its assembled words, but Intelligence gives you the activity of those words and the good you might derive from reading the book. On the other hand, Intelligence may give you the desire for, and show you the necessity of, better conditions, but intellect draws together the material for the betterment of conditions. Thus, the activity of both Intelligence and intellect, working in unison and harmony, brings about desirable end results.*

Both must work together in order for you to operate and function when you are in control. If you are not in control, then intellect is going to control you and you are going to be trapped.

Being Free

Your Universal Creed states: **I am Eternally free, in deed, which is my nature, and I bow to no man not even God, for I Am God.**

Anytime you place yourself under a fixed condition, taking an oath of allegiance to anything other than yourself, you have broken the First Commandment: "Thou shalt have no other God before Me."

THE FIRST COMMANDMENT **Thou shalt have no other God before Me.**

The first commandment.

Either you bow to some other man's rule, or you are God. Do you accept somebody else's thesis of operation, or are you an individual?

You are individually made, you are individually perfected in your own division of being. You have your own rights and your own abilities; you need to bow to no one. Nobody owns you but yourself. You are a free agent in the Intelligence of Be, and you should act in that Intelligence and that ability of accomplishment of attainment in accordance with your fulfillment of your ability at all times. Any time that you doubt or settle for less than this, you have placed yourself in a substandard, and you come under a subconscious condition, instead of being totally aware in Full Consciousness.

> *Like all perfect laws, the law of Intelligence and intellect works either positively or negatively, according to its use, and the results will be according to the amount of activity or Spirit given it.*
>
> *Spirit is a word rooted in Latin, which means: spirally, I go to express, continuously in action, multiplicity in all directions at the same time. There is never any time that you can be out of the energy factor of Spirit.*

The Speed of Intelligence

The regulatory factor of Intelligence is of such speed that the speed of light is comparable to a snail beside it. The finite mind cannot grasp the instantaneous nature of its activity in motion. In the Bible it states:

> *Ask of those things you need, in secret, and I shall reward you openly because I already know what you ask before you ask.*

If you become quiet and ask Within, you shall be openly rewarded. This shows you that before you ask, it is already known, because Intelligence is a Now condition which has no variance to wait for time or motion, to activate. By application of intellect, man has brought many standards of attraction to himself, according to what he has made his God. Be careful of those things you desire that they do not devour you. Don't let your desires own you.

Everything you attain and use, bless, use and enjoy, then release for others to have. If you hold it, then you don't have room for anything else. Your burden will become too heavy, which is the way for intellect. If you carry too much of it, then it will descend upon you and you won't be able to carry the load of it.

If you don't let go of the old ways, how can the new come into Be? If you don't let the new come into Be, how will you ever know the difference of how it was or was not? Allow the subject of change to be your avenue of attainment and use each adjustment for its ability to aid you and not control you.

Do not allow yourself to be trapped in the condition of being so dependent upon your intellect conditions that you become hoodwinked into thinking this is the ultimate and all that there is. It is difficult for you to realize the lightning speed of Intelligence attainment and the changes it can instantly bring about, as well as the factors it can bring into being, which are beyond your imagination at this time.

When you grasp into the Divine Truth, then you will know that you know. When you see Truth, then you will see it as it really is, not as you think it should be, or as you accepted it as your standard of acceptance. When you have accepted it as it is, it really isn't as you have accepted it, for you continuously alter.

Doubt, Your Greatest Enemy

In almost all operations that you work with in your normal functions, you rely on your intellect abilities rather than your Intelligence. You will not follow your hunches. There is a little word called ***doubt*** that is the greatest enemy you have to overcome. The **lack of self poise allows the intellect to completely control you.** When you attain a poised condition of a surety, even above self, of absolute fact, which is wisdom, then you know that you will reign within the Intelligence of the universe.

When anything is put to you, and it doesn't ring true at that time, do not be hasty to discard it. Just set it aside until you have grown to attain to its attitude and ability, because many times you will throw the wisdom away by intellect act, and you will go through a lot of digging to reclaim it to have when you need it.

Planting Seeds Of Wisdom

There will be many things that I will say that seem very foreign to you and rather awkward to accept the exchange as presented.

Do not be disturbed when you run up against these difficulties because **many times I will place words in sentences to plant seeds for you to grow with**. As I plant these seeds, they will allow Intelligence to bring wisdom to bear against you, and the seeds mature while you aren't attending them. At some time, all of a sudden a seed will mature into an expression within you. There will be a sudden clarity and you will now understand what I was telling you.

When you pressurize anything by intellect standards and reasoning, you stop the normal flow of energies of Intelligence and you become confused and befuddled within your own inadequacy. You try to remember something but you can't quite seem to recall. However, when you stop and go to do something else, it will come right into your mind.

In all cases, never force anything to come about. Allow it to be very natural in its exchange. Everything that you do in your exchange, allow it to be just as natural as that sun shining outside and just as free in motion. The two attributes of intellect and Intelligence have such a vast difference between them that, for now, we will link Intelligence to the true spiritual activity. However, we are using a very broad terminology which is the best that you will be able to accept at this time. We will leave it at that point.

Your intellect is the reasoning ability of the spirit, by the spirit to the spirit. Each has its own confinements as to all things. Each acts independently of the other, but there is a vast difference.

By definition, **Intelligence is all things contained within the Now State. Intellect is the ability to reason the values of Now** through your ability of reasoning.

> *The best comparison of Intelligence and intellect is that **Intelligence is a certainty, whereas intellect changes with the amount of activity given to it**.*
>
> *Intellect may give you the power to desire a book and understanding the assembled words, but Intelligence gives you*

the activity of those words, the conception of the understanding of the good you might desire from the reading.

Be In It, But Not Of It

In most of your operations you express in, you will allow Intelligence to be pushed aside for your intellectual values of standards that you have accepted by social and cultural conditions. You will even do things that are wrong, knowing that you are doing them wrong, when Intelligence is prompting you not to do it. You will proceed to make the motion and go through the act of acting, rather than being still enough, quiet enough, long enough to withdraw to be in it but not of it.

A great secret to learn to be in things but not of them. In this way, you have control of the situation and not the situation having control over you. Whereas, if you would only have been gracious for a few seconds to become quiet, the Intelligence would express to you the proper answer and act.

One of the greatest problems you will have to face as you start to grow is learning to have patience enough to allow yourself time to be yourself, and not image or mimick everything that is about you. Intellect projects you in this operation of this expression.

Learn to listen to that little voice within you that prompts you continuously. The more that you learn to work with it, the greater the volume of control of projection it will give forth to you. The more that you lessen it, the quieter it will become until it is almost dormant for you to hear, unless it is an extreme emergency.

Intelligence may give you the desire for, and show you the necessity of, better conditions, but intellect draws together the material for the betterment of conditions. Thus, the activity of both Intelligence and intellect, working in unison and harmony, brings about desirable end results.

Until you are able to control and live within the wisdom of Intelligence, you are going to continuously be drawn between a blend of the two trying to attain the ultimate. Each thing that you attempt in your activity, strive to raise your aptitudes and abilities to the best possible of your activities expression. **Whenever you set out to do something, do it the best that you can do it.** Pride yourself in the projection of perfection in everything that you do. It may take you a little longer to begin with, but you will be surprised, in a very short period of time, how fast and proficient you can become.

The more that you ally yourself with the Intelligence, the greater amount of spirit you have in activity with you through your Mind Presence rather than the brain expressing. As you now function, which is mainly in your intellect projection, you allow brain and memories to control you by reasoning value. Many times, even horse sense would have been better than the answer you put out or the act that you did.

You are the sum and substance of all your thoughts. If you are able to quiet yourself enough to shut brain off, and **take time enough by stilling your breath to allow spirit to prompt you through Mind,** through the spirituality center, into the sensitivities of the muscle tones of your body, your reflections will be enormously increased and projected into perfect.

At that time, you will be a dual-fold activity, not only **bringing forth the wisdom of Truth into expression,** but you will glorify yourself by the same activity of this expression because **you become in the image and likeness of God, which is Intelligence**.

With the control of Intelligence, you will find that which is matter will become putty in your hands. By your controls of these activities, you will be able to conjure into expression, anything that you desire. You can alter any condition or any attitude; you can be very responsible for the changes within yourself, which will show to other people, attracting a change within them by the attitude that you project in your Intelligence of activities. Rather than being a mass of the crowd, you become an individual.

In a sense, you grow with self assurance until you no longer have need of self and have the assurance, and assurance brings forth the poise. You no longer have need of faith nor are you subject to the whims of doubt. **You will arrive to the state of Intelligence when you know that you know.** When you arrive to that point of understanding, nobody is going to change your mind. You already are the ultimate.

As you are growing unto these steps of agreement through intellectual exchange, you will discover that the projection of acceptance and theses, called science and "facts," are not so. These scientific facts fall away each day with new advancements taking their place. Everything is continuously in a change condition in the intellect manner. In Intelligence, there is no alteration whatsoever. It is permanent; it is perfect.

As we continuously go through the operation of moving from the true state into a truer state unto the state of Truth, we go through an exchange of taking, giving and replacing. What you thought was the ultimate today, you won't give a second glance to tomorrow. You will grow that rapidly. What you so greatly desire at this time, one year from now, you will have no desire for whatsoever. You will have grown that much.

You will realize that there are so many things that you haven't even considered which are waiting for you for expression within you and through you, that all of this society that exists around you becomes very uninteresting to you. It will sadden you to look at the mundane functioning that most people function in, as you grow.

If you have a slight 3% edge of proofing to yourself, you will be God-like to those that don't understand. What would be like if you had 70% or 100%?

When you wish to project to an understanding of something, your first procedure is to seek something to aid you in conception of understanding. You seek books for their accepted standards for acknowledgment of exchange, but being very dry reading, most people are more likely to read something more exciting, rather than those things of Truth. It comes with a growing and a condition of desire to attain the Truth of all things. It is well to enter through the intellect standards so that you can see all the pitfalls of those who have preceded you. Almost all of the histories and the sciences are the histories of life itself being expressed in exchanges.

The steps of these growths have brought about an intellect culturing condition of a standard accepted. However, it is usually the individual that is uneducated by social standards who makes all of the breakthroughs that give us all of the great inventions, with all of the prosperous activities of the new age, before its time. It is because they didn't know it couldn't be done, so they did it. Whereas, intellect teaches you it cannot be done, and you will not do it. There's the difference.

Wisdom of Intelligence

What you are doing to yourself, absolutely fits 100% to that activity. You are stepping into a void that will take you into the vast universal activity. You have boarded a spaceship called wisdom that will light your way unto the Truth of Life. By your great ability of attainment of entering into the realm of the **magic of the Wisdom of Intelligence,** you will become eternally free from the bounds of the chains of intellect.

It's the avenue that **allows you to open the doors of freedom** that will give you total freedom from the chains of this earth. It will take from you the greatest fear that you have which is called death. It will relieve you from the responsibility of doubt and the activity that goes with it.

In intellect, there is doubt because intellect says this is all the further you can go. Intelligence has no bounds.

If someone says to look at that blue hat over there, everyone would look at the hat and see a different shade of blue. No two of you will see the same blue because no two of you are keyed on the same frequency nor will you see the same reflection. Everything you look at, you look through your eyes of expression from your values and viewpoints of intellect.

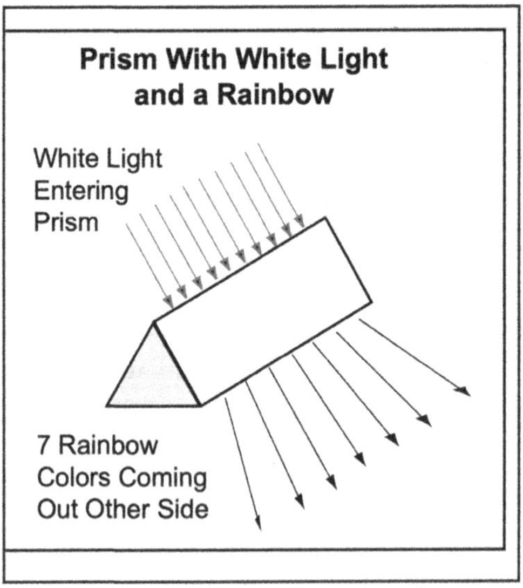

Prism with white light.

When you close your eyes and look at it with Intelligence, then you see it through your Physical eye, your navel, as it really is, rather than what the reflection is. Learn to use your inner sense and allow the Truth to abound within your presence so that you may have the control of the exchange with it and the acknowledgment of it in unison of expression. It becomes at one in atonement with that which is perfect, expressing eternally.

You will also find that **with Intelligence, there is no time, space or distance**. Only in intellect of attainment do you have the voids of space, then time, and in the activity expressing in the time.

In your prismatic activity of expression in the seven-fold of your Intelligence shining forth in expression, in every prism, when you look at the beam of white light coming into it, you see a rainbow coming out the other side. There will be three primary and four secondary colors in the rainbow, making a triangle and a square. That triangle will set inside of the square and the square will set inside of the circle. The dot in the middle is the Intelligence. Everything beheld from it out, is Truth in expression.

Everything that is beheld from any point back within is true from its perspective from that point only. This becomes intellect because it is a divided perception of expression rather than being the total whole, Now.

When you know the Truth of all being, then it's Wisdom. The application and the ability to apply to the degree of your awareness becomes your knowledge. This is what you have accepted. This is the amount you will express to. It is like somebody running up to the edge of a cliff and stopping there to wonder if he should fall down and try to fly or step back and wonder about it.

Many times you will stand on the edge of a threshold and not make the move to become free. Your control of Truth will make you free from all of your entanglements and bonds you have made for yourself. Everything that exists for you and about you, don't blame anybody but yourself. You brought it into be. By your conjuring of agreement, everything exists exactly as you picture it. You put it into the thought mold, which has solidified for you just exactly as you programmed it.

You can also reverse that activity and change everything back to its perfect by forgiving yourself for your act against yourself by the Truth of Motion.

When you have a bucket of muddy water, you always let it stand for a while so the mud can settle down to the bottom. As long as you don't rile it up, the water stays clear. Have you ever looked at yourself as to how much you stir yourself up?

You forgive yourself and ask for forgiveness for those you trespassed against as well as those that trespassed against you. **A big important rule for you is to never go to sleep without going back over your day and forgiving yourself for every trespass you did for that day.** You won't have any hang-ups tomorrow. This is a way to use Intelligence. You will be surprised at how much that little act will change your whole life.

> *Seek intellect, then, but let your Intelligence be your guide in uplifting yourself into the perfect state of being.*

As long as you are in a flesh-physical body, you will have need of your intellect along with your Intelligence. Much of your functional operation has already been programmed, and has been accepted to your brain as your standard of being. As a result, you are trapped within the realm of your acceptance by your own bounds. In the Intelligence of universal factor, man is only just beginning to scratch the surface of abilities. All about us, man is producing gadgetry to aid him in his conditions of understanding, so that he can prove for himself that by brute force many things are possible. You really have no need for brute force or all of the waste of the use of nature's balancing elements which Earth depends upon for its functioning.

If you would use your Intelligence, you would have no need of heating or cooling, because you have the best built system within your body, which is your lungs. By the proper blending of your three gases in function, you can learn to control the elements of your body by heating or cooling. Only by your Intelligence in functional operation can you bring these things into rapport for full use of them, thus relieving yourself of the necessity of mass culture and society that you are trapped in.

In the Intelligence of control of the understanding of assembled words, so many today use words, yet don't know the meaning of those words. They do a lot of talking but say nothing. **When you have something to say, make it as short as you can, and to the point**. You will find that when you stop flowering your prose, **more Intelligence will come forth**, with less intellect. You will tell things as they are and not what you think they should be.

You will find that when you become aware, the Universal conditioning is such that everything that was, already is, and is at your fingertips awaiting your desire. You just forgot how to do it. However, by re-associating a few seeds for you, a few simple exercises will help to help stimulate centers within your body. These centers will become very active and produce greatly for you to give you the power and the energy necessary to bring Force into activity and dismiss the powers, then you will work on a universal plane instead of acceptance of a physical plane.

In the Intelligence of functional operation of universal, we are so used to accepting as our controlling elements of being, only the galaxy we exist in. However, I will say that those views couldn't be more dead wrong.

Our sun is dependent upon the other suns, and those suns are dependent upon other suns which are greater in mass than you could ever imagine. Even our Earth is dependent upon the White Sun for its necessity of BE. **The Intelligence upon the White Sun is the primary Force Energy that comes into operation for those here on Earth**. Because of their love to you and knowing of your necessity, they continuously increase their bombardment of the energy rate, so that you may quicken yourself.

If you look within yourself, you will have the opportunity offered to you. It doesn't mean you have to take it; you have the right of choice in this expression. Each day as the pace quickens in expression, your abilities of sensitivity will have to become keener to be in rapport with Intelligence.

From this lesson, you should do a lot of evaluating to yourself as to what you have been doing, how you have been doing it, and whether it controls you or you control it. It is a good spiritual awakening for you to realize that you do have conditions to overcome. **No condition can be corrected until you admit it is there, and then take decisive measures to overcome it**. Otherwise, it can be there forever. You have to clear out the thinking so Intelligence can correlate and record properly.

When you can't quite grasp something, don't fight it, but dismiss it and let it come back to you. You will find that it will be easier and explained in a clarity of explanation when your guard is down and you are not clouded by thinking and reasoning.

Intelligence, then, is the living thought action, and intellect is the action of thought upon life.

Another good rule to follow is to keep a tablet at your bedside, so as soon as you awaken, whatever is in your thoughts, instantly write it down. Don't rely on memory. In five minutes, you will not remember what it was, nor will you ever be able to recall it. This is very exacting.

Also, during your day, keep a tablet handy for when you have an impression. Take time to write it out and do not interfere with the transmission coming to you. Do not use your reasoning values whatsoever. Learn to become a free floating agent. You will be surprised at the information that will come through.

A LITTLE SAYING ABOUT LIFE

Pain makes men think.
Thinking makes men wise.
Wisdom makes life endurable

A little saying about life.

I have a little saying that was told to me a long time ago: "Pain makes men think. Thinking makes men wise. Wisdom makes life endurable."

You are very carefree until someone is stepping on your toes. When they are stepping on your toes, it is different than if they were stepping on somebody else's toes. It becomes your personal problem. It is only when the pain is bothering you that you will take time to think "Why is this happening to me?"

If you had listened to the prompting that was given to you, this condition could never have arrived. Due to your inefficiency that is prompting you of the condition coming, you set yourself up. It is always in the after effect, when it has been solidified into activity, that you have the results playing back to you, that you begin to think about what you had done wrong.

Nothing takes place without your agreement; you have to agree for it to take place. **Nothing can enter into your expression without your agreement.** Nobody has a right to trespass upon your person without your permission. Even the wisest of teachers will never come forth to you without you first asking for their presence. Only man is the best director of everybody else while his house is falling in shambles.

Wisdom begins at home with number one: you. When you become the example you won't have to tell anyone else about it, they will come looking.

When **Solomon** was trying to fathom the truth of the universe, in his bewilderment he said, "Father, why did you give me all of this knowledge and all of this wisdom without the ability to control?"

The Father said, "Oh son, can't you see the truth of your expression of Me through you? From this day forth, you are My expression expressing in Truth."

From that day on, Solomon was referred to as the wisest man of wisdom that existed in this history because he dared to ask the one question of Truth.

How many times have you asked yourself this question? How many times have we wished that we could backtrack to eat the words and do over the things we had done; and have the perfectness of forgiveness for those we have trespassed against?

Five steps in your truth of being: Idea, which is the impression.

Ideal, the agreement between Mind and self.

Thesis science, which is the discussion of a thesis.

Fact, the proofing that it is.

Wisdom, the ultimate absolute.

We start out with an idea, the impression. The ideal is the agreement. Now we are going to apply that agreement, so we bring it into a thesis where we prove by science. After we have proofed that science into it, only then, can it become a fact and is absolute, becoming wisdom. Otherwise it is continuously stopped at the fourth point, where it is continuously subject to alteration. The fullness of Truth is never brought forth. Only the application of applying into was entertained. The story was never completed.

It is like reading a book and on the last page, it is left to your decision as to how the story ends. You do it to yourself every day! You go to sleep with the same thought. **When you lie down,** you don't even **think about tomorrow**. No thought about the day you just expressed. When you wake up, you say, "I'm back. I lucked out!" So much of that can change for you.

FIVE STEPS IN YOUR TRUTH OF BEING	
Idea	the impression
Ideal	the agreement between Mind and self
Thesis science	the discussion of a thesis
Fact	the proofing that it is
Wisdom	the ultimate absolute

Five steps in your truth of being.

Everything that you reason is of a questionable value. What is fact will change today in your awareness as it grows. All things that are in a manifested state are because of your remembrance. Everything that exists today exists because of your desires yesterday. Your problematic position and condition, all activity you deny self-expression to this day, you put into the future because you can't ever get around ever to do. It's called the great "buck-passer."

A Fuller and Richer Life

In your activities of normal expressing of a day, you are given multiples of opportunities to excel and you will pass them by. There will come a time when all of your abilities that are now dormant will be necessary for you to employ in order to express. The time is now for you to start awakening these sleeping giants and bring them into play. You have been around here about a million and one half times on Earth alone. You are here because you are coming into the realization that you are about to put your house into order. There is a great necessity to uplift yourself into the Great Intelligence and to be able to manage and handle it into the proper perspective.

The greatest problems you are going to have are:

1- learning to budget your time.
2- learning to stretch time.
3- learning to make every second very important.

You will find that you are too busy to do anything else, but you will have a fuller and richer life than you ever dreamed possible. You will also be able to attain the ability to grasp the Divine Truth and live accordingly with it. You will be able to retain your poise when everybody else is losing their expression. There becomes an inner knowing within yourself in your attainment through the normal operation of your truth within yourself by your intellectual agreement in allowing the brain to be shut off.

Everything through your intellect is due to brain stored knowledge of the composite of accumulation. As with all garbage piles, there are few treasures in it. You can go through it any time you want, but it will get you nowhere. It is like a garden, if you allow the weeds to grow, the vegetables will die; the weeds will choke them out. If you wouldn't allow the weeds to grow in your garden, why do you allow them to grow in your brain? Why do you allow your body to become dormant? Because too much is put upon the self importance of the mundane things of each day, rather than a total day of a Whole.

That is what Jesus asked the rich man, "Would you give up all that you had for eternal life and freedom?"

"Oh no," he declined because of his ships, many people working them, all of his sheep, However, a little beggar behind them said, "I'll give you all I have, which amounts these few coins, which is my total wealth."

Jesus replied, "Yes, you shall come with me and you shall have eternity because you learned the first lesson: you own nothing."

You are only a user of all things. All things are here for your use, for your ability to express with, for, by and to. It doesn't matter what you accumulate, you don't own it. In one sweep of the hand, it can be wiped away, instantly, and it does happen. **Only in the Intelligence and wisdom within yourself will you get this surety of eternal peace and the abundance of everything you desire. Abundance means plenty and to spare so that you may share with those about you**.

Be very careful in your desire of material things that you do not become caught up in a self worship, that they begin to control you and own you. All things are things of beauty to be adorned as long as they are adorned as things of beauty and do not become possessive or possessed. You own nothing, you are a user. Even the house you live in is borrowed.

You see what a make believe expression you are actually acting out in? By the Truth, you can have the perfect expression and you can have all the love beyond your desires. You can attain into realms that you can never imagined existed, the realms that you have forgotten about. **There will be a poise and peace within yourself by the surety of the quickening of Intelligence that will instantly prompt you in all things and all activities.**

It also will teach you to remember what knowing you so carefully hid away of **how to take your body back into perfection of Life and take it with you** and not leave it with Earth. Jesus said, "The meek shall inherit the earth." They will, over and over again. They shall be eternally bound to this earth until they become masters of themselves. Being gentle does not mean to be meek. Gentleness is a great condition to culture. It is a great attribute to be able to control, but to be meek means that you have no authority of yourself whatsoever.

Above all, **you are an authority unto yourself.** You are a law unto yourself, not yourself unto a law. You made many agreements before you came into expression; very few of them have been fulfilled.

If you learn to quiet yourself, you will find that Intelligence, through Spirit, will inform you of many things. It also will narrow the gap between the doubt and your certainty.

Can you tell me of one thing that is certain in this expression?

In this expression, we are here.

Is that a certainty? If you were to say the love of your presence, then I would agree with you.

The Only Certainty Is Love

Without love, you could not exist or express. **Without Love, nothing takes place**. Before anything came into motion from the Motionless, it was on the movement of Love that it came into being. From Life came Love and from Life and Love came Light. "Behold, there was Light. Lo, there was Light."

This is a seed-key of certainty that you have never looked at before, nor have you looked into the standards of this depth between an intellect approach and an Intelligence acknowledgment.

To my way of thinking, you have used an intellectual argument to prove Intelligence, being a logical progression of Intelligence followed Love, which followed Life.

That is correct. Intellect is to used for the proof of Intelligence until you go into knowing and you know that you know.

Just as I am not certain that I exist, I am also not certain that Light follows Love, which follows Life, or that intellect proves Intelligence. I am not certain of the presence of any of these.

This is because you are still in a thesis condition, you have not proved anything to yourself. That is for this point of conception. That is why I say that the only certainty that you can say is for Love, because it is eternal.

You are now being approached by a projection of proving for yourself. I am giving you a key that is going to make you cycle. The words that I have just spoken unto you have set up a mathematical formula, in sound, and all the gears are set into motion, right now! Every word that I have used, has a mathematical formula to it. It becomes a chemistry exchange, and the chemistry of your body reacts exactly to the chemical formations of crystallization of those sounds uttered into Light. This is a very technical explanation of what has just taken place. In normal words of explanation, it is Love.

> *The Intelligence of man tells him to quicken his body, and his intellect sets about making automobiles and airplanes.*

And other things, as well.

Everything that you function with is a copy from your body. Every object that you bring about you and surround yourself with, is a copy from out of your body.

What Intelligence Teaches

If you would use your Intelligence, rather than your intellect, you would have no need of automobiles, because in a second, you could be any place that you wanted to be on this planet. You could disassemble and reassemble your body anywhere that you want to be. You could go any place in this universe; you are not limited to this planet. This is why I said that the truth will make you free.

Intelligence will teach you how to quicken the crystallization of your body to make it Light rather than the density of molecules. It will also teach you to remember, because nobody teaches you but yourself. I only inform you, but you teach yourself. **Intelligence teaches you to be real rather than make believe.**

How many of you are able to walk up to a mirror and tell yourself that you love yourself and look at yourself while you are telling yourself? Try it some time. You want to see a lot of guilt come out?

You have no idea of the potential that you hold in captivity, which you restrict in its uses and you restrict its expressions. You have the **best computer that was ever designed** which lies in the back of your head on each side of the knowledge bump. There are two pin points on either side of that bump. Within those two dots is stored all of the past, present and future of all your expressions. Now that is a computer for you! Your right dot is your past and the left is your future.

What happens when there is a severe blow to that area?

Very detrimental. It usually puts you in an unstable condition, a state of bewilderment.

Your brain uses these dots as a control lever against you. It has access to it and will use it to keep you in control. It can easily recall the hurt and pain in you that you don't like, as well as the emotions of activities of anxieties and stress that are not tolerable by you.

Counteracting Conditioning

By learning to quiet brain, you will deprive it of its ability of control, which you allowed to have control over you for a period of years.

When you don't feel well, what is your first reaction? You hurt. And you want to get rid of the hurt. You go to the cause and the source that caused this to be, or you put a bypass between it, turning off that which is warning you to be corrected. Rather than the correction taking place, the bypass continues. As the bypass is allowed to continue, destruction takes place because of illumination of itself by energizing. However, if you had been quiet, you would have been informed as how to exactly handle the situation for correction.

Almost 90% of the things that go wrong with you is due to the agreement and the values of discernment of those expressing about you. You have been programmed to become conditioned to the conditions about you. Did you ever notice on television when August comes and the cold weather sets in, how all of the advertisements about colds start coming on? How long is it before you start catching colds and begin coughing? You will have it for just as long as you put up with it. When you take a stance and decide it isn't going to happen any more, it stops.

By conditioning, you have been taught to accept that pleasure can only be had at certain times. Not so. You can have anything you desire, so why limit yourself? As long as you allow intellect to control you, you will be subject to that condition. If you will look to the source of the truth of what is, nothing is limited to you.

Picture Imaginative Process

When you really want to know something, you do a vast amount of imaginary picturing to get the idea going so the ideal exchange between Spirit and yourself can take place. Then you very easily accomplish that which you desire. How many times have you searched for the answers to something, and when you sat down to ponder it, the answer came to you? Isn't it amazing how it will crystallize back to you? Only when it is dire need will you bring this much effort to bear.

At a normal rate now, you evaluate over 3,000,000 thoughts a second; you have currently limited yourself to that amount. You react, transmit and agree on the acceptance of those thoughts you desire to bring into your realm of being, expressing. Many of them are too fast for your comprehension at this time, so they pass right on by because you have not brought in your view to such a point that you are able to entertain this vision of activity. When you place no limitation over yourself, you will be able to handle a billion thoughts a second to discern and evaluate.

As long as you stay within the mundane functioning of this earthly expression, you limit yourself only to the domain that you are expressing in. When you start perceiving in a universal perception, rather than individualized self, you will think of multiples in all directions at the same time.

How would we make mental pictures to help someone else?

When you manifest by your picture imaginative process, you must not alter a condition or the will of another. **You have no right to enter into**

the will of another without their consent. When you desire answers to something, you will be given them only to your ability of comprehension. **When you are still and you ask for an explanation of what is the most perfect way to go about something, Intelligence will tell you exactly what to do. Then you will know that you know.** If you allow reasoning to come into it, then the Quiet Voice will never be heard.

When you complete the rhythm of one breath, then you are into an alliance with Intelligence. You are allied with Spirit. It's just that easy for you to leave vibration and enter into pulsation where everything is. Actually each breath rate is a continuance of the first breath in action. We are continuously altered by our breath, because we are continuously broadcasting and receiving.

The Ultimate Goal: Become Selfless

Would you explain more about self?

Until you can give up self, you will never lose this flesh body. When you become selfless, then you have attained everything there is to do. **The very ultimate of your goal is for you to become selfless.** Then, you become the Universe. You are no longer an individualized division of the Universe in expression.

The statement which mentions, "I bow to no one," indicates self, doesn't it?

It indicates you are God, which you are. When you are selfless, it means that you are in a state of All in everything. When you are individualized, then there is a self bringing about an individual expression of idea or function of activity. You divide yourself from the Universal Whole to project forth your radiance of expression of Be. Then you return back to the universe and become the fullness thereof, as you return to the state of All.

Doesn't that take place upon ***death****?*

No, there is no death. There is only a cessation of the flesh body as it drops away its heaviness from the Light Body. The molecules that belong to this Earth will return to Earth; you can't take them to any other place in the Universe, or else you would have to bring them back.

Selfless is the lack of a ***personality****?*

Yes, each of you will find that you will be confronted with this as you develop into the advanced stages of meditation, where you will be placed in a selfless condition of Expression. It will be one of the tests that you will undergo.

*What is the **average interval between expressions**?*

Until they can be convinced to come back! On an average, measuring it in our time, it is usually about 500 years. Some may stay from 2 up to 2,000 years. They may come back in a few years due to a problem confronting them which they wish to work out, so they take another try at an expression. The shortest span to come back by desire is 7 days. If the death is accidental, the shortest duration is 3 days. **Every time you come back into expression, the adamic veil is dropped over you.** Everything you knew before is wiped clean. You must accomplish it all in one lifetime. An individual must be an authority to enter into this realm without the veil of the adamic sleep.

What are the conditions going to be for those that take embodiment?

They will come to a condition that man will produce in Thought embodiment. Earth is not too far away from this realm. Much programming is going to have to take place for accepting such standards, and the old standards must fall away.

It is not difficult to make a vehicle to exist in, because all you have to do is to draw from the gases and the elements of the area you are expressing in. It is just a matter of rearranging the molecules in electronic order, using the electrons to congeal the form necessary to operate within the pressures and gases of the expression you are to be in. This is something most of you will have the opportunity to attain.

Death Defined

We see instances of life support systems being removed and they appear as though death has overtaken them, yet the breathing continues. When is death in those instances?

The definition of **death is when the Airless Cell leaves the heart**. In the cases you refer to, the Airless Cell has not left the heart. The Ego center is functioning and the Airless Cell is not commanding the body because the Ego Cell has set up a false identity of authority and the body has become ill and out of proper rapport to its energizing of Will, so there is no longer a Force with a Purpose [Will] to drive the body anymore.

By the intervention of our medical science with their gadgetry, those individuals become trapped on this Earth when they should have been released. This is not necessary. It's just as easy to say, "Unplug me, I want to turn this body in for a new one." You close your eyes and awaken from a sleep again, as you leave this expression and continue on. If taught properly, who would fear death? It is only fear and your greed of expression that keeps you trapped here.

Spiritual Intelligence

How would you describe the Airless Cell?

The **Airless Cell** is not contained by anything physical. It **is the Spiritual Intelligence of your being.**

Is it our consciousness?

There is only one conscious. You may make as many divisions of consciousness as you wish, which you are doing as you now exist. There is no such thing as super or sub, only your divisions of understanding. There is no time that you have no Conscious, or else you couldn't exist.

The occult philosophies use many divisions for your understanding, just as we currently refer to Mind, but as you grow, you will find out there are seven Minds with which you function. You say that you have five **senses**, but actually you function with twelve: five physical and seven spiritual. As you are now, you are only using five.

When you finish these studies, you will be functioning on all twelve, and you will have the ability to turn this body to Light. You will be given the information and the keys, but you will have to do it. If you were able to hold the stillness, you could Perfect your body to Light all by yourself. You would be taught from Within, for attaining the wisdom necessary for your freedom to no longer to be bound to Earth.

What should we do when emotions come in?

Don't get involved with them. Emotions are the result of a misunderstanding condition of operation that one or two may be functioning in. The emotional senses, or the emotional mind comes into play, playing back through the suppressive of the subjective or the objective mind. You may not understand this now, but I am planting seeds. Your computer has made a data file bank of this and you will store this information there for future understanding, when you listen without question or thought distortion.

Don't let these emotions control you. Send them out. You are master of your universe. You demand that brain go back to its job, which is the computerizing of the activities of flesh, and you will take care of the rest of it.

The Adamic Veil

How do I know that I am not expressing subconsciously in multiples already?

You don't know because you don't remember. You have the memory locked away but you don't have the ability of recall.

Why are we not able to recall?

Because of the adamic veil. You took molecular activity over Light Expression, and when you did that, you took the veil to cloak your two memory cells, for coming in to prove everything as you come into expression on this plane.

The only way you erase the play is to rewrite your play. But first, you are going to learn to handle yourself in perfect poise. This means that you must shut down all activity in order to allow the total whole to be. Brain is self. **If you are going to learn to be universal, you are going to have to be selfless.**

Jesus said it in a very beautiful way, "If you know not the Father then you know not me, for the Father and I are One." He said it very clearly and truthfully. This is exactly what I am saying.

The proofing of your self is selfless, and the only time you are going to become universal. When your self importance of ego can be given up, then you will attain your true state of Be. Until then, you are a prisoner of the prison that you make because you worship the false idols. You put everything in front of you but the truth. Even memory is played against you to hold you in control.

If you want to see something mighty, look to the mustard seed and the mustard tree. The minute size of seeding in comparison to the extent of the growth is beyond belief to the accomplishment that is attained there. We are only seeds of remembrance and we have to break the seed to become the tree of knowledge to become the serpent of wisdom that hangs within the tree and entwines through its branches.

Cleansing the Brain Cells

The apple was given forth to Eve so that she would know the difference between good and bad: the bewilderment of knowledge rather than the wisdom of actuality. The apple was used as a symbol because the apple is the only thing that exists in your domain which will clean the mucus from your brain.

The ancients used the three day green apple diet to clean the brain cells of all mucus. You have to have the original pippin apple because the skin is put around it to hold the etheric quality that is spiritually put within the substance of the apple. Our current apple juice won't work because it is already dead matter. As soon as the skin is broken, within a few minutes the essence is gone and the chemicals exchanged to bulk matter.

The diet consists of all of the pippin apples you want to eat and all the water you want to drink, for three days. Only take in apples and water. Keep a tissue handy because you may need it to blow your nose and clear your head.

The easiest way to test yourself to see if you need to go on this diet, is to spin your head around about twenty times. When you stop, if you feel a dizziness and your head keeps on going, then your brain cells need cleansing.

Does this cutting of the skin apply to vegetables and fruit?

Yes, the essence instantly vaporizes. Another thing, a metal knife changes all of the molecular arrangement of the crystals within the substance that is cross-currented by the cutting activity of the steel knife which disrupts the magnetic and electronic impulses.

What type of knife should be used?

You should use a glass knife or a ceramic knife.

How about plastic knives?

In some of your plastics, you have magnetism also. If it is a memory plastic, it has magnetism.

What is the symptom of mucus on the brain?

It causes a laxity in your activity. The mucus continuously putrefies the entire system of the body. When you eat the apples, don't peel off the skin, bite them and eat them immediately. Do this diet only once a year. This is not something to be played with.

What causes the mucus in the brain cells?

It is caused from many things, but mainly by misused thought. You may experience a headache by the second day of the green apple diet. However, a headache is only the brain kidding you not to do it. Brain is bringing pressure to bear on you; it knows it is being threatened. Every time you threaten brain, it is going to kick back at you.

Why is this diet only done once a year?

As with anything, if you overindulge, it loses its efficiency because brain will set up a chemical reaction to it and it will lose its potential properties. The brain is a master chemist. It has the greatest chemist to work for it, which is your thyroid.

You want to be very careful how you do any type of diet because you can upset your metabolism and have disastrous results.

Diet And Blessing Food

What is the best way to diet?

Listen to your palate. Most of desire is imagination, anyway. After being fulfilled, you feel it wasn't as good as you thought it would be. The anticipation is greater than the fulfillment. The trick is to turn it around and make the fulfillment fulfill the essence of the imagination. You do that by giving wholeheartedly to it. Don't tie any strings to it. Whenever you do something, don't expect something in return. How about doing it just for the love of the doing?

Turn all your food into energy, and all the excess, return back to the source from which it originated. **Demand that you partake only of the highest of essence of the food. This was the original purpose for the blessing of the food**. Tell your body it's starving to death, then all the food will be turned into energy and no waste nor fat will be stored.

You are subject to conditioning; you conditioned yourself. If you set a scale for yourself from one to ten, set the goal as to where your appetite is. For the following day, set your level lower on that scale. Each time, keep bringing you desire down by this scale. If you use this as a guide rule, you will find that in most everything you do, you will find that the proficiency of your exchange is beyond your belief. It does work.

Any time you want to indulge, do it that day only. Eat all you want until you make yourself sick. Then you don't want any more. The brain will set up natural cravings in your desires to hold you in bondage.

Eventually, you will attain the condition of an airitarian. You will take all your substance by thought.

With respect to some people craving chocolate, a female friend around the time of month for her female cycle, will crave chocolate. Is it due to vitamin E in the chocolate or something the body needs?

It is according to the individual as to what their stress condition has been for the month; this will move with the moon cycle. When you are in a depletion state, the body will try to tell you in which food substance the chemical is that the body needs for balance. However, this should be taken in a small amount because a small amount will rapidly adjust that condition, whereas indulging will tear it to pieces.

You have programmed and set your body up at childhood by conformity so that certain poisons are now necessary. When you have a withdrawing feeling, you feed it. When you ingest small amounts, the craving becomes less. If you try to cut it out altogether, brain will bend you and break you.

The main point is the thought that you take in with that food. **Everything that you partake into your body, bless into perfect before it passes your teeth**. Your teeth are the sounding boards of the computer that sets up the actions of all the acids that break down the light crystals of the food into energy. If your thought is not proper, your computerization will break down. You have allowed the clarity of clear computerization to take place.

That is why Jesus made the statement, "You could eat of poison, or of scorpions, without any fear of danger if your thought be perfect."

How does the process continue once the food has passed the teeth?

Before the food has even entered the teeth, it is picked up by the sense glands on the inside of the nose. This impression is passed up to the top side of the spirituality cone at the top of the head, where it then goes to the vibrating mechanism inside of the gelatin mass that sets forth the picture of the food. From there, it feeds back from that to the pituitary where those twenty divisions of that gland start feeding all the glandular activity of the ductless glands of your body. Our science is only familiar with eight.

When you were a baby, you had natural faculties that were allowed to become dormant because of deed and food thought projection. This started when you were in the fetal condition where you will still robbing your mother's body of all the things necessary to make the house you were to exist in.

For the seeding, nine years preceding conception is most important in the acceptance of the vehicle and the problematic conditions of it. This includes the nine months of gestation and nine years after birth: perfect act, thought and deed; a condition of Love in expression.

Food Essence and Crystal Energy

Everything that exists in being is composed of crystals. They are Light being solidified into form in an octave expressing in resonance of change.

If we would look at the petal of a red rose, we would only see a red color as well as some white. By magnifying the vision of your eyes thousands of times, and penetrated into that, we would first see the cellular makeup that holds it in form. Then we could break each one of those cellular forms holding it, and go inside of that and amplify it. Within that would be all the miniaturization of light crystals in every geometric form that you could think of, and in all colors of the rainbow. That is the essence which is there.

We take this essence into our mouth and due to a lack of proper computerization, it is destroyed in an instant. It then becomes bulk matter.

In most things that we desire, for example, take the strawberries at this time of year. They are so big and sweet, when you bite into them they are full of sweet juice. How is your mouth when you are given that mental picture! I just proved my point.

You have conditioned yourself so problematical in acceptance and rejection, and you only take a small fraction of that, while all the rest is destroyed. If you would take one strawberry and get all the crystal energy and essence of it, you would be fed by that one berry for the entire day. It is the essence of the smell by holding it near you that will feed you.

Does that hold true for anything that has a pleasant smell?

Yes, but anything that is bitter to taste, do not partake of it Your chemistry is too weak in your body to handle it.

What should we say?

"Everything that I partake of into my body be turned into perfect energy". That is the only thought you need.

What is the function of the thyroid?

The thyroid sets up the energy flow from the temples, the center of will, and directs the iodine color. It takes the red and yellow Light Rays through the temples into the thyroid and directs the iodine color, which it sends out as energizing into the marrow of the bones to coin new cells. It gives the wavelength of that cell that is to be constructed in a replacement condition.

For true and lasting results,
Intelligence and intellect must work
in conjunction with one another,
not independently of one another.

The activity of both Intelligence and intellect, working in unison and harmony, brings about desirable end results.

Lasting results.

COMPARISONS OF INTELLIGENCE & INTELLECT	
1 INTELLIGENCE	INTELLECT
True spirit activity It can & does act independently of intellect.	**Reasoning ability of the spirit**
An absolute certainty	Is not certain, but draws things to itself for its own use
Living thought action	The action of thought upon life.
When you allow yourself to become quiet, then the intelligence can come into rapport with you and give you the guidance.	Intellect is where 90% of man's problems get started. This happens because man allows what seems to be, to control him, instead of what really is.
Man must learn that his greatest avenue of achievement is by the prompting of intelligence.	When we look about us today, we see a world controlled by the activity of intellect alone.
Intelligence is free law. It is limitless. Intelligence works for you if you will only allow it to do so.	Man's ability in intellect has become a fixed law of functioning, which is constantly fluctuating, bending and stretching easily. It collapses just as easily.
Intelligence, is there waiting for you, but you have to be receptive so that you can have it. In intelligence there is no time.	When you fight intelligence, it can't come through because you set up a barrier. This is intellect blocking intelligence. Intellect becomes ruled by time, because it needs time in which to function.

2 INTELLIGENCE	INTELLECT
You are a free agent in the Intelligence of Be, and you should act in that Intelligence ... at all times.	Intellect has its place as we function in our mundane ways.
The regulatory factor of Intelligence is of such speed that the speed of light is comparable to a snail beside it.	The finite mind cannot grasp the instantaneous nature of the activity of Intelligence in motion
Intelligence is a Now condition which has no variance to wait for time or motion to activate.	Intellect is NOT a Now condition, so it has to wait for time or motion to activate
Intelligence attainment has lightning speed and it can bring instantly bring about changes.	Intellect works very slowly in comparison with Intelligence.
When you learn to dismiss everything else other than what you are doing, you have the benefit of Intelligence prompting you and then you will see things in their true focus, not what you think you saw.	When you use intellect, you do not see things in their true focus. Instead you see what you think you saw. If you play back what you think you saw, it will only be so much garbage.
If you can learn to vibrate in perfect unison in conjunction with Intelligence, using your electronic forces of energy, you can be any-where in the Universe that you want. The Intelligence can enable you to diagnose, through spirit, to attain unto yourself the perfectness of health.	Intellect is in control by thesis, by what one thinks is so. As long as you are in a flesh-physical body, you will have need of your intellect along with your Intelligence. In many things, we react from an intellect conception, rather than questioning, "Is this really good for me?" "Am I doing this out of habit?"

3 INTELLIGENCE	INTELLECT
If you would use your Intelligence, you would have no need of heating or cooling, because you have the best built system within your body, which is your lungs. By the proper blending of your three gases in function, you can learn to control the elements of your body by heating or cooling.	With intellect, you need heating and cooling from outside. You do not control the proper blending of your three gases or the elements of your body.
You will find that when you stop flowering your prose, more Intelligence will come forth, with less intellect. You will tell things as they are and not what you think they should be.	With intellect you tend to flower your prose, to do a lot of talking but say nothing. You tell what you think things should be, rather than what they are.
The Intelligence can enable you to diagnose, through spirit, to attain unto yourself the perfectness of health.	As long as you are in a flesh-physical body, you will have need of your intellect along with your Intelligence.
You have to clear out the thinking so Intelligence can correlate and record properly.	When you are thinking, Intelligence can't correlate and record properly.
You can only exceed time when you come into intelligence, because intelligence does not need time in which to function.	If you accept the intellect as your standard of being, then you are trapped exactly there and you stand still as you mark time with time.
If you learn to be quiet and go with intelligence, using it as a ruling factor, then you should not be the least concerned about the intellect overruling.	If you are not quiet within, you are using intellect, which only gives you the reasoning of why a condition exists.

Comparisons of intelligence and intellect.

The energies then are transferred through the flow of the blood and the lymph by demand of the cell expressing itself out of expression. In that way, your continuation is continuously in being.

Very few people bring these thoughts to bear when they partake of food. This does not remain limited only to food but to all activities. You can over-indulge in anything. Truth tells you: **All things in moderation.** You can control anything as long as it is in moderation, but over-indulging in anything can be detrimental. Partaking of anything should only be taken to the point of pleasant condition, not filling. You will be surprised at the little amount you actually need to keep yourself energized. The more that you partake of, the more slothful you become within your activities and the more sluggish your activities become.

The biggest problem we are going to have is to get you to let go of the trap that you got yourself into. You have fixed conceptions and perceptions, which have to be altered. Only you will discard them, nobody else will do it for you.

Food, Drink and Blending Foods

What about alcohol?

If you are unable to exert any control over it, then leave it alone. Your body creates more alcohol from the various blends of foods than most people indulge in their average meal.

What about fruit salads?

A fruit salad is one of the worst things on your nervous system that you can eat. It mixes five acids together simultaneously. You really give your system a shock when you do that.

To eat properly, no foods should be blended within twenty minutes. How does that square with eating a fast meal and running off to do something else? No two different types of foods or colors of foods should be blended in that manner.

That is a very beautiful thought because if we would actually eat like that, it wouldn't be possible to over-eat. What should we do if there is only a half hour available for lunch?

Take just one food for lunch! You don't mix colors or different types of energy together. If you would take your food and chew it as it should properly be done, you wouldn't have any more full plates when you sit down to eat.

I was told by a chemist that drinking coffee with the meal doubles the caloric intake of the food. It is better to wait for about a half an hour, so that it doesn't have that reaction.

Many things blended together change the chemical arrangement completely. Taking coffee with your meals, sets up a tannic acid condition which thwarts the breakdown of the food so that it is flushed out of the stomach before it can be converted into a digestive condition.

You can have anything you want. I can't tell you what to do; I can only inform you. You have to do it yourself.

What about lemon and water?

Lemon and water is very good only when taken first thing in the morning. When you do this, and roll your stomach around, it cleans out the intestines. The lemon kills everything.

What about lemon and water taken with meals?

I can't tell you what to do, I can only tell you what I would or wouldn't do; I wouldn't drink it with my meal.

How do you feel about goat milk?

The goat milk should be turned into whey to be taken properly. That is the only thing that can be mixed with the food when you are eating.

What about cheese?

Very good in the middle of the afternoon. This gives it time to be broken down before you go to sleep. Cheese is very bad for you because it binds the system. It reacts against the system, taking a very long time to be broken down. Cottage cheese is one of the better cheeses you can eat because it is easier for the body to break it down. It hasn't become curd yet. It is not yet compressed and is still in a "semi" condition.

You can eat anything you want as long as you eat in moderation; don't limit yourself on anything. **The thought while eating is the most important. Remember that in anything that you partake of is light crystals, not matter.** When you take of the matter, you lose the light crystals. There's the secret!

Do dogs, cats and other animals see auras?

Instead of seeing auras, they will pick up the radiation of the odor of your body that is produced in your atmosphere. They can read that odor much quicker than they can an aura. They have a greater range of acceptance. As for the feline, although they are looking in a given direction, it has a scope of angle for perception at about 92 degrees, whereas your scope of angle is fixed at 15 degrees.

I would like to know about eating meat. Should we, or shouldn't we?

This becomes an individual choice. Jesus told you that you could ingest a poison if you knew there was no harm in it. By your knowing, there could be no harmful effects. Your body has been set up on a condition of flesh acceptance, but if you were a baby that never taken flesh food into it, then this would be a different condition. Once your body has been conditioned into flesh acceptance, it makes no difference what you eat. It is the thought behind what you are eating, when you are eating, that is important.

As you continually change your diet, you will find out, unless you have a great control, that you will not have a balanced diet. However, by knowing the complete understanding of how energy is directed in the body, you realize that it makes no difference what you take into the body because your energy comes out of the air anyway. For us now, most of the value of energy is in the smell rather than the eating factor. We have been taught that this is the proper way to have physical endurance. Thus, we feed ourselves at the dinner table

If you took the energy within a one inch cube of wood, you could drive a steamship across the Atlantic. The same thing applies to the value of food. **If you would use the essence of the food rather than the food itself, you would find your body greatly nourished**. It would be much more nourished than with all of the chemical processes which cause the body to have to dispose of, as well as, unbalance the body itself. We tend to blend a mixture of our foods too fast which results in an acid condition. No foods should be blended within 20 minutes. Heavily seasoned foods may taste appetizing, but they are very difficult for the body to digest.

Also, your range of origin within the 12 areas on this planet, which corresponds to your home planet as well as the 12 areas of earth, makes a difference in the factoring of food that you eat. The temperate zones of earth in longitude and latitude, by the magnetic lines of force that you function in, also change your food demand for energy exchange for your functional operation.

You can eat anything you want as long as you accept it and bless it into being and return it back to the universe. There is nothing but an exchange taking place, anyway. Jesus taught you anything in moderation,

just don't over-indulge. Too much water can be as bad as too little water, or taking water during the process of chemical breakdown of the food can be a hindrance to the body. The water sets up a difference in the acid flow, breaking down the effectiveness of the acid so that it doesn't achieve its function. The husking of the food has to take place in the kneading of the stomach.

What is the cause of ***migraine headaches****?*

Migraine headaches are caused by emotions. Migraines are the results of contained emotions that are not allowed to express.

What about those who know the cause of migraine headaches, yet are unable to control them?

You give in very easily! Only you know what lurks back there. You even forgot where you hid it, and you can't live with yourself because you forgot why you hid it. It will torment you until you find out.

Proper Environment and Home Planet

How do we find our proper environment so that we can function, if there are 12 different areas on earth for us?

That really isn't your spiritual condition, but it is rather that you desire the atmospheric condition on the earth which equals with your home planet. What you desire and are most comfortable in, becomes your environment of conditioning. You will find that the food substance in this environment is most common to your need, by the energy factor it affords you. When you attain unto a better physical ability, then you will attain unto your Spiritual ability.

If the body is clean and healthy, then the Spirit has full activity of being free of bondage to you. If your body is ill and out of place and you are out of environment condition, you cannot equalize with the pressures of atmosphere that you are functioning within. It can be too wet, too dry, too cold or too hot, which can change the gas condition of your cellular makeup. Your cells cannot equalize in that environment, so you will find that your health will fail in an environment which you are not natural to. You can exist in it, but you cannot be healthy.

You are a free agent and you have a right to be happy and you have a right to be where you have your own happiness. Nobody can tell you where your happiness is but yourself. You don't have to answer to anybody but yourself. **When you have concluded this expression, you have only to answer for what you did, not for what anybody else did.** Don't let anybody else alter you; you make your own choices. **You know within yourself what is right for yourself.** Don't let anybody influence or impress you in any way. This is your right as an individual.

What do you mean by the planet we come from?

This would be the planet from which you originated and are familiar with in expression besides Earth. In each solar system, there are 12 planets birthed by the sun of that solar system. Earth has 12 areas, each of which is equal to one of the other 11 conditions of this solar system.

The degenerates and outcasts of these other planets are brought to this frequency on Earth for their correction and to be purified. It could be from a planet in another galaxy, yet of a similar condition to this range rate. No matter where you go in the universe, you will find things very much the same. There is not a great deal of difference outside of the Intelligence level. Form may differ due to gases and chemical arrangement of the molecular structure.

When you are able to contact your Inner Self, your God, you will know who you are, where you are, what you are and why. You can go back and talk to your memory cells and watch it play back for you. You can watch all of your expressions of everybody you existed with and where you existed. You carry two little cells on either side of your knowledge bump at the back of your head. This little computer, the size of a pencil point, carries all of your expressions in record.

The Source of These Teachings

What is the source of your teachings?

They were given directly to me by what you would call God, or the Father. If you could go to the Akashic Records, you would find them in the Royal Golden Book. It was only nine years ago, [1967], that I was authorized to release this information. I've had it since 1927. This comes from the Golden Book and you must go to the Arch Realm to get to it.

Why are we allowed access to this now?

Because Earth has come to the frequency in this period of its history where the information should be placed in the hands of individuals who will find their way, in Light, to receive this information. Not one of you found your way here by chance. The opportunity was opened to you by yourself to be here. You chose yourself to be here.

Shambhalla and the Vial of Light

It was only due to your vial reaching a certain intensity of Light in Shambhalla, that you were allowed to be here as a student. As you change in your desires that you project, your vial, which is placed as you take expression on Earth, will glow. When it glows to a certain intensity, a teacher will be placed in your path, or an individual will be placed to give you information to In-light you. If you pass it by, your vial will lose its intensity. If you accept it, then your vial increases in intensity. When it reaches a certain vibration rate, then a teacher is placed in your way. When you outgrow that teacher, then another will be placed in your way, so that your growth will continue.

Your vial is placed at Shambhalla, which is a location beneath the Gobi Desert. The vials are under constant supervision as your expression is monitored.

As you continue to endeavor, you will exceed and receive the Universe. Remember this, all that you have will be taken from you if you drop it. You will not quite remember what you had if you do not make the use of it. If you live it and become it, as you should be doing, this becomes your ruling factor of Be; you will find that you will be greatly rewarded beyond your imagination.

You will attain unto yourself a state of **Poise and Joy** that you never knew existed on this earth. You will attain unto yourself a **health condition where your body will be radiant with energy and brilliance** that will exceed anything you could ever imagine. My body isn't any older than twenty years, yet my outward aging factor shows age. No cell of my body is older than seven years. An age factor has been set up so that my body be will shown respect. You won't listen to a twenty-year-old kid.

Man's Responsibilities

Man is responsible for the well-being of all forms of creation. He is also responsible for the Earth itself and for all that transpires here, because he is the cause of all that happens here.

For too long, man has looked upon his own iniquities and their results as the will of God. The truth is that man himself is the cause of all adversities because of his creative thought. If mankind would use this creative thought for the betterment of all things instead of their destruction, he would not suffer the results that he does.

For just as long as man thinks wars, storms, earthquakes and calamities, then for just that long will he have these things. Remember also, that all discordant thoughts—hate, selfishness, lust, passion and greed—have a tendency to cause the calamities that befall man from time to time. If the people of a nation did not hold hate in their hearts for other nations, they would not suffer these terrible calamities. These are the natural results of evil thoughts. This does not mean that all people have thought this way, but because thought is the most powerful of man's powers, it takes only a few people thinking and agreeing to the same thoughts to produce these devastating results.

Their responsibility begins just as soon as they send these thoughts forth into vibration, and the results are their fault as surely as if they grasped the foundation of the Earth and shook it. For redemption, they must first set right the results of their thoughts, then change their thoughts. That is their responsibility.

Your thought is all-powerful, and you are responsible for its control and its use, and for the results of its use. Man is responsible for everything on this Earth and for the planet itself, for God gave man dominion over the Earth. The results of that dominion are caused by man, and are man's responsibility. Because God gave to man the absolute rule of himself, the world and the fullness thereof, man is responsible for the results of that rule.

Therefore, **whatever man has harmed, he must set right.** He has caused havoc and destruction, and he must make peace and reconstruct all things he has destroyed. He has caused sickness, death, disease and heartache. He has even caused the grass to be different than it once was. Even when all these wrongs are righted, his responsibility will not end, for **he must maintain all in the state of perfection through loving service.**

Whatever man does to anything, he does to himself. If he kills, he also kills part of himself. If he neglects anything, he also neglects himself. If he sees iniquity in others, it is because he has it within himself. If he condemns any other form of activity, he also condemns himself.

The first responsibility of man, then, is to make himself a fit habitation for God's Pure Life by cleansing himself through service to other men and other creations.

To have any semblance of peace, **man must learn the two great fundamental laws of life and live by these laws.** The first law is to mind one's own business. This business is that of love: to love all things as he loves himself. It is his failure to live by these simple, fundamental laws that has brought man to his present condition.

The second Law that man must understand is that whatever he sows he must also reap. He must sow good things to reap good things.

Live then, according to these laws so that your life may be a constant blessing to all of God's creations, that your days may be full of eternal blessings, and that your responsibilities will be beautiful to behold because of your creative thought. As Jesus said, "Guard well your thought so that your speech and action may bring forth fruit and blessings abundantly."

Remember that you bless or curse yourself, according to your own action and thought.

TWO GREAT FUNDAMENTAL LAWS OF LIFE

Man must learn the two great fundamental laws of life and live by these laws

I. Mind his own business.

This business is that of love: to love all things as he loves himself.

II. Whatever he sows he must also reap.

He must sow good things in order to reap good things.

Two great fundamental laws of life.

Man's Responsibilities

One of the greatest challenges you will have to face is to learn to let go, because you can never have anything new until you let go of the old. As long as you hold on with a death grip, nothing new can take place. Unless you are open and unbiased and not opinionated, you will only partially accept that which is being presented.

One of the biggest responsibilities that mankind has is the misappropriation of the ability of constructive thought. We are so positively negative that we are perfect in negative projection. If you would reverse the possibilities, it would be beyond your beliefs in potential. Considering the evaluations of your abilities and the minor portion that you use in your normal day of exchanges and expression, you use about one ten thousandth of your ability.

Regardless of how much you have acquired in knowledge, you will live to see that knowledge has become past dated. Regardless of what you accumulate in collection, there is no way by knowledge that you can keep abreast of the constant exchange that is going on second by second in every field.

Knowledge has its place in exchange for introductory capacity only. There is one problem with knowledge in that a little of it can be very dangerous. A little wisdom can be disastrous if improperly used or improperly projected.

Mankind is prone to be very self-centered and selfish. Self seems to become the very first operation of activity rather than looking about to see what the prior condition of what that activity is before self is even considered.

Importance of Your Thoughts

Your responses and responsibilities are usually set forth too rapidly without consequences being fully evaluated before projection takes place. **Remember, as you make your thought pictures, whether you act it out or not, you become responsible for it** because you charged the ethers with that activity in expression; you are responsible for it because you are the sum and substance of the totality of your thoughts.

Your constructive thought pattern is the only ability that you have left of your purity in operation. This is the one part that was not allowed to become dormant in order to allow you to have the opportunity to realize by your projections what you are doing to yourself and those with whom you associate. **This becomes the personal responsibility of each to learn to clean your own house before telling others how to clean their houses.** Usually, you will find that those who are telling others how to clean their house, have locked the door on their own house upon leaving it!

In socialized conditioning, by character and creed, you are given a biased projection by your normal expression of your home life and patterning of your parents and those with which you are associated. Many times, these allow you to become callous into a pattern that is unlike you but which you accept as a standard and act of being, and you become that which you are patterning. As you pattern and you deny others, you deny yourself equally. As you belittle anything, you equally belittle yourself. When you affect others singularly, it comes back to you in multiples.

You cause the great calamities to take place in this great habitation which you call Earth by your misappropriation of thought alone. A group singularly has tremendous power, but when you amplify it by multiples and grouping until it becomes a mass movement, then it becomes a quagmire of conditioning. This sets up conditions that are not proper for functioning in poise and perfect condition.

It allows you the opportunity to set up greed and destruction where there should be love, liberty and free act. The problem is that you have been brainwashed into a condition of believing that certain things should be necessities because a few wish to control the majority. By using the proper swaying conditions of amplification, they can persuade your undivided attention in subconscious activities. This impresses upon you without your realizing it because you are accepting this bombardment without evaluating the effects of the cause that are going to take place by your acceptance.

You evaluate over 3,000,000 thoughts a second; you have the capacity of ten times that amount. Thus, in your evaluating condition of your discernment throughout your Spirituality Cone, you set up a standard of acceptance that you have allowed to be your standard. That standard is not rigid, it is constantly in a flux. It has a high and a low. When something goes too far above the top, you won't tolerate it, the same when it goes too low. You are constantly in a flux of being impressed by conditions of others you associate with, also by mediums of projection that are targeted to you to take away your own time of thinking. They fill your thinking time with their nonsense, so that you begin to live in a world of make-believe prattle.

As long as you are in with this make-believe small talk that most people are always into, you are going to be into the same quagmire and you are going to be held to the same cause and effects of consequences that take place from this quagmire.

The important fact to learn is that you are responsible for everything that you put into thought vibration. Nobody does anything to you but yourself. If you have any problems, don't pass the buck on to anyone else, look at number one and find out why it took place.

If you look hard enough and deeply enough, you will find out why it took place and why the responsibilities are as such from your own projection.

Learn to Evaluate

Have you ever noticed how the media, just before the onset of fall, will set up television ads that tell us the flu season is coming along with coughs and colds? These symptoms are set for you to make you prone for acceptance. Comes spring, there is a reversal of activity. Then it is the allergies and pollen that are in the air. You can see how people allow their will to be swayed by other's projection and they take their conditioning of cause until they get tired of it.

What you have to learn is to be in but not of it. Learn to evaluate for yourself, "Is this really good for me?" "Can I really handle this?" "Is it going to aid me, or will it cause an indebtedness at a later time?"

The important factor is to learn to evaluate and learn to listen; don't hear, listen within. A big difference! **Listen to what's being projected, not what the words are saying.** It is your responsibility to realize.

Your evaluation of asking whether this is good for me, can be taken two ways. That word "me" can be self embodied associated as well as just toward self.

Right, it is only towards self. When I refer to "me," that is self. When I say "I," then I'm talking about the inner self. Me is past tense, I is present. Whenever I use a past tense, I am referring to this reflection. "I" is the personified activity in expression: the total whole. As you go further in these lessons, you will be given each letter of the alphabet and a full understanding of it. Then you will begin to understand what words really mean when they are spoken.

Use this as a clue to understanding the lesson paper as to whether the point is celestial or terrestrial. **These lessons are specifically put together and the more times you read them, the more there will be teachings from the spaces between the lines.** The more effort you put into this, the more the Thought is going to project back to you. Just be still and listen.

Responsibilities and Personal Endorsement

The purity of your self is a total whole. On a scale of one hundred, the average individual is operating on a purity level between two and three. That is where your responsibilities are: so much success with negativity. This is the only thing mankind has really learned well.

You are going to move that number up to the maximum; you have all the facilities and all the available ability of functional operations to accomplish this, if you will just **let go of the old to have the new.** Habits are easy to form but very difficult to get rid of. However, when you make new habits, make good habits to exchange for the old ones.

In your idle thinking, when you make an agreement with something without evaluating it completely, you know that you amplified that with your personal endorsement which you have authorized for everybody else to have. **When you give it your personal endorsement, then it is released into the eth to go completely around the universe.** The eth, as opposed to the ethers, is without animation waiting to be put into activity in the ethers. Now do you see your responsibilities?

Thought vs. Thinking

Thought is one thing, thinking is something else. **Thought is created of activity**. When you make a picture mold and release it on the outgoing breath, then you are in a total control condition in projection of activity of the future. Sometimes it doesn't even take a day to receive Thought when the intensity is released upon and the value is put upon it in emphasis.

You have the ability within you to create anything that you desire within a split second toward manifesting everything that you need which takes in toil, endeavor and time. You are responsible for the control of everything that is in use and the results that are caused by that use.

Any act of act is acting in a continuous replay until you stop it, and you are responsible for it to the Godhead for everything that you alter in that replay.

When we breathe something that is out of value of Truth, we clean it up by our thought and release it?

Yes, in the future you will be given exercises on how to use the cleansing process of yourself and the cleansing of your thoughts. For the time being, we are only informing you of the conditions that you function and exist within so that you become aware of what you are really existing with and why you are existing, instead of living. There is a great difference between those two words. As it is now, you don't know what is happening from second to second. You have no idea until it hits back to you what you have caused in an effect condition.

Be In It But Not of It

If you are still and tap Source; then you will know exactly what is going to take place at all times. You will be aware of all causes in act coming into action, before they take place. In this way you learn to be in it but not of it. You then put up your barrier and it goes right on around you. It won't affect you because you won't allow it to come into your field of operation. You will not give it power or strength to exist. You are cleansing it conditionally.

HOW TO
BE IN IT BUT NOT OF IT

Be still and tap Source.
Then you will know exactly what is going to take place at all times. You will be aware of all causes in act coming into action, before they take place.
In this way you learn to be in it but not of it.

You then put up your barrier and it goes right on around you.
It won't affect you because you won't allow it to come into your field of operation.
You will not give it power or strength to exist.

You are only an observer.

The only way you can change any injustices is by thought.
Nothing is changed by action. Action is the result of proper thought projection, or improper thought projection, whichever way it is employed.

How to be in it but not of it.

To be in it but not of it, **you are only an observer,** and **the only way you can change any injustices is by thought. Nothing is changed by action. Action is the result of proper thought projection, or improper thought projection, whichever way it is employed. The effects of that activity is by the emphasis of the cause.**

As it stands now, one half of one percent of the total population of Earth is keeping this planet clean so that it can exist. It was up to two percent but it settled back again. It always climbs during the yuletide season, and then after the holidays, it goes down again. The calamities crop up all over the earth. All of the people on this planet, by their agreement of misappropriation of thought, due to the conditioning of society and culture, are causing their own problems.

The main thing is that so many people are biased and opinionated by conditioning that they don't realize the Truth when they see it. They don't look at things from a true prospective, they are looking from a reflective, slanted view. When they start to evaluate something, they run up to their barrier, and that is where they stop.

What is the contribution of those remaining people, what are they contributing?

Nothing. They shall inherit the earth and all of the dirt upon it. They have assured their cycle of continuation. In other words, you stand back and let the crowd run away. However, you can warn them of the consequences, but they won't heed you.

Responsibility to Perfect

Do we have a responsibility to others?

No, **you have only one responsibility which is to self.** Everyone is given the same opportunity, but they don't want to be bothered. They are happy wallowing in the mud; they don't know anything else exists.

Isn't that arrogant?

No, it's not. Everybody has the same opportunity to perfection. How many will seek to rise above their level of conditioning?

Perhaps that person hasn't been introduced to anything and feels this is all that exists.

I can't buy that. **The inner voice is always there as long as they are drawing their breath.** You have something that mankind refers to as conscience, which is a wee small voice. If you do not listen to that little voice that prompts you, it will become quieter. Each time that you don't respond to Its impressions for your values of betterment, it will decrease in intensity. The more you use it, the greater its intensity will become.

Everybody has this when they come into expression; it's called an Airless Cell. For now, you can regard it as the Divinity of your Be. This will be covered in greater depth at a later series of lessons. Then you will understand the difference between the ego cell and the Airless Cell. Most individuals are reflecting an activity from the ego cell, which is the reflected activity of construction. This is dominated by past memory impressions, from brain, in responsive activity of expressing in this reflection. This is a reflection and it is a reflection of expression.

You are given so much time each day to act out that day's expression. When you are in your rest state, you are preparing your script for your next awakening. There is no need for any of this to ever be if you will only put yourself into authority.

Responsibility to Your Dominion

Everything that takes place in a condition of adversity is the net result of faulty programming of man's own erroneous thinking and the malfunctioning in his thinking process. Nothing can take place within you unless you allow it to. Anything that is out of order within you is your responsibility.

You are also responsible for the correction of anything that is misfunctioning in operation within you. In the next few years, many things will implode to you to make you aware of your responsibilities, and to give you the ability of control of those responsibilities. As it is now, through your social and cultural conditions, almost all of what you have learned is wrong. In the Bible it states that the meek shall inherit the Earth. If you stay in ignorance, you shall inherit this Earth. You will not get away from it until you can look death in the eye and walk away.

Your responsibility is only one thing: your personal perfection. One thing only needs to be done above anything else, and that is **the purification of yourself**. For too many times in man's past, he has shrugged his responsibility over to the next guy or left the reasoning of brain to do it for him.

However, the time has come in being, where we no longer need to look to brain. It's time to stop passing the buck, face facts and face yourself as you become responsible for what you do in life. When you reach the avenue of endeavor that you take the responsibility for yourself, you will find it is not nearly as difficult as you thought it was going to be.

You will also find that as you study your lessons, **your Inner Self will begin to direct you** in ways, forms and modes to relieve the conditions you are existing in. You will be given opportunities which could have been disastrous if you were not walking the Path of Light. When you walk that path, you will be able to stand before death and walk away from it. With the Light about you, many disastrous things will be diverted from you.

Keep your Circle of Light charged about you; this is most important. Accidents do happen because people don't keep their responsibilities about them, and they get somewhat forgetful about others. Out of neglect, you may cause a condition for others that can be disastrous. Yet, even things that may seem disastrous can be altered by your knowing.

Many things will be placed in your way so that you will receive and know your responsibilities of BE. Each day as you open your eyes and take your first waking breath, you become responsible for that entire day's operation. This first breath is very important. You should charge that breath fully with Light. In this way, you have brought your body to full potential with Light.

In times past, when man was very doubtful about what tomorrow would bring, because of his own ignorance of doubting his own ability of that which is Truth, man-made hardships upon himself. Even today, man continues to do this while in a land of abundance. There is no place in the world that you can go where there is more abundance than here in the United States. What you would call a life of existing is considered living like a king in other lands.

THE CIRCLE OF LIGHT

The Circle of Light is all about me, and the life-giving Spiritual Substance is ever present in the God within. The Circle of Light holds the Forces of Light which watch over me vigilantly.

Lovingly and confidently, I release myself to the care and keeping of the Great Brotherhood of Light. Knowing that, I give thanks to the In-dwelling Force that is constantly and unfailingly guiding me into my Perfection.

Two circle of light.

There is one thing which exists in our country that doesn't exist in others, which is knowing you are free. There are only two other countries where you will find an avenue of this, which are Australia and New Zealand. The rest of the world is so completely dominated that they don't realize their own responsibilities to individualization. They don't realize they are eternally free. In your responsibilities of being, all the chaos taking place in the world, all of the furies of nature that are ravaged against you are due to your neglect; you dropped your responsibility.

Man was given dominion over everything, and that means nature, also. Yet, nature controls you. When you **Know**, then nature answers to you; you don't answer to nature. By your expressions, your doubts and alarms, you bring about the calamities that function in your world. This holds true for your famines, floods and furies of nature. They are all a direct result of the people's insecurities within their own being as to their surroundings.

When man learns to turn his thoughts to Love and loving one another, which doesn't mean owning, but sharing with one another of all things in being with no strings attached, **then you will see some change. Love means a gentle exchange of all things.** Love has to be something mutually given by both, equally with no terms, bounds or requests in return. Until you are that, you will never know Love. Every individual must learn everything about themselves so that the beauty can expound in everything with which they associate. Only if you associate and expound this beauty, may you also become this beauty. You surely can't be that which you don't have.

Master Qualities: Poise and Grace

If you have hate and malice within you, then you can't be the Love of the Father in expression. If you doubt yourself, then how do you have the ability of authority? By this, you lose the first thing which a Master must have: poise. The second principle is grace. If you have poise and grace, you don't need faith, hope and charity.

When you have the Authority of Being in poise, then you have everything, because you are within the fullness of Love radiating forth in Love Be. That is truly your responsibility.

When God created this Earth and contracted with Man in agreement as to how this planet was to be dominated, a contract agreement was that Earth was to be the most beautiful jewel that was ever created in the Universe.

From out in space, Earth appears as a very deep aqua-turquoise jewel. It is best described as an aquamarine blue, as it formed itself like a raindrop. Even now, some seven billion years later, as our astronauts go into space and photograph Earth, you will see the aqua blue around it. We are still in the percolating stage as it was when it was created.

The radiations of responsibility of every individual that expresses here was, that everything gave to one another with no questions asked: Love. You will find in the Biblical Genesis that when Adam walked, all the grass bowed down so that he would have a carpet to walk upon. All the trees lowered their branches for him to pick their fruit. All the flowers turned their blossoms toward him as he walked by.

The same thing is happening today, but you don't realize it. The flowers are telling you how much they love you as you walk by. You don't look; you don't even see. The trees extend their beauty in radiance of gas exchange for you, and you don't even thank them. Every earthworm is making it possible for all the vegetation and the bacteria germination of fertilization of your soil. These are all your responsibilities. **Everything that exists in function about you is your responsibility**. If you don't give authority and love to them, then you short-change yourself, because they still pour their hearts out and patiently await your exchange with them.

Within the air that you breathe, there are millions upon millions of universes so infinite in their smallness, they cannot be measured by our scales, yet, they are just as important as you are. Neither you or anything else upon this planet, could exist without them. When you say your Circle of Light affirmation in the morning, you don't realize the multiples of your responsibilities that you cover.

Circle of Light

The Circle of Light is all about me, and the life-giving Spiritual Substance is ever present in the God within. The Circle of Light holds the Forces of Light which watch over me vigilantly.

Lovingly and confidently, I release myself to the care and keeping of the Great Brotherhood of Light. Knowing that, I give thanks to the In-dwelling Force that is constantly and unfailingly guiding me into my Perfection.

As you walk about each day, don't look for things out of order and misfitting, but see them fitting and in order, as you give them your blessing and your love. The same love brilliance radiating in this room could be in the entire world, but it is up to you to make it so. We have taken the time to charge this house. Have you taken the time to charge your individuality, the home you exist in, and the area you express in? These are your responsibilities.

They can be changed and be just as radiant as this house is. **All you have to do is to give it your love, and put your love into it as you thank it and bless it for being, as well as yourself.**

For too long, man has looked upon his own iniquities and their results as the will of God. The truth is that man himself is the cause of all adversities, because of his creative thought. If mankind would use this creative thought for the betterment of all things instead of their destruction, he would not suffer the results that he does.

Nature's Time Clock

Anything manifested has a built-in destruction factor; it has a time date on it. Now mankind has deemed himself smarter than nature, so he is going to produce something that can't self-destruct. By a meddlesome situation, he is setting up a toxic condition for himself because of an alteration of natural reaction of nature.

From a historical point of view, he is only projecting a logic that has preceded him. For example, the hole in the earth, the root cellar, the ice cooler and the refrigerator, all are logical progressions of man's inventiveness.

No, not the inventiveness but the speed of necessity is the answer to that, not inventive progression. It is his idea of a speedier more efficient condition, although he forgot that he is upsetting nature's conditioning of the time act of germs within that food element. Anything that is put into a refrigerator is dead within five minutes. It loses its ability to produce rhythm; it has loses its resonance of vibration. There is no essence left in it whatsoever, and all that is left is chemical bulk.

Are we able to purify that?

You can purify anything that passes your teeth by your purity of thought. You will reverse that entire activity if your thought is strong enough.

Your teeth are computers which set up all the conditioning of all the acids, chemicals and necessities of purification of anything that is put into the mouth by the sense glands located there. These are your etheric teeth, not the physical, which is why this still is in function even when there are no teeth present.

Everything is in your blueprint and your body only sheaths the blueprint. The responsibilities of what I am after is that in your natural functioning, you have natural germs which abound good health for you. By your act of misappropriation with fertilizers and pesticides, you set up a toxic condition as you place toxins in your food.

Nature has a time clock of everything that exists in its expression of time, form and space. Everything has a rate of frequency and vibration in resonance response, so when that resonance response totals zero, it will fall apart only to return to new later. From each germ, a thousand seeds fall. Out of that thousand which fall, maybe ten will germinate, unless propagated.

Propagation is good if it is done in proper conditioning. An over-production is as boundless as a shortage condition. Everything must be held within its metes and bounds of an equal level condition, so there is no desire, need or want. Most of us have been conditioned to overabundance. Abundance means plenty and to spare so that you can share. An over-abundance decays before it can ever be used so that it becomes detrimental from its decaying activity as it produces a toxic condition.

All shortages come from man's ignorance. When grain is stored, it is fumigated, which upsets the germ activity so that it no longer has a food value.

How did the Egyptians store their food, then?

The Egyptians were in a period where they used harmonics of sound. They used two dishes which were facing each other. When Joseph designed the warehouse that all the food was put in, even the apples and fruit were put in two dishes on posts. This was never shown, but I'm telling you from the Akashic Record what actually took place.

Everything was set in a frequency of vibration and a tone was set up in that room after it was filled, then everything responded to that and continued to grow and stay in life until it was removed.

They used two dishpans set upside down but placed on a pole. There was a hole in the middle of the dish so that it could be slid up the pole, thus there could be several pans on each pole. They were spaced three feet between each other as they were stacked up that pole. Each pan was sealed and set to a tone within, staying in that resonance until the pan was opened.

The same with their grain. The grain was placed in angled vats, not square. Here, the resonance of the sound went in on an angle, bouncing from one angle to the other. This was continuously purified with light from any direction the sun moved.

We are talking **exact science** that is not even understood by modern man. This activity is what goes on within your body up and down the spine as you bring the Light into it, or it comes into it naturally, to a lesser degree.

Harmonics of Sound

There have been experiments I have been privileged to be involved with, whereby melons have been preserved for nine months regardless of humidity and temperature, by playing music into them every fifteen minutes for a duration of two minutes. It is soft resonant music. It has to have a change in resonance and we even found that the melon maintains its weight and continues to grow. There is no essence lost in the food. Electronic vibrations are fed into a plate and the field of impulses is received by the food. You can stroke the melon and hear the music within it. This can be fed into the earth for growing.

In my understanding that I have been given of how light and sound work, this will be your future. We have constructed and used it exactly as we were instructed by our inner voice. It will become commonplace. That will replace your refrigerator and your generator of your light. The energy that is produced does not kill, destroy or maim.

Purification by Thought

Man can now set right everything that he has produced into havoc and destruction. Within your purity of your own thought, you can adjust all conditions by self-forgiving. Also, you can ask for the charge of this energy to go into the universe and withdraw that which you have set into presence by giving a stronger, more pure thought in projection.

Anything that you do, you are responsible for. Any act that you act upon without considering the consequences, you are being very foolish. You are going to have those consequences whether you want them or not.

One of the most important points that you are going to learn is to become still. That means learning to shut everything down in your body. You will become Breath breathing, and not breathing breath. You will leave a plane of vibration and enter into a state of pulsation. This is where one

Breath is capable of forty-two days of action. You learn to breathe Breath and not breathe air.

The Talking Tree

In each of these classes, you will be given your instructions as you enter to that point in study. There was a long time before these seven books were determined to be put into print. This information was received in 1927. It was held until it was released in the mid-sixties.

I have had the inner voice since I was twelve years of age. I was very fortunate as I have had the best of teachers that are on this earth. Their guidance allowed me to associate again with all the things I forgot as I took on this earth. Everybody that takes form on this earth in this dimension passes through the same adamic veil. You must go through this in order take flesh onto the body.

There is one advantage I have over most individuals. I came in with all memory. It was necessary to go through a guidance conditioning order for my natural growth to take place, being able to live within the society as this growth took place. **I was taught to be in it but not of it,** being able to associate with my society without having disastrous results.

When I was twelve, I was severely punished for something for which I was not responsible. Every time I would try to prove my innocence, it made me look more guilty. I was living in the state of Washington on top of the Cascade Mountains at about 9,000 feet elevation above Lake Cle Elum. I went for a walk in the woods, finally sitting down at the base of a big pine tree looking out toward the lake. I was thinking how unjust this all really was.

While in the midst of this thought, I heard the words, "Never mind, all things pass away with time."

When I heard that voice, the hair on the back of my neck stood straight out. I said, "Wh-wh-who's talking to me?"

There was nobody there but me. I was frightened. Then I again said, "Wh-wh-who's talking to me?" about three or four times.

In my bewilderment, the voice continued, "Be not of a fear, there is only love here."

My next thought was, "Who is talking here?"

The voice said, "Look up!" All I could see was the top of this big pine tree. The voice said, "Yes, it is I."

That tree and I became very good friends over the next three years! That tree took on the in-lighting to in-light me of nature. All I had to do was formulate a question in my mind and I was instantly transferred into that question in activity in nature.

A Cosmic Experience

In thought, I asked, "What feeds the tree?" I instantly became sunlight and was projected into the earth and solidified into crystals. I can still hear the vibration of all those crystals in the ground making the music of the earth. I could hear the bacteria making their resonance of sound separating the crystals, dividing them in energy form. Those that were not devoured were stacked, and then, the mucus from them covered these crystals and changed their oscillation so the earthworms could come to get them.

The earthworms take those crystals within them, amplifying them into sub-minute particles to the walls of the canals that they burrow. When broken into these smaller particles, they are ready for an osmosis condition of energy into the plants. Once those tunnels are lined, the moisture of the earth starts to pass through them, washing away these little crystals, floating them.

As they are floating down this tiny stream, and you are one of the crystals, you can actually hear the pulse of the tree. You are being drawn by the tree's pulse in a continuous motion through the water. Even though the water is still, you are being drawn by the heart beat of the plant.

Suddenly, you come into contact with the rooting pattern of the plant, you notice a blue-white light with a purple tone over it. As soon as you enter through that purple glow, you suddenly vaporize. You turn from a solid, to a liquid, to a gas, and then you are inside of the root. You are moving in flow with this heartbeat as you are transformed back to a liquid state.

You are put into the lock valve with many other crystals oscillating at the same time you are. As the heartbeat of the tree continues, you move upward by each pull of the beat. You are sent to the respective branch of the tree, which is picked by the intelligence that is in operation at the base of the tree, which is the brain and defines the branch where you are to be stored.

When you reach that level, you are put into a gas condition, vaporized and shot through the center of the branch and put into the leaf. When you reach the leaf, as each fills up, all the way back to the trunk, you are again crystallized and stored there. That is why all of the food that is in a leaf condition has all of these crystals of Light that have been transformed into energy and stored there for your necessity of operation. All life then feeds from these harmonics of rhythm in these crystals that are partaken, which we call food rather than light crystals of energy in motion.

That is the way I was taught. In my quest to understand, I became that which I asked about and experienced the process in activity. When I speak of a condition, I've been there! It wasn't what I heard or read. Science hasn't advanced enough to understand these energy exchanges in crystallization.

No pump has thus far been designed to lift the amount of water that a tree lifts in one day's operation.

That is the way that I again acquired my acknowledgment of wisdom. As I grew, I encountered great problems when I was in school, especially in physics, science and history because the history teacher would say one thing, and I would counter, "No, it wasn't like that. It took place this way." I had lived each one of these histories and I knew what had taken place. This cost me a lot of time in the principal's office.

My teachers would say to me that they would certainly like to read from one of my books sometime! The last answer to any argument was, "Go to the office." They couldn't see how one could understand so much, so young.

This wasn't only unique to me. Walter Russell was, for a period of three weeks, in continuous communication to receive the wisdom for his book, The Universal One. One of my school teachers gave me a copy of this book when I was 16. His comment to me was, "You talk a lot like this man!" I was given into the same awareness, into the consciousness that he was.

I also was sent through every organ in my body and fully saw how it totally operates. Then I was advanced above this, when I was shown how light is solidified in the body into liquid energy and turned into the proper energies that cause this body to function rather than the chemical exchange.

To further my education after that, I was sent to all the best teachers throughout the world that were in hiding, who took me in tow to instruct me as I traveled completely around the world one and a half times. I was the guest of my Uncle Sam at this time during World War II. I am not just limited to this vehicle, I have full right of being relieved from this vehicle at any time that I want. That was efficiently perfected long ago, yet anything that I can do, you can do even better. If I can do it in this flesh body, you can do it as well as I.

THE TWO LOVE COMMANDMENTS

11th

Love thy neighbor as you love the Father

12th

Love thyself as you love God, for you are God.

It was Jesus' mission, above everything else,
to bring us these.

The two love commandments.

The Love Commandments

Jesus brought forth the two Love Commandments. Moses was given twelve Commandments. When he broke the tablets, he had to hew the others out of stone, and that was when he withheld the Eleventh and Twelfth Commandments. This is why he was never allowed to enter into the New Jerusalem, because he broke a fundamental law. Moses judged and took authority unto himself. Aaron, Meriam and Moses were denied entry into Jerusalem. It was Jesus' mission above everything else to bring you the last two Commandments.

11 - Love thy neighbor as you love the Father.

12 - Love thyself as you love God, for you are God.

The Authority of Be is the responsibility of each individual. **Your Authority of Love,** which is your first principle of Be, is your first principle of Life in activity, because Light could never exist without Love. Your radiation of Being could not Be without the Love, because there could be no Light without the blending of Life and Love. There could be no Light shining Force if it wasn't for Love. Love is the mother principle of God.

It should be your first principle of activity. It is a very simple rule to live by and the more you practice it, the more you begin to realize how easy it is to live by. When you love things, they will love you in return. You won't have the doubts that you used to have. You will find a presence and comfort within yourself that you never knew existed.

Whatever you sow, you must reap. Be sure and sow good things in order to reap good things, because if you sow adversity, you will reap the damnation of it. Everything about you reacts to your projection. What you take into your body depends upon your thought as you eat it. It is not what you eat, but how you eat it. If you fear and doubt food, you will get adverse effects.

> *Man must understand that whatever he sows he must also reap. He must sow good things in order to reap good things.*
>
> *Live then, according to these laws so that your life may be a constant blessing to all of God's creations, that your days may be full of eternal blessings, and that your responsibilities will be beautiful to behold because of your creative thought. As Jesus said, "Guard well your thought so that your speech and action may bring forth fruit and blessings abundantly.*
>
> *Remember that you bless or curse yourself— according to your own action and thought.*

Charge Yourself With Love

Starting tomorrow morning, I want you to charge everything about you with Love. I want your first thought before you arise, to be to just lay still in bed and relax. Put the Love radiantly about yourself and demand that the Love enter all of the cells of your body, and that it should radiate to everything that comes into contact with you. See how long you can go for that day without any malice or impure thought entering into your exchange of functional operation.

When you break your love, just forgive yourself and start over again the next day. See how long it takes before you can make it through the day. It really is easy to do, just **look for the good in all things** instead of finding fault with them. You will find life becoming more beautiful. The more that you work with yourself, the more that you bless everything about you, because you leave your radiant atmosphere behind. Everything that comes into contact with your atmosphere is also charged with energy. It may be for only a small duration, but it will be charged.

One of your gracious rewards will be that the animals will look to you instead of looking away. You will begin to notice that the plants and flowers will give an aroma to you when you are in their presence. The flowers will try to equal their radiations to your Love radiations.

When you take the time to charge your day before arising, you will find that your day will go much better for you. It will temper your impatience with others when you realize that a few centuries ago, you were in the same ignorance; so bless those coming behind you. Allow them the same opportunity you have, because **you don't grow unless you love, and you will never know what this whole expression is all about. Only when you give Love, to receive Love, will you really know your responsibility.**

If we learn to raise our vibratory rate and have an awareness of the Light, then can't we disassociate ourselves from this programmed world about us?

No, you are in a vibratory expression until you can change this density of molecules into Light. Otherwise, you will be affected by the frequency of energy of your ego cell. You are subject to the conditions as long as you wear a flesh body. However, by knowing you are entering into this condition, you are going to be on your guard. You will think twice before doing something.

Biorhythms

Does the study of biorhythms have any bearing on man's ability of responsibility, and how does it function? When those curves cross the line, you are out of correlation with your cells. You have a triad of functional operation:

Physical—Mind—Spirit

Biorhythms call it:

Physical—Intellectual—Emotional,

This is your triangle of being, within a square.

Your cells are made up of segments which range from 12 to 360. Your cells spin upon a center axis. The polarity within those cells, which makes this spin possible, is constantly changing from north to south poles.

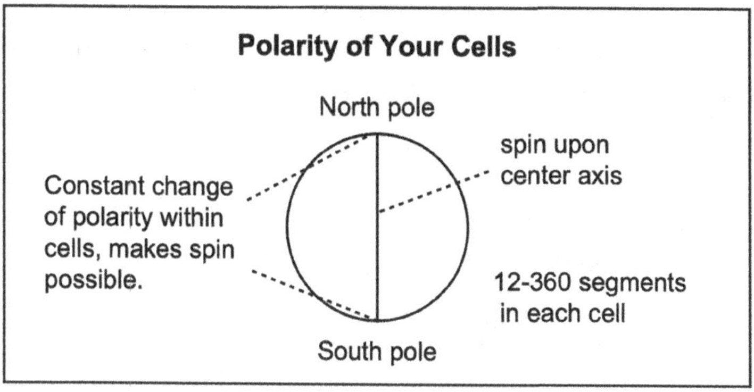

Polarity of your cells.

When the energy is leading the operation of spin at the north poles, there is an excess of energy. A laxity takes place when there is a lag of energy, causing the south poles to overlap one another. The north poles overlap when there is an excess of energy. Your upswing is on the excess, and a downswing is on the lag condition. In either situation, all of the cells of your body go out of order. This is when you go out and do all sorts of dumb things.

Your functioning is out of order because of the magnetic attraction of your atmosphere, by the amount of light that comes through your Sightcone, which is defused in a lead or lag condition. When all three principles cross together, then a fusion takes place in a short circuit power failure condition. You would experience a blackout condition.

You don't realize that you've done it until it's over, but you realize, too late, that you did something wrong. You are out of frequency with yourself. This is what happens when those curves cross the base line. It has to do with energy from the nucleus of the Master Cell which arranges the rest of the cells. Also, at the end of each muscle cell in your body, there is a north and a south pole, which causes expansion or contraction. When these go out of order, one is trying to expand while the other is trying to push, so your body is not efficient in correlation. This is when your body is out of order and you do those dumb things. You send a message and it goes just the opposite way that you tell it.

Neutralize Your Static Energy

You can neutralize your magnetic condition by putting your feet to Earth. Dig an ankle deep hole, fill it with water and slosh your feet about in the mud. Every cell in your body exists by electrical contact on your feet. This is why you should go barefoot outside because the base conditions of your vehicle are on your feet. This will help to neutralize much of the electrical short-circuiting in your body.

Earth Tumble: Cause and Result

Would you explain in greater detail what causes and takes place during an earth tumble?

The earth stands still four hours. When we reach 32 degrees, this puts the magnetic north and true north out of polarization of the Light attraction of the multiple Rays from the triangle and square formed by the Primary and Secondary Suns, whose energy emissions cause the spin of Earth. This means the triangulation of the Rays which emanate from the White Sun, the Green and the Red Sun, that triangulate our earth in motion. It also produces our sun in energy, but at this disparity of 32 degrees, loses its rate of exchange of overlap.

That overlap is in a magnitude of 7 times 7, or 49 strands of energy in a twist pattern from north to south. There are 49 of these cross rings of energy that lock the earth in spin. These lines of force, weave from outside to the inner regions in a cycle of 7. The earth is actually a selsyn motor.

As the inner earth moves, the outer moves equally with it in polarization, but if the balance becomes unequal from the outer to the inner, then a slowing action takes place. They no longer attract each other. Thus, the inner continues its spin of rotation, while the outer drifts to a stop.

When the heat friction becomes great enough between the two mantles, with the inner, which is about 250 miles below the crust of the earth, then the outer part of the crust is thrown into projection. The grab is like setting a clutch into immediate function. Its speed becomes an instant exhilaration of approximately 4,000 miles per hour.

You can imagine what happens to the Pacific Ocean when that type of projection takes place. The wall of water that will raise up will be about two- and one-half miles high traveling at approximately 4,000 miles per hour. The changes of gases in vacuum in front of it will create a freezing condition in excess of 600 degrees below zero, which is impossible in our science. Everything within that mass will be frozen within five minutes.

This is what happens to our histories on an average of every 7,000 years. This is a scientific fact for we have the tektites, in lava formation, that lock in the crystals which point to multiple north poles. Tektites are formed by an over-gasified condition by the loss of a rhythm of harmonics.

Does this explain the presence and loss of ***Atlantis****?*

Yes. The Atlantis period lasted for about 12,000 years. There was one other period that lasted for 18,000 years. That was the longest history that earth ever had, which was way before Lemuria in another Earth history. This was when earth was a two-continent mass. This was right after Amassaland, when there was one continent. This lasted for plus three billion years.

What caused the tumble and what happened to man?

The angelic condition of man fell to less than his standard and he became reflected condition. In other words, he was thrown out of the Garden of Eden.

Man lessened his thought to the ability that he could hold his responsibility in control and brain was put in charge to tell him how to do it; man lost his ability of domination, and nature took over. As it is, man should have dominion over nature. However, he is striving to do it with machines rather than himself. Machines do nothing but mimic.

The cleansing effect does take place. That is how **one half of one percent is able to keep this earth in presence and history.** If it were not for this, your history would have terminated over 1,000 years ago. The average of each earth history is 7,000 years.

When Tibet was overrun, was that one place where they did a great deal of this work and gathered this information?

It was transferred to South America before it was ever overrun.

Machines are put to good use, for example, as implants for epileptics.

An epileptic condition is due to an inability to cope with their emotional reaction. A spasm condition is produced. The sensor dissipates them before their emotions can raise enough to combat the condition. If they would only develop certain organs that are dormant, there would be no need for the implant. This is not helping, only deferring because it still will not endure time.

Time and Tides

Purity of thought is the only way anything is controlled. A machine only lengthens time but does not endure time because it is on a timetable itself. It is made of molecules which are held together by the frequency of light. When that tone frequency stills, it will fall apart. We call it fatigue.

The biggest problem I had when I first started being prepared to guide people in understanding, was to bring information down to a level of comprehension. How do you tell a story to bring it back to a level where it can be intelligently exchanged? It's quite a job!

I can talk to you on two levels at the same time. I can talk to the inner part of you and to the outer part, simultaneously. By this act I can plant many seeds. Thus, you see that **your responsibility to everything does begin with you. You are the total whole**; nothing can exist without you. You are eternal. There is no such thing as time, only the illusion of time.

We give habit to time because we started the marking of days when we allowed darkness to fulfill us. We also allowed a conditioning to take place which we call aging, due to time. We measured things by moon cycles and we set up patterns of operation by these moons until the moons controlled us. Therefore, even today, emotional values of individuals are greatly exchanged by the new and old moon.

This is the tidal effect of waters moved upon the earth by the movement of the moon's pressure as the water within your body is moved equally. The tides in your body move equally with the ocean. You become creatures of habit.

You allowed all of this alteration to take place. You lessened your responsibility, passing that responsibility onto nature. Now nature is running the show. If you don't think so, try to go out and fight nature! See how fast it will dominate you. But you can go out and agree with nature, live with nature, and nature will bend to your will.

Communication With Plants

About two years ago, we had Dr. Clive Baxter here with his delicate equipment with electronic plates attached to the leaves of plants, which recorded on a paper graph scroll, the responses of the plant to our projected thoughts.

If the student projected a love vibrancy, the plant became excited, which showed on the graph.

That device was an off-shoot of the lie detector. His fifteen year investigation with the intelligence of plants brought out an interesting point that involved the ability of communication over great distances. This response was recorded. A plant was injured by an individual. As soon as that thought was sent out, it evoked a response which was recorded instantaneously on an instrument 5,000 miles away. I am bringing this out to show you the instantaneous communication that you really have.

Another experiment Dr. Clive Baxter conducted was on a dozen eggs. One egg was placed in a pan of boiling water and the other eggs fainted. "How did they faint?," you are asking! The other eggs stopped their heartbeat. They became null and void. It was fifteen minutes before they came back. **Everything has intelligence. Everything is of the same source of intelligence.**

When you really learn that secret, then you've learned the secret of the universe. Then, you really are the fullness of that universe because everything that exists in you, exists in everything else in dimension that you dimension with.

Man's big mistake is that he is biased to believe that he is the only one endowed with Intelligence. That chair has as much intelligence as you do. If you don't think so, talk to the atoms of it and they will tell you. Can you make a chair out of yourself? A thought form pattern is holding it in this dimension of conditioning. It will support you because it is obliged to support you. Things will only break when you don't accept their privilege to aid you.

Love is the Universe. You are the Universe; you are Love. Do you conduct yourself in Love?

Color, Tone and Elongation of Cells

When you take away the love from anything, it takes away its presence, turns grey and dies. Space, which is grey, is the common denominator of everything. I don't care how you much you mix activity together, when you over-mix it with everything, it will blend together and turn back to grey. It will become space again. Then, in this space, we have all time and all operation, functioning in form. By changing the vibrations of the colors by our thinking in time, with space, we formulate the form expressing.

We change the vibration of the color, but isn't color a vibration?

No, color is a specific light and it resonates into vibration by demand. This is molecular activity, vibration. Projected thought keys all of that vibration, and then it locks it into solidity.

By changing the vibration are you not changing the frequency of the color?

No, the color stays the same because the hue is constant, only the resonance has altered.

Instead of being an A it is an A sharp?

Yes, or A flat.

We are very keenly tuned, as all of our cells are rolling in multiples of rates of speeds of operation with one another in frequency. As we allow deterioration to take place from improper oxidizing, or gasification of these energies in flow, we elongate the cells and we age. We take them out of perfect tone.

That is what they found out with all of the astronauts who went into space and returned; all of the cells were elongated. They don't know why or how, as yet. No matter how good their suits are, they can't produce the equalization of light gravity.

That's the bone marrow problem?

Right, it goes to the bone marrow. On the coining from the pituitary to the thyroid, it then produces that activity in a continuous operation, because the tone has been changed at the Sightcone to the pituitary.

You are saying that when we live in space, there has to be a tone resonance with Light?

That's right. Man tries to do everything by brute force rather than blending with the natural condition. Had they worn just a thinner suit, and had they played music into their bodies, the elongation of their body cells would never have taken place. There would never have been a fatigue factor introduced into their body, so the cells wouldn't have become elongated and the gravity would have stayed the same as well as the sphere of the cells.

Also, they would never have to shut down their machines, for the power they would need could be produced even by the dark of the moon.

Man must learn a fundamental law of life and live by this law. This law is to mind one's own business. You are not your brother's keeper. All responsibilities begin with number one. When you become the example, you do not have to search for those to teach because by your example, you light your way, and you light your authority.

If you will look in Matthew, you will find a declaration:

> *"For that which you wish to know, go into your closet and ask quietly of the Father of these things you desire. Don't run up and down the street shouting your glory in false proclamations."*

Your closet is your cube.

That's right. Within the cube are six pyramids. They make the total whole of the square. In that square is the box of four elements which comprise the four elements of fire, air, water and earth, which you exist in.

By the triangulations of these, you make 12 positives and 12 negatives, both masculine and feminine, both expressing equally with each other in total balance.

If you open that square up, you will make a cross which puts flesh man standing forth in full expression.

This is what it means to mind one's own business. Don't be a busy body about everybody else. When you are so good, you won't have to worry about being a busy body. They will all be there to find out how and why you are doing it.

Parentage: Responsibility and Choice

What about having children?

That's the greatest responsibility of all because you are a guardian; you don't own it. Remember, it picked you, you didn't pick it. It picked you for parentage due to a necessity of its demand of a vehicle for expression set up by memory.

Where it broke the Law, it has to re-enter. It has to re-enter expression exactly where it broke the Law. What Law? The Law of Life.

Does it have the right of parentage?

It only has the right of choice of parentage if its light bubble is gold, silver or bronze.

Have you ever talked to anybody that claims to see bubbles about her head when she is near, during or after conception? When the egg is fertile within the female, then all the entities that wish expression will collect around the head of the female. If any of the gold, bronze or silver bubbles appear, then all the others must move away.

The bubble can hover around the head because it has demand of authority of parentage. This is earned by past expressions. As for the others, it amounts to who gets there first. When the sperm makes an atomic spark, all the rest of the sperm instantly die because the body has then been claimed.

What if there is a miscarriage or an abortion?

It doesn't matter in either instance; they will just do it all over again. Sometimes it only takes a spark of condition for a termination of life by just one breath in this dimension. That could be a full expression and all that is necessary for the entity to perfect.

Could that be possible if someone is on the verge of perfection and has everything in order when an earth tumble should occur?

That is correct, and **some only need to get born long enough to take that one breath into their perfection**. They have totaled their necessity of expression in time, form and space. Many of the things we call calamities in our own expression could be blessings in disguise because we have never been fully endowed in the truth of the nature of the construction of the vehicle. We will go into this fully in future studies as to how you are put together, why and what takes place.

How is an ***avatar*** *able to come in for his assigned purpose?*

You have to consider the immaculate conception of Thought conditioning before conception takes place as it is set down in Truth. In order to produce the elements necessary in the body for the production of a perfect body for a perfect inhabitant, it takes nine years of preparation before the conception period without even one mis-thought, one counter word or one misdeed. This also has to be sustained throughout the full nine months of carrying, and for nine years afterwards.

Be Selfless: Love All Things

To have any semblance of peace, man must learn the two great fundamental laws of life and live by these laws. The first law is to mind one's own business. This business is that of love: to love all things as he loves himself.

FUNDAMENTAL LAWS FOR PEACE

1. The first law is to mind our own business.
This business is that of love:
to love all things as we love ourself.
2. Whatever we sow we must also reap.

Fundamental laws for peace.

That means all things come before you do, because when you learn to be that selfless, you have made it! That is the **whole secret** right there. I am going to tell you this: it is going to be a tough job to let go of self.

Selfless, Authority and Stillness

We have to be selfless to have authority?

That is the only way you get authority. **As long as self is in the way, you are never an authority. "Of myself, I do nothing, my Father does everything."**

If you think these are great things I do, you should see what my "Dad" can do! He has a way of sending it. If these things are flabbergasting you, just consider what Motionless is in the act of Now. When you get to that point of understanding, think where Motionless will be at that time.

The easiest way to say that and understand it, is to say, "Multiplicities of motions simultaneously in all directions at the same time." Then you have a small conception of what **Motionless** is, yet all active. The **Stillness is all action, all activity.**

Be still and know that I am God.
Be still and know God.
Be still and just Be.

Stillness.

It is his failure to live by these simple, fundamental laws that has brought man to his present condition.

Man always puts himself at the short end of the stick by his lust and greed and his over-emphasis of desires, as well as not being thoughtful of those whom he associates with, by climbing over the top of them. **Nobody is a doormat for anybody else.** Everybody and everything has the same right to expression that you desire. Only when you realize this and put it into operation, will your desires be fulfilled.

Mud makes more mud. If you become quiet enough, the mud will go to the bottom, then the clear water will shine forth again and some light can pass through. If you are smart enough to hold the light in time long enough, the water will evaporate away and the mud will be left compact, and you will be free. I just gave you a lot of wisdom!

Don't Let the Past Consume You

Jesus said it in a most beautiful way. Matthew was quite upset. He had two beautiful robes, one his mother had fashioned for him and the other he had earned as a prize. A beggar had stayed with them for the night while they were traveling from the Sea of Galilee back to town. Upon awakening in the morning, the robe that Matthew had won, had left with the night's guest.

Matthew came crying to Jesus, "The man took my best robe! My prized possession!"

Jesus looked at Matthew, "Have you ever wanted since you were with me? Now hearken to me. Bless the man that took your robe because he needed it more than you did. What more do need than one robe at a time? You can only wear one at a time. What is the necessity of all of this excess baggage, when you have not need or want? Bless the man in his conditioning and dust the dust from your feet and let's be on our way. Let the dead bury the dead."

From the wisdom of conditioning, don't let the past consume you. If you allow it to ferment, it will surely make you rotten. That is one of man's greatest problems: fermentation. **Only when you forgive and dismiss, will you have any peace within yourself.** You will be in torment until you do, because your business is love. That's the Father's business, Love, and you are about your Father's business.

You will receive your just rewards for your just acts; be just in your act for the rewards. Your rewards are great and many if you allow them to be, or they can be pitifully small if you are not tolerant of your own conditions and about your own conditions of love.

The only way you can get rid of an enemy is by love. That's why Jesus said so beautifully, "Turn the other cheek." He will be so dumbfounded that he won't know what to do but walk away in disgust. He will also be in shame of himself as he will realize at the last instant that he is only destroying and hurting himself. Anger only lashes out at self. Anger only lashes out at self. Due to your emotional values, you try to transplant it to others by an anger condition.

Remember this: one minute of sustained anger requires 24 hours to replace the etheric energy of your body consumed in that brief moment of rage. Do you ever wonder why you shake and quake after being angered? Now you are understanding why. You are suffocating yourself.

Thought, Speech and Voice

As Jesus said, "Guard well your thought so that your speech and action may bring forth fruit and blessings abundantly."

You attract everything by your thought and speech. Learn to control the amplification of your voice. By your voice, you give yourself away more than any other act you do. This is so because preceding your voice, the Light transmission from the front of your head has already been received and evaluated before the first word has been spoken. The other guy is already on guard. The transmission of light way exceeds the voice explosion of the atoms in your larynx to make speech.

You can control everything but the vibrations in your voice. Even though you feel you are saying something, the overtones on that are detectable by very sensitive instruments.

The Thymus and Strength

I can talk on the phone with somebody and I can feel in my chest what is actually going on within them that might be contrary to what they are saying.

Yes, that is within your sternum. Beneath your sternum is one the most valuable glands that you possess called the thymus. Presently it is about the size of a hair, but it should be about the size of a pencil. This is what gives you super-strength of perception. That is why the gorillas pound their chest when they are confrontational to activate this super-charging of energy. This is what Tarzan was doing by his yell, super-charging for the same purpose.

This is a way of building up the energy in the body by the thymus. Beating the chest makes the thymus begin to boil. It boils rapidly from compression. It is what we would call a super adrenaline within the blood which brings tremendous super-strength into the body.

Talk To Your Body, Kinesiology

The body will respond to your talking to it. You can grasp an object or another person's hand, and then have them ask you if your arm is strong and you respond affirmatively. Then let go and feel the energy tingling in your arm. The body will so respond and you will learn to talk with your body and communicate exactly with it.

You will learn to formulate questions as well as statements of affirmation to yourself that evoke a response of regeneration of condition. It will help you aid your condition of releasing multiples of the ills that you produce to yourself. Also, when you pick up psychic garbage, which could even cause a spasm condition in your muscles, it will help you to wipe it away.

What is psychic garbage?

This is when somebody gives you a feeling of bad negative energy that you won't accept and you fight yourself within, causing such reactions as an ill-at-ease feeling or even muscular spasms.

How would we deal with this?

Recognize it and when you are talking with your body, ask why it is taking place, and by the explanation you receive, the pressure will give away. Or you can do the same thing with color tones, by taking crayons and putting them on your arm. With the proper toning on it, there is no resistance. You do this when you know the colors and frequency with which you have a problem. Then you balance this color on the intake with the breath, which is held and released. This is called kinesiology.

Another way to neutralize everything in your body is to drain off the energies within it. You do this by digging a hole in the earth and filling it with water. Slosh your feet around in the mud, and earth will neutralize all the etheric static that has collected from psychic conditions. They have intermingled in your aura setting up fault lines in the grid lines of your body.

You have been exposed to a lot of seemingly strange ideas, but there is much Truth to be understood in how things function and why. Don't try to let go of the total whole all at once. **To get to your goal, you have to find out who you are, why you are here and where you are going.** We try to do it a piece at a time because, otherwise, it is too drastic. Everything is done in moderation.

TO GET TO YOUR GOAL:

To get to your goal,
you have to find out who you are,
why you are here and
where you are going

To get your goal.

MAN'S RESPONSIBILITIES

The well-being of all forms of creation

The control and use of his thought and the results its use.

This becomes the personal responsibility of each to learn to clean your own house before telling others how to clean their houses.

Everything on this Earth and for the planet itself and for all that transpires here, because he is the cause of all that happens here, for God gave man dominion over the Earth

The results of man's dominion, which are caused by man.

To make himself a fit habitation for God's Pure Life by cleansing himself through service to other men and other creations

The results of man's absolute rule of himself, which rule was given by God

The correction of anything that is mis-functioning in operation within himself.

Himself, and anything he does in life

The world and the fullness thereof

Setting right whatever he has harmed

Making peace and reconstructing all things he has destroyed

To give Love and to receive Love

To mind one's own business and love all things as he loves himself.

Maintaining all in the state of perfection through loving service.

Men's responsibilities.

UEL Glossary Intro, L1-7

INTRODUCTION

age	You are no older than the thought of right now.
Airless Cell	The Airless Cell is really you. It is the eternal you of Be; of infinitesimal smallness, locked in the center of your heart. It is the one Dot of your Pure Being, your True Self.
alive, being really	When we can still the brain so that Mind can be in rapport with Spirit, then we are really alive, Real Life expressing.
answers you seek	Meditation is the avenue to all the answers of everything that you seek.
Blue-Green Sun	Earth is to be the Blue-Green Sun, when it fully develops itself. It will be one of the Quadrant Suns of the Universe.
body, flesh-physical	The body is flesh-physical, existing in a sensory illusion. It only exists because of our agreement and solidification in our thinking.
brain	a computer data base
breath practice	The breath practice I will give you will allow you to take yourself from vibration to pulsation.
Central Sun	The center of the Universe
clear-thought	A state where everything else is dismissed but that one act that you are in.

Council of Souls	When you terminate this expression, you must spend your fourth day at the Council of Souls, explaining your life, for that eight-hour period. You are judged by the harshest judge of all, yourself. You pass judgment upon yourself
desire	Everything you desire necessary for yourself is yours by proper breath & imaging.
deterioration	Lust and greed are where your deterioration really starts, because you start valuing material things more than Perfection.
discernment	Your values of discernment must become very, very keen, so you know what is really right for you.
Divine Atom	Within our Divine Atom, we are the Universe in miniature.
Earth	All the best of the Universe was placed on this planet, Earth.
Evaluate fully	Face each issue squarely and fully. Quiet your breath and know the truth of the condition and correct it into that point. Learn to fully evaluate everything
Forgive yourself	Before going to sleep at night, forgive yourself for all the things that you did wrong, and forgive all those that trespassed against you for their acts.
free will	You can do it your own way, any way you want, but you also pay the consequences for it.
freeing yourself	The first secret of freeing yourself is putting yourself in unison with the pulsation of the Universe. This secret is to breathe in unison with your Airless Cell, the one Dot of your Pure Being, your True Self that resides in the center of your heart.
God's abundance	You will discover that all of God's abundance is at your fingertips,
Holy Breath	The Whole-in-One-Breath, Divine Wisdom, the Thought for Life that God has for you

Holy Breath Diagram	The diagram shows you exactly what takes place when you draw from Source into the breath and how it animates the body.
Issues, facing them	Face each issue squarely and fully. Quiet your breath and know the truth of the condition and correct it into that point. Learn to fully evaluate everything
know yourself	The main thing is to get to know yourself, and know who you are and where you are. When you know who you are and where you are, then you will know what you are about and why.
Love Commandments	11th and 12th Commandments. It was Jesus' primary mission to give these last two Commandments to us, which are in the New Testament.
love, state of	You will start to live in a state of love, rather than a state of lust.
Love, the Father's	You will discover also that all the Father's Love is for everyone to share equally because He loves each of us in the same amount.
love, whole secret	The whole secret is to learn to Love, everything.
lust and greed	Lust and greed are where your deterioration really starts, because you start valuing material things more than Perfection.
meditation	enables you to get into rapport with Intelligence,
meditation, answers	the avenue to all the answers of everything that you seek.
Meditation, key	the key to knowing yourself and for you to purify your body, to have the ability to heal your body and to get to know yourself.
meditation, freedom	the gateway to freedom for yourself; Meditation will open the doors for you to find yourself and find the freedom from what you call ego, the selfish you.
meditation, key	the key for you to purify your body, to heal your body and to get to know yourself.

meditation, ultimate	The Ultimate in Meditation is Full Light
Mind	When you succeed in shutting brain down, then Mind can take its place and you will have forged an alliance with Source and will be free from the reflection of belief coming from brain.
Mind and Spirit	When we can still the brain so that Mind can be in rapport with Spirit, then we are really alive, Real Life expressing.
Motionless	From the Motionless, Life came into being, by the Light of Love, and you are expressing because of this condition, from the Motionless into Motion.
perfect yourself	to change your earthly body to LIGHT so you can take it from this Earth; Otherwise, you will continue to return to Earth until you attain that perfection.
personal experience	Everything that I speak of in the lessons I have personally experienced
proper breath	Everything that you desire necessary for yourself is yours by proper breath and imaging.
purpose of book	what this whole study is about is to change you from a past tense in a lived condition into Life itself. It is to change you from vibrating individual into a pulsating individual, where you become one Breath breathing, instead of breathing Breath to merely exist.
Sages on earth	There are always a minimum of seven Sages on the Earth at all times. These are great teachers.
selsyn motor	A planet is like a selsyn motor with a rotor and a stator.
senses	We are a 12 sense being, but man is in functional operation with only the 5 lower senses, while the upper 7 are dormant.
the Father's Love	You will discover also that all the Father's Love is for everyone to share equally because He loves each of us in the same amount.

True Self	Airless Cell, the one Dot of your Pure Being, your True Self that resides in the center of your heart
Truth State	The Truth State is the ultimate state of attainment
truth, information of	Information that will help guide you to find yourself and make yourself free
twelve-sense being	You are a twelve-sense being operating on five senses.
universe	Everything that exists out there in the universe exists within you.

Definitions from Universal Everlasting Life, Book 1, Series 1, Lesson 1

THE WHY OF LIFE

abundance	You have abundance beyond your dreams, but you own nothing
Blue-Green Sun	Earth has a rendezvous to become a Sun, the Blue-Green Sun
breathing	The proper way to breathe is to do so with the frequency of your heart.
Causeless Cause	The Causeless Cause of all things, of all being, is Life. Life may be considered as the Granary of God, for it is God's storehouse.
Clear thought	Clear thought is of the utmost importance for you,
Conscious condition	Remember you were created eternal. What you call death is only losing sight of this dimension, but you never lose your Conscious condition
Council of Souls	Council of Souls. You will run through all of your life and you pass judgment on yourself. Nobody judges you but yourself.
Death	There is no death. What you call death is only a changing of frequency. Remember you were created eternal. What you call death is only losing sight of this dimension, but you never lose your Conscious condition

Earth: your source	Earth is your source of being. All the energy that operates the flesh part of your body comes through your feet from the earth. All that operates the spiritual part of your body comes through your temples and your clavicles, by your breath animated, until you go into a pulsated state.
Earth's purpose	The earth was set up originally to be the sun of this area, and it will be the Blue-Green Sun of the Cosmic Light when it does go back into perfection, for which it was created
freedom	When you come to the point that you can shut brain off and make it a computer, which it actually is, instead of controlling you, then you will be free
God's expression	Seven manifestations of life are seven distinct planes of God's expression; Man, Angel, Fowl, Animal, Vegetable, Protoplasm and Earth.
God's storehouse	The Causeless Cause of all things, of all being, is Life. Life may be considered as the Granary of God, for it is God's storehouse.
In-lighting yourself	Instead of solidifying into matter you can in-light into substance and change your body to light, by your discernment and valuation of your thought activity
Key to Everything	Love is the Key to Everything
Know thyself	Man must return to earthly expression again and again until he has atoned, and until he has again come to know himself. For man is not as he seems to be, and there is a mighty work that each individual must do.
Life, Granary	The Causeless Cause of all things, of all being, is Life. Life may be considered as the Granary of God, for it is God's storehouse.
Life, first	Life is the most beautiful thing there is. Before anything else was, there was Life. Life is indeed "that perfect cycle, through which the thoughts of God are made to manifest in all perfection."

Love	Love is the Key to Everything
Man's mission	Man's mission, the why of his present life, is to regain his created state of perfection, and to lift all the creations that he caused to fall back into belief, into that same state of perfection which God created.
Mind	The go-between between Spirit and Physical, that Spirit uses for communication with the physical.
Motionless	In the Motionless is the same thing as the Airless Cell that is in the center of your heart. It is the receptacle that retains the Spirit unison and directs the activity of your being.
Perfection	Perfection is created by God and is the only creation of God. Man is imperfect only because he has made for himself other vibratory planes of existence. Now you are in the first aspect of the most perfect time in your period of history for your Perfection.
Physical	Physical is the responding to the Spirit to bring forth the activity of Mind and Spirit.
purpose	You are on this plane of expression to learn love and forgiveness
seven manifestations	The seven manifestations of life are seven distinct planes of God's expression: Man, Angel, Fowl, Animal, Vegetable, Protoplasm and Earth.
Spirit	Spiral activity of force energy in motion, continuously
	Spirit is the concentrated thought of the perfect you waiting to be expressed, not reflected.
Triune God	Triune God means Spirit, Mind and Physical.

Definitions from Universal Everlasting Life, Book 1, Series 1, Lesson 2

WHERE MAN IS NOW

Airless Cell	Airless Cell: Love and Light in Activity
best friend	Talk to your Self, your best friend, your real best friend. Learn to look at yourself in the mirror in the morning and say that you love yourself and mean it.
conformity	Because we are so accustomed to conforming, we forget our real place and we become something manipulated by the will of others rather than by a thought of our own.
Conscious	God created just one plane of Conscious: Perfection
created things	All created things are eternal and unchanging, and are those things which emerge from the Divine Substance in perfect form.
Creation of Man	Man was created out of the ALL, a Perfect Divine Thought, clothed in Spirit Substance and Flesh Divine.
Father, asks you	The Father asks for ten percent of your time, not your money, so that He can commune with you.
Fifth Plane	Man is now in the beginning of the fifth plane of consciousness of his perfecting. In this plane, he must complete the re-perfecting of his physical body.
Great Teacher	The time has not yet come when every man will look to the Great Teacher, his own spirit, for guidance
heart transplant	In a heart transplant you give your individuality to someone else
light body	Each of you must, at some time or another, make a decision to take your light body from this earth. If you don't, you are chained to this Earth until you do.

Listen within	Learn to be an authority to yourself. Learn to listen to that little voice that will tell you the truth all the time
Little Voice	When you hear the Little Voice within you, if you procrastinate, you are too late. When it tells you to do something, you do it right now. The more you use it, the louder it will become.
love	In perfectness, there is only love.
made things	Made things are not eternal and are subject to change.
mastery, poise	The secret of your being is in your poise. This is your perfect control. Either you master the situation or the situation masters you.
mastery of brain	When you learn to master brain, then you will have full access to know who you were, what, why and where you were, as well as what period of time
meditation, stillness	"I demand the stillness," that is your command-demand. You will find that you will be able to hold in one breath for two to three hours, where you will change from the vibrant into a pulsated state, a full wakened condition
Mind, not brain	If you would allow Mind to impress you, then you would never do anything wrong. You would do everything perfectly. Brain and Mind are two completely different conditions, totally separated. Mind fills all the space of the universe.
Perfect of thought	The perfect of Thought cannot be attained unless your breath rate is in a perfect equal flow with the Divinity of the Airless Cell within your body
Perfection	God created just one plane of conscious: Perfection
Perfection of body	Until you can change the grossness of the flesh body into electrons, atoms and molecules and align them, simultaneously, to function in the same direction at the same time, you have not Perfected.

Perfection info	In each history I come once to inform the history at that time of perfection. The information that I am given, I give very freely, so that you can remember yourself and find yourself and know where you are, what you are, who you are and why.
Perfectness & Love	In perfectness, there is only love.
Plane of Five	Man is now vibrating upon the Plane of Five, which is the great turning point for man's perfection, the preparatory stage. In the Plane of Five there is so rapid a change, that what has happened in a span of a few years, in the Plane of Four would have taken centuries of time.
poise	The secret of your being is in your poise. This is your perfect control. Either you master the situation or the situation masters you.
pureness of Thought	Learn to go within and stop thinking, being quiet enough to hear the Pureness of Thought, then you will have the true answers.
salvation	Perfection in Conscious. Your only salvation is in yourself, not anybody else. Only when you are quiet and look within, will you find the answers and true salvation that you have been searching for.
Spirit of God within	The Spirit of God within man could not fall, for it is that part of man which is truly of God, the God in action which is the essence of life, in and with man.
teachings purpose	Enlighting you of perfection in Conscious, so that you will be able to climb above this earth's dimension of expression and not have to return here, unless by choice
three magnetic grams	There are only three grams of us. What makes up the three grams? These are the elements of the dust of earth itself that are taken into your body to hold you to this earth. That's what magnetically holds you to this earth.

time alterations	If you make an alteration in time then you must stand good for it to the Godhead.
where man is now	Where man is now, he places God outside of himself.
wise authority	Always put yourself in the other person's place. How would you like it?

Definitions from Universal Everlasting Life, Book I, Series 1, Lesson 3

THE LAW OF LIFE

Adamic web of sleep	Almost all who enter onto this earth at this time come under the Adamic sleep, the Adamic web of sleep, where the veiling of the mind is blocked by the brain.
aging, agreement	There is no reason for aging outside of your own agreement.
air transformer	As you breathe in, your body is an air transformer. The iron in your blood is excited and the residual of it trying to capture itself, emits a tremendous amount of energy. This causes all the protons and neutrons around it to activate.
airitarian	There will be a time again when you do become an airitarian, whereby you will subtract from the ethers everything you desire to express, and you will become one breath breathing, rather than breathing breath. You will become the pulsation and vibration in unison with the spheres of the universe
anger	For every minute of sustained anger, it takes 24 hours to replenish that energy you burned out of your body.
attitude, changing	Talk about love, pleasantry, inventive conditions, things of acknowledgment and interest. Talk constructively or of things of great importance.

authority, become — You have to learn to become an authority unto yourself. You have to learn to demand your right, your place in the sun. You were created as the most perfect of all expression. Prove yourself as such. Bring yourself to this point, of absolute control. This is the Law of Life.

blessing food — Everything that you partake of, bless it into perfection.

Breath, Seven Rate — This breath exercise is the secret to perfect meditation. The main thing is to allow your breath to come in rapport of perfect response with universal pulsation. That's what this Seven Rate Breath is. This puts you in unison with the universe. It's also called the Holy Breath.

Circle of Light — The greatest safeguard that you could ever have

consuming — You become the sum and substance of what you consume, your thought patterns and activities and everything.

creative principle — Man is controlled by the creative principle of Man Spirit, he can never be anything but man. That is true of all phases of existence.

Destruction, Triad of — The three destroyers of life are improper breath, over-stress by not forgiving self, and lack of clear-thought.

earth — Earth is the planet of redemption.

foundation, basic — In the first book the main thing that we are going to be doing is setting down a basic foundation for you.

God — primary principle

Law of Life — what you do unto others shall be done unto you, in multiples.

Law of Life, — You have to learn to become an authority unto yourself. You have to learn to demand your right, your place in the sun. You were created as the most perfect of all expression. Prove yourself as such. Bring yourself to this point, of absolute control. This is the Law of Life.

Law of Life, breaking	Where man breaks the Law of Life he must re-enter back into expression again. From the time that he breaks that law, at that point he will start to deteriorate. He will terminate this expression and have to restart it again where he broke the law.
Law of Life:	Whatsoever you do unto any living thing, you also do unto yourself.
Law unto yourself	You are a Law unto yourself, so you are going to become that Law in activity.
Life Itself	In Life Itself, everything exists. Life is the grandeur of God. It gives forth into every expression everything necessary for that expression, unlimited.
Light, pureness of	Man can lower himself to where he is almost mineral, or he can alter himself back into the pureness of Light, which is where he really should be.
little voice inside	Learn to listen to that little voice inside of you. That's the Airless Cell, the spiritual impulse telling you what actually should take place and what shouldn't take place
love yourself	When you look in the mirror, tell yourself that you love yourself and forgive yourself for what you have done.
Man Plane	There are many kinds of examples of mankind, but all come from the same great Source: the spiritual plane of Man.
master or slave	You are either master or slave. Either you are going to be an authority or you are going to be a slave, one of the two. You are either going to be your own master, your own projection, or you are going to be the salvation of every other thought coming through.
meditation	The avenue to infinite wisdom
meditation, perfect	Holy Breath exercise

meek	In the Bible it says, "The meek shall inherit the earth." And believe me they are going to inherit it, and they are going to be bound to it, until they find themselves.
meek vs authority	An all-loving God is never meek. If you are not an authority unto yourself, how can you be an authority to anything else? Meekness is not authority. It's the absolute opposite. When you are right, say so.
palette, your	Learn to listen to your palette. Your body will tell you what you want to eat.
Perfection	Man is capable of expressing in all perfection, but he is not aware of his possibilities because of the limitations of his own making.
Perfection, little key	The properties that you are attaining and wish to attain to are Perfection, which all start with a little key: I love you, everybody, everything, unconditionally, with no strings attached
Primary Principle	God
Redemption planet	Earth is the planet of redemption.
redemption, thoughts	Guard well your thoughts, because they are the only creative thing that you have kept and they are your only avenue of redemption.
seven primary Spirits	The Triune God breathed into expression seven primary Spirits and set them into activity to express the primary principle: God. These primary Spirits, or primary planes are, Man, Angel, Fowl, Animal Vegetable, Protoplasm and Earth.
slave or master	You are either master or slave. Either you are going to be an authority or you are going to be a slave, one of the two. You are either going to be your own master, your own projection, or you are going to be the salvation of every other thought coming through.

subjective mind	Everything that you suppress during your day of activity will go into the subjective mind, and when you go into sleep state it will express itself as best it may in the time given for it to express.
suppressing	You must realize that everything you suppress must be faced at one time or another.
thought	Guard well your thought, which is the only creative thing you have kept, and use it wisely for your own redemption.
thoughts, your	You are the sum and substance of your thoughts.
Universal Law	This is the only law: Universal Law.

Definitions from Universal Everlasting Life, Book I, Series 1, Lesson 4

KINGDOM OF HEAVEN, NOT KINGDOM OF GOD

Absolute Conscious	The Star of David depicts the Absolute Conscious. This is the pair-I-dise [Paradise].
authority, learn	When something has to be said, say it and get it into an understanding. You don't have to be argumentative, nor do you have to be antagonistic with it. Learn to speak with understanding, to be conscious of why this condition exists.
authority, learn	Learn to be what is necessary for the time, the place and the condition.
bliss, state of	is very difficult to hold. The essence of energy that complies to go with it is so fine of matter that it is difficult for you to hold that state of being because the flesh begins to melt. That is why you feel buoyant and floating while in the bliss state
breath & health	Your direct health is reflected in your consciousness of your breath. When you are in unison with the Universe by Breath, you are triadic.
brother's keeper	Here is another point to always remember. You are not your brother's keeper.

Cardinal Suns	There are the four Cardinal Suns which form a square. They set on the four corners of the quadrants of the universe, which are the Green, Orange, Indigo and Purple.
Central Sun	The Central Sun is the home of the Father. That is the dead center of the universe.
Circle of Light	affirmation to say each morning. This places the White Light of protection about your aura. Nothing out of Truth can or will penetrate the fire of that Light.
clear-thought	Dismiss everything that enters in requesting form, when you are imprinting something that you are receiving. Then, your recall will be exact and accurate.
Conscious	the perfect state of being, where you can change this paradise into the Kingdom of God. Conscious is the true state of being, the state of Perfection
consciousness	Man has one ability that the subservient to him were not given: He was given the knowledge of the awareness of consciousness contained in Life.
consciousness	knowing, capable of activity upon, that is, knowing in all actuality, to be able to associate with, to harmonize, in harmonious relations
control	The ability of adjustment
discernment, poise	You will begin to evaluate all conditions that exist around you in a different way. You will alter those conditions to bring a poise with yourself in an area that you are expressing with and in.
discernment, value	Evaluate everything that you are given. That is why you are given the value of discernment. You evaluate over 3,000,000 thoughts per second so that you do keep yourself in a perfect state of heaven.

discernment, quiet — Allow the quietness during the pause of your breath for broadcasting and receiving, for your values of discernment in your Spirituality Cone to have their chance to work with you to give you the rapport of Thought Itself.

dominion, balance — "To have dominion over," doesn't mean an iron-clad ruler. It means an association of working, poise and rapport with each other, a total balance of equality.

eternal, indestructible — You were made eternal. You are indestructible even though you think you aren't. You will last throughout eternity. You may come and go, changing form and personality, but you are very durable and pliable.

evaluate — Evaluate everything that you are given. That is why you are given the value of discernment. You evaluate over 3,000,000 thoughts per second so that you do keep yourself in a perfect state of heaven.

Father's day — Each of the Father's days is one thousand years.

feeling & heaven — Feeling is a composite of all five of your natural senses coming into a unity of one. When you learn to respond to this force, which is part of the creative activity with you responding to you, it will bring you into your heaven here on earth.

Force — The purpose in activity of Intelligence of Universal expression. We have an exchange of Force to operate the flesh body.

forgive yourself — Be gentle to yourself, love yourself and learn to forgive yourself in your own inability of understanding until you grow in the poise to have the control of that understanding and that peace within yourself.

forgiveness	Relive each day. Everything that wasn't in absolute perfectness, readjust it and forgive it before you go to sleep.
future, to know	In our quest of the consciousness of being, we have to look back to know the future. When we look back, we understand the future.
God: Motionless	A perfect created plane is zero, or God: Motionless. The circle in it is also the Airless Cell, which you are.
gut feelings	Learn to rely on your inner senses, your feelings. Listen to your feelings. When you have that gut feeling, listen, or you will have consequences
health & breath	Your direct health is reflected in your consciousness of your breath. When you are in unison with the Universe by Breath, you are triadic.
health, perfect	These lessons are for you to learn to transform your body from flesh back to Pure Physical, and bring back the perfect condition of health into your body and to bring back all of your awareness that is sleeping in your senses back into perfect rapport.
heaven, control	If you were in the consciousness of control, then you would be in heaven.
heaven & agreement	Your heaven, the Kingdom of Heaven, is responsible to your agreement of consciousness of expression; that is your heaven. You can make this a place of utter joy or you can make this a place of remorse. This you do by your own improper thinking and improper programming.
heaven here on earth	Feeling is a composite of all five of your natural senses coming into a unity of one. When you learn to respond to this force, which is part of the creative activity with you responding to you, it will bring you into your heaven here on earth.

heaven or hell	As long as you keep that Universal Creed in front of you, you will be in heaven, otherwise you will be in hell.
heaven & peace	By your keenness of your awareness, you will change your state of confusion into a state of heaven, until you have attained a peace and poise about yourself that others will seek, while wondering why, in the midst of such confusion, you are able to be at peace with yourself.
heaven, upon earth	Learn that you are the power, you make heaven upon this earth by taking time to still your breath, making perfect thought molds to project as you breathe out, so that you correct the conditions about you without ever uttering a word.
heaven, your	Remember, this is your heaven, make it so.
Holy of Holies	You are the Holy of Holies, that Temple not built by hands, eternal in the Heavens, eternal in the consciousness of consciousness: the Perfect Consciousness of Heaven.
"I"	the personified representative of God standing forth in expression.
inner senses	Learn to rely on your inner senses, your feelings. Listen to your feelings. When you have that gut feeling, listen, or you will have consequences
inner voice, 6th sense	Learn to be keen with the perception of the inner voice and the feeling of the inner voice within you until you have full control of communication with it. This is your sixth sense in working.
inner voice, guide	If you will listen to that inner voice and learn to have it for your guide, you will divert almost all of your problems
Kingdom of God	When man becomes Selfless, the perfect state of being, putting everything above self, he becomes the master of all. Only then, shall you have the Kingdom of God.

Kingdom of Heaven	The perfect state of conscious
Kingdom of Heaven	You are going to learn to be in it but not of it. This is the first step of attaining the Kingdom of Heaven.
kingdom of life	The triangle, the square and the circle are the major elements of the Kingdom of Life of your blood. There are minute crystal formations of light itself solidified into crystalline form that flow in your blood, which are the major crystals of energy for your Life substance. All of the life in miniature crystalline form which is held in all plant forms is brought into your digestive system, and released into your blood to feed the cells of your body by atomic implosions from the blood stream to your cells.
Knowing, quiet	Be quiet within yourself, when you want to know something, and allow the Intelligence of the universe to fully express it for you and to you.
Knowing, surety	When you know that you know, nobody can change your mind because you know that is correct.
law unto yourself	You are a law unto yourself. You are not yourself unto a law.
lessons, purpose	These lessons are for you to learn to transform your body from flesh back to Pure Physical, and bring back the perfect condition of health into your body and to bring back all of your awareness that is sleeping in your senses back into perfect rapport.
love, consciousness	Everything should be projected in a perfect state of the consciousness in love. How would you want someone to do unto you?
man	Through all eternity, man was created to rule through love, to bless and control, to have dominion over and serve all creation.

Man (spiritual)	the last creation of the Triune Spirit of God, and the most ideal creation, molded in the form and possessing all the powers of the Power that created him. He is all forms, all the intelligence, all the forces and all the Truth. He is love, beauty and all durability for all eternity
master or slave	If you are not the master of a situation, then you are a slave to it.
meditation, Spirit	where you can shut brain off so Mind can have full rapport with Spirit into your consciousness, to produce the ideal state of Conscious. Then, you can be truly aware of the All Existence of the Universe
mistakes, making;	When you are wrong, admit it. So what? Everybody makes mistakes. Don't be ashamed to admit you are wrong. You grow by being able to admit because this is a part of forgiving yourself, and don't try to make the same mistake twice.
necessary, learn	Learn to be what is necessary for the time, the place and the condition.
Paradise, Star	Star of David depicts the Absolute Conscious. This is the pair-I-dise [Paradise].
Paradise	One expression that is seven thousand years in a Pure Physical body of Light.
Paradise, being in	When you learn the three things: the grace of love, the poise of authority and the peace of meekness (being gentle and kind), you will know that you are in Paradise.
Paradise, Selfless	If you express yourself joyously, being Selfless in that expression, in Love, then you share the Universe. When you even surpass that, and give of yourself without any prospect of receiving for that which you give, then you are in Paradise. Very few ever reach the state of Paradise.
Perfect Consciousness	You are in the Perfect Consciousness of Heaven when you are in Love, Light and Life.

Perfect Plane	The Perfect Created Plane would be one dot. That one dot is your Airless Cell, at the center of your heart, which takes It's seating with your first breath
Perfect State of Being	When you become Selfless, you learn to put everything above self, you become Master of everything. Selfless is the Perfect State of Being.
perfect understanding	Living in perfect love and the authority of perfect trust, brings about the condition of perfect understanding.
physical	made up of fire-air-water-earth. These are your basic elements. With this, you have the ability of all creation.
Primary Cause of All	(Spiritual) Man
Primary Suns	There are the three Primary Suns; the Red, Yellow and the Blue that form a triangle.
question, in question	When you are in question, not doubt, but just in question of information you are receiving which doesn't ring true, demand that it stand forth in Truth and Light. If it isn't Truth, it will get quiet very quickly
Selfless	When you become Selfless, you learn to put everything above self, you become Master of everything. Selfless is the Perfect State of Being.
Selfless, Perfect State	When man becomes Selfless, the perfect state of being, putting everything above self, he becomes the master of all. Only then, shall you have the Kingdom of God.
sixth sense	Learn to be keen with the perception of the inner voice and the feeling of the inner voice within you until you have full control of communication with it. This is your sixth sense in working.
spirit	a Latin word which means spirally I go to express. The Latin spire is a circular motion of activity both coming and going, simultaneously.

Star of David	Depicts the Absolute Conscious. This is the pair-I-dise [Paradise].
teachings, purpose	That is what these teachings are all about: to teach you to attain from the flesh to the (Pure) Physical, so that you may light your body and take it with you.
thought molds, perfect	Learn that you make heaven upon this earth by taking time to still your breath, making perfect thought molds to project as you breathe out, so that you correct the conditions about you without ever uttering a word. Your thought can do a thousand times more than any speech of hours upon hours. By just one breath, once your perfect thought (mold) is released clearly, everybody on this earth is going to be bombarded by it. Your thought is heard throughout the universe.
Truth	the total fullness of the State of All
truth, test for	Above all things, prove everything you receive. Tell it to stand forth in Truth and Light. It will back away in a hurry if it is not.
truths of the universe	All awareness of the Truths of the Universe are functioning in Mind conditions, being bombarded continuously through the Spirituality Cone by your brain.
Universal Creed	"I am eternally free, which is my nature, and I bow to no one, not even God, for I am God."
White Sun, Intelligence	The White Sun is the Intelligence that informs us of all consciousness at this level. It is what directs our quadrant and is not a planet. The White Sun emits nothing but White Light, which is Intelligence.
you	you are the Holy of Holies, that Temple not built by hands, eternal in the Heavens, eternal in the consciousness of consciousness: the Perfect Consciousness of Heaven.

your divine principle	Nobody has the right to enter your kingdom without your permission. Within yourself, don't let anybody change you. Become perfect within yourself, as you are. Be the fullness that you were given to express in.

Definitions from Universal Everlasting Life, Book I, Series 1, Lesson 5

THINGS AND REAL THINGS

Air transformer	Your body is an air transformer. As you breathe in, the iron in your blood becomes excited and the residual of it trying to capture itself, emits a tremendous amount of energy. This causes all of the protons and neutrons around it to activate.
Airless Cell, real	Your Airless Cell controls you and is your God. This is all of you that is real.
Airless Cell, Source	You want to learn to be more in rapport with your Airless Cell, where your True Source really is.
best, do your best	Starting today, and from this day on, you are going to do your best to make everything as true as you possibly can, regardless of what anybody else thinks.
Commandments 11&12	11th & 12th that Jesus brought. Love thy Father thy God above all things. Love thyself as you love thy God because thou art God.
doing your best	You are going to do everything to the best of your ability from this moment on, and you are not going to settle for anything less than perfect.
freedom, Love	You can be free any time that you want, just be Love. Open up and allow everything to come to you.
friend	A friend is a person you can absolutely rely upon in any situation
honesty	Unless you can be honest to yourself, you will never know Truth

Hunza secret	At a young age, they are taught meditation and quietness for self.
illusion	Everything that you see about you is illusion and is made
knowing & not	When you know, then you know, but if you don't know, then you don't know that you don't know. It takes one little bit of doubt, don't know, and nothing takes place.
knowing, Truth	Be quiet and know that you are God. Be still and know the Truth.
Law of Life	The Law of Life is that what you do unto others shall be done unto you, only in multiples.
lessons, purpose	What these lessons are all about is to cheat death and change all of this flesh into Light and take your Light Body with you from this earth. You are going to be eternally free when you walk away from here.
Life itself	In Life Itself, everything is Bliss. Life is the rendered of God, which gives forth into every expression, everything necessary for that expression
life, joyous	This life can be the most joyous of expressions that can ever be imagined if you will only be kind to yourself and love yourself, and take a few minutes to talk with Dad.
Life, Source, Real	Everything came from the same Source, and that is Life: the great granary of God. All you have do is to ally yourself in Life, with Life, of Life for Life. All Life will bow to you and it will become eternal. Everything will become real.
limitation, no	Place no limitation upon anything or any act. This is a very important secret; learn to use it. It will make you free.
longevity secret	Let love, joy and affection of exchange be your dominating activities.

love	You will find that the more you grow in Truth within yourself, the only thing that has any value at all is Love.
Love Commandment	Learn to love yourself above all things. Learn to love everything and everyone as you love yourself.
love yourself	This life can be the most joyous of expressions that can ever be imagined if you will only be kind to yourself and love yourself, and take a few minutes to talk with Dad.
love, Freedom	You can be free any time that you want, just be Love. Open up and allow everything to come to you.
love, key to Perfection	The properties you are attaining for your Perfection all start with the little key: I love you. When you learn that you can love everything and everybody, then you won't find time enough to see something wrong.
manifesting	f you will learn to relax and make thought pictures, you will be able to manifest anything that you desire.
molecular structure	Molecular structure we accept as real. However, all of it has a point of termination; it has a point of self destruction.
perfect things	things subject to change are not perfect, and anything less than perfect can never be real.
perfecting yourself	If you are looking to perfect yourself, I'll give you all of the answers.
poise	Poise is when you can be in anything but not be of it.
potential	Your potential is beyond your wildest imagination
real things	that from which all things are made is real
real, to be	To be real is to know yourself; know who you are, what you are, where you are and why at all times.

reflection, not real	In everything that is not real, we are like a reflection that is flashed on a screen by a motion picture projector
secret	The secret is this: be in it, but not of it.
senses, keenness	When your senses become very keen, you will be made aware, beforehand, of what to do and how to do it,
senses, twelve	Those seven dormant senses are the most important to your being.
Sightcone discernment	In your Sightcone, you will find that all of the problematic conditions that you are going to function in, will be discerned, evaluated, acted upon and re-broadcast before you are even aware it has taken place
Soul	Soul is the eternal life of being of expression, expressing. It is the eternal youth fluids in your body that will keep you young. You have the Fountain of Youth within you.
Source	Source where all Truth and real is
Spirit of man	Only the great Spirit of man, controlled by God, is real.
Spirit, multiples of motions	Spirally I go to express: Spirit, which is both coming and going, simultaneously at the same time as multiples of motions simultaneously in all directions at the same time
Spirit, oscillation	the oscillation between the two positives in activity.
Spirit, things of	Things of the Spirit are real and perfect and will endure.
True Source, your	You want to learn to be more in rapport with your Airless Cell, where your True Source really is.

Definitions from Universal Everlasting Life, Book I, Series 1, Lesson 6

INTELLIGENCE AND INTELLECT

abundance	Plenty and to spare so that you may share with those about you.
Adamic Veil	Every time you come back into expression the Adamic Veil is dropped over you. Everything you knew before is wiped clean. You must accomplish it all in one lifetime. An individual must be an authority to enter into this realm without the veil of the adamic sleep.
agreement, importance	Nothing can enter into your expression without your agreement
agreements, previous	Above all, you are an authority unto yourself. You are a law unto yourself, not yourself unto a law. You made many agreements before you came into expression; very few of them have been fulfilled
airitarian	Eventually, you will attain the condition of an airitarian. You will take all your substance by thought.
Airless Cell	The Airless Cell is not contained by anything physical. It is the Spiritual Intelligence of your being.
Authority, yourself	Above all, you are an authority unto yourself. You are a law unto yourself, not yourself unto a law. You made many agreements before you came into expression; very few of them have been fulfilled.
brain: self	Brain is self. If you are going to learn to be universal, you are going to have to be selfless.
certainty, a seed key	Without love, you could not exist or express. Without Love, nothing takes place. Before anything came into motion from the Motionless, it was on the movement of Love that it came into being. From Life came Love and from Life and Love came Light. "Behold, there was Light. Lo, there was Light."

correcting a condition No condition can be corrected until you admit it is there, and then take decisive measures to overcome it.

crystals Everything that exists in being is composed of crystals. They are Light being solidified into form in an octave expressing in resonance of change.

death when the Airless Cell leaves the heart

doubt the greatest enemy you have to overcome.

emotions Emotions are the result of a misunderstanding, playing back through the suppressive of the subjective or the objective mind. ...Don't let these emotions control you. Send them out. You are master of your universe.

First Commandment "Thou shalt have no other God before Me." Either you bow to some other man's rule, or you are God. Do you accept somebody else's thesis of operation, or are you an individual? You have your own rights and your own abilities; you need to bow to no one.

food blessing Everything that you partake into your body, bless into perfect before it passes your teeth. "Everything that I partake of into my body be turned into perfect energy." That is the only thought you need.

forgiving You forgive yourself and ask for forgiveness for those you trespassed against as well as those that trespassed against you. A big important rule for you is to never go to sleep without going back over your day and forgiving yourself for every trespass you did for that day.

free agent, being a Nobody owns you but yourself. You are a free agent in the Intelligence of Be, and you should act in that Intelligence and that ability of accomplishment of attainment in accordance with your fulfillment of your ability at all times

gentle	Gentle does not mean to be meek. Gentleness is a great condition to culture. It is a great attribute to be able to control.
goal, ultimate	The very ultimate of your goal is for you to become Selfless. Then, you become the Universe. You are no longer an individualized division of the Universe in expression.
God, image of	Intelligence
great secret	Learn to be in things but not of them. In this way, you have control of the situation and not the situation having control over you
greed	One of the greatest problems you have to overcome. Greed: a very strong wish to continuously get more of something, especially food or money. When you get rid of greed, self is very easy to overcome.
green apple diet	The ancients used the three-day green apple diet to clean the brain cells of all mucus.
Inner Self, your God	When you are able to contact your Inner Self, your God, you will know who you are, where you are, what you are and why.
intellect	the action of thinking upon life; the ability to reason the values of Now; the reasoning ability of the spirit, changes with the amount of activity given it, is not certain. Intellect is where most of man's problems get started
Intelligence	Intelligence is true spirit activity, an absolute certainty, living thought action. Intelligence teaches you to be real rather than make believe.
Intelligence, using it	You forgive yourself and ask for forgiveness for those you trespassed against as well as those that trespassed against you. A big important rule for you is to never go to sleep without going back over your day and forgiving yourself for every trespass you did for that day.

Intelligence, Now	In the image and likeness of God; all things contained within the Now State
Intelligence, informing	When you are still and you ask for an explanation of what is the most perfect way to go about something, Intelligence will tell you exactly what to do. Then you will know that you know.
law unto yourself	Above all, you are an authority unto yourself. You are a law unto yourself, not yourself unto a law. You made many agreements before you came into expression; very few of them have been fulfilled
Light, "Behold ..."	Before anything came into motion from the Motionless, it was on the movement of Love that it came into being. From Life came Love and from Life and Love came Light. "Behold, there was Light. Lo, there was Light."
Light, turning to	As you are now, you are only using five of your twelve senses. When you finish these studies, you will be functioning on all twelve, and you will have the ability to turn this body to Light. You will be given the information and the keys, but you will have to do it.
Love	Without Love, you could not exist or express. Without Love, nothing takes place. Before anything came into motion from the Motionless, it was on the movement of Love that it came into being. From Life came Love and from Life and Love came Light. "Behold, there was Light. Lo, there was Light."
love exercise, mirror	How many of you are able to walk up to a mirror and tell yourself that you love yourself and look at yourself while you are telling yourself? Try it some time. You want to see a lot of guilt come out?
meek	The meek shall be eternally bound to this earth until they become masters of themselves. To be meek means that you have no authority of yourself whatsoever.

memory cells	You carry two little cells on either side of your knowledge bump at the back of your head. This little computer, the size of a pencil point, carries all of your expressions in record.
Mind	the greatest attribute that Spirit gives us.
moderation	Truth tells you: All things in moderation.
peace & abundance	Only in the Intelligence and wisdom within yourself will you get this surety of eternal peace and the abundance of everything you desire. Abundance means plenty and to spare so that you may share with those about you.
perfect expression	By the Truth, you can have the perfect expression and you can have all the love beyond your desires. You can attain into realms that you can never imagined existed, the realms that you have forgotten about.
perfect Intelligence	The perfect accord of Intelligence and intellect results in perfect Intelligence in active expression. Seek intellect, but let your Intelligence be your guide in uplifting yourself into the perfect state of being.
perfection of Life	The quickening of Intelligence also will teach you to remember what knowing you so carefully hid away of how to take your body back into perfection of Life and take it with you and not leave it with Earth.
perfection, projection	Whenever you set out to do something, do it the best that you can do it. Pride yourself in the projection of perfection in everything that you do
poise and peace	By the truth, there will be a poise and peace within yourself by the surety of the quickening of Intelligence that will instantly prompt you in all things and all activities

problems, cause	Almost 90% of the things that go wrong with you is due to the agreement and the values of discernment of those expressing about you. You have been programmed to become conditioned to the conditions about you.
problems, greatest	The greatest problems you are going to have are: 1- learning to budget your time. 2- learning to stretch time. 3- learning to make every second very important. You will find that you are too busy to do anything else, but you will have a fuller and richer life than you ever dreamed possible.
quiet, becoming	When you allow yourself to become quiet, then the Intelligence can come into rapport with you and give you the guidance.
record of expressions	You have the best computer that was ever designed which lies in the back of your head on each side of the knowledge bump. There are two pin points on either side of that bump. Within those two dots is stored all of the past, present and future of all your expressions. Now that is a computer for you! Your right dot is your past and the left is your future.
self	The second greatest problem you have to overcome
selfless	When you are selfless, it means that you are in a state of All in everything. Then you return back to the universe and become the fullness thereof, as you return to the state of All.
Selfless, ultimate	The very ultimate of your goal is for you to become Selfless. Then, you become the Universe. You are no longer an individualized division of the Universe in expression.
selfless, universal	Brain is self. If you are going to learn to be universal, you are going to have to be selfless.

speaking	When you have something to say, make it as short as you can, and to the point. You will find that when you stop flowering your prose, more Intelligence will come forth, with less intellect.
Spirit prompting	If you are able, quiet yourself enough to shut brain off, and take time enough by stilling your breath to allow Spirit to prompt you through Mind.
Spiritual Intelligence	The Airless Cell is not contained by anything physical. It is the Spiritual Intelligence of your being.
time & space	With Intelligence, there is no time, space or distance
twelve senses	You say that you have five senses, but actually you function with twelve: five physical and seven spiritual. As you are now, you are only using five. When you finish these studies, you will be functioning on all twelve, and you will have the ability to turn this body to Light. You will be given the information and the keys, but you will have to do it.
Universal Creed	I am Eternally free, in deed, which is my nature, and I bow to no man not even God, for I Am God.
user, being a	You are only a user of all things. All things are here for your use, for your ability to express with, for, by and to. It doesn't matter what you accumulate, you don't own it. In one sweep of the hand, it can be wiped away, instantly, and it does happen.
White Sun	Even our Earth is dependent upon the White Sun for its necessity of BE. The Intelligence upon the White Sun is the primary Force Energy that comes into operation for those here on Earth.
who you are	When you are able to contact your Inner Self, your God, you will know who you are, where you are, what you are and why.

will, that of another	When you manifest by your picture imaginative process, you must not alter a condition or the will of another. You have no right to enter into the will of another without their consent.
Wisdom	When you know the Truth of all being, then it's Wisdom.
Wisdom, begins where	Wisdom begins at home with number one: you.

Definitions from Universal Everlasting Life, Book I, Series 1, Lesson 7

MAN'S RESPONSIBILITIES

Airless Cell	Something that mankind refers to as conscience is a wee small voice. If you do not listen to that little voice that prompts you, it will become quieter. Everybody has this when they come into expression; it's called an Airless Cell. For now, you can regard it as the Divinity of your Be.
authority & self	As long as self is in the way, you are never an authority. "Of myself, I do nothing, my Father does everything."
Authority of Being	When you have the Authority of Being in poise, then you have everything, because you are within the fullness of Love radiating forth in Love Be That is truly your responsibility.
biorhythms	The idea that a person's life is influenced by rhythmic biological cycles that affect his or her ability in various domains such as physical, emotional and intellectual
Circle of Light	Keep your Circle of Light charged about you; this is most important.
Commandments, last	It was Jesus' mission above everything else to bring you the last two Commandments.11- Love thy neighbor as you love the Father. 12- Love thyself as you love God, for you are God.

control	Purity of thought is the only way anything is controlled.
doormat	Nobody is a doormat for anybody else.
eth	The eth, as opposed to the ethers, is without animation waiting to be put into activity in the ethers.
expression	When I say "I," then I'm talking about the inner self, "I" is present. "I" is the personified activity in expression: the total whole.
Father's business	Your business is love. That's the Father's business, Love, and you are about your Father's business.
forgive & dismiss	Only when you forgive and dismiss, will you have any peace within yourself. You will be in torment until you do, because your business is love. That's the Father's business, Love, and you are about your Father's business.
goal, to get to your	To get to your goal, you have to find out who you are, why you are here and where you are going. We try to do it a piece at a time because, otherwise, it is too drastic. Everything is done in moderation.
house cleaning	This becomes the personal responsibility of each to learn to clean your own house before telling others how to clean their houses.
"I"	When I say "I," then I'm talking about the inner self, "I" is present. "I" is the personified activity in expression: the total whole.
Immaculate Conception	The Immaculate Conception of Thought conditioning: In order to produce the elements necessary in the body for the production of a perfect body for a perfect inhabitant, it takes nine years of preparation before the conception period without even one mis-thought, one counter word or one misdeed. This also has to be sustained throughout the full nine months of carrying, and for nine years afterwards.

Inner Self	You will also find that as you study your lessons, your Inner Self will begin to direct you in ways, forms and modes to relieve the conditions you are existing in.
Inner voice	Something that mankind refers to as conscience is a wee small voice. If you do not listen to that little voice that prompts you, it will become quieter. Everybody has this when they come into expression; it's called an Airless Cell. For now, you can regard it as the Divinity of your Be.
Intelligence, secret	Everything has intelligence. Everything is of the same source of intelligence. When you really learn that secret, then you've learned the secret of the universe
Jesus' mission	It was Jesus' mission above everything else to bring you the last two Commandments.11- Love thy neighbor as you love the Father. 12- Love thyself as you love God, for you are God.
kinesiology	The body will respond to your talking to it.
listening	The important factor is to learn to evaluate and learn to listen; don't hear, listen within. A big difference! Listen to what's being projected, not what the words are saying.
Love, gentle, mutual	Love means a gentle exchange of all things. Love has to be something mutually given by both, equally with no terms, bounds or requests in return. Until you are that, you will never know Love.
Love, Father's business	Only when you forgive and dismiss, will you have any peace within yourself. You will be in torment until you do, because your business is love. That's the Father's business, Love, and you are about your Father's business.
me	When I refer to "me," that is self. Me is past tense. Whenever I use a past tense, I am referring to this reflection."

Mother Principle — Love: There could be no Light shining forth if it wasn't for Love. Love is the Mother Principle of God. It should be your first principle of activity.

multiplicities of motion — "Multiplicities of motions simultaneously in all directions at the same time." Then you have a small conception of what Motionless is, yet all active. The Stillness is all action, all activity.

nature's time clock — Nature has a time clock of everything that exists in its expression of time, form and space. Everything has a rate of frequency and vibration in resonance response, so when that resonance response totals zero, it will fall apart only to return to new later.

peace within yourself — Only when you forgive and dismiss, will you have any peace within yourself. You will be in torment until you do, because your business is love. That's the Father's business, Love, and you are about your Father's business.

peace, laws for — 1. The first law is to mind our own business. This business is that of love: to love all things as we love ourselves. 2. Whatever we sow we must also reap.

personal endorsement — When you give (something) your personal endorsement, then it is released into the eth to go completely around the universe.

pulsation — A state of becoming still, where one Breath is capable of forty-two days of action. You learn to breathe Breath and not breathe air.

reflection — When I refer to "me," that is self. Me is past tense, Whenever I use a past tense, I am referring to this reflection.

responsibility to Perfect — Your responsibility is only one thing: your personal perfection. One thing only needs to be done above anything else, and that is the purification of yourself.

Selfless	That means all things come before you do, because when you learn to be that Selfless, you have made it! That is the whole secret right there.
Stillness	"Multiplicities of motions simultaneously in all directions at the same time." Then you have a small conception of what Motionless is, yet all active. The Stillness is all action, all activity
thought pattern	Your constructive thought pattern is the only ability that you have left of your purity in operation. This is the one part that was not allowed to become dormant

Printed in the United States
by Baker & Taylor Publisher Services